The
HAIR AND MAKE-UP
Artist's Handbook
A complete guide for professional qualifications

Beverley Braisdell
Jennifer Lenard

HODDER
EDUCATION
AN HACHETTE UK COMPANY

This publication has been developed by Hodder Education.

Hodder Education has taken all reasonable care in the preparation of this publication but Hodder Education and the City & Guilds of London Institute accept no liability howsoever in respect of any breach of the rights of any third party howsoever occasioned or damage caused to any third party as a result of the use of this publication.

Products and services that are referred to in this book may be either trademarks of their respective owners. The publisher and author/s make no claim to these trademarks.

These materials have been developed by Hodder Education and all the content and the accuracy are the sole responsibility of Hodder Education. The City & Guilds of London Institute accepts no liability howsoever in respect of any breach of the intellectual property rights of any third party howsoever occasioned or damage to third party's property or person as a result of the use of this Work.

Orders: please contact Bookpoint Ltd, 130 Milton Park, Abingdon, Oxon OX14 4SB. Telephone: +44 (0)1235 827720. Fax: +44 (0)1235 400454. Lines are open from 9.00a.m. to 5.00p.m., Monday to Saturday, with a 24-hour message-answering service. You can also order through our website www.hoddereducation.co.uk

If you have any comments to make about this, or any of our other titles, please send them to educationenquiries@hodder.co.uk

British Library Cataloguing in Publication Data
A catalogue record for this title is available from the British Library

ISBN: 978 1 444 13838 2

First Edition Published 2011
This Edition Published 2011
Impression number   10 9 8 7 6 5 4 3 2 1
Year   2016, 2015, 2014, 2013, 2012, 2011

Hachette UK's policy is to use papers that are natural, renewable and recyclable products and made from wood grown in sustainable forests. The logging and manufacturing processes are expected to conform to the environmental regulations of the country of origin.

Cover photo from © Image Source Ltd/Getty Images
Typeset by Pantek Arts Ltd., Maidstone, Kent
Printed in Italy for Hodder Education, an Hachette UK Company, 338 Euston Road, London NW1 3BH.

CONTENTS

WITHDRAWN

Foreword

After nearly 30 years working in the beauty-related industry I am honoured to be asked to write a foreword for this inspiring textbook.

Hair and Media Make-up is a fantastic industry to work in; it's visual, dynamic and anyone entering it has to have artistic vision and flare. This textbook is a real inspiration and will enhance any learners studying a qualification at Levels 2 and 3 in Hair and Media Make-up.

Achieving your qualification can take time, hard work and determination. You will need to successfully complete the knowledge requirements as well as the practical skills. This industry is an innovative and visual industry and is fast becoming a popular choice when deciding on career pathways in the hair and beauty-related sectors.

Beverley and Jenni are both inspirational tutors with a huge amount of experience behind them; they are passionate about the industry and education, which means they are the ideal authors of this textbook. The step-by-step visuals will really help you to see the process of achieving the finished looks. I would encourage everyone to practise these skills and develop your own ideas and create fantastic visuals of your own.

I would like to take this opportunity to wish you good luck with your qualifications and your potential future career within the Hair and Media Make-up industry.

Anita Crosland

Portfolio Manager, Creative and Business, City & Guilds

Introduction

Welcome to *The Hair and Make-up Artist's Handbook: A complete guide for professional qualifications*. This book is written to the new standards in the beauty industry, to specifically meet the needs of the make-up route. It includes hundreds of photos to inspire you (including step-by-step guides on how to complete different looks) as well as lots of other useful features to help you complete your course.

Features include:

Quotes from industry professionals, to give you an insight into what it's really like to work in the beauty-related industry.

 Key term

Key term boxes with definitions of important terms.

 Tip Useful hints and tips to use in your own work.

End of Chapter Knowledge Test

End of chapter knowledge tests allow you to test what you have learnt. You can check your answers at the back of the book.

 Health and Safety

Important health and safety points to remember.

Remember . . .

Remember boxes to highlight important points.

Anatomy and physiology

Anatomy and physiology boxes in the practical chapters signpost you to the relevant material in the dedicated anatomy and physiology chapter.

Activity

Activities to help you practise your skills and test your knowledge.

About the authors

Authors Beverley Braisdell and Jennifer Lenard are on the HABIA panel for make-up and nails and have worked closely together at City & Guilds in writing the questions for their mandatory and non-mandatory paper-based and online GOLA testing for Nail Services & Make-up, giving them a unique and up-to-date understanding of the knowledge requirements for the new Diplomas and VRQs.

Beverley works for City & Guilds as an Examiner (question writing) and External Verifier. She also has the unique role of Qualification Advisor for City & Guilds, advising them, centres and lecturers on any aspects of Nail Services. Beverley is currently a full-time lecturer at Wigan and Leigh College, specialising in Special Effects Make-up & Nail Services, with nine years' experience in teaching. She has had over 20 years' experience in the industry and has owned her own salon businesses. She has been a competition judge and educator both in the UK and Athens, Greece. She has also worked as a professional make-up artist on set and at photo shoots and has been a feature writer for the worldwide trade magazine 'Scratch' – a nail magazine that has a monthly distribution of around 45,000 copies per month. It was in this role she earned the title of 'The Voice of FE', writing about the great work going on in colleges.

Jennifer is the Principal of The Biz Media Make-up and Hair Academy. She is a professional make-up artist and has worked on numerous major productions with Cartlon Studios. Jenni worked on a BAFTA-winning team for make-up and hair for a major period drama and has worked on numerous TV productions, including Dalziel and Pascoe, Pride and Prejudice, Atonement, Emmerdale, Dr. Who, Police Bravery Awards, Strictly Come Dancing, Dancing on Ice, Celebrity Circus, BBC Restoration, Antiques Roadshow, Question Time, and many more.

Over the years both Beverley and Jenni have built up professional reputations that have taken them to the top of the industry; they have both made so many contacts over the years, some of whom provide advice and guidance in this book.

Acknowledgements

To all the wonderful models and photographers who were so patient and have helped make our ideas come to life: Christopher Roberts – an awesome guy, who sat in the make-up chair so patiently while we 'zombified', 'guylinered' and made him into a tramp; Scarliee Bee – my beautiful princess, you made an amazing witch; Amy Jones – thank you for letting us use your gorgeous eyes.

Special thanks go to Katie Garbett, Maria Pantellis and Nikki Staley for all their help and hard work, for being at all the photo shoots, helping to make prosthetics, dress and clean wigs and modelling, and doing any jobs that we asked of them. We are so thankful to you; you are all little angels.

Thank you to: Katie Garbett, Katie Atchinson, Maria Pantellis, Breda Shorten, Charlie Shorten, Billy Shorten, Ellenora Dean, Courtney Brogan Thompson Randles, Julie Atkins, Ian Philliskirk, David Pagett, David Hope, Karina Mehta, Heather Jones, Brad Coxshall, Jessie Coxshall, Beth Smout, Nikki Staley, Kate Staley, Scarlett Braisdell, Christopher Roberts, Amy Jones, Todd Watts, Louise van Heerden, Genevieve van Heerden, Caitlyn van Heerden, Titch Page and Kimberley Drexel.

A special thank you to Jackie Sweeney from Wigs up North, for your support and fantastic contribution in the wig section, Joanne Etherson from Beauty Express, Debbie Drew and everyone at Tan Solutions. Thanks also to Silhouette, Fake Bake, Ashleigh Halvorsen at Artdeco Cosmetics, Liz Whittingham at Lizbeth Photography and Brian Whittaker at Royal Brushes for all the photos, and to everyone at Hodder.

This whole experience has been amazing – such hard work, but anything worth doing is worth doing right! Our hearts and souls have gone into this, it's our passion and we really hope you enjoy reading it!

A big thank you to every one who gave up the time to help make this dream we had come to life. Once more a very big thank you to a fantastic crew – in front of the camera and behind the camera – for modelling, being part of the make-up team and organising corsetry/dresses and costumes. Also thanks to all that helped with making food and cups of tea to keep us all going!

Bev Braisdell

I would like to thank some incredible people who have made my dream possible: Jenni Lenard – who was crazy enough to follow me on this adventure, your knowledge and skills amaze me; your attention to detail and pure passion for this industry are infectious, love you tons!

To my amazing family – my fab kids, Josh and Scarlett you two are the most fantastic kids in the world, I'm so lucky to have you; the gorgeous CJ, thank you for cuddles, your love and keeping me sane! To the very beautiful Amy for looking after Josh and for listening! I really couldn't have done this without all your love and support, thank you for tidying up and cooking!

To my lovely friends and my special 'Sister from another Mother' – sorry I dumped you guys for a few months, missed you!

Jennifer Lenard

A very special thank you to Beverley Braisdell, who is a fantastic make-up artist, very focused and passionate about her work and a credit to the industry. Bev is also a very good friend and a pleasure to work with – I have thoroughly enjoyed the opportunity I have had to work with you, and I am looking forward to the next Braisdell and Lenard adventures.

To my Nan, Carmel Cushen, who encouraged me from when I was a child to follow my dreams and goals in life and never give up on what you want – one of my dreams was to write a book. Thank you for your wise words, Nan, you're a star. From your little flower xxj. Also to my mother and father, Breda and Charlie Shorten, and to my brother, Clive Shorten, and family for being very loving and supportive and encouraging me in everything I have set out to do. Thank you for being a fantastic family, you all mean the world to me.

Ian Philliskirk, thank you for all your help and support throughout this journey. You are a very kind and understanding person for letting me and Bev take over your brand new showroom at Provençale Kitchens and turning it into a photographic studio, and for letting us work late into the night for the duration of the making of this book. You're a very dear and special person to me; you're one in a million.

Thank you to Heather Jones for all her contributions and skills in the fashion and photographic/camouflage chapters. Richard Page: thank you for your help and support throughout the writing of this book, spending time with the reptiles and walking Nikita and Billy-bobs. **Your help, support and friendship mean a lot to me, you're a star.**

To all my students at The Biz Academy who have been models and let us use their fantastic photos from their Level 3 Theatrical, special effects media make-up coursework.

Thanks to Louise and David for being fantastic photographers.

The authors and publishers would like to thank the following for photos used in this volume:

The following photos are © David Simon Pagett: p. 8 (bottom); p. 17 (top); p. 234; p. 252; pp. 257–61 (day make-up); p. 268; pp. 286–88 (bun); pp. 293–301; p. 305; pp. 307–326; p. 330; p. 335; pp. 336–37; p, 338 (top); p. 340; p. 341 (top); pp. 346–47; pp. 351–64; pp. 404–407; p. 410; p. 413–21

The following photos are © Louise van Heerden: p. 22; p. 57; p. 58; p. 142; pp. 147–48; pp. 154–58; p. 211 (bottom); pp. 220–31; pp. 261–63 (evening make-up); pp. 263–65 (special occasion make-up); p. 266; p. 275; p. 277; p. 283; pp. 284–86; pp. 303–4; p. 306; pp. 342–43; p. 348; p. 350; pp. 374–78; p. 382; pp. 408–9; pp. 411–412

p. 1 © Beauty Photo Studio/Age footstock/Photolibrary.com; p. 5 (from top) Darren Baker – Fotolia, John Burke/Getty Images, Art Deco Cosmetics; p. 7 Ken McKay/Rex Features; p. 8 (top) © imagebroker/Alamy; p. 9 fStop/Getty Images; p. 17 (bottom) OJO Images/photolibrary.com; p. 26 Health and Safety Executive – contains public sector information published by the Health and Safety Executive and licensed under the Open Government Licence v1.; p. 34 GraphicHead – Fotolia; p. 36 CHW – Fotolia; p. 40 Paul Gibbings – Fotolia; p. 42 (from top) somenski – Fotolia, Ken Ng – Fotolia; p. 43 (from left) © Mark Richardson – Fotolia.com, Steve Woods – Fotolia; p. 47 © Paul Gill; p. 52 Beauty Express; p. 53 Beauty Express; p. 54 Beauty Express; p. 61 © Andres Rodriguez/Alamy; p. 63 © Paul Gill; p. 64 Hufton + Crow/View Pictures/Photolibrary.com; p. 65 pixel&korn – Fotolia; p. 69 © RubberBall Productions/Getty Images; p. 77 © Paul Gill; p. 83 © Ralph Mercer/Getty Images; p. 128 (from top) DR P. MARAZZI/SCIENCE PHOTO LIBRARY, DR P. MARAZZI/SCIENCE PHOTO LIBRARY; p. 129 (from top) CNRI/SCIENCE PHOTO LIBRARY, BIOPHOTO ASSOCIATES/SCIENCE PHOTO LIBRARY, ERICH SCHREMPP/SCIENCE PHOTO LIBRARY; p. 130 (from top) DR H.C.ROBINSON/SCIENCE PHOTO LIBRARY, © Cristina Lichti / Alamy, DR P. MARAZZI/SCIENCE PHOTO LIBRARY, DR HAROUT TANIELIAN/SCIENCE PHOTO LIBRARY; p. 131 (from top) DR P. MARAZZI/SCIENCE PHOTO LIBRARY, SCIENCE PHOTO LIBRARY, DR P. MARAZZI/SCIENCE PHOTO LIBRARY; p. 132 CNRI/SCIENCE PHOTO LIBRARY; p. 136 Hollywood Lashes; p. 138 All photos © Paul Gill; p. 140 Hollywood Lashes; p. 141 Hollywood Lashes; p. 145 both photos Beauty Express; p. 149 © Frances Roberts/Alamy; p. 151 Beauty Express; p. 159 (clockwise from top) Hollywood lashes, Beauty Express, Beauty Express; pp.162–66 © All photos Paul Gill; pp.167–68 All photos © Louise van Heerden; p. 169 Hollywood Lashes; p. 171 All photos © Paul Gill; p. 174 Elixea; p. 177 © Paul Gill; p. 178 Wolfgang Ott/Getty Images; p. 179(from top) Ingram Publishing/Photolibrary.com, © Ranald Mackechnie/Photonica/Getty Images; p. 180 (from top) André Schuster/Imagebroker/Photolibrary.com, © Catchlight Visual Services/Alamy; p. 181 (from top) Cultura/Getty Images,

Image Source/Photolibrary.com; p. 186 (from top) Silhouette, Elixea; p. 187 Silhouette; p. 188 Beauty Express; p. 189 Elixea; p. 190 Silhouette; p. 192 Elixea; p. 193 Silhouette; p. 194 Elixea; p. 195 Beauty Express; p. 196 Beauty Express; p. 199 Beauty Express; p. 202 Beauty Express; p. 203 Beauty Express; p. 204 Beauty Express; p. 205 (from left)Elixea, Silhouette, Silhouette; p. 211 (top) Beauty Express; p. 217 © Paul Gill; p. 219 © Paul Gill; p. 233 Beauty Express; p. 236 College Kits Direct; p. 237 Beauty Express; pp. 238–41 all photos courtesy of Art Deco; pp. 242–44 all photos and artworks courtesy of Royal and Langnickel; p. 270 (top left) © Tony Nylons/Alamy, (top right) Philippe McClelland/Getty Images, (bottom left) Alastair Muir/ Rex Features, (bottom right) ScreenGem/Everett/Rex Features; p. 273 Liz Whittingham; p. 292 C Squared Studios/Photodisc/Getty Images; p. 327 © Natasha Jordan; p. 331 (from top) Image Source/Getty Images, © Philippe Regard/The Image Bank/Getty Images, Beauty Express; p. 338 (second from top) Heather Jones; p. 339 (from left) (1) Natasha Jordan, (2) Natasha Jordan, (3) make-up by Louise Young, Hair by Paul Harvey, photo by Dougal Waters Photography, image copyright Louise Young Cosmetics; p. 341 (second from top) Heather Jones, Heather Jones; p. 344 © Philippe Regard/The Image Bank/Getty Images; p. 366 © Louise van Heerden; p. 368 (top) DR P. MARAZZI/SCIENCE PHOTO LIBRARY, (bottom left) DR P. MARAZZI/SCIENCE PHOTO LIBRARY, (bottom centre) DR P. MARAZZI/SCIENCE PHOTO LIBRARY, (bottom right) DR HAROUT TANIELIAN/SCIENCE PHOTO LIBRARY; p. 369 (from left) DR P. MARAZZI/ SCIENCE PHOTO LIBRARY, HUMBERT/AMEL/BSIP Medical/Photolibrary.com; p. 370 (from top) BSIP Medical/Photolibrary.com, Koshy Johnson/Oxford Scientific (OSF)/Photolibrary.com, DR M.A. ANSARY/SCIENCE PHOTO LIBRARY, Haramis Kalfar – Fotolia; p. 371 © Paul Gill; p. 397 © SCPhotos/Alamy; p. 422 courtesy of Fake Bake; p. 423 Tan Solutions; p. 424 (from top) Fake Bake, Tan Solutions; p. 425 all photos Tan Solutions; p. 426 (from left) Tan Solutions, Fake Bake, Tan Solutions; p. 427 Tan Solutions; p. 428 DR P. MARAZZI/SCIENCE PHOTO LIBRARY; p. 429 DR HAROUT TANIELIAN/SCIENCE PHOTO LIBRARY; p. 433 Tan Solutions; pp. 436–37 all photos courtesy of Fake Bake; pp.438–43 all photos Tan Solutions.

Every effort has been made to trace and acknowledge the ownership of copyright. The publishers will be glad to make appropriate arrangements for any copyright holder whom it has not been possible to contact.

NVQ and VRQ mapping grid

This table maps the content of this book to the NVQ and VRQ units.

Chapter	1	2	3	4	5	6	7	8	9	10	11	12	13	14	15
LEVEL 2 VRQ UNITS															
Working in beauty related industries	✓														
Follow health and safety practice in the salon		✓	✓												
Client care and communication in beauty related industries			✓												
Provide facial skin care				✓ (A&P)		✓									
Apply make-up				✓ (A&P)	✓										
Provide eyelash and brow treatments				✓ (A&P)			✓								
Instruction on make-up application				✓ (A&P)				✓							
Create an image based on a theme within the hair and beauty sector															
The art of photographic make-up				✓ (A&P)							✓				
Body art design				✓ (A&P)								✓			
Apply skin tanning techniques				✓ (A&P)											✓
Shaping and colouring eyebrows				✓ (A&P)	✓										
The art of colouring hair									(part)						
The art of dressing hair									(part)						
Make and style a hair addition									✓						
LEVEL 2 NVQ UNITS															
G20: Ensure responsibility for actions to reduce risks to health and safety		✓													
G8: Develop and maintain your effectiveness at work			✓												
G18: Promote additional services and products to clients			✓												
B5: Enhance the appearance of eyebrows and eyelashes					✓										
B4: Provide facial skincare treatment						✓									
B8: Provide make-up services							✓								
B9: Instruct clients on the application of skin care products and make-up							✓								
B10: Enhance appearance using skin camouflage													✓		
LEVEL 3 VRQ UNITS															
Working with colleagues within beauty related industries		✓													

Unit									
Monitor and maintain health and safety practice in the salon	✓								
Client care and communication in beauty related industries		✓							
Provide self tanning			✓ (A&P)			(part)			✓
Creative hairdressing design skills									
Apply individual permanent lashes			✓ (A&P)	✓					
Design and apply face and body art			✓ (A&P)						
Fashion and photographic make-up			✓ (A&P)						
Apply airbrush make-up to the face			✓ (A&P)						
Media make-up			✓ (A&P)					✓	
Camouflage make-up						✓			
Style and fit postiche						✓			
Provide hair extension services						?			
Style and dress hair using a variety of techniques						✓			
Studio photography						(part)			
Principles of studio photography						(part)			
Create and cast small prosthetic pieces and bald caps						✓		✓	
Apply prosthetic pieces and bald caps						✓		✓	
Fantasy hair design for performers									
Productions arts planning									
Design and Apply Mendhi skin decoration		(part)							
Cut women's hair to create a variety of looks		(part)		✓					
Promote products and services to clients in a salon									
Display stock to promote sales in a salon									

LEVEL 3 NVQ UNITS

Unit									
G22: Monitor procedures to safely control work operations		✓							
H32: Contribute to the planning and implementation of promotional activities		✓							
B15: Provide single eyelash extension treatments			✓						
B12: Plan and provide airbrush make-up					✓				
B11: Design and create fashion and photographic make-up						✓			
B22: Provide specialist skin camouflage services							✓		
B25: Provide self-tanning services									✓

CHAPTER 1

Working in the beauty-related industry

Units covered by this chapter:

Level 2 VRQ – Working in beauty-related industries

This is a generic unit for beauty therapy and hair and media make-up. The knowledge and understanding within it is transferable and can be adapted for use in both of these industries.

▲ A make-up artist at work

Chapter aims

This chapter will look at:

- Job types, careers and opportunities in the make-up industry
- Employment rights and responsibilities
- Legislation
- Competitions
- How to search for jobs
- Good working practices
- Developing and promoting professional image
- How to create and present a curriculum vitae (CV)/ portfolio suitable for the make-up/hair artistry industry
- Appearance, personal hygiene and professionalism
- Professional etiquette.

This is such an exciting industry to work in, and one in which the role of the make-up artist is to bring ideas and visions to life. Make-up can help make a project a success and there are many accolades to aim for, but we want you to be under no illusions – the aim of our book is to be as frank about the industry as possible.

This is a very demanding industry with irregular hours – you are often working under pressure with tight deadlines, and timing, professional etiquette and teamwork are of the utmost importance. Working to a budget and having to adapt your creative ideas to suit a client's budget or personal choice can sometimes be frustrating. Sometimes work may not be steady or it comes along all at once; then you have to decide which job would be the best career choice overall. Sometimes the job that pays a little less but would raise your profile and make you more contacts may be the best choice.

This is not the career for the person who wants a '9 to 5' job. It may involve travel and changes to plans at the last minute. It requires flexibility, commitment and quite often the ability to think on one's feet.

> "Working in the hair and make-up industry isn't at all glamorous; it's not uncommon to work 12-hour days and sometimes more! But I am positive it is the most rewarding and enjoyable industry in the world, providing you work hard. I was always taught with this industry you only get out what you put in and it's so true!"
>
> **Ellenora Dean**, Hair Stylist

> "I love hair and make-up artists. They're the ones who truly transform you from the person you are in day-to-day life, to the character you're portraying on screen. These people enhance your image so that you can really believe in your character, and thus create an enhanced version – which comes across better on screen."
>
> **Calum O'Toole**, Actor

Routes into make-up artistry

Professionals should only ever carry out the treatments they are qualified to do, otherwise if something goes wrong the insurance could be invalid as this is the professional standard as set by the standards-setting body: Hair and Beauty Industry Authority (HABIA). HABIA's Codes of Practice (COP) set out clear guidelines on working practices within the beauty therapy industry, which can be adapted for media make-up and make-up artistry. The standards-setting body for the media make-up industry is SkillSet (Sector Skills Council for Creative and Media).

Further education learning providers

This may be a college or a private training provider that has been approved by an awarding organisation to run the courses and certificates. There are full-time and part-time courses available in make-up and this qualification has grown vastly over recent years. Historically a few make-up units were completed as part of a beauty therapy qualification or via a basic part-time course. Now there are full Levels 2 and 3 qualifications in make-up, making it a stand-alone qualification that covers all aspects of the industry, including hair design. Level 4 qualifications are currently being considered by various authorities and awarding organisations. Many learning providers will ask that the potential learner has a GCSE or similar qualification in art as an entry requirement. Many further education colleges will be looking for two C grades or equivalent as an entry requirement for a Level 2 course – this is because of the level of academic skill also needed to complete the qualification.

Awarding organisations now must work together so the standards are the same but their assessment material may look different to allow them to keep their individual brand identity. The awarding organisations are shown in the spider diagram.

▲ Awarding organisations

Apprenticeships

Apprenticeships are a great way into the industry, so you can earn money whilst gaining experience in the job. They can be undertaken in many industries including the hair, beauty therapy and make-up industries. Usually the apprentice will work four days a week and attend a course with a learning provider one day per week. A learner can begin at Level 2 on an apprenticeship and then progress to Level 3. However, if a learner completes their Level 2 qualification with a learning provider and then decides to become an apprentice at Level 3, they must have employment in place. There are many changes happening in this area currently; a learning provider or job centre will have details.

Skill Set

Many learning providers use these recognised qualifications. There are many short courses available so that the learner can build their own qualification and specialise in a particular area or these can be used to 'up-skill' on previous training.

Higher education

Many universities offer courses in media and fashion/photographic make-up, advances in prosthetics, casting and moulding techniques, which may be:

- Foundation degrees
- BA (Hons) degrees.

Careers, opportunities and types of jobs available within the make-up industry

There are a range of careers, opportunities and types of job available within the make-up industry, as shown in the spider diagram.

> **Key term**
>
> **Apprenticeship** – a 'learning-on-the-job' opportunity. Usually, an apprentice will work four days a week and attend a course with a learning provider one day per week.

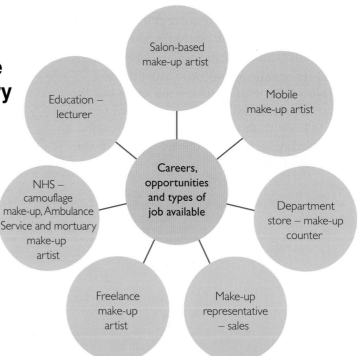

▲ Different types of work available

Salon-based make-up artist

Work within a salon environment, which could be in a hotel or spa, may include a permanently set up make-up area and retail products available for the client to purchase. This job is sometimes combined with beauty therapy and nail technician jobs to maximise profitability.

Status

Employed or self-employed.

Job description (Level 2/Level 3)

You may be expected to provide: 1) special occasion make-up, 2) evening make-up 3) bridal make-up, 4) prom make-up, 5) cosmetic camouflage make-up, 6) airbrush make-up, 7) make-up lessons.

▲ Salon-based make-up artist

Mobile make-up artist

You may travel out to different locations as and when required; work may be for straight or media make-up.

Status

- Employed
- Usually self-employed.

Job description (Level 2/Level 3)

You would be expected to provide: 1) special occasion make-up, 2) evening make-up, 3) bridal make-up, 4) prom make-up, 5) cosmetic camouflage make-ups, 6) make-up lessons, 7) airbrush make-up.

▲ Mobile make-up artist

Department store – make-up counter

Promotion and sales of the make-up is a vital part of this job role. Make-up lessons and advice on product suitability and colour choice will also be necessary so in-depth knowledge of the product range is imperative.

Status

Employed.

Job description (Level 2/Level 3)

The make-up artist will gain promotion and sales through various media such as special offers, promotional events and the application of make-up at the counter. The types of make-up required may be: 1) special occasion make-up, 2) evening make-up, 3) bridal make-up, 4) prom make-up, 5) fashion make-up, 6) cosmetic camouflage make-ups, 7) make-up lessons.

Some companies pay commission on sales to add an incentive for the make-up artist to sell their products.

▲ Department store make-up counter

Make-up representative – sales

This position could involve lots of travel to promote the wholesale of the company's products but a lot of companies will provide a company car with the job.

Status

Employed.

Job description

This job role could involve the make-up representative working towards sales targets, making appointments with various sides of the business such as salon owners, freelance make-up artists, educational establishments etc. to sell the products for re-sale. Excellent communication and organisational skills are required for this job role alongside great personal selling skills and a good underpinning knowledge of the industry. Many companies pay their representatives commission on sales to add an incentive to sell their products.

Freelance make-up artist

This may involve a variety of jobs being undertaken. It would be working on a self-employed basis. Most media make-up artists begin their career as a junior and work their way up to work as a make-up artist then make-up designer.

Status

Usually self-employed, often on short-term contracts.

Job description

The job could involve: 1) special-occasion make-up, 2) evening make-up, 3) bridal make-up, 4) prom make-up, 5) cosmetic camouflage make-ups, 6) fashion and photographic make-up, 7) airbrush make-up, 8) theatrical make-up, 9) special-effects make-up, 10) safe removal of make-up, 11) setting and dressing wigs, 12) styling and fitting postiche, 13) laying on facial hair/setting, 14) styling hair, 15) applying hairpieces and 16) applying hair accessories.

Many make-up artists are also fully qualified hairdressers or have some hair-styling qualifications.

> "A lot of responsibility rests on the make-up artist during a media production; continuity is a vital piece of the production process. The make-up artist must ensure that everyone working on the make-up team is fully aware of any changes and keep thorough records for continuity."
>
> **Melanie Doyle**, Freelance Make-up Artist and Lecturer

Junior media make-up artist/make-up assistant

This may involve assisting the make-up artist, lots of setting-up areas, tidying up and cleaning brushes etc. It is important to be a proactive junior to try to get noticed by your peers; this is how to build a professional reputation and gain further work. Never, ever overstep the mark and know your job role.

> "For me a make-up artist is vital to any professional production. Their role not only improves the quality of the film but helps to take some pressure off myself. Spotting continuity errors is always a difficult and painstaking process, but a very necessary one. Having a make-up/wardrobe specialist on hand not only gives me peace of mind but lets me concentrate on my job a little better. The best kind of crew member is always professional, knows their role inside out, is enthusiastic and knows when they are needed."
>
> **Gareth Britton**, Director, camera operator/filmmaker

Media make-up artist

You may be working as part of a team, taking direction and instruction from the make-up designer and be responsible for some continuity records, liaising with others such as in hair and wardrobe. A senior make-up artist may be appointed on a larger production to also oversee the juniors; this will help support the make-up designer.

▲ Media make-up artist

Media make-up designer

The make-up designer is responsible for liaising directly with the production crew. They will initially be given the script and attend production meetings to develop ideas with the production team. These ideas will then be presented to the director and producer in a professional portfolio, either as hard or electronic copies. Further meetings will then follow whilst the ideas are finalised and budgets agreed.

The designer will then order the products and equipment with their allocated budget. They will assemble the make-up team and divide the job roles and areas of responsibility. They will hold make-up team meetings and finalise the designs with the team.

> "Working on any set is always pressure-filled and exciting, whether in a controlled environment like a studio or exposed to the elements outside. But one thing that stays consistent with the changing locations is the expectations of every crew member. Professionalism is constantly required. A good make-up artist knows their job is never done; they must always be aware of how the shoot is going, what is expected of them, and be ready on set at a moment's notice. Long hours, difficult circumstances and battling with continuity are just a few things they face, but the rewards and positives are endless."
>
> **Gareth Britton**, Director, camera operator/filmmaker

Theatrical make-up artist

This is similar to the media make-up artist, where there may be a junior, a make-up assistant, a make-up artist and a make-up designer. The job roles are similar in a theatrical context. Timing is imperative in the theatre as it is very fast moving, live production, and with lots of quick changes involving other members of the production team.

Wig master/mistress/designer

This involves liaising with the client (the client could be a producer or director), who gives you a remit in which the wig will be designed from. Often the wig master/mistress is a make-up artist too. In the Theatre or Media setting there could be production meetings to develop the designs for the wigs and agree budgets. Wardrobe and make-up are also usually involved in this process as the total look has to work in all these aspects. Practicalities, for example quick changes, must be taken into consideration, especially in the theatre, so that the wigs don't get ruined and are easy to fit securely when a performer has changed costume. The wardrobe department and costume designer will usually work closely to find ways of changing costumes so whenever possible they don't have to be put on or taken off over the head.

The wig masters/mistresses usually head the team of wig dressers to ensure that things run smoothly. Some larger production companies employ the wig master/mistress on a permanent basis, where smaller companies offer short-term contracts but often use the same people.

The wig master/mistress may also be responsible for teaching the cast how to apply their own make-up, so that the team can work on hairstyling, postiche and make-up on the rest of the cast.

Wig dressers

Wig dressers are responsible for the wig and postiche during a performance and are often make-up artists too! More junior roles in this aspect of the industry include assistant wig dressers.

Special-effects make-up artist

This type of make-up artist specialises in special effects make-up, prosthetics, moulding and casting, and may liaise with the other members of the special effects production team. The special effects make-up artist would be involved in the production meetings to develop the effects and agree budgets. The job role/structure may be similar to that of a media make-up artist.

▲ Theatrical make-up

▲ Wig master/wig dresser

"I have been a professional make-up artist for over 30 years, working in all areas of the industry from film and TV through to fashion, theatre and special effects. I was fascinated with films as a child and loved the golden age of Hollywood – I collected old film annuals from the age of around 10 and used to make up the pictures of the Hollywood film stars with crayons, so I think I was destined to do this as a career!"

Louise Young, make-up artist

Fashion and photographic make-up artist

There are many areas to work in as a fashion and photographic make-up artist. It is often very high-profile work and very demanding, where you have to think on your feet and work to a budget and a remit with demanding schedules and timescales.

For those working in this job it is necessary to do lots of research into current fashion trends, historic/period design, colours, design trends in art, interior design etc.

▲ Fashion and photographic make-up artist

NHS – camouflage make-up, Ambulance Service and mortuary make-up artist

These types of job role may require a sensitive approach but can be very rewarding.

Camouflage make-up artist

This often involves working with people who may have been referred via the NHS for a variety of reasons. Occasionally clients will seek the help of a make-up artist for this type of work themselves.

Status
- Employed
- Self-employed.

Job description
Clients may require areas on the face or body to be covered because of many of the following reasons:

- Scarring
- Birth marks
- Skin grafts
- Pigmentation disorders
- Vascular disorders
- Varicose veins
- Acne rosacea and vulgaris
- Tattoos

Tip Professional etiquette is so important; experience has told us this. I always remember one overzealous junior make-up artist, overstepping the mark, desperately trying to impress the make-up designer went to touch up an 'A list' celebrity's make-up, who had their own make-up artist they worked with regularly, who remarked 'Oh who are you?' Needless to say the junior didn't work with the team again.

- Moles
- Dark circles around the eyes
- Age spots.

Face shapes and features can also be corrected using camouflage make-up techniques.

Working with the Ambulance Service

Usually special-effects make-up is required for this role.

Status

- Usually self-employed.

Job description

Often make-up artists agree short-term contracts with the Ambulance Service or sometimes the other emergency services to assist them with staff training activities. Often special-effects make-up is used to add realism to actors in a training scenario.

NHS wig service

The NHS wig service offer help to people who have problems with all types of hair loss. Highly trained specialists from the NHS send the patient to a specialist wig centre that has been approved by the NHS. The wig specialists are trained in measuring and making handmade lace wigs, fitting for lace front wigs, mono wigs, machine-made wigs and hair pieces, and are responsible for cutting the wig to suit the client's needs. The specialist will need to have very good interpersonal skills to gain the client's confidence, so they feel happy talking about what may be to them a very painful subject. It is important to be as helpful and understanding to the client as possible to help make easier the very stressful and difficult choice of choosing hair style and colour.

You may have to make visits to clients' homes and work around treatments such as dialysis. Some clients may be housebound or severely disabled, so driving is a good asset.

You may be working with:

- A terminally ill person who does not have long to live
- Clients who are on chemotherapy and don't yet know the outcome
- Clients suffering with alopecia
- Male or female clients in all age groups including children, teenagers, middle-aged persons and pensioners.

You will find that the clients' families often become involved and this can be a very emotional time for all of them.

This is a very rewarding job for the right person.

Status

- Employed
- Self-employed.

Job description

Often with lace wigs the measurements are taken and then the foundations of the wigs are made and posted out to a freelance wig-making specialist to hand knot. This is freelance work, although wig shops will employ staff.

Mortuary make-up artist

This type of job role involves applying make-up to a corpse prior to burial.

Status

- Usually self-employed.

Job description

Often camouflage make-up is required to cover blemished areas that may have occurred during or after death.

Education – lecturer

This job role may take different forms:

- Working for a product company as a trainer/educator
- College/university lecturer – teaching qualifications (usually the Certification in Education is required for college lecturers and PGCE for some college and all university lecturers or anyone teaching to foundation degree level or above) are required along with industrial experience.

Status

- Usually employed, full or part time.

Job description

Planning, preparing, delivering and evaluation of lessons/lecturers to learners of all ages and abilities. Pastoral care of learners, for example:

- Ensuring their well being
- Equality and diversity
- Differentiation strategies (for different learning styles and abilities)
- Equal opportunities.

"I started working with HABIA around four or five years ago and am on their Skills Team, travelling the UK training and doing photo shoots and videos."

Louise Young, make-up artist

Average rates of pay for a standard eight-hour working day

Pay may vary depending on where in the world you work and the size of the production:

- Junior make-up/hair artist – £100
- Make-up/hair assistant – £120
- Make-up/hair artist – £140
- Make-up designer – £180–200
- Special-effects make-up designer – £180–200

> ⭐ *Tip* Gain as much work experience as you can – this will help build your professional reputation and portfolio.

Legislation

The law protects you from discrimination (see Chapter 2 Health and Safety and Chapter 3 Client care and communication in the beauty-related industry for more information on the specific acts) due to your gender, age, race, beliefs, religion, disability or sexual orientation. Here is a list of the relevant Acts to be covered:

- Equal Opportunity and Discrimination Acts
- Working Time Regulations, National Minimum Wage
- Employment Rights Act
- Employment Act
- Health and Safety at Work Act
- Performing Rights regulations
- Data Protection Act
- Trade Description Act
- Consumer Protection Act.

Competitions

The competition circuit is an exciting arena to show off creative work. It is great experience for students and professionals to showcase their talents. Many colleges and trade shows put on student competitions. Trade shows also hold competitions for professionals too.

Competitors work to a design brief and examples of the categories include:

- Catwalk make-up
- Face and body painting (including sponge and brush, airbrush and prosthetics)
- Fantasy face make-up.

There are often cash prizes and goodie bags for competitors placed first, second or third.

Job searching in the make-up industry

Jobs in the make-up industry can be found by using any of the following:

- Internet
- Trade magazines
- Newspapers
- Jobs fares
- In-house
- Word of mouth
- Agencies
- Photographers.

Internet

Of course the internet is a useful tool when searching for work; there are many websites that advertise job vacancies. There are some websites specifically designed for all aspects of media work and students and novices often advertise for work as make-up artists on short film projects, often as university media students' final year projects. This is often unpaid work and is a great way to gain experience and make contacts; this is also a great way to build your professional reputation.

Many professional media make-up artists also have their own website to advertise their skills to potential employers, to display their CV/portfolios and show reels.

Trade magazines

Many jobs are advertised in these publications, sometimes worldwide.

Newspapers

Selected newspapers may advertise jobs.

> ☆ *Tip* You never know who you will meet along the way – treat everyone with respect!

> ☆ *Tip* Never think that the job is too 'low budget' as everyone has to start somewhere and you don't know who those people may become in the future!

Make-Up Artist

Reference:
Vacancy: Make-Up Artist
Employer: West End Studios
Location: London
Duration: 4 days from 18/07/2011

We are looking for a talented make-up artist to work on set for a new short film. This is an excellent opportunity for any make-up artist with experience of working on a film set. The ideal applicant will be able to bring their own ideas to the film and to work with other members of the crew to give each character a distinctive look. Reasonable expenses for travel and make-up products will be provided.

Please apply to David Hayes at david.hayes@westendstudios.co.uk, providing your CV and stating previous experience, availability for the dates shown, and why you'd like to be involved.

Only successful applicants will be contacted.

▲ Jobs can be found in newspaper ads or trade magazines

Jobs/careers fairs

Look in your local job centre, large shopping centres, newspapers, radio and the internet for these events. Lots of companies come together under one roof to recruit new employees. You can approach the companies with your CV and talk to their representatives about available positions and their requirements.

Tip Most novice/budding production companies will pay expenses!

In-house

Often new positions are advertised on staff notice boards, newsletters, e-mails and staff intranets. This is a good way to work your way up the career ladder, as people often take any job positions, just to get into a company and then they can progress through this route.

Word of mouth

This is often how jobs in the media are gained – professional reputation follows you.

Agencies

Many media make-up artists have an agent to help find them work through their contacts and support them in advertising their skills and talents, just like an actor or model would. The agent will charge a fee, usually per job and there may be an initial fee when the agent takes a new client onto their books. The make-up artist would need a professional portfolio of their work; this is often displayed on the agent's website.

Photographers

A photographer often works with a few make-up artists who they have worked with previously and work is often gained through word of mouth, by professional reputation.

Speculative applications

You may send your CV directly to production companies and fashion or make-up designers to see whether they have any suitable jobs.

Employment rights and responsibilities
Employment rights
Contracts of employment

This is an agreement between an employer and an employee that sets out their employment rights, responsibilities and duties; this becomes a contract as soon as you accept a job offer. It doesn't have to be in writing but you are entitled to a written statement of your main employment terms within 2 months of starting work. If you start work it will show that you accepted the job on the terms offered by the employer, even if you don't know what they are. Having a written contract could cut out disputes with your employer at a later date, and will help you to understand your employment rights.

You and your employer are bound to the employment contract until it ends (usually by giving notice) or until the terms are changed (usually in an agreement between you and your employer).

National minimum wage

At the time of writing the minimum wage rates are as follows:

- £5.93 – the main rate for workers aged 21 and over
- £4.92 – workers aged 18–20
- £3.64 – workers aged 16–17 (older than school-leaving age but younger than 18)
- £2.50 – apprentices under age 19, or 19 or over and in the first year of their apprenticeship

As from 1 October 2010 the age at which you become entitled to the main rate was reduced from 22 to 21 years old. The apprentice rate was also introduced at the same time.

If you are of compulsory school age, you are not entitled to the National Minimum Wage.

Employment responsibilities

It is a legal requirement to work safely – a professional should only carry out treatments that they are qualified to do. Salon owners and employers usually have their own workplace policies too.

Safe working environment

Follow industry COP.

Good working practices

The make-up and hair artist should be fully aware of good working practices, including:

- Personal Protective Equipment (PPE)
- Control of Substances Hazardous to Health (COSHH)
- Health and safety
- Hygiene – sterilisation and disinfection.

Developing and promoting a professional image

Professionalism is imperative at all times whilst working in any aspect of the make-up industry, no matter how small or low budget the job is. You never know who you might work with again; a good reputation will follow you! How can you develop and promote a professional image?:

- Be well organised
- Be punctual
- Be prepared for the unexpected
- Ensure personal hygiene is of a good standard
- Be well groomed
- Work to commercially acceptable timings
- Good interpretation and presentation of ideas to clients
- Know your job role
- Teamwork is vital
- Never gossip
- Treat everybody with respect – professional etiquette counts for a lot!
- Observe a high standard of hygiene, health and safety at all times
- Know the organisational requirements – a set of work rules issued by the employer
- Ensure you are up to date on new techniques, products and training through continual professional development (CPD).

These things will help you build a good reputation and that's often what helps you get further work. Teamwork is essential but on set it is vital, so the targets, timings and budget are met. This also promotes a professional image.

"Teamwork on set is massively important from an actor's perspective. It is a necessity if things are to work smoothly. Without teamwork, filmmaking just wouldn't work. The tight shooting schedules call for all members of the team to pull together, so that each day's goals are achieved. If crew members don't work together well, nothing would get done, sets wouldn't be constructed, hair and make-up wouldn't be designed and applied, the actors would have no stage on which to perform."

Calum O'Toole, Actor

'When working on set it is absolutely imperative that you work as a team. It is far too easy to overbear yourself with logistics. Have people you can trust and who are just as passionate about the industry/project as you are. Always plan the shoot well in advance and remember, fail to prepare and you prepare to fail. But most of all, HAVE FUN!!'

Dane Jones, Independent Producer

Appearance and personal hygiene

When working in close proximity as therapists and make-up artists do with their clients and models, it is important to pay particular attention to personal hygiene.

How can the therapist promote a professional appearance?

- Wear clean, low-healed, fully enclosed footwear – for comfort and safety
- Keep jewellery to a minimum – usually a wedding band and small unobtrusive earrings; this will help avoid injury to the client
- Nails should be clean, short and free of enamel/polish – so as not to interfere with the treatment and to help avoid injury and possible allergic reaction for the client
- Hair should ideally be tied back – to avoid contact with the client or product and so it does not interfere with the treatment
- A freshly laundered uniform should be worn; this should be clean and pressed (this may not be a traditional 'overall' type uniform, but it should be 'suitable sufficient clothing'). This is a health and safety requirement under the PPE regulations.

While it is good practice for a make-up artist to always maintain a professional appearance, it will not always be practicable to apply the above rules (especially when working on set in varying environments).

▲ A professional make-up artist

Professionalism

The first impressions you make are usually lasting ones. If you are a clean, professionally turned out make-up artist, this will help to instil the client's confidence in your professional abilities. No matter how well you know the client you must remain professional at all times because your reputation is everything and you never know who may be around. You should remember that a lot of media jobs are gained through word of mouth.

Professional etiquette

This is very important when working in the media sector. Know your job role and be proactive but do not overstep the mark.

How to access information on industry standards
Hair and Beauty Industry Authority (HABIA)

Information on HABIA can be accessed via the internet on www.habia.org.

HABIA is the government-appointed standards-setting body for hair, beauty, nails, spa therapy, barbering and African-type hair. It also creates the standards that form the basis of all qualifications including National Vocational Qualifications (NVQs), Scottish Vocational Qualifications (SVQs), apprenticeships, diplomas and foundation degrees, as well as industry COP and assessment strategies, which are then used across the industry in the education sector and by awarding organisations.

▲ A professional therapist

HABIA provides guidance on careers, business development, legislation, salon safety and equal opportunities, and is responsible to government on industry issues such as education and skills.

HABIA also raises the profile of its industries through the press and media, and is the first port of call for news organisations and broadcasters on news items and background information.

Codes of Practice

Information on the COP for beauty therapists can be accessed via the HABIA website www.habia.org.

The COP contain clarification on a range of generic issues such as proper client consultation, infection control, operational procedures (including preventing repetitive strain injury (RSI)), salon safety, following manufacturers' guidance, insurance, personal protective equipment, waste disposal and training and education, as well as a section on health and safety law.

Although compliance with the codes is voluntary, they have been promoted widely throughout the beauty and nail industries, as well as to the consumer press and to environmental health officers in order to encourage good practice based on nationally agreed standards. This code can also be adopted for media make-up and make-up artistry.

Continual professional development

Information on CPD can be accessed via the HABIA and awarding organisations' websites and publications. A generic list of awarding organisations for the industry can be found at the front of this book.

It is good practice for the professional make-up artist to update their skills by training, refreshing or updating and becoming aware of:

- Techniques
- Latest treatments
- Products
- Equipment
- Business developments.

Keeping knowledge up-to-date in these areas is vital to success in any industry. For NVQ qualifications it is compulsory for an assessor or internal or external verifier to complete a set amount of CPD hours. For other qualifications, while not compulsory it is good practice.

Awarding organisations

An awarding organisations is a validated, professional organisation, that provides qualifications and relevant materials, against National Standards for industries. Information on awarding organisations can be accessed via the HABIA and awarding organisations' websites and publications.

Health and Safety

The make-up industry should follow the HABIA COP for Beauty Therapy.

Tip There is always something new to learn in this industry as techniques and products develop and evolve; this is what keeps skills fresh, interesting and challenging.

Tip It is often the old cliché of 'it's not what you know, but who you know', that applies in this industry!

How to create and present a CV/portfolio suitable for the make-up industry

A traditional CV may be appropriate for some aspects of the industry but not others, for example:

- Salon work – hair or make-up
- Make-up counters
- Sales jobs.

Often in the media sector people are so busy that they don't always have time to read through a traditional style CV. This is a generic guide on how the CV/portfolio should be presented:

- Visual – include lots of photos of your relevant work
- Type of media job you worked, i.e. TV drama, special-effects film etc.
- Production title you worked on
- Who you worked for – what company?
- Cast members may be included
- Position/job title you held
- Show reels, e.g. videos, PowerPoint presentations, websites etc.

As a make-up/hair artist you may work with other professionals in the beauty-related industry and the media industry, such as:

- Beauty therapist
- Electrologist
- Nail technician
- Manicurist/pedicurist
- Masseuse/masseur
- Aromatherapist
- Reflexologist
- Complementary therapist
- Cosmetic consultant
- Sales representative
- Receptionist
- Salon manager/owner
- Teacher, trainer
- Production crew, including hairdressers and designers, wig specialists, wardrobe etc.
- Actors/performers
- Photographers.

> ⭐ *Tip* Look up the credits at the end of productions to find out the production company and contact them direct with your CV/portfolio.

Model release forms

One mistake photographers often make when they take photos is to believe that they can use their images whenever, wherever and however they wish. This is not the case; they do not own that image.

Regardless of whether you are photographing people you know, people who know they are being photographed, or buildings, if you want to place those images with an agency, sell them, publish or syndicate them you must ensure that you have a signed 'model/building release form'. You may be required to have separate forms for children to also cover child protection issues.

The rules regarding the use of these forms may vary greatly from country to country and you should never expect a signed release form to be fail-safe; however, it's a vital first step into protecting yourself from possible expensive litigation.

Model release form

I, the undersigned, do hereby consent and agree that West End Studios, its employees or agents have the right to take photographs, videotape or digital recordings of me beginning on *14 July 2011* and ending on *17 July 2011* and to use these in any and all media, now or hereafter known. I further consent that my name and identity may be revealed therein or by descriptive text or commentary.

I do hereby release to West End Studios, its agents and employees all rights to exhibit this work in print and electronic form, publicly and privately, and to market and sell copies. I waive any rights, claims or interest I may have to control the use of my identity or likeness in whatever media used.

I understand that there will be no financial or other remuneration for recording me, either for initial or subsequent transmission or playback.

I understand that West End Studios is not responsible for any expense or liability incurred as a result of my participation in this recording, including medical expenses due to any sickness or injury incurred as a result.

I represent that I am at least 18 years of age, have read and understand the foregoing statement, and am competent to execute this agreement.

Name: *K. Young*   Date: *14/07/11*

Address: *13 Clarendon Road London SW1 4PB*

Signature: *K Young*

Witness: *T Clarkson*

▲ Example of a model release form

End of chapter knowledge test

1. State **one** type of job available to the make-up artist.
2. Name **two** methods of searching for work.
3. State **one** reason why it is important to work as a team whilst on set.
4. State **one** piece of legislation used for good working practices.
5. State **two** ways of developing/promoting a professional image.
6. What organisation set the standards for the industry?
7. Where could information on Codes of Practice (COP) be accessed?
8. State **one** reason why it is important that a photographer use model release forms.

CHAPTER 2

Health and safety practice in the salon

Units covered by this chapter:

Level 2 VRQ: Follow health and safety practice in the salon

Level 2 NVQ Unit G20: Ensure responsibility for actions to reduce risks to health and safety

Levels 2 and 3 VRQ: Working in beauty-related industries

Level 3 VRQ: Monitor and maintain health and safety practice in the salon

Level 3 NVQ Unit G22: Monitor procedures to safely control work operations

This is a generic unit for beauty therapy and hair and media make-up. The knowledge and understanding within it is transferable and can be adapted for use in both industries.

Chapter aims

This chapter will show how important health and safety practice is and how it relates to the beauty-related industry. It looks at:

☞ all health and safety laws

☞ monitoring and maintaining health and safety practice in the salon

☞ hygienic and safe working practices

☞ consultation, record cards, treatment planning, make-up charts and sterilisation/ disinfection

☞ brush care.

Health and safety is important to ensure everyone in the workplace is safe. Many harsh chemicals are used within the make-up industry; the make-up artist must be able to apply, store and dispose of them correctly so as not to pose a risk to themselves or others.

Codes of Practice

This refers to a set of guidelines that we as professional therapists and make-up artists will follow. Some organisations and professional associations may have their own guidelines. These ethics are there to ensure that members of the public are protected from improper practice.

The code will:

● establish appropriate conduct

● establish acceptable practices

● protect clients from improper practices

● maintain professional standards of behaviour towards:

    1 other members of the organisation

    2 members of the public and clients

    3 other professional therapists and make-up artists

    4 members of other professional organisations

    5 colleagues within the industry.

In general all professional make-up artists should:

● comply with statute law and local by-laws

● apply treatments/services for which they are qualified

● not treat a client who may be contraindicated

● consult with the client's medical practitioner when necessary

● maintain client confidentiality

● treat colleagues with respect

● not criticise other businesses

● not deliberately poach clients from a competing business.

Statute law

This is the written law of the land and consists of Acts of Parliament and the rules and regulations that relate to the Acts.

Bylaws

These are the laws that are made at local rather than national level and are made by a council, for example:

- Planning permission
- Building regulations
- Certificate of registration (covering treatments such as epilation)
- Licensing (some councils charge a yearly fee to license a therapist for body massage or other treatments; they set standards and conditions for you to adhere to).

Health and safety legislation

The Health and Safety Executive (HSE) enforces and supports health and safety law. This legislation is in place to protect employees and members of the public and has identified three important areas of health and safety:

- Risk
- Hazard
- Control.

Hazards

Hazards are shown in the diagram below.

Key term
Risk – the chance, whether it be high or low, that someone could be harmed by the hazard with an indication of how serious the harm could potentially be.
Hazard – anything that may cause harm, such as chemicals, electricity, working from ladders, an open drawer etc.
Hazardous substance – a substance that could harm anyone who comes into contact with it, for example a harsh chemical.

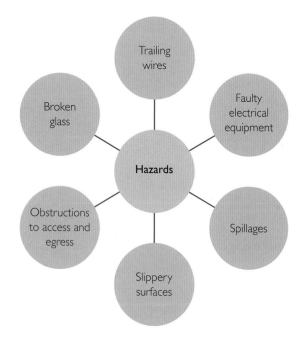

▲ Hazards

Trailing wires

Where possible do not let wires trail. They can be secured by the use of tape or cable tidies. Ensure there is no water near to the electrical equipment.

Faulty electrical equipment

Take the equipment out of service, label it as faulty for others to see and ask a qualified electrician to check it or return it to manufacturer if still under warranty.

Spillages

Place the 'wet floor' warning sign to alert people to the danger if a spillage has gone on to the floor. Clean up using a disposable cloth, paper towel or mop. Leave the sign there until the floor is dry. If a spillage has occurred on a surface, alert people to the hazard and clean up using an appropriate method.

Slippery surfaces

Deal with these in the same way as spillages.

Obstructions to access and egress

Remove the obstruction within the limits of your own authority and report the obstruction to the person in charge. If the obstruction is too big or heavy, a trained member of staff may need to use a special trolley to remove it. In this case report the obstruction to the person in charge and make arrangements for its removal.

Broken glass

Alert people to the hazard and report it to the person in charge. Do not use your hands to pick it up – a dust pan and brush is safer. Place it in paper or cardboard, carefully wrap it up and place it in the COSHH bin. Empty the bin.

▲ Wet floor sign

Safe working methods

It is important to work safely at all times. Health and safety Acts form the basis of safe working methods alongside industry codes of practice. This involves working in a manner that will not increase the risk of someone being injured in the workplace.

Workplace policies

Individual workplaces may have their own rules/policies regarding issues relating to health and safety. The basis of these is usually formed from the Health and Safety at Work Act and industry codes of practice. These policies are usually displayed within the premises and should be outlined during staff induction training; any updates to these policies should be identified to the staff.

> **Key term**
>
> **Control** – the means by which risks are identified, eliminated or reduced to 'acceptable levels'.
>
> **Legislation** – the laws affecting the way a business conducts itself.
>
> **Environmental factors** – things that surround you within the workplace.

Acts relating to the make-up industry

Health and Safety at Work Act 1974

This is the main piece of legislation from which all other health and safety regulations are made. Employers have a legal duty under this Act to ensure as so far as is reasonably practicable the health, safety and welfare at work of the people for whom they are responsible and the people who may be affected by the work that they do. Employers should make their staff aware of their workplace policies through regular training. Everyone in the workplace has a duty to take reasonable care to avoid harm coming to themselves or others in the workplace from the work they carry out.

Health and Safety (Information for Employees) Regulations 1989

This Regulation requires employers to display a poster telling employees what they need to know about health and safety.

Health and Safety

Remember everyone in the workplace is responsible for health and safety.

▲ Health and safety law poster (Source: Health and Safety Executive)

Employers have a legal duty under the **Health and Safety Information for Employees Regulations (HSIER)** to display the approved poster in a prominent position in each workplace or to provide each worker with a copy of the approved leaflet, outlining British health and safety law.

It must include the following information and details of:

- chemicals that are stored on the premises
- details of the stock cupboard or dispensary
- records of checks carried out by a qualified electrician on any specialist equipment
- escape routes and emergency evacuations
- names of key holders.

Regular checks should be carried out to ensure that safety is being adhered to at all times.

Management of Health and Safety at Work Regulations 1999

This Regulation states what employees are required to do to manage health and safety under the Health and Safety at Work Act. Like the Act, they apply to every work activity.

The main requirements are for employers to carry out a risk assessment and, if appropriate, implement necessary measures to ensure safety, including arranging appropriate training and information from competent people.

Employers with five or more employees need to record the significant findings of the risk assessment. If any risks have been identified, an action plan must be drawn up and all staff must be aware of the risks and the procedures that will be enforced to control the identified risks. The health and safety training for all staff must be ongoing.

The Workplace (Health and Safety and Welfare) Regulations 1992

This Act covers a wide range of health, safety and welfare issues including heating, lighting, ventilation, seating, workstations and welfare facilities.

Manual Handling Operations Regulations 1992

All people at work have the duty to minimise risks from lifting and handling heavy objects. Training should be given on this to ensure it is done correctly. For example, weight should be distributed evenly.

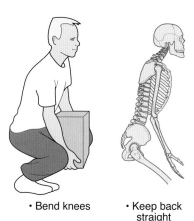

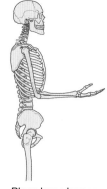

- Bend knees
- Keep back straight

- Do not lift heavy weights – get someone to help you

- Place large heavy boxes on the floor – do not lift onto high shelves

▲ Correct lifting technique

Provision and Use of Work Equipment Regulations 1992

This states that all equipment must be fit for its purpose, properly maintained, and all staff must be trained in the use of the equipment. This applies to all new and second-hand equipment.

Control of Substances Hazardous to Health (COSHH) Regulations (recently consolidated in 2002)

Many substances that seem to be harmless can sometimes prove to be hazardous if incorrectly used or stored. The employer has to carry out a risk assessment to assess those that could be a risk to health from exposure and to ensure that these are recorded; this must be carried out regularly.

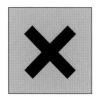

Highly Flammable

Harmful

Explosive

Toxic

Corrosive

Oxidising

Fire alarm call point

▲ Hazardous substances and symbols

Hazardous substances must be identified by symbols and handled and stored correctly.

Make-up products must be used by qualified professionals and must be correctly labelled, stored and disposed of under COSHH Regulations. However, some make-up products such as latex, collodion, adhesives and solvents are more hazardous and therefore great care must be taken. Wherever possible high risk products should be replaced with appropriate low risk products.

Waste

There are different types of waste:

- General waste
- Waste chemical products
- Contaminated waste/sharps (such as needles).

Contaminated waste

This should be disposed of in a sharps container that is disposable. The local authority would be able to advise individual areas on their disposal arrangements.

An assessment must be carried out on all members of staff who may be at risk.

Personal protective equipment should be provided and staff training should be carried out if required.

Hazardous substances can enter the body via:

- eyes – contact
- nose – inhalation
- mouth – ingestion
- skin – contact/absorbed
- body – injected or via cuts.

All suppliers must legally provide guidelines on how their materials should be stored and used.

All COSHH waste should ideally be disposed of in a metal bin containing a bin liner and a lid to help minimise vapours being released into the air. If a plastic bin is used it could be melted by some chemicals such as solvents. The COSHH waste bin should be regularly disinfected in a well-ventilated area and protective gloves should be worn while doing this.

Personal Protective Equipment (PPE) at Work Regulations 1992

The main requirement of these Regulations is that personal protective equipment (PPE) is to be supplied and used at work wherever there are risks to health and safety that cannot be adequately controlled in other ways. All employers must provide suitable personal protective equipment to all employees who may be exposed to any risk while at work.

Types of PPE

Types of PPE that may be used in the hair, beauty and media make-up industries include:

- Uniform
- Apron
- Powder-free vynal or nitrile gloves
- Protective mask and safety glasses (may be used when airbrushing and using some special effects/theatrical products, for example latex).

What do the Regulations require?

To ensure the right type of PPE is chosen, carefully consider the different hazards in the workplace. This will enable you to assess which types of PPE are suitable to protect against the hazard.

The Regulations also require that PPE:

- is properly assessed before use to ensure it is suitable
- is maintained and stored properly
- is provided with instructions on how to use it safely
- is used correctly by employees.

Training

- Make sure anyone using PPE is aware of why it is needed, when it is to be used, repaired or replaced and its limitations.
- Training and instruction must be given on how to use it properly.

CE marking

Ensure any PPE you buy is 'CE' marked and complies with the requirements of the Personal Protective Equipment Regulations 2002. The CE marking signifies that the PPE satisfies certain basic safety requirements and in some cases will have been tested and certified by an independent body.

▲ Make sure you wear correct PPE

Provision and Use of Work Equipment Regulations (PUWER) 1998

These Regulations refer to the health and safety controls on the provision and use of work equipment, addressing the specific Regulations that concern the potential risks and dangers that could occur when using the equipment. They state both the duties for employer and employee. This Regulation affects both old and new equipment.

It identifies the requirements in choosing suitable equipment and maintaining it, and the information that the manufacturers provide instructions and training in safe use of the equipment.

Data Protection Act 1998

The Data Protection Act is in place to protect client confidentiality.

- All information held must be kept in a secure place, whether held on a computer or record card.
- Information held must be accurate and necessary to the service or treatment being carried out.
- Information must be available for the person whom it is about to see at any time if they request to do so.
- Information must not be disclosed to a third party.
- Any out-of-date information no longer required must be disposed of in a secure way (not just thrown into the dustbin).

Computerised and paper-based record cards

When storing computerised record cards the make-up artist or business owner must register with the Information Commissioner under the terms of the Data Protection Act. This does not apply to paper-based written records; however, you must still uphold the principles of the Data Protection Act and comply with the following terms:

- All information must be stored securely, for example password-protected computer files and authorised access to paper records.
- You must not divulge information about clients to a third party, whether that is personal details or details regarding the service that has been provided or products that have been purchased. The consequences of failing to keep client confidentiality would be loss of clients, a bad reputation for the salon, the client could sue, or you may receive a warning from your employer.

Electricity at Work Regulations 1989

Any electrical equipment used must be maintained so it is in good working order and in a safe condition. It should be PAT tested every 12 months by a qualified electrician. It is the user's responsibility to report any faulty electrical equipment as unsafe for use to the relevant person in charge. This equipment should be labelled as faulty to ensure others are aware.

Regular checks of electrical equipment should be made by a trained member of staff. A general recommendation is that this is done around every three months and a record should be kept of the checks. A workplace may have its own policies on this to check for potential hazards and unsafe working practices such as:

- exposed wires
- warn or damaged cables
- damaged casing for plugs or sockets

- damage to the equipment itself
- trailing wires
- electrical equipment being used close to any liquids
- equipment should only be used by a person qualified to do so and for its intended use.

Reporting of Injuries, Diseases and Dangerous Occurrences Regulations 1985 (RIDDOR)

These Regulations cover the reporting of injuries, diseases and dangerous occurrences. Everyone in the workplace has a responsibility to report to the relevant person in charge if any of these things occur.

Cosmetic Products (Safety) Regulations 1989

This law governs the strength and volume of different hydrogen-based products depending on whether they have been prepared for professional or non-professional use. Manufacturers' instructions must always be followed when using professional products in a professional capacity. It is important to check the strength of the product to ensure it is suitable for the intended use. Guidance on this can be obtained via manufacturers and the Hairdressing and Beauty Suppliers Association.

The Consumer Protection Act 1987

This Act safeguards the consumer against unsafe products. It covers general safe handling requirements, product liability and prices that are misleading.

Disability Discrimination Act (DDA) 2005

Under this legislation access should be provided for disabled people at the premises.

Working Time Regulations 1998

These Regulations are concerned with working hours, holidays and rest periods for both full-time and part-time staff.

An employee cannot work more than, on average, 48 hours over 17 weeks unless the employee agrees in writing and a period of notice is agreed in which the employee can withdraw. If the employee also works elsewhere these other hours must be adjusted accordingly.

Those under the age of 18 are entitled to two days per week off and all adult employees are entitled to at least one day per week off.

Holidays

When an employee has been employed for 13 calendar weeks they are entitled to at least four weeks paid holiday; bank holidays can be counted towards these.

Minimum rest periods

All employees are entitled to at least a 20 minutes rest, if they have worked more than six hours. A young person is entitled to 30 minutes if they have worked more than four and a half hours.

Environmental Protection Act 1990

This Act states that all waste must be disposed of safely. It is important to exercise care when disposing of surplus/out-of-date stock and manufacturer's guidance should be sought. If in doubt, ask the manufacturer to dispose of the stock for you.

Waste Electrical and Electronic Equipment (WEEE) Regulations 2007

These Regulations affect the disposal of electrical equipment in the UK. They aim to reduce the amount of electrical equipment going to landfill and affect the way businesses get rid of old electrical equipment. Any equipment with a symbol of a crossed-out wheelie bin will need to be separated from standard rubbish. These Regulations also apply to the general public in relation to their household rubbish.

What you should do?

Contact your local waste collector or council to see if they have a local scheme to deal with electrical waste (arrangements vary across the country so you will have to ask them).

If you have old business equipment and you do not have an appropriate local scheme, you can contact:

- the company that is supplying new equipment, if you are replacing the old equipment
- the producer whose brand appears on the item if you are not replacing the equipment and you bought it since August 2005.

Employers Liability Compulsory Insurance Act 1969

This is the law if you employ anyone and you should display the certificate.

Inspection and registration of premises

The local authority's Environmental Health Department enforces the Health and Safety at Work Act. The environmental health officer/inspector visits and inspects the premises to check that people are sticking to the rules. Any area of danger is identified by the inspector, and it is then the employer's responsibility to remove the danger within a stated period of time. The inspector will issue an improvement notice stating the required improvements. If the employer fails to comply, this then can lead to prosecution. The inspector has the authority to close the business until he or she is satisfied that all dangers to the public and employees have been removed. This will involve the issuing of a prohibition notice. Inspectors investigate some accidents and complaints but they enforce only when something is seriously wrong.

Some treatments within the beauty therapy sector may require a certificate of registration; this will follow inspection of the premises to check that it can offer certain services safely, for example piercing and hair removal by epilation. Some make-up artists may already have beauty therapy skills.

Professional indemnity insurance

This provides cover for claims brought against the policyholder due to their professional negligence.

Health and Safety (Display Screen Equipment) Regulations 1992

If you have an employee who is working with display screen equipment, such as a receptionist, you will need to pay for eye tests given by an optician or doctor and special spectacles if required. It is also the employer's responsibility to provide information and training for display screen equipment users and ensure there are regular breaks or a change of activity.

It is also the employer's responsibility to provide information and training for display screen equipment users and ensure there are regular breaks or a change of activity.

▲ The Health and Safety (Display Screen Equipment) Regulations 1992

Risk assessment

The Health and Safety Executive sets out guidelines for risk assessment entitled 'Five steps to risk assessment'.

Apart from carrying out a risk assessment, employers should:

- make arrangements for implementing the health and safety measures as identified as necessary from the risk assessment
- appoint competent people (often themselves or company colleagues) to help them to implement the arrangements
- set up emergency procedures/policies
- provide clear information and training to employees
- work together with other employers sharing the same workplace if appropriate.

Why would a risk assessment be carried out?

To ensure safety in the workplace.

When should a risk assessment be carried out?

- When any change is introduced to the salon environment
- With any new service or product
- When there are any changes within personal/staff circumstances (for example, a change of job role).

What are the hazards?	Who might be harmed and how?	What are you already doing?	What further action is necessary?	Action by whom?	Action by when?	Done
Products and chemicals	Staff and clients may get skin irritation or allergy or breathing difficulties	• Staff to follow manufacturer's instructions • Wear non-latex gloves when mixing and using products • Salon and stock room well ventilated • Clients to be protected with towels	• Staff to check for customer discomfort • Staff to perform a skin allergy test before treatment • Manager to check with staff for skin allergies or problems every three months • Owner to buy eye baths in case of splashing incidents	All staff All staff Manager Owner		
Slips and trips	Staff and clients may be injured if they trip over trailing cables, or if they slip on spillages or wet floors	• Salon to be kept tidy • Any spillages to be cleaned up immediately • No trailing cables • Staff to wear appropriate footwear	• Staff reminded to check routinely for spills • Floor surface to be kept in good condition	All staff Owner		
Electricity	Staff could get electrical shocks or burns and there is a fire hazard from wet or faulty electrical equipment	• Staff to report any damaged plugs or cables • Staff to know how to turn off electricity in an emergency • Electrical equipment stored and used away from water	• Owner to visually check cables every six months • Manager to ensure all electrical equipment stored away from water • Electrics to be checked by an electrician every five years	Owner Manager Owner		
Standing for long periods	Staff may suffer back pain, pain in their feet and legs and neck or shoulder injuries	• Client chairs and couches fully adjustable • Wheeled stools provided for staff to use	• Manager to make sure all staff take regular breaks • Manager to check conditions for individuals and make any necessary special arrangements (e.g. pregnant women)	Manager Manager		
Fire	Staff and clients could suffer smoke inhalation and burns in the event of a fire	• Fire risk assessment completed	• Keep aerosols and flammable products away from windows	All staff		
Blades and sharp instruments	Cuts and grazes to staff and clients. Possible blood transmission and risk of blood-borne infection	• Sharp instruments cleaned and sterilised • Disposable sharp instruments disposed of in sharps box • Stocked first-aid box	• Staff to wear gloves • Spot checks to ensure sterilising procedures are followed	All staff Manager Manager		
Heavy lifting	Staff may suffer from musculoskeletal injuries	• Not to lift heavy objects unless necessary and to check weight before lifting	• None	All staff		

▲ Example risk assessment form

How can staff stay up-to-date on any risks within the workplace?

- Clarification of existing requirements and updating of information via team meetings, e-mails, staff manuals etc.
- Induction for new staff, including manual
- Specific training.

This should be recorded and displayed for staff to see and staff should be made aware of any changes.

What is meant be a necessary action?

The action needed to reduce the risk, such as:

- recording the risk assessment
- report to the salon manager or owner
- an update of risk assessment information
- informing staff.

It is important that the employer provides a safe and healthy environment, and if a hazard is identified it must be reported to the designated person in order for the problem to be rectified.

Spillages

It is important to establish if a spillage is potentially harmful to health and the action that must be taken in the event that a spillage might occur. It is important to remember to whom it must be reported to, what equipment is required to remove the spillage and how it should be disposed of. If any spillage occurs in the workplace it is essential that it is removed immediately to avoid someone slipping and falling.

Obstructions

An obstruction is anything that blocks the traffic route in the workplace.

If a fire exit was blocked this would delay people from exiting the building, or prevent the emergency services entering the premises.

▲ Fire exits should not be obstructed

Registration, Evaluation, Authorisation and restriction of Chemicals (REACH)

This is a new chemicals policy for the European Union (EU) concerning the Registration, Evaluation, Authorisation and restriction of Chemicals. It came into force on 1 June 2007. This replaced a number of European Directives and Regulations with one single system.

It sets out to:

- provide a high level of protection to human health and the environment from the use of chemicals
- make the people who place chemicals on the market, i.e. manufacturers and importers, responsible for a managing and understanding the risks associated with their use
- enhance innovation in the competitiveness of the EU chemicals industry
- allow the free movement of chemical substances within the EU market.

Health and Safety

Don't put yourself at risk when in the workplace – stay alert to hazards.

Correct positioning

Correct and safe positioning of yourself and the client/artist throughout the service is important to avoid injury to either of you. As a make-up artist you may not necessarily be working in a treatment or make-up room, you could be in the middle of a field on location! Repetitive strain injury or carpal tunnel syndrome, bad backs, aching shoulders and knees are just a few examples of what may happen if posture is repeatedly poor or incorrect positioning of the client/artist leads to strain on the make-up artist's muscles, joints etc.

The client/artist should be positioned at the correct height for the make-up artist to work so that they are not straining themselves. Ergonomically designed equipment is preferable as it is often adjustable.

Also correct positioning of tools, products and equipment could help prevent repeated strain. For example, ensuring that these items are within easy reach to avoid overstretching for them.

Equipment that can help prevent strain

- Footrests may be provided when sitting for any long periods of time in case the make-up artist cannot comfortably place their feet flat on the floor.
- Try to position yourself and your clients directly away from sunlight to prevent discomfort.
- A rest pad may be provided for leaning on when providing certain services.
- Any chairs should be height adjustable with good back support.

A freelance make-up artist will travel and work in lots of different types of location; you are your best resource so you must look after your well being. Always work as safely as possible even when out on location.

Accidents and emergencies

The Health and Safety (First Aid) Regulations 1981

All businesses/workplaces must have an appropriate level of first aid treatment available. All employees should receive training and information on:

- who is responsible for first aid in case of accident or illness
- where the first aid box is located
- who is responsible for maintaining the first aid box

These Regulations apply to all workplaces in Great Britain, including those with less than five employees and the self-employed. The Regulations set out the aspects of first aid that employers need to address and offer practical advice on training.

First aider

As from 1 October 2009 changes were introduced to the first aid training regime. While the legislation remains the same, the supporting guidance has been updated. There are no rules on exactly how many first aiders may be needed but it would be sensible to ensure there is a sufficient number to cover the amount of staff within the business.

The first aiders in the workplace codes of practice for the first aid regulations (ACOP) recommend an annual refresher training session to be taken for first aiders to help maintain their skills but this is non-mandatory. These regulations require employers to provide suitable first aid equipment, facilities and personnel to offer immediate assistance if an employee is injured or becomes ill at work.

The Regulations state:

- A person shall not be suitable to carry out first aid unless they have undergone such training and have such qualifications as the Health and Safety Executive may have approved for the time being in respect of that case.

- First aiders must have a valid certificate of competence in first aid at work (FAW) or for emergency first aid at work (EFAW). This training enables the first aider to give emergency first aid if someone is injured or becomes ill at work. EFAW training involves at least 18 hours of training and FAW training lasts for at least six hours. Training organisations offering these courses must be approved by the Health and Safety Executive. These certificates last for three years and a re-qualification course needs to be taken before this time lapses to continue to be a qualified first aider.

The employer should also:

- Appoint a trained person to take charge in an emergency and to look after the first aid equipment. There should always be an appointed person available during working hours.

- A first aid box must be provided and maintained. The box should also contain guidance on the treatment of injured people. For example:

  1 How to deal with unconsciousness
  2 How to control bleeding
  3 How to give artificial respiration.

- Notices must be displayed which state:

  4 The location of the first aid equipment
  5 The names of the persons responsible for administering first aid.

- The first aider must update their training every three years. It is also the employer's responsibility to ensure this happens.

Larger businesses require a first aid room with fully qualified first aiders who must be registered through the Employment Medical Advisory Service (EMAS). The first aid box must be stocked well enough to cover the number of employees within the workplace.

All employees should have a basic knowledge of first aid, so that assistance can be given for minor injuries that can occur. However, a qualified first aider, nurse or doctor should only deal with those conditions involving acute pain, unconsciousness or serious bleeding (more serious injuries).

Accident book

Au Natural Beauty Salon

INCIDENT REPORT FORM

This form must be completed following an inccident or illness by the person making the report. It should be completed immediately following the incident and handed to the salon manager who will forward to the Health and Safety Officer as appropriate

Date _____ Time incident took place _____

Location of incident _____

Name of injured person _____

Address _____

Email address _____ Tel. No _____

Description of accident/illness:

Account of injury/illness (tick the relevant boxes):

First aid given ☐   Ambulance called ☐   Taken to hospital ☐

Relative called ☐   Treatment continued ☐

Signature of injured/ill person _____

Signature of person(s) attending the incident _____

Any preventative action or safety recommendations _____

Signature of Salon Manager _____

▲ Accident book

All accidents that occur should be recorded in an accident register/book. This should contain details of the accident that has occurred, with the date and details of what happened. If possible, the person who has had the accident should sign the report as a true reflection as to what occurred. Any witnesses' names and contact details should be recorded. Staff should be informed by the employer where the accident book is kept and whose responsibility it is to record any incidents. The injured person has a right to see what has been recorded regarding the accident. If any claim of negligence is made against the company this may be required as a piece of evidence by law.

First aid kit

There should be a first aid kit available that is clearly marked and clear signs showing the location of it. It should be kept in a damp-free, clean area.

▲ First aid box

The contents of the first aid box may vary according to the number of staff employed. The basic items you require:

- One guidance/information card
- Sterile eye pads with attachments
- Individually wrapped sterile adhesive dressings
- Medium and large sterile dressings – unmedicated
- Triangular bandages
- Safety pins
- Wound cleansing wipes
- Phials of sterile saline.

Some general first aid additions that are useful are:

- Scissors
- Disposable gloves
- Gauze
- Surgical adhesive tape
- Instant ice pack
- Emergency telephone numbers, such as local health centres and hospitals, standard local numbers for police etc.

Fire and evacuation procedures

All employers and employees should have knowledge of the fire and evacuation procedures if they are to ensure a safe working environment. Employers must make sure that there is up-to-date fire-fighting equipment and their employees are trained to use it.

This equipment must be located within easy reach. Failure to comply with the laws can have serious consequences and can be very costly for the salon.

The salon should clearly display notices detailing the evacuation procedures. The salon should appoint a fire marshal to oversee the evacuation procedures. The fire-fighting equipment should be in good working order and checked regularly.

Tip Information regarding health and safety can be gained from the HSE website or by writing to your local Health and Safety Executive.

Regulatory Reform (Fire Safety) Order 2005

The law on fire safety changed in October 2006 with the introduction of the Regulatory Reform (Fire Safety) Order 2005. The requirement for businesses to have fire certificates has been abolished and any previously held are no longer valid.

The law now:

- emphasises preventing fires and reducing the risk of fire
- makes it your responsibility to ensure the safety of everyone who uses your premises and in the immediate vicinity.

A set of guides has been developed to tell you what you have to do to comply with fire safety law, help you to carry out a fire risk assessment and identify the general fire precautions you need to have in place.

Previous legislation

Previously there were two key pieces of legislation for fire safety:

- **The Fire Precautions (Workplace) Regulations 1997; amended in 1999.** These Regulations updated the Fire Precautions Act 1971 and Fire Regulations Act 1976. Businesses in the UK had to carry out a fire risk assessment that looked at preventing fire in the first place and how to escape a fire safely. When the Regulations were amended at the beginning of December 1999 it had major implications for businesses. Then employers were responsible for fire safety and required to carry out a full fire risk assessment even if the workplace was covered by a fire certificate.
- **The Fire Precautions Act (1971).** This was very prescriptive piece of legislation. If you had a fire certificate, it would have been issued under this and it determined your level of fire safety. The focus was to reduce risk to life once fire has started.

Emergency personnel

In a fire, emergency personnel must suggest all the occupants within the building are evacuated.

Fire wardens

It would be sensible to have fully trained fire wardens who could coordinate evacuation procedures during an emergency. These fire wardens will also be trained in how to extinguish fires correctly.

Health and Safety

No one must use the lift during a fire as you could get stuck in there. Most businesses have a designated refuge area (usually at the top of a landing) for people in wheelchairs to wait for the designated trained person to assist them.

Fire detection equipment

Smoke Detectors Act 1991 (this Act applies to England and Wales only)

New premises must have one or more smoke alarms fitted. It is an offence not to comply with this law.

Smoke alarm

All businesses should have a smoke alarm fitted that is regularly checked to ensure it is in good working order. The fire safety officer for the business should be responsible for this. This can help save vital time during a fire by alerting people to the emergency as soon as it is detected.

Fire alarms

The fire alarm should be tested on a weekly basis to ensure it is in good working order. Staff should be made aware of evacuation procedures during the induction process, and regular simulations of the evacuation procedure are a sensible option.

▲ Smoke alarm

Fire-fighting equipment

Equipment to fight fires should be located in specific designated areas. All staff should be made aware of these locations during induction procedures and should be given any further staff training or updates as necessary. Relevant staff should be trained in the use of fire-fighting equipment and this equipment should only be used when the cause of the fire has been identified. Using the wrong extinguisher could make the fire worse. Never use fire-fighting equipment unless you are trained to do so and never put yourself at risk.

Fires can be fatal; they spread very quickly and it may be safer to leave the building once an alarm is raised, to telephone the emergency services on 999 and to let the professionals deal with the incident. No one should return to the building until the fire crew say that it is safe to do so.

▲ Fire alarm

Fire blanket

These are used to smother a small local ice fire or if a person's clothing is on fire.

Sand bucket

These are used to smother a fire if the source of the fire is a liquid by soaking up the liquid.

Water hoses

These are used to extinguish large fires caused by paper and similar materials. Electricity must be turned off before the water is used. Buckets of water may be used to extinguish a very small fire of this type if appropriate and safe to do so.

▲ Fire blanket

▲ Sand bucket

Fire ratings

All fires are grouped into classes, according to the type of materials that are burning. The classes of fire for the UK and Europe are different to those used in the USA and Australia.

The latest fire extinguishers to conform to BS EN3 Regulations are all red and have a coloured panel to show the contents and state the size in kilograms or litres.

	Fire type
Class A	Those involving free-burning materials such as paper, wood, fabrics and other textiles, and also plastics.
Class B	Flammable liquids and solids, such as diesel, petrol and oils (but not cooking oils), as well as solid fuels such as wax.
Class C	Flammable gases, such as propane, butane and methane.
Class D	Flammable metals such as sodium, potassium and magnesium. Electrical equipment fires involve electrical equipment such as switchgear or computers. (These are sometimes accidentally referred to as Class E fires, although the category does not officially exist in the UK.)
Class F	Cooking oils and fats.

Types of extinguishers

Each type has been specially designed to extinguish different types of fire.

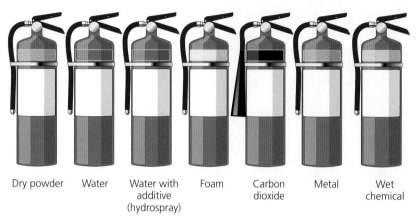

Dry powder Water Water with additive (hydrospray) Foam Carbon dioxide Metal Wet chemical

▲ Types of fire extinguisher

Dry powder

These are excellent all-round fire extinguishers that are painted red with a blue panel.

Water

These are filled with ordinary tap water and are ideal for use on Class A fires. They are solid red in colour.

Water with additive ('Hydrospray')

These are often referred to by the popular brand name of 'Hydrospray' and are up to 300 per cent more effective than normal tap water extinguishers. These are suitable for Class A fires and are painted completely red.

Foam

These are suitable for Class A and Class B fires. These are aqueous film-forming foam fire extinguishers (AFFF). Foam fire extinguishers are red with a cream panel above the operating instructions.

Carbon dioxide (CO_2)

Carbon dioxide or CO_2 fire extinguishers are the only ones recommended for fires involving electrical equipment – Class D fires. Carbon dioxide fire extinguishers are painted bright red with a black panel above the operating instructions, with a distinctive horn-shaped nozzle at the side or hose and horn on larger sizes.

Metal

A variety of specialist fire extinguishers are required to tackle Class D flammable metal fires. All flammable metal fire specialist extinguishers are categorised as powder extinguishers, so UK ones are painted red with a blue panel above the operating instructions.

Wet chemical

These were developed specifically for use on deep fat cooking fires (Class F fires). They are coloured red with a yellow panel above the operating instructions.

Fire extinguishers using DuPont FE-36 (Hydrofluorocarbon-236fa or HFC-236fa)

The US manufacturing company DuPont created FE-36 or Hydrofluorocarbon-236fa (HFC-236fa) as a replacement for the now-banned Halon fire-extinguishing agent. It is a clean, non-toxic agent suitable for use on fires near expensive electrical equipment. Small automatic extinguishers are commonly seen in the UK.

Halon

Halon fire extinguishers are now illegal in the UK (due to their ozone-busting potential), except in aircraft, for military use and in the Channel Tunnel. Halon fire extinguishers are painted a distinctive green or red with a green panel.

Scenario

You are working in a salon that has two floors and employs 20 people. You are giving a client a make-up service on the first floor and hear the fire alarm sound. What would you do?:

- Give the client a robe to wear
- Quickly and as calmly as possible leave the building. Walk, don't run, and never use a lift
- Make your way to the fire assembly point and report to the fire marshal
- Dial 999
- Stay out of the building and do not go back in until a member of the fire brigade says it is safe to do so.

Employer duties

The duties of an employer are shown in the flowchart opposite.

Other emergencies

Emergency situations may arise involving flooding, gas leaks, chemical leaks or excessive toxic vapours or fumes being released into the air. Evacuation procedures must be followed, but if appropriate and safe to do so the designated trained person should know the location of the relevant stop-cock to turn off a supply.

Employer duties

To provide a means of escape in case of fire for staff and the public

↓

Fire exits must be clearly marked and fire doors kept closed to prevent a fire from spreading

↓

To ensure that the escape area is kept clear of obstruction at all times

↓

To ensure means of escape is properly maintained and fire-fighting equipment is properly maintained and easily available

↓

To ensure all employers are aware of escape route and fire procedure notices are clearly displayed

▲ Employer duties

Carbon monoxide

Carbon monoxide (CO) is a colourless, tasteless, odourless, poisonous gas produced by incomplete burning carbon-based fuels including gas, oil and coal. Carbon-based fuels are safe to use; it is only when the fuel does not burn properly that excess carbon monoxide is produced, which is poisonous. When this enters the body it prevents the lungs from bringing oxygen to cells, tissues and organs.

Because you cannot see or taste this smell, carbon monoxide can kill quickly without warning. Levels that do not kill can cause serious harm to health if exposed to over of a long period of time; in extreme cases paralysis and brain damage can be caused.

How to prevent the risk

- Ensure any work carried out in relation to gas appliances is undertaken by a gas safe registered engineer, who is competent in that area of work.
- A landlord has a legal duty to carry out an annual gas safety check of gas appliances and flues and to maintain gas appliances. They must provide you with a copy of the completed gas safety check certificate.
- Always make sure there is enough fresh air in the room containing your gas supply and that vents are not covered.
- Chimneys should be swept from top to bottom at least once a year by a qualified sweep.
- Carbon monoxide alarms can be purchased as a precaution but guidelines for safety must always be followed.

Bombs

Staff should be trained in appropriate emergency procedures in the event of a bomb alert. This would involve how to recognise a suspect package and how to deal with that threat. Evacuation procedures should be followed and the emergency services contacted.

Security procedures

Any business regardless of size should have adequate security of its premises. This is a legal requirement and it is necessary when obtaining insurance cover and for leasing and mortgage procedures.

It is very difficult to make the salon premises completely burglar-proof, but steps can be taken to reduce the chances of a burglary and possible damage once the building has been entered.

The salon should also be fitted with security locks for windows and doors. Check with the insurance company if there are any special requirements with security. If the salon has a large shop front window, it is a good idea for it to be made of toughened glass. An alarm can be added to it in the form of a metal strip across the full length of the window. Metal shutters are ideal to protect the windows from breakage but can be costly to install. Decorative metal grills are also an alternative. A security light that works on a movement-detecting sensor is ideal however you must make sure that it is pointing at an appropriate angle and not into another person's window as there are laws regarding light pollution.

If retail stock is on display it should preferably be displayed in a glass cabinet that can be locked to prevent theft. Often these types of display are located in the reception area. Empty boxes can be displayed to protect stock.

Stock should be regularly checked by completing stock taking. This will record what stock is left and can then be used to indicate what stock is low and needs ordering. This is also a security measure to see if stock is going missing or it may act as a deterrent if staff know regular stock checks are in place.

Stock should be regularly rotated to ensure it does not go out of date. Older stock should be displayed at the front of the shelf and newer stock behind it. Be careful not to over order stock to avoid waste; it could be sat on the shelves and go out of date.

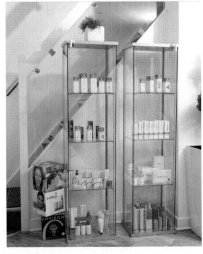

▲ Displaying retail stock in lockable glass cabinets prevents theft

Salon equipment

These items are often expensive to buy so they must be looked after. Ensure equipment is secure wherever possible. Rooms should be locked and equipment locked away where appropriate. Equipment can be included within regular stock checks.

Till point

If money is kept at the salon it should be secure in a cash register or safe. Banking should be done as often as possible to avoid money being left on the premises. Where possible only one person should be responsible for handling the daily takings. If the money has been banked you could leave the till drawer open at night to show that it is empty. Your local crime prevention officer can advise you on crime prevention and security measures, such as burglar alarms. These alarms can be linked to the security provider or the police. This enables a quick response to the alarm signal. A key holder is usually named together with a contact telephone number and registered with the police or security provider, and these people will be called out in the event of the alarm going off, regardless of the time! These key holders should be the only people responsible for locking and unlocking the premises. Some insurance companies charge extra premiums per key holder.

Staff belongings

Staff should try not to bring expensive items or large amounts of cash to work as a security measure to safeguard themselves against theft. The employer may or may not provide lockers or a locked cupboard or room in which staff can place their belongings while in the workplace.

Client/artist belongings

The client or artist may need to remove items such as jewellery and perhaps some clothing to have a make-up service carried out. In an ideal situation these possessions can be placed somewhere visible so that it is the responsibility of the client/artist to look after them. In some situations a locker, locked cupboard or room may be available for this purpose.

Insurance

The law expects a business to be insured, whether you own or rent it. This is in case of theft, accident or injury. If a business is not insured it could prove very costly for the owner.

Many make-up artists work on a freelance basis, meaning that they are self-employed. The main types of insurance needed for the make-up industry if you were self-employed are listed below.

Public liability

Public Liability insurance will cover you if someone is accidentally injured by you or your business operation. It will also cover you if you damage third party property while on business. The cover should include any legal fees and expenses which result from any claim by a third party.

Product and treatment liability insurance

In product liability insurance terms, a product is any physical item that is sold or given away. Products must be 'fit for purpose'. You are legally responsible for any damage or injury that a product you supply may cause.

If you supply a faulty product, claimants may try to claim from you first, even if you did not manufacture it. You will be liable for compensation claims if:

- your business's name is on the product
- your business had repaired, refurbished or changed it
- you imported it from outside the European Union
- you cannot clearly identify the manufacturer
- the manufacturer has gone out of business.

Otherwise, the manufacturer is liable (or the processor, where the product involves parts from multiple manufacturers). However, you must:

Activity

1. What other measures could you use to ensure stock control?
2. How could you ensure the safety of a client's belongings when in the salon?
3. How could you ensure staff's personal belongings are secure?

- show that you gave consumers adequate safety instructions and warnings about misuse
- show that the products were faulty when they were supplied to you
- show that you included terms for return of faulty goods to the manufacturer or processor in any sales contract you gave to the consumer
- have good quality control and record-keeping systems
- make sure that your supply contract with the manufacturer or processor covers product safety, quality control and product returns.

What is covered

Product liability insurance covers you against damages awarded as a result of damage to property or personal injury caused by your product. If damages are paid for personal injury, the NHS can claim to recover the costs of hospital treatment, including ambulance costs. This applies to incidents that happened after 28 January 2007.

Employer's liability insurance

This covers small businesses if an employee is injured or falls ill while at work. All employers must take out this type of insurance, although there are a few exemptions (for example, if you are the sole employee of your limited company and also own at least 50 per cent of the share capital in the company). If you are a sole trader and do not employ anyone (or you only employ close family members), you should also be exempt. However, if you occasionally hire staff or use temporary staff or seasonal workers, you must take out insurance.

Salon records

Any contraindications or contra-actions must be recorded on the client's record card for future reference. Client records may be stored manually or electronically; these should be updated at every visit. A record card should contain:

- client name, address and contact telephone number
- emergency contact name and telephone number
- any necessary medical information relevant to the service
- contraindication checks and, if appropriate, findings
- client requirements
- client lifestyle
- limitations or restrictions to the service
- details of the service
- follow-up recommendations
- any retail products purchased or recommended

Activity

1. What are the main types of insurance you would need for the make-up industry if you were self-employed?
2. What do the employers and employees have to do to make sure this insurance is covered and complied with?
3. List the main points to remember if a client makes an insurance claim against you.

- aftercare and homecare advice
- client/artist and make-up artist's signature and date (this should begin prior to treatment as it indicates the client is giving consent for the treatment plan to go ahead).

If a record card is not up-to-date and does not contain a history of services provided, the make-up artist's insurance may be invalid in case of a claim.

How long should record card be kept for?

Three years. Medical claims can be made in a period of three years following the survey. If the client is under 18 years of age the recommendation is that the record card is kept until they are 21.

The client record card is protected under the Data Protection Act.

Anyone under the age of 16 years should be accompanied by a parent/guardian who must sign the consent form and remain present throughout the treatment/service.

If a contraindication is identified during the consultation this can be discussed prior to the service and the appropriate advice given. In the case of medical referral where GP's permission is required to be able to continue with the service, a copy of the GP's letter can be kept alongside the client record card.

Workplace hygiene

The workplace needs to be spotlessly clean or you could risk the spread of infection. A clean, tidy workplace will also look professional, giving a good first impression.

It is rare that an infection is caught due to a make-up or skin care treatment; however, it is a possibility and we therefore must protect ourselves, our clients and our work areas regardless of whether that is in a salon environment, a make-up counter, or on location. It is good practice to reduce the risk of cross-infection (the transferring of infection by person-to-person contact) by practising good hygiene. It is possible that the person may not realise they have an infection or the symptoms may not have appeared at the time of treatment.

Preventing cross-infection

To prevent cross-infection the following procedures should be taken:

- A selection of disposable wooden spatulas should be available to remove cream-type products from their jars.
- Therapists and make-up artists must wash hands before and after each client/artist.
- The area to be treated must be cleansed and checked for contra-indications prior to carrying out the treatment.
- Towels should be washed at 60°C to kill bacteria.

- The massage couch should be covered with disposable tissue roll.
- All work surfaces, couches and trolleys should be wiped down with a chemical solution.

Waste disposal

This must be handled, bagged and disposed of according to the local environmental health regulations.

Infectious agents

There are four main types of infectious agents:

- Bacteria
- Viruses
- Fungal infection
- Infestations.

Bacteria

These are single-cell living organisms that exist in two ways: in single-cell vegetative form; or as spores. The spores are much more difficult to destroy but can be destroyed easily by chemicals. Often extreme heat is used to destroy bacteria, for example an autoclave. Most bacterial infections can be treated successfully with the use of antibiotics.

Viruses

These can only reproduce within living cells but can mutate to form new strains of virus. They are minute particles that are not treatable by antibiotics. Viruses such as herpes, hepatitis B and C and HIV/AIDS are a concern due to their transmission through blood-borne viruses.

Fungal infection

A consequence of the overuse of antibiotics to fight bacteria can be the increase in fungal infection production as the fungi are often kept at bay due to competition from bacteria. Some fungi can cause skin and mucous membrane infections, for example ring worm.

Infestations

Common infestations in humans include lice and the scabies mites, which burrow into the skin, often causing intense itching which when scratched can cause damage to the skin tissues, resulting in secondary infections.

Roots of entry for infectious agents

- Direct contact
- Inhalation

- Ingestion
- Injection/puncturing the skin.

Direct contact

Bacteria can be passed from person to person and often come from a lack of or poor hand washing technique, particularly after visiting the toilet. Urine or faecal matter could be passed on through direct contact and this may contain infectious organisms. This risk could be increased with the presence of an open wound.

Cross-infection

Effective hygiene is necessary in the salon to prevent cross-infection and secondary infection:

- Cross-infection occurs through micro-organisms that are contagious and are transferred through personal contact, through touch or by contact with infected equipment that has not been disinfected/sterilised.
- Secondary infection can occur as a result of the client having an open cut or wound, and bacteria penetrating the skin and therefore causing an infection, or by an injury caused during the treatment.
- Sterilisation and disinfection are methods used to destroy or minimise harmful micro-organisms that can cause infection.

Disinfection and sterilisation

Sterilisation is the total destruction of all living micro-organisms and **disinfectant** is the destruction of some but not all micro-organisms. Sterilisation and disinfectant techniques that are carried out in beauty salons involve the use of heat and also chemical agents such as antiseptics, disinfectants and vapours.

Heat

A very effective method of sterilising tools is with use of an autoclave – a piece of equipment that heats water to a very high temperature – higher than boiling. It creates what is known as super-heated steam and this is hot enough to quickly kill most common bacteria found in salons. Autoclaves are used by doctors, dentists and other professionals. Small, hand-held tools are put into the autoclave, it is sealed and the water inside it is brought to the required temperature. The temperature is maintained for the time necessary to ensure that all bacteria are dead and then the water is allowed to cool before the tools are removed.

You must ensure that you have sufficient supplies of tools to allow you to work on other clients while the autoclave is in use. This is the main drawback of this method of sterilisation. You must also buy tools that can withstand very high temperatures if they are to go into the autoclave.

> ### Key term
>
> **Antiseptic** – prevents the multiplication of micro-organisms but does not kill all micro-organisms.
>
> **Disinfectant** – destruction of some but not all micro-organisms.
>
> **Sterilisation** – total destruction of all living micro-organisms.

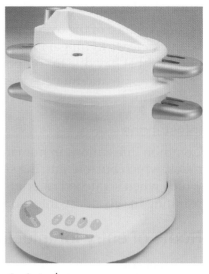

▲ Autoclave

Dry heat

This method of sterilisation is rarely used in salons. It is a method that uses an oven to create high temperatures. Although bacteria are effectively killed by this method, tools can be damaged because they are held in the heat for an extended time.

UV light rays

This method of disinfectant uses ultraviolet (UV) light rays to kill bacteria. Tools are cleaned then placed into a UV cabinet and the rays disinfect only the surface areas that the rays touch. This means that you must turn the items so that all surfaces are treated.

Many therapists and make-up artists tend to use the UV cabinet to store their tools in after they have been sterilised by another method such as the autoclave.

Chemicals

This method is often used in salons and is effective if used correctly. Tools must be washed before placing them into the chemical solution otherwise the dirt on them will contaminate the solution. The chemical must fully cover the item – many therapists and make-up artists place their tools into a sterilising jar that is only three-quarters full. The tools must be left in the chemical long enough for it to sterilise the tools; this time varies depending on the cleanliness of the item and the strength of the chemical solution, but it can take as long as an hour. As with using an autoclave, this means that the therapist or make-up artist must have enough tools to allow for the time taken to sterilise.

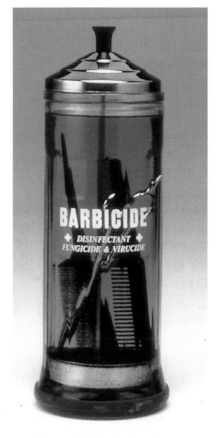

▲ Chemicals can be used to disinfect tools

Disinfectants and antiseptics

Disinfectant

A disinfectant destroys some but not all micro-organisms and the following should be noted:

- If for some reason an object cannot be sterilised, it must be wiped with surgical spirit and placed in a chemical disinfectant such as a quaternary ammonium compound or glutaraldehyde.
- Once implements have been removed from the disinfectant they must be rinsed in clean water to remove all traces of the solution in order to avoid an allergic reaction occurring on the client's skin.
- The quickest method of sterilisation is cleaning with alcohol, either by immersion or wiping the exposed surface of the implement with the alcohol before placing it in a dry steriliser. Alcohol wipes are easily used for this procedure.
- Containers that are used for disinfecting should be washed out on a regular basis with hot, soapy water and the

disinfectant should be discarded after one use as it will become unsterilised.

- All equipment must first be washed in hot, soapy water to remove surface debris, rinsed in plain water and dried thoroughly with the correct method of sterilisation.

Antiseptic

This prevents the multiplication of micro-organisms; it does not kill all micro-organisms. This is much milder than an antiseptic and can therefore be applied to the skin to cleanse it at the beginning of the treatment, but it does have limited effects.

Single-use Items

Items that cannot be cleansed or disinfected such as orangewood sticks, cotton pads and disposable paper coverings. These should be disposed of after each service and not reused.

▲ Single-use items cannot be sterilised and should be thrown away

Hygiene measures

- Wipe trolleys and work surfaces with disinfectant prior to use.
- Use clean towels and disposable covering for each client/artist (towels should be freshly laundered at 60°C in line with Codes of Practice).
- Use disposable products where appropriate.
- Use a spatula to remove products from containers to avoid cross-contamination.
- Clean bottle necks prior to putting lids on.
- Maintain a clean and tidy work area.
- The make-up artist should wash their hands before and after each treatment with anti-bacterial handwash/gel.
- Sterilise/disinfect all tools before and after use or dispose of them depending on type.
- Metal tools can be sterilised.
- Make-up brushes, sponges and other tools can be disinfected by washing them in warm soapy water to clean them then placing them in the chosen method for disinfecting.
- When working around the eyes use fresh cotton pads, mascara wands etc. for each eye.

Contraindications

This is a condition that may prevent or restrict a treatment from taking place.

If a condition is contagious it would prevent the treatment being carried out. Once the condition has cleared then the service could be carried out. If a condition is not contagious or there is open wound, red or swollen skin you could work around the area. If it is not located in the area where you are carrying out the treatment then you could make a note on the record card.

If a contraindication was identified during the consultation the client should be referred to a medical practitioner or GP for medical advice, a diagnosis and, if appropriate, medication.

Exposed cuts or abrasions may be covered with a waterproof dressing to prevent cross-infection.

Contra-actions

This is an negative reaction that has occurred due to the treatment or products used, for example an allergic reaction.

Contact dermatitis

This condition is an auto-immune response to an allergen. If this reaction occurs the irritant must not be used and a cold compress may be applied. If the condition worsens refer the client/artist to their GP for advice.

Acute dermatitis

This reaction is the skin's response to being exposed to an irritant and will occur almost immediately following exposure for the first time.

Chronic dermatitis

The reaction has occurred as the skin has been exposed to an irritant over days, weeks, months or even years. The skin may not have shown signs of irritation to the allergen immediately, but with repeated exposure it has become sensitised to it.

Personal hygiene

The appearance of both yourself and the workplace is a reflection of your professionalism, which will enable your client to make a judgement. Remember first impressions count.

Clients/artists will have confidence in you if you always look clean, well groomed and smart.

As you are going to work in close proximity with your clients/artists it is essential that body cleanliness is achieved, through daily bathing or showering. This will remove the sweat, dead cells and bacteria that cause body odour. An antiperspirant, applied under the arms daily will help reduce perspiration, as this has a tightening effect (astringent), and the smell of sweat. Underwear should be clean and changed daily.

Oral hygiene

Teeth should be cleaned every morning, evening and after every meal. Dental floss should be used to remove plaque. Breath fresheners and mouthwashes may be required to freshen the breath throughout the day. Remember to visit the dentist regularly, to maintain healthy teeth and gums.

Remember . . .

It is important that the make-up artist does not name specific conditions/contraindications as they are not medically qualified to do so and they may be wrong.

Key term

Contraindication – a condition that may prevent or restrict a treatment from taking place.

 Anatomy and physiology

For a full description of contra-actions, see Chapter 4.

 Health and Safety

"It is important that the hands are protected against dermatitis. This can be a very painful condition so protect the hands with before- and after-creams when using chemicals such as hair colour. Remember prevention is better than cure!"

Diane Griffiths

 Health and Safety

"Hygiene should be embedded into everything we do to avoid cross- infection and safeguard ourselves and our clients/artists." Louise Gray, Wigan and Leigh College.

Hands

It is essential that you wash your hands regularly, as they are covered in germs. Most of the germs may not be harmful, but some can most certainly cause ill health and/or disease.

It is important that you wash your hands before and after working on your client and if need be to wash/cleanse them during the treatment. This will minimise risk of cross-infection and also portrays a hygienic and professional image. When washing your hands it is always more hygienic to use an antibacterial liquid soap from a sealed disposable dispenser. Disposable paper towels should be used to dry the hands.

If you have any cuts or abrasions on your hands it is important you cover them with a clean dressing to prevent the risk of secondary infection.

Nail enamel should never be used when treating a client, as the client may be allergic to it and therefore develop an adverse reaction. Even though enamel will hide dirt that is present underneath the nails, it is better to present an enamel-free nail that is clean, so as to inspire confidence.

Feet

To ensure fresh and healthy feet, they should be washed daily and always ensure they are dried thoroughly.

Make sure the shoes are comfortable and are of the correct fitting, with a low, comfortable heel. It is important to remember you are on your feet all day long.

Foot sprays and powders can be used to keep the feet dry and cool.

Hair

If hair is long it should be tied back securely, to ensure it does not fall forwards, either over your own face, or the face of the client when working. Hair should always be clean as well as tidy.

Posture

Posture is the way you hold yourself when walking, sitting and standing. Correct posture will enable you to work much longer without becoming tired, preventing stiff joints and muscle fatigue. It is important to stand with the head up and body balanced centrally. Shoulders should be relaxed but held slightly back, with the weight evenly distributed and the feet slightly apart.

Uniform

The therapist must wear a protective, clean and pressed uniform each day. An apron can be worn to protect the uniform, made normally of lightweight fabrics that are comfortable to work in. Cotton is ideal as it allows air to circulate, allowing perspiration to evaporate and therefore discouraging body odour. The uniform should be fairly loose fitting and not too short if a dress style.

Jewellery

Jewellery must be kept to a minimum. A flat wedding ring is acceptable. Avoid wearing a watchstrap or bracelets that may catch on the client's skin during treatment.

Every salon or studio has its own rules on dress, jewellery etc. to reflect their own professional image; it is therefore best to stick to their rules.

Well being

A make-up artist may work long, unsociable hours and therefore it is important to take care of yourself to ensure your own health, vitality and well being.

- Eat a sensible well-balanced diet.
- Drink plenty of water to keep the body hydrated.
- Herbal teas can have a therapeutic effect upon the body.
- Take regular exercise.
- Try to take regular breaks.
- Hand, arm and shoulder exercises can be performed to stretch out and relieve tension between treatments.

Set up of the workstation

The workstation/treatment area should be well organised with the products, tools and equipment needed to perform the treatment/service to hand. If they are placed in order of use that may help too!

The workstation should not be cluttered. However, often in the make-up industry many products may be required to carry out the service.

A make-up artist may work on their client/artist on a make-up chair, treatment couch, stool or anywhere if out on location! The aim is to work as safely as possible at all times, this may mean you need to adapt.

▲ A treatment room: make-up artists often work on location rather than in this type of environment

Client preparation

The client should get onto the treatment couch or make-up/chair carefully. They must never sit on the end of the treatment couch as it may tip. They should be correctly positioned so that they are comfortable but also so the make-up artist is positioned correctly too. You should not be leaning downwards or stretching upwards.

For treatments such as skin care and most eye treatments the client's/artist's hair should be secured off the face by the use of a headband. However, often a client will have a make-up treatment/service after having their hair dressed. In this case, or where appropriate, a kirby grip could be used.

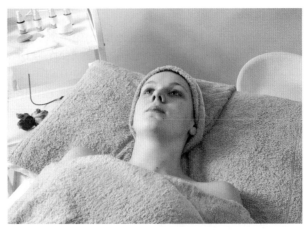

▲ Safe client preparation on treatment couch

Hand-washing technique

Following the guidelines shown ensures that all parts of the hands are cleaned. It should take at least 15 seconds to complete.

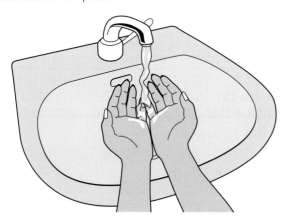

1. Wet hands with water.

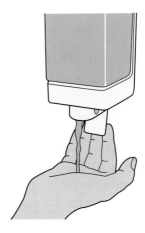

2. Apply antibacterial liquid soap to hands.

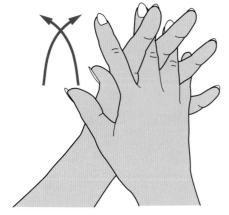

3. Ensure liquid soap is applied between fingers.

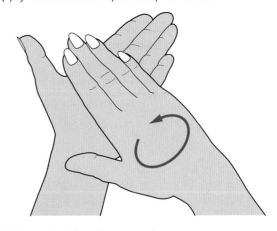

4. Rub hands with palms together.

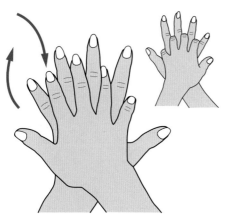

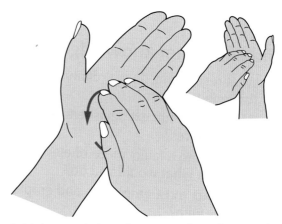

5. Rub the back of each hand with the palm of the other hand, with fingers interlaced.

6. Make sure lathered soap reaches all parts of hands.

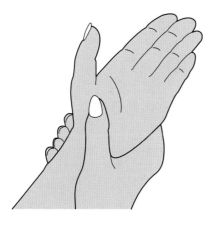

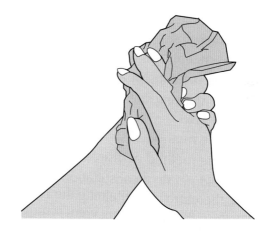

7. Rub each wrist with the opposite hand.

8. Dry hands thoroughly.

It is important to remember the following:
1. Remove rings or jewellery before washing your hands.
2. Wash hands before and after eating.
3. A gel type, non-rinse hand sanitiser may be used.
4. Wash hands after using the toilet.
5. Wash/sanitise hands before and after treatments.

End of chapter knowledge test

1. What regulations do we follow when disposing of waste in the salon?
2. What type of fire extinguishers can be used on electrical fires?
3. If you found a faulty piece of electrical equipment in the salon what would you do?
4. Which Act must employers and employees comply with?
5. How often should electrical equipment be checked by a qualified electrician?
6. What is the name of the insurance a salon owner must have in order to ensure the safety of the public?
7. What is meant by a contraindication?
8. State the meaning of a contra-action.
9. When employing staff what insurance cover do you need by law?
10. State one method of sterilisation.
11. State one method of disinfecting tools.
12. If you did not do a consultation and fill in a record card, therefore not obtaining the client/artist's signature and something went wrong with the treatment, what could happen with regards to your insurance?
13. A large glass gets broken in the salon. How should you dispose of it?
14. Why do we use disposable equipment/covering in the salon environment?
15. Why do we maintain high standards or personal hygiene in the salon?
16. If an accident occurred in the workplace how would you safeguard against a client or artist claiming other injuries occurred?
17. Why is the record card important?
18. What is meant by sterilising equipment?
19. How could you ensure staff's personal belongings are secure?

CHAPTER 3

Client care and communication in the beauty-related industry

Units covered by this chapter:

Level 2 VRQ: Client care and communication in beauty-related industries

Level 2 VRQ: Working in beauty-related industries

Level 2 NVQ Unit G8: Develop and maintain your effectiveness at work

Level 2 NVQ Unit G18: Promote additional services and products to clients

Level 3 NVQ Unit H32: Contribute to the planning and implementation of promotional activities

This is a generic unit for beauty therapy and hair and media make-up. The knowledge and understanding within it is transferable and can be adopted for use in both of these indusries.

Chapter aims

This chapter will look at:

- Importance of communication in relation to the industry
- Client care
- Promoting additional services and products to clients
- A retail area for make-up, i.e. make-up counter and display cabinets
- Contributing to the planning and implementation of promotional activities – teamwork, marketing, advertising, personal selling skills and unique selling point (USP).

Client care is such an important aspect of the industry. A client must be made to feel special and important; they should have your full attention throughout the service. This will keep clients coming back to you time after time, which will also help to increase your profits, reputation and client base.

Importance of achieving the correct environment

Creating the right environment is important with all treatments and each treatment area may be created specifically to suit delivery of each treatment. For example, most skin care treatments require a calm and relaxing environment. The colour scheme and music played could be chosen to reflect this. All working environments, regardless of whether static – set in a salon environment – or mobile, should comply with health and safety regulations and have adequate warmth, ventilation, privacy, appropriate volume and type of music/sounds, and a pleasant aroma.

Room

The treatment room should be:

- well ventilated to avoid headaches and fatigue and prevent a build up of unpleasant odours/vapours from some products
- comfortable – temperatures should be kept to a minimum level of 13°C where the work involves physical activity or 16°C for 'sedentary' workplaces, but there is no maximum limit
- adequate in size
- in good repair
- set up so that products, tools and equipment are within easy reach so the treatment is not disturbed.

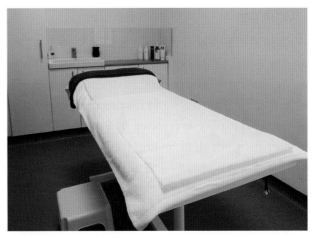

▲ The correct environment is important

Creating a relaxed atmosphere

It is important that:

- the atmosphere is conducive to achieving the treatment objectives
- a professional standard is maintained.

Creating a professional environment

Decor should be:

- relaxing, with a calming, soothing colour scheme
- tasteful and appeal to both male and female clients
- pastel shades – they are more calming and relaxing
- colour coordinated. Matching towels and blankets will create a 'cared for' feel and give the image continuity
- not be too clinical, e.g. all white.

General lighting

Lighting can be either:

- natural lighting
- overhead lighting. A cold magnifying lamp will help in assessing skin and during eye treatments.

Music

Music must create the right atmosphere and appeal to all ages.

Hygiene

Excellent hygiene must be maintained by:

- disinfecting work surfaces before and after use
- disinfecting work surfaces during treatment, if appropriate
- using clean towels and disposable coverings for each client
- using spatulas to remove products from containers
- sterilising or disinfecting tools before and after use
- disposing of any waste products, coverings or consumables
- cleaning the bottle neck prior to replacing a lid to a product
- maintaining a clean and tidy work area
- washing hands before and after each treatment
- washing then placing brushes, sponges and powder puffs before and after use in a UV cabinet
- cleaning make-up palettes after use
- using disposable products such as mascara wands and spatulas etc. whenever possible.

A client deserves your:

- personal care
- total commitment
- professional skills.

A satisfied client will:

- return to the salon
- speak well of you and the salon
- keep you in business.

Communication skills

Make-up artists may have to take on other roles, for example:

- Manager
- Personnel/human resources.

To complete these tasks you would need extra skills:

- Good listening skills
- Understanding
- Organisational skills
- Tactfulness.

Communication can be:

- verbal (words used, tone of voice, silence)
- non-verbal (body language, personal space, eye contact).

Body language often coveys a different message to what is being said. Eye movements can be a giveaway and eye contact is important. Your tone of voice and the manner in which you speak and present yourself is all-important.

▲ Good listening skills are important when communicating with a client

Any instructions should be clear and concise, so that they can be understood easily. You should always be approachable so that the client feels comfortable, as you will be working in their personal space.

Throughout the course of a working day it may be necessary to communicate with other members of staff. You must always remain professional and treat them with respect, as you would wish to be treated.

On occasion it may be necessary to communicate in writing. A memo is ideal in this case and can help to:

- prevent mistakes
- act as a reminder.

Remember without clients there is no business, so always be polite and consistent.

Contracts of employment

All employees must have a contract, whether it is a formal, written one or a verbal one; this is the Law according to the Department of Employment. A verbal contract is known as an **unwritten contract**. If this contract is broken it is difficult to prove so a formal written contract is always advisable.

Employment Rights Act 1996

It is advisable to have these contracts drawn up by a solicitor. It is usually a formal agreement signed by both the employer and employee. What kind of details would you need on it?

Fixed-term contract

A 'fixed-term' contract is an employment contract that ends on a particular date, after a certain event or on completion of a task. Examples of fixed-term employees are seasonal staff who are employed for a short period of time (for example, six months) during a peak period, specialist employees taken on for the duration of a project, or someone employed to cover during another employee's leave (for example, maternity leave).

Short-term contract

A 'short-term' contract is one that extends over a limited period.

Open-ended contract

An open-ended contract has no set end date.

Activity

Which approach is appropriate with a client? (Please circle.)

1. Easy and sincere
2. Arrogant and dictatorial.

Memo

Date:
To:
From:
Re:
CC:
Message:

▲ Memos act as reminders and prevent mistakes

▲ A contract of employment

Termination of contract

Employment can be terminated either by the employee or employer giving the correct notice as stated and agreed in the contract. It should be remembered that employment legislation changes frequently. Some general guidelines from The Employment Protection Act 1978 state that the **employer** must give:

- one week's notice after four weeks of continuous employment
- two weeks' notice after two years of continuous employment
- one week's notice for each year of continuous employment; this is capped after 12 weeks. The employee must have been with the business for a minimum of two years.

The **employee** must give:

- one week's notice after four weeks of continuous employment, unless the contract states otherwise. This can be done verbally or written and the employer must reply within 14 days.

Consultation

Information is obtained at the consultation by asking questions and by examining the area to be treated. If you keep eye contact with your client and listen carefully to what they say to you it allows a personal relationship to develop between client and therapist, which should promote confidence in your professional abilities.

The consultation and record card process also provides a ready-made mailing list of clients to use for promotions.

If a course of treatment is recommended, you must make sure that the client understands why the treatments have been recommended, the expected outcome from the treatment, what the costs are, frequency of appointments or specific home care.

It is important to keep the records in a safe place, so that only the necessary people have access to them. The client has entrusted these personal details to you; it is professional practice to keep this private. The last thing you want is a client's personal business being gossiped about. You are also bound by the Data Protection Act (1984). Some businesses keep records on a computer, but even if the information you keep is only a list of names you will still need to comply with the Act.

Facial treatment card								Name:				
Address:								Tel:				
Medical history:								Medication:			Date of birth:	
Skin assessment	Date	Date	Date			Date	Date	Date			Date	Date	Date
Seborrhoea				Open pores					Milia				
Comedones				Acne					Scars				
Sensitive				Dry					Dehydrated				
Mature				Flakey					Loss of firmness				
Skin colour				Dilated capillaries					Pigmentation				
Superfluous hair				Skin blemishes					Lines/ageing				
Other													

Treatment		Products used	Advised for home use	Products purchased
Date				

Treatment progress:
Client comments:
Homecare checklist:

Client signature:	Date:
Therapist signature:	Date:

▲ Example of a client record card

Activity

Telephone enquiries

You are working as a make-up artist in a busy town centre salon. You have many duties, which include answering the telephone when appropriate. A new client rings, enquiring about a make-up treatment/service:

1. How would you answer the call?

2. What information could you give about the treatment?

3. When you book the appointment, what information will you need from the client?

Complaints

A client has a complaint about a make-up treatment/service treatment she received the day before. She is very cross and is raising her voice and her arms are folded:

1. How would you deal with the situation?

2. What could you do to calm her down?

3. How could you maintain the salon's good reputation?

Staff problems

You overhear another therapist/make-up artist within your salon inappropriately calling another salon to a client.

1. As the salon manager how would you approach this?

2. What guidelines do we work within to ensure this does not happen?

Staff selection

Staff selection requires managerial skills. Finding the right staff is extremely important as regular clients usually return to the same therapist each time. It is important that the right choice is made the first time as a high turnover of staff can have an adverse effect on the business. You need to employ members of staff who are going to help make your business a success. Staff need to be highly trained amongst other qualities such as being: 1) hard working, 2) friendly, 3) reliable and 4) honest.

When advertising for staff you will need to begin with a job description, which provides details of the job specification including:

- Job title
- Employee's immediate superior
- Duties and responsibilities
- Pay and package, including hours to be worked
- Qualifications and experience required (this could also include personal and physical skills).

Next you would place the advertisement in the appropriate place. Remember you are paying for the advert, often depending on number of words, so try to be as brief as possible.

A more detailed job description or specification should be available. It should contain such information as the following:

- Job title
- Location
- Salary
- Aim
- Staff responsibilities
- Duties
- Working hours
- Special tasks
- Education
- Previous training
- Experience
- Specialised skills
- Personal attributes
- Communication skills
- Closing date for application
- Application contact.

Activity

Provide examples of places where you could advertise.

Selecting job applicants

When candidates reply to the advertisement they should fill in an application form. This will help you choose the candidates that match the requirements and eliminate unsuitable candidates. Usually a letter is sent out to all the candidates, telling them whether their application has been short-listed or not. You can now arrange interviews for the prospective candidates.

Activity

What information do you think would be on an application form?

Interview

Once you have received the applicants' CVs you should make a list of suitable candidates and ask them to attend an interview. This should be done in writing, clearly stating all of the details.

In the beauty-related industry, you may be required to do a 'skills test', to demonstrate your practical skills. Remember you may need your uniform!

A good interviewer allows the applicant to talk about themselves. You should be calm and relaxed to try to put the interviewee at ease. Remember they could be nervous. Try to be aware of the applicant's non-verbal behaviour; are their actions telling you something different to what they are telling you verbally?

Activity

List the skills you would need as the interviewer.

▲ Interviews are used for staff selection

The **interviewer** should:

- Use the CV as a basis for the interview
- Ask open questions
- Be attentive and listen carefully to applicant's replies
- Check the motivation and career aims of the applicant
- Ask the applicant to expand on information on their CV, if necessary
- Allow the applicant to ask questions
- Be led by the applicant's answers.

The **interviewee** should be:

- Smartly dressed
- Prepared to ask questions
- Honest
- Knowledgeable about their work and current trends
- Able to draw on strengths and lesser strengths, and be able to analyse these in a positive manner.

Data Protection Act

The Data Protection Act is in place to protect client confidentiality. The principles of the Act are that:

- Information held must be kept in a secure place, whether held on a computer or record card
- Information must not be disclosed to a third party
- Information held must be accurate
- Information held must be available for the person whom it is about to see at any time if they request to do so
- The salon must be registered with the Data Protection Register if holding files on a computer
- Any out-of-date information no longer required must be disposed of in a secure way (not just thrown into the dustbin).

You must not divulge information about clients, whether this is personal details, service that has been provided or products that have been purchased to a third party. The consequences of failing to keep client confidentiality could be: 1) loss of clients, 2) a bad reputation for the salon, 3) the client could sue, 4) you could receive a warning and 5) you may even lose your job.

Prices Act

Product prices must be displayed to prevent the buyer being misled.

Resale Prices Act 1964 and 1976

A manufacturer can supply a recommended price, but the seller is not obliged to sell it at the price that was recommended.

Sale and Supply of Goods Act 1994

This replaced the Supply of Goods Act 1982 in order to include service standards requirements. Goods must be fit for their intended purpose and described of merchantable quality. This Act also covers all the conditions under which a person can return goods.

Consumer Protection Act 1987

This implements the European Community directive to ensure that the consumer is protected against products and services being used or sold that are unsafe. The Act covers general safe handling requirements, product liability and prices that are misleading.

Clients who are unsatisfied may contact several organisations that deal with legal advice on consumer protection. If a business is found to be at fault it will face legal action.

Consumer Safety Act 1978

This Act aims to reduce the consumer's risk from products that are potentially dangerous.

Consumer Protection (Distance Selling) Regulations 2000

The Regulations are derived from a European directive that covers the supply of goods and services made between suppliers acting in a commercial capacity and consumers.

The Regulations concern purchases made by digital television, telephone, fax, mail order and the internet.

The consumer must receive clear, written information on services and goods, including payment, delivery arrangements, supplier details and consumer cancellation rights.

The consumer has the right to cancel their purchase during the 7-day cooling-off period.

Equal Opportunities

The UK has equality legislation specific to protecting employees, and covers the goods and services provision.

Race Relations Act 1976

This Act makes it unlawful to discriminate on the grounds of colour, race, nationality, ethnic or national origin.

Disability Discrimination Act 1995 (DDA)

This Act makes it unlawful to discriminate on the grounds of disability. Under the DDA from 1996 as a provider of services, goods and facilities your workplace has a duty to ensure that no one is discriminated against on the grounds of disability.

It is unlawful because of a disability to:

- Provide a service to a lesser standard or on worse terms
- Fail to make adjustments that are reasonable to the way the services are provided
- Fail to make reasonable adjustments to the service premises physical features, in order to overcome physical barriers to access.

Services can only be denied to a person who is disabled only if it is justified and other people would be treated in the same way. It is the employer's responsibility to ensure adequate training is provided to the employees to prevent discrimination practices taking place and reasonable adjustments are made to the workplace to facilitate access for people who are disabled.

This Act was also introduced to prevent people who are disabled being discriminated against during selection, recruitment and employment. Employers have a duty to adjust working conditions to prevent discrimination of a person with a disability.

Equal opportunity policy

The Equal Opportunity Commission (EOC) states that it is best practice for all workplaces to have a written equal opportunities policy. This policy will include an equal opportunity commitment by the employer and details of a structure on how the policy will be implemented. All employees should know and understand this policy and it should be monitored regularly to review its effectiveness.

Sex Discrimination Acts 1975 and 1985 and the Equal Pay Act 1970

This was implemented to prevent less favourable treatment of a man or woman on the basis of gender. It was designed to promote equal opportunities and covers such issues as pay and conditions.

Trade Union and Labour Relations Act 1992

This Act prevents members of the trade unions being treated less favourably than non-members and vice versa. Employees who feel they have been discriminated against can complain to an employment tribunal.

Information systems

Information systems can be either computerised or manual. Manual systems need to be indexed into an organised filing system. Computer systems allow you to input client information, which will include treatment details, personal details etc. Data can be held on staff members, targets they have met, salon performance, as well as current stock levels, retail sales and daily takings.

Information systems are used to ensure that the business runs smoothly and provides all the legal information required for external agents and the supervisor, including information required by Inland Revenue at the end of each financial year.

Resources

Resources are time, stock, staff and consumables. If these resources are not used to their full potential they end up being wasted, which costs money. For all salon resources you must ensure that there is a procedure for their storage, safety and maintenance.

Electrical equipment must have a maintenance record that shows when the equipment was purchased, when it was checked by an electrician and when the next check is due. Stock should also be checked regularly, so that the stock can be ordered correctly. These records should be checked and dated by a supervisor.

Activity

1. Why do we have trading standards officers?
2. When selling retail stock you must have a full understanding of the relevant legislation. Describe the principles of the following Acts:
   (a) Trade Descriptions Act 1968/1977
   (b) Consumer Protection Act 1987
   (c) Sale and Supply of Goods Act 1994
   (d) Re-sale Prices Act 1964 and 1976
   (e) Cosmetic Products Regulations 1989

Principles of finance and selling

These include:

- Pricing of products and services – legislation
- Handling payments – correct techniques
- Product knowledge – know your product and gain feedback from your client on what services, products, colours etc. they might use
- Positive body language
- Stages of the selling process – identify need, identify the product to meet the need, demonstrate the product, overcome obstacles and close sales.

Good book keeping

It is important to keep accurate records when working in the make-up industry. It is also a good idea to keep them as orderly as possible, as this will not only benefit you but if you have an accountant it will help them work out your expenses and what you might owe to HMRC (Inland Revenue). Orderly records also cut down time when you come to present or claim your expenses.

Making sure that your record accurate benefits in more ways than just one, the information that you keep in records will help you track the progress of your business. If you decide to go for a loan at a bank or other lending organisation they will require you to prove your finical records accurately as this will reflect the progress of your business.

Forms of marketing and publicity

These forms include:

- *Internet and text messages* – e-commerce is an excellent way of reaching a wide audience
- *Leaflets* – these should be eye catching, easy to read, have clear and concise information, with relevant images if appropriate and perhaps special offers. Usually the word 'free' or 'money off' attracts a reader's attention.
- *Promotional articles in magazines and newspapers* – as well as promotional activities, such as open evenings, taster sessions and promotions events.

Promoting facilities and services

Promoting facilities and services is another way to keep the customer satisfied. You must keep up to date with all the treatments and products that are on offer. Don't be embarrassed if a client asks you a question that you cannot answer, but try to find out for them.

Read the literature from providers of equipment/products and keep the information close to hand so you can refer back to it if needed. If you are enthusiastic about the services and products your salon offers you can pass this on to the client, which can help boost revenue.

Ways to promote products and services

- Advertisements in the press and within your workplace
- Leaflets and posters
- Open days

- Special offers, discounted prices and/or free gifts
- Incentives to introduce a friend
- Gift vouchers
- Working with other businesses
- Website
- Fridge magnets
- Cut-out cards
- Notepads
- Point-of-sale cards

Your clients will expect you to have an understanding of services and products within the salon, including cost, time and how this will benefit them.

Advertising

All businesses need to advertise in some way. Word of mouth is advertising despite the fact that it cannot be controlled. Advertising is all about image. Businesses must decide what image they wish to present to the public, for example:

- Organised
- Trendy
- Upmarket
- Warm and friendly.

Choosing your method of advertising is extremely important. You need to be consistent in your image, so as to portray professionalism.

Forms of advertising

- Internet/website
- Newspaper
- Trade magazine
- Shop window
- Supermarkets
- Radio
- Posters
- Leaflets
- Word of mouth
- Other businesses.

Measuring effectiveness of advertising

A form similar to this can be used to measure the effectiveness of advertising.

Enquiry contact form

Date: - - - - - - - - - - - - - - -

Name: - Address: -

- -

Tel No: -

Enquiry:	1). Phone ☐
	2). Personal call ☐
	3). Mail ☐
Source of enquiry:	1). Advert ☐
	2). Mail shot ☐
	3). Exhibition ☐
	4). Other ☐
Type of Enquiry:	1). Information ☐
	2). Order/booking ☐
	3). Product ☐

Action:

By whom:

▲ Advertising effectiveness form

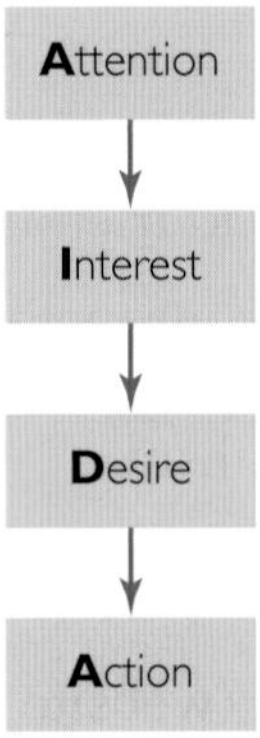

Attention

↓

Interest

↓

Desire

↓

Action

▲ Advertising (AIDA)

Advertising can also be made more effective by using a business model known as the AIDA format (See flow chart opposite).

Print advertising

This can be divided into three parts:

1. Illustration
2. Headlines
3. Main body.

Illustration

This is the part that catches the eye and ensures the reader is paying enough attention to it to continue reading. The reader should immediately know what the product or service is from this.

Headlines

This should be written in a clear font and should help to pinpoint the target audience.

Main body

This should sell the product or service and invite a response, i.e. a telephone number, address, e-mail etc. The body of the ad should be written in clear, short sentences.

The layout is also important as people normally read from top to bottom, so putting the most eye-catching part at the top makes sense.

USP

The effect of advertising builds up over time. The more you continue to advertise the more you will attract the customer's attention. You need to promote the **unique selling point** (USP) for your product or service. Be distinctive about it.

The consumer will be interested in the benefits of your product or service, so state them clearly in your advertising.

Never overlook the importance of internal promotion, for example use letterheads, business cards, logos, distinctive labels and packaging. There should be continuity in the image you present.

It is difficult to be prescriptive about how much money you should spend on advertising, but a typical figure is 3 per cent of the annual turnover. For example, a company with a turnover of £200,000 might reasonably have an advertising budget of £600.

Personal selling skills

Attention to detail is imperative as is developing your own selling technique. To improve your selling skills you need your own strategy, which should be something that you are comfortable with.

Some rules to follow that can help your selling ability are:

- Know your product
- Listen to your buyer
- Plan your strategy for each customer, so you know your targets
- Relate what you are selling to your customers' needs and wants
- Work out clearly presentations, promotions or demonstrations
- Where applicable, make sure you know who the decision maker is within the business.

▲ Developing your own selling technique is important

Developing your own sales approach

You should not try out your selling approach for the first time in front of a customer. Instead you should practise, perhaps with a friend or relative in a role-play situation.

Three stages of a sale

1. Opening
2. Building the sale
3. Closing.

Marketing

Marketing is vital for the success of any business. Once you have decided on your business idea you must look at the likely market for your services. You need to talk to other people, for example potential customers to get their views on your idea, but be careful that you don't give too much away! Without marketing, how would you expect your customers to know about your products or services?

You would need to check on market trends and identify the cause of those trends. If your line of business is in a declining market, how would you make it a success? If your business appears to be in a thriving market, how would you persuade your customers to use your service instead of your competitor's?

A very important function of any business is to increase turnover and profits. Marketing is a key managerial function, particularly in the beauty business because it is so highly customer orientated. This does not stop once your business is up and running. You must always be aware of what the client's needs are and be prepared to respond. Marketing activities include:

- Creating the right image
- Market research
- Testing products
- Advertising
- Selling
- Promotions.

It is essential to:

- Assess the client's needs
- Monitor changes in the marketplace
- Anticipate future trends
- Promote the business.

The importance of marketing in the beauty-related industry has increased over the past 40 years for several reasons, which will be discussed in turn.

Economic growth

There has been an increase in the disposable income of many consumers, which has resulted in a growth in demand for beauty products and services; this then resulted in a wider range of choice and therefore competition.

Fashion

There has been considerable change in fashion, taste and lifestyle of consumers. Many more people consider a visit to the hair or beauty salon a necessity rather than a luxury and men are becoming increasingly more aware of the therapeutic treatments that are available. Celebrity culture and make-up trends also have an influence on people.

Technology

Firms are constantly inventing, designing and launching new or more advanced products onto the market offering increased benefits to the consumer.

Competition

The number of businesses competing for the consumer's attention is constantly increasing, therefore marketing is vital to each business in maintaining its market share.

Marketing mix

To achieve marketing objectives a business must consider the 'marketing mix':

To meet consumer needs the business must produce the right product at the right price, make it available in the right place and let consumers know about it through promotion.

Think of a product you would like to sell and how you would promote it. Answer the following questions:

1. **What is the brochure's/leaflet's purpose?**
   - Will you be mailing the brochure by itself or as part of a larger promotional package?
   - Is it for an exhibition, show or demonstration?
   - How will you distribute it?

2. **Who is your target audience?**
   - Are they existing or prospective customers? Do you want to reach all of them or just a section? Think about who will be reading it and is the language appropriate to reach a wide variety of people.

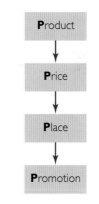

▲ Marketing mix (the 4Ps)

3. **Who should be involved?**

   It's best to get decision makers involved at the early stages. Have a meeting/session to thrash out your ideas.

4. **How much can you spend?**

   It is best to know your budget from the start. That way you can find the most appropriate method without breaking the bank.

5. **Who is going to write it?**

   - You may wish to write it yourself. Remember some forms of advertising charge per word so if you can use half the words, do.

6. **How much photography or imagery will you use?**

   - Have you got photos to use already, or will you need some taking?
   - Or will stock photos do the job?
   - How many will you need?
   - Who is going to design it?

7. **What are your competitors doing?**

   - Gather together your main competitors' promotional literature such as leaflets. This may help decide what you need to cover. You need to look at least as good, if not better.

8. **How much detail should you go into?**

   - It is tempting to include every little scrap of information but great promotional materials are often uncluttered, with lots of white space. They should be eye-catching, to the point and tell you immediately what the product or service is offering and how to get this product or service. Anything to cluttered often puts people off reading it.

9. **Who is going to proof read it?**

   - Not anyone who has been involved in its writing! People tend to read what they think they've written.
   - Use a fresh pair of eyes and meticulously check every detail. It is worth the effort.

Branding

The quality of your branding can mean the difference between success and failure. No matter what size your business is, branding is essential to differentiate yourself from the competition. It is your personality and it needn't cost the Earth. How you are perceived may depend on your marketing communications.

Your logo is important to your brand identity. Without a logo, or with a poorly designed one, your business may look amateurish. A great logo will help your customers identify with you and is more likely to help you succeed.

Keep a similar 'look and feel' through all your communications to help people become familiar with your brand. Familiarity leads to trust, trust leads to sales.

Mail

Mail is only junk mail if it is not targeted correctly. You will get a much better response if you follow these golden rules of direct mail:

1. *Contact your current customers first* – They are a gold mine! Get the most from them first with mailings specifically targeted to their individual needs. Use e-marketing to your advantage (for example email or text messaging).

2. Often a better model is to mail the same person three times rather than to mail three different people. It takes repetition for your message to sink in.

3. *Make it personal* – In this electronic age, it is easy to personalise your letters.

4. *Write like a friend* – When you are writing, imagine you are speaking to an individual and your business will sound much more friendly and appealing.

5. *Keep it simple* – Give them enough information, but don't overwhelm them.

6. *Sell benefits not features* – Sell the benefits of your product or service to entice them into purchasing.

7. *Test it* – Try different mailings with different groups and figure out what works best for your business. Keep track of postcodes to see where your mailings have been effective.

8. **Always mail to a person** – Avoid lists with just a 'Proprietor' or 'Owner'.

Power words that sell

Here's some examples of power words used in selling

- Amazing
- Breakthrough
- Discount
- Endorsed
- Exciting
- Exclusive
- Experts
- Famous
- Free

Louise James
Make up artist

tel: 01392 190000

louise.james@mail.com

1A Bristol Street
Exeter

EX1 4GB

▲ Business cards should contain your branding

Key term

Unique selling point (USP) – Your product's offering; it can be a problem solved with use of your product.

Unwritten contract – A verbal contract, which is much harder to prove or enforce.

Written contract – The best way to record terms of employment.

- Guaranteed
- Professional
- Profitable
- Quality
- Revolutionary
- Reduced
- Successful.

SWOT analysis

SWOT analysis is a business model used when analysing your own and other businesses. It encourages you to look at how to identify areas for improvement and to check out your competition.

▲ Gift vouchers are a good way to promote products and services

▲ SWOT analysis

End of chapter knowledge test

1. Strengths, weaknesses, opportunities and threats; what do we call this method of analysis in marketing?
2. Can you name the 4Ps?
3. When recoding information about clients, what Act do we comply with for issues of confidentiality?
4. Name **one** way of advertising.
5. Name **two** methods of payment.
6. State **one** reason why it is important to know the products you are selling.

CHAPTER 4

Anatomy and physiology

This chapter provides a basic knowlege and understanding of anatomy and physiology to be used in conjunction with the practical units in this book. This is not a stand-alone unit and you will not necessarily be assessed on all of the content in this chapter.

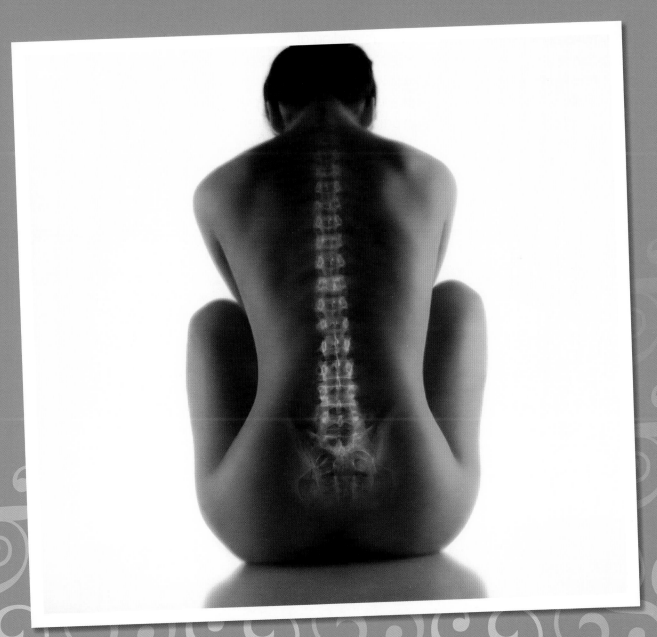

Chapter aims

This chapter will look at:

- Skin structure
- Bones of the skull and body
- Muscles of the head and body
- Hair structure and growth cycle
- Blood and lymphatic systems
- Heart and circulatory system
- Diseases and disorders.

The make-up artist must have an understanding of associated anatomy and physiology so they understand how the body works and therefore do not work on an area when it is contraindicated. A knowledge of anatomy and physiology will also allow a therapist/make-up artist to know the correct course of action to take to protect themselves and the client.

In this chapter we focus on anatomy and physiology related specifically to the practical units in this book.

Chapter	5	6	7	8	9	10	11	12	13	14	15
Skin, hair and nails	✓	✓	✓	✓	✓	✓	✓	✓	✓	✓	✓
Skeletal system		✓	✓				✓				
Muscular system		✓	✓								
Lymphatic system		✓	✓								
Cardiovascular system		✓	✓								
Diseases and disorders	✓	✓	✓	✓	✓	✓	✓	✓	✓	✓	

▲ How anatomy and physiology is relevant to the units in this book

Skin

This is the largest organ of the body and has three layers:

- Epidermis
- Dermis
- Subcutaneous layer.

The average person's skin covers about 1.6 metres square and is the largest organ in the body. Two and a half centimetres of skin contains millions of cells and hundreds of nerve endings, plus lots of muscles, blood vessels, hair follicles, sweat glands and oil glands.

The inside layer of the skin is called the **dermis**. Above it lies the outer/surface layer called the epidermis.

> ★ *Tip* Epidermis is Latin for 'upon the dermis'. 'Derm' means 'skin' and forms the basis of many medical terms relating to the skin, like dermatologist (a doctor who treats problems of the skin, hair and nails).

Functions of the skin

The functions of the skin are:

1. Sensation
2. Heat regulation
3. Absorption
4. Protection
5. Excretion
6. Secretion
7. Production of vitamin D.

Sensation

There are sensory nerve endings contained in the dermis, which when stimulated by external stimuli, send messages to the brain that respond via the **motor nerves**. For example, motor nerves supply the **erector pili** muscle, which is attached to a hair follicle and cause it to stand on end and produce other feelings such as heat, pain, cold touch and pressure.

Heat regulation

The body's temperature control system. The sweat glands, hair and the arrector pili muscles which cause the hair to stand on end all help to maintain the normal body temperature of 37°C.

Absorption

The skin acts as a waterproof barrier and very little absorption takes place. However, the superficial layer of the **stratum corneum** (the outermost layer of the epidermis) absorbs minute amounts of water, which may be absorbed over a large surface area. Vitamin D is also produced in the skin in the presence of sunlight, which is vital for healthy bones. This process is known as the **synthesis** of vitamin D.

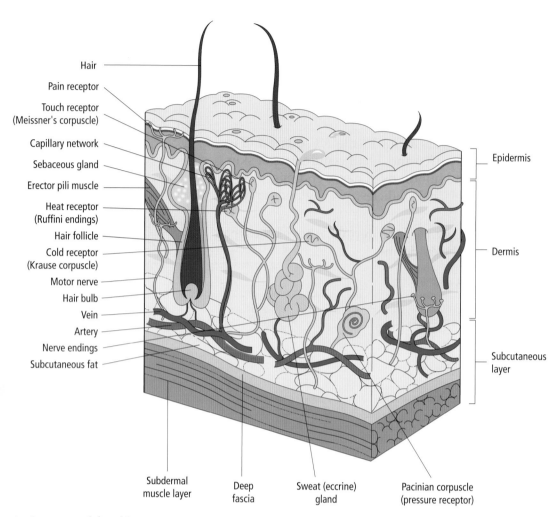

Hair

Pain receptor

Touch receptor
(Meissner's corpuscle)

Capillary network

Sebaceous gland

Erector pili muscle

Heat receptor
(Ruffini endings)

Hair follicle

Cold receptor
(Krause corpuscle)

Motor nerve

Hair bulb

Vein

Artery

Nerve endings

Subcutaneous fat

Epidermis

Dermis

Subcutaneous
layer

Subdermal
muscle layer

Deep
fascia

Sweat (eccrine)
gland

Pacinian corpuscle
(pressure receptor)

▲ Structure of the skin

Protection

The skin forms a tough, flexible barrier that keeps excess water out and body fluids in. Melanin pigment in the skin helps to filter out harmful rays of the sun and the oil and sweat it produces are acidic, which help to prevent bacterial growth.

Excretion

Waste products such as **urea** and salt are passed out of the body via the sweat glands (**sudoriferous glands**), which cause perspiration.

Secretion

Sebum is secreted from the sebaceous glands, which acts as the skin's natural moisturiser, keeping it soft and supple.

Epidermis

The epidermis is the outermost layer of the skin. It protects the other layers of the skin that lie beneath it. This layer is made up of **stratified squamous epithelium tissue**, which comprises of flattened **epithelial cells** that lie in layers on a basement membrane at the bottom of the epidermis. This membrane acts as a sticky layer between the epidermis and the dermis. Some of these epithelial cells may not yet be flattened and in the deeper layers, the cells may be cuboidal or columnar. There are no blood vessels in the epidermis and nourishment comes from interstitial fluid (tissue fluid), which is a solution that fills in spaces between the tissues and surrounds and bathes the cells.

Stratified squamous epithelium tissue also has keratin present, which is formed in the deeper granular layer. This is a tough protective protein also found in the hair and nails.

The epidermis is the outer covering of the skin and consists of the following five layers:

1. Stratum corneum/horny layer
2. Stratum lucidum/clear layer
3. Stratum granulosum/granular layer
4. Stratum spinosum/prickle layer
5. Stratum germinativum/basal layer.

> ⭐ *Tip* A person has about 11 litres of interstitial fluid that provides the cells of the body with nutrients and waste removal.

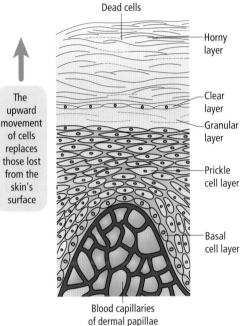

▲ Layers of the epidermis

Stratum corneum/horny layer

This is the surface layer of skin. It consists of flattened, dead, irregular-shaped keratinised cells around 25–30 cells deep that overlap each other and reflect ultra-violet light. This layer of skin acts as a waterproof protective covering, which prevents excessive dehydration of the tissues, hence the term 'horny' layer. It is also thicker in black skins.

> ⭐ *Tip* It takes around three weeks for the cells to travel from the stratum germinativum to the stratum corneum.

Stratum lucidum/clear layer

This layer lies below the stratum corneum and is around 3–5 cells deep. It is a transparent layer consisting of flattened and closely packed cells. They contain a substance called **eleidin**; this is a similar substance to keratin and is a product of keratohyalin, a protein structure of lifeless matter deposited within the protoplasm of living cells. These cells have an indistinct outline and no nuclei, hence the term clear layer. This layer is seen in thick, hairless skin, for example on the palms of the hands and soles of the feet.

> ⭐ *Tip* Eleidin can be found in the red border of the lip where the blood supply shows through, giving the lips their colour.

Stratum granulosum/granular layer

This is the third layer of the epidermis and is 1–3 cells deep, consisting of flatter cells. The nucleus begins to break down here and cells contain keratohyaline granules. These are irregular-shaped granules (later becoming keratin) that are thought to aid cell adhesion and retain some water, hence the term granular layer.

Stratum spinosum/prickle cell layer

This layer is up to eight cells in depth, with round nucleated cells that vary in size and shape. They produce **fibrils** which interconnect them with neighbouring cells, hence are often referred to as the prickle cell layer.

Stratum germinativum/basal layer

Within this layer cells are one cell deep, rounded and clearly defined with a nucleus and rest on the papillae of the dermis. These epithelial cells are able to divide and reproduce themselves by a process called **mitosis** hence the term germinative. As these cells form they push themselves up towards the skin surface. Within this layer there are also melanocyte cells, which produce the pigment melanin, which gives both the hair and skin its colour density. **Langerhan** cells are also found within this layer and absorb and remove foreign bodies that enter the skin.

> ⭐ *Tip* Squamous epithelium comes from the Latin word squama, meaning 'scale'.

> ⭐ *Tip* Basal cell carcinoma and squamous cell carcinoma are cancers of the squamous epithelium.

Dermis

The largest layer of the skin also known as the 'true skin'. It has a very rich blood supply, though no blood vessels pass through to the epidermis. It is a dense structure that is composed of **areolar connective** tissue and contains the protein **collagen**, **elastin fibres**, **fibroblasts**, **macrophages**, mast cells, enzymes, numerous blood vessels, lymph vessels, nerves, sweat glands, hair follicles and arrector pili muscles.

The skin contains various types of **mechanoreceptors/sensory nerve endings** which run through the dermis; these branched nerve endings are found in the hair root and papillary layer, which allow us to feel pain, heat, touch and pressure by sending a signal to the brain.

There are several different types of special sensory nerve endings in the dermis, the main types are:

- **pacinian corpuscles** – for pain and pressure
- **meissner corpuscles** – for touch.

The dermis is composed of:

1. **Collagen fibres** – These are made by cells known as fibroblasts. The thickness of collagen depends on different factors such as age, sex and body areas. The collagen layer is organised into a smooth superficial layer under the epidermis at the level of papillae and is coarser in the deeper layers. The collagen fibres give the skin its toughness and elasticity.

2. **Elastin fibres** – are associated with the collagen fibres and both are surrounded by **mucopolysaccharides**.

3. **Ground substance** – The base of the dermis is a supporting matrix or ground substance which is composed of **polysaccharides** and protein. These are linked to produce **macromolecules** with a remarkable capacity for holding water. There are two kinds of protein fibres: collagen, which has a great tensile strength and forms the major part of the dermis; and elastin, which forms only a small proportion of the bulk.

The dermis is composed of two layers called the **papillary** and **reticular** layers.

Papillary layer

Lies directly under the germinativum layer of the epidermis and provides nourishment to it. There are small cone-shaped projections contained within this layer of the dermis called papillae; these contain looped blood capillaries, others contain **tactile corpuscles** and **nerve endings**.

Reticular layer

The larger of the two layers containing cells called fibroblasts, which produce the **yellow elastin fibres**, which make up 4 per cent of connective tissue and give the skin its flexibility and ability to recoil. White protein collagen fibres give the skin its strength and make up 75 per cent of connective tissue. Reticular fibres run between the dermis fibres and structures helping to support them and hold them in place.

There are also specialised cells within this layer: macrophages and mast cells.

Macrophages destroy bacteria and tissue debris, while mast cells secrete histamine, a substance which enlarges small blood vessels and heparin, an anti-coagulant that stops the blood clotting.

Tip If injury occurs below the reticular layer, scarring usually occurs after healing.

Subcutaneous layer (hypodermis)

The function of the subcutaneous layer is to form and store fat for energy; it provides warmth and protection. It has two different tissue types:

- **Adipose tissue** – this contains fat cells
- **Areolar tissue** – this contains loose connective tissue and elastic fibres, which makes this layer flexible and elastic.

There are larger blood vessels and nerves found in this layer than are found in the dermis. The types of cells that are found in the hypodermis are adipose cells, fibroblasts and macrophages.

Skin appendages

Hair and nails are '**appendages**' of the skin (something that grows out of the skin) and are located in the dermis.

The skeletal system

The human skeleton is made up of about 200 bones, which vary greatly in size and shape. It has three distinct areas:

- Skull: cranium, face and lower jaw
- Trunk: spinal column, ribs and sternum
- Limbs: which include the shoulder and pelvic girdles.

The structure and classification of bone

Bone is a porous connective tissue containing living cells, blood vessels and nerves. It has a matrix that is hardened by the minerals calcium, phosphate and calcium carbonate. Collagen fibres within the matrix form a system of scaffolding on which the minerals are deposited. This collagen makes the bone tissues less brittle.

There are three types of bone tissue:

- compact (hard)
- cancellous (spongy)
- bone marrow.

> ☆ *Tip* Females have a little more fat stored in the subcutaneous layer. This is there to help protect the foetus during pregnancy.

The bones of the skeleton are classified as follows:

- Long: these bones form the limbs.
- Short: these bones are found in the wrists and ankles.
- Flat: these bones are for protection (for example the skull) or for the attachment of certain muscles. They are made from a sandwich of hard bone with a spongy layer in between.
- Irregular: these bones are varied in shape. The vertebrae are an example of this type of bone.
- Sesamoid: these are small bones that develop in the tendons around certain joints (for example the patella in the knee).

The growth of bone

Bones are active living tissue. **Osteoblasts** are bone-forming cells which when calcified become **osteocytes**. **Periosteum** is a tough fibrous sheet covering the surface of bones, except where the bone forms a joint and is covered by hyaline cartilage. Most bones have protuberances and ridges for the attachment of muscles and tendons.

The process by which bones form is called **ossification**. The osteoblasts secrete substances composed of collagenous fibres, forming a framework into which calcium salts are deposited. This process is called **calcification**.

The bones develop hollow centres, which contain marrow in which the manufacture of blood cells takes place.

The function of the skeleton

The skeleton:

- provides shape
- allows for movement (attachment for skeletal muscles and leverage support)
- protects internal organs
- produces blood cells
- stores calcium.

The structure of the skeleton

The skeleton has two distinct parts: the axial skeleton (the central core, including skull, vertebral column, sternum and ribs); and the appendicular skeleton (shoulder, pelvis, upper and lower limbs).

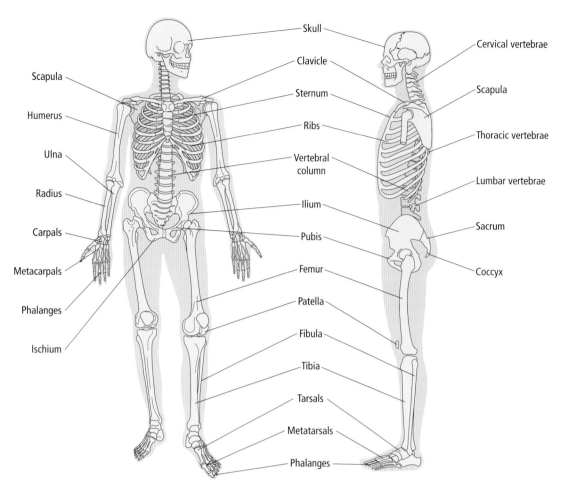

▲ Anterior and posterior of the skeleton

The bones of the head

The main functions of the bones of the head are to protect the brain and to provide face structure.

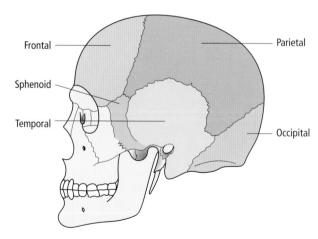

▲ Bones of the skull

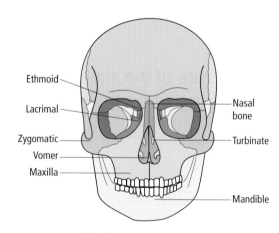

▲ Bones of the face

The bones and structure of the spine

The main functions of the bones of the spine are to protect the spinal cord and to provide a structure for bones (for example, ribs) and muscles to attach to.

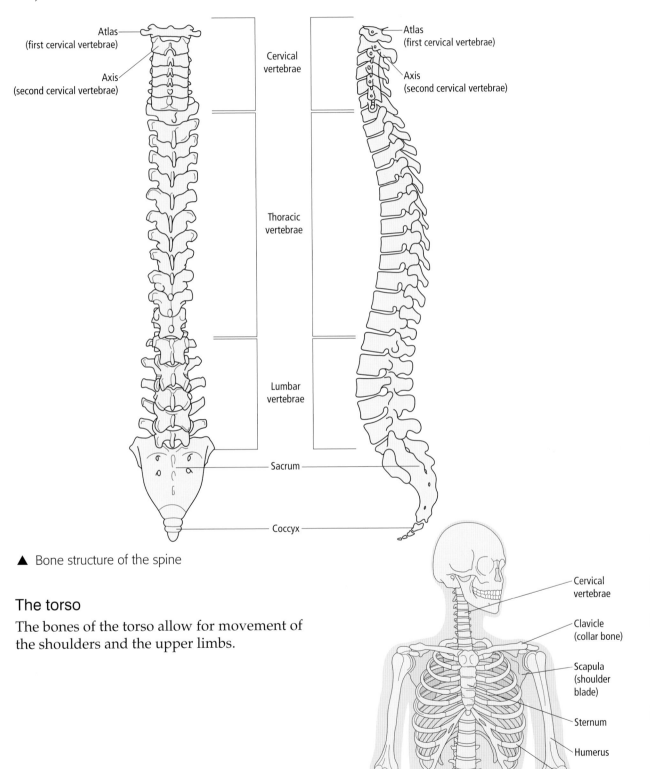

Atlas
(first cervical vertebrae)

Axis
(second cervical vertebrae)

Cervical vertebrae

Thoracic vertebrae

Lumbar vertebrae

Sacrum

Coccyx

Atlas
(first cervical vertebrae)

Axis
(second cervical vertebrae)

▲ Bone structure of the spine

The torso

The bones of the torso allow for movement of the shoulders and the upper limbs.

Cervical vertebrae

Clavicle
(collar bone)

Scapula
(shoulder blade)

Sternum

Humerus

Ribs

▶ The torso

Basic types of joint

There are three basic types of joint:

1. **Fibrous:** these are also called fixed joints. They are immovable. Examples of these can be found in the skull.

2. **Cartilaginous:** these are capable of slight movement. Examples include the joints of the vertebrae.

3. **Synovial:** these are able to move freely.

Synovial joints

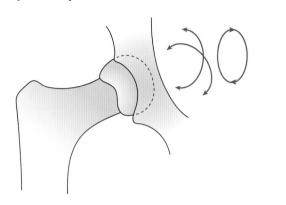

Ball and socket joint

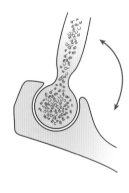

Hinge joint

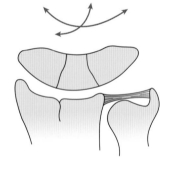

Condyloid joint

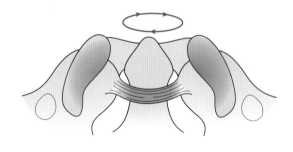

Pivot joint

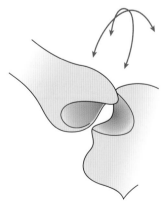

Saddle joint

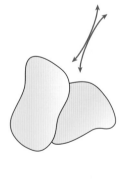

Gliding joint

▲ Synovial joints

- Gliding joints are found in the vertebrae.
- Hinge joints are found in the knees and elbows.
- Pivot joints are found in the vertebrae.
- Ball and socket joints are found in the hip and shoulders.
- Condyloid and saddle joints are found in the wrist and the thumb.

Anatomical terms associated with joint movement and their meaning

- Flexion – bending of a body part at a joint so that the angle between the bones is decreased.
- Extension – straightening of a body part at a joint so that the angle between the bones is increased.
- Abduction – movement of the limb away from the midline.
- Adduction – movement of the limb towards the midline.

Contraindications associated with homeostatic disorders and conditions of the skeletal system

- Arthritis (osteo, rheumatoid and gout)
- Bursitis
- Torn cartilage
- Tendonitis
- Sprain
- Dislocation
- Osteoporosis
- Rickets
- Bunions
- Hammer toes.

Contraindications or disorders of the spine

- Scoliosis
- Kyphosis
- Lordosis
- Herniated (slipped) disc.

Muscular system
Skeletal muscle

A muscle is a bundle of many cells called fibres. The basic action of any muscle is contraction; this occurs by the brain sending a signal down a nerve cell telling the muscle to contract. The body's endoskeleton is under the skin; it is covered and moved by the muscles. It is made of connective tissues and cartilage.

Common properties of muscle tissue

- Ability to contract in response to nervous stimuli.
- Ability to return to its original shape and after contraction.

Types of muscle tissue

- Skeletal: voluntary; striated; attached to bone.
- Visceral: involuntary; non-striated (smooth).
- Cardiac: involuntary; only found in the heart.

Functions of skeletal muscles

- facilitate movement
- maintain posture
- raise body temperature
- assist venous return.

Structure and organisation of skeletal muscles

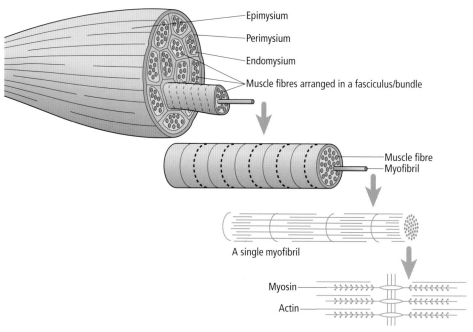

▲ Structure and organisation of skeletal muscles

A muscle fibre contains many **myofibrils**, which are cylinders of muscle that allow a muscle cell to contract. Myofibrils contain two types of **filaments** that run along the long axis of the fibre and are both thin and thick.

Contracting a muscle

The thick and thin filaments do the work of a muscle. They are made of a protein called myosin. A thick filament is a shaft of myosin molecules arranged in a cylinder. A thin filament is made of a protein called **actin**. During the process of contraction the thick filaments attach on to the thin filaments to form **crossbridges**. The thick filaments pull the thin filaments past them, making the **sarcomere** shorter.

Contained within the grooves of each thin filament are two structures that allow the thin filaments to slide along the thick ones: a long, rod-like protein called **tropomyosin** and a shorter protein called **troponin**. These proteins control the interaction of actin and myosin during contraction.

These sliding filaments shorten the muscle, but to shorten the muscle must create a force.

Isotonic versus isometric contraction

The shortening of the fibres creates mechanical force, or **muscle tension**. The muscle itself may change in length (**same-force** or **isotonic contraction**), or it may not (**same-length** or **isometric contraction**). For example, the bicep muscle is attached to the shoulder blade at one end and to the ulna in the forearm at the other end. When the bicep contracts, it shortens and pulls the ulna towards the shoulder blade (the ulna is attached to the elbow joint). This movement allows you to lift your forearm and any load you may be carrying. If you are carrying a heavy load, which prevents you from lifting your forearm, the bicep does not shorten significantly. The force that the muscle generates helps you to carry the heavy load.

Triggering contraction

The contractions of all muscles are triggered by electrical impulses, either transmitted by nerve cells, created internally (for example, with a pacemaker) or applied externally (as with an electrical-shock). The electrical signal sets off a series of events that lead to crossbridge cycling between myosin and actin, which generates force.

The process differs slightly between skeletal, smooth and cardiac muscle. Within a skeletal muscle, during the move from excitation to contraction to relaxation, an electrical signal (**action potential**) travels down a nerve cell, causing it to release a chemical message (**neurotransmitter**) into a small gap between the nerve cell and muscle cell. This gap is called the **synapse**.

The neurotransmitter crosses the gap, binds to a protein (**receptor**) on the muscle-cell membrane and causes an action potential in the muscle cell. The action potential spreads along the muscle cell, entering through the T-tubule. The action potential opens gates in the muscle's calcium store (**sarcoplasmic reticulum**).

Calcium ions flow into the cytoplasm, which contains the actin and myosin filaments. Calcium ions bind to troponin-tropomyosin molecules in the grooves of the actin filaments. Normally, the tropomyosin molecule covers the sites on actin where myosin can form crossbridges. Upon binding calcium ions, troponin changes shape and slides tropomyosin out of the groove, exposing the actin-myosin binding sites. Myosin interacts with actin by cycling crossbridges. The muscle therefore creates a force, and shortens.

After the action potential has passed, the calcium gates close, and calcium pumps located on the sarcoplasmic reticulum remove calcium from the cytoplasm. As the calcium gets pumped back into the sarcoplasmic reticulum, calcium ions come off the troponin. The troponin returns to its normal shape and allows tropomyosin to cover the actin-myosin binding sites on the actin filament. Because no binding sites are available now, no crossbridges can form, and the muscle relaxes.

Muscle contraction is regulated by the level of calcium ions in the cytoplasm. In skeletal muscle, calcium ions work at the level of actin (actin-regulated contraction). They move the troponin-tropomyosin complex off the binding sites, allowing actin and myosin to use energy in the form of adenosine triphosphate (ATP). The energy from ATP is used to reset the myosin crossbridge head and release the actin filament. To make ATP, the muscle does the following:

- Breaks down **creatine phosphate**, adding the phosphate to ADP to create ATP
- Carries out **anaerobic respiration**, by which glucose is broken down to lactic acid and ATP is formed
- Carries out **aerobic respiration**, by which glucose, glycogen, fats and amino acids are broken down in the presence of oxygen to produce ATP.

Muscles have a mixture of two basic types of fibres: fast twitch and slow twitch. **Fast-twitch fibres** are capable of developing greater forces and contracting faster. They have greater anaerobic capacity. In contrast, **slow-twitch fibres** develop force slowly, can maintain contractions for longer and have higher aerobic capacity. Training can increase muscle mass, by changing the size and number of muscle fibres rather than the types of fibres.

Other muscle cells

Compared to skeletal muscle, smooth muscle cells are small. They are spindle-shaped, about 50 to 200 microns long and only 2 to 10 microns in diameter. They have no striations or sarcomeres. Instead, they have bundles of thin and thick filaments (as opposed to well-developed bands) that correspond to myofibrils. In smooth muscle cells, **intermediate filaments** are interlaced through the cell much like the threads in a pair of fishnet stockings. The intermediate filaments anchor the thin filaments and correspond to the Z-disks of skeletal muscle.

Unlike skeletal-muscle cells, smooth-muscle cells have no troponin, tropomyosin or organised sarcoplasmic reticulum.

The location and action of skeletal muscles
The head and face

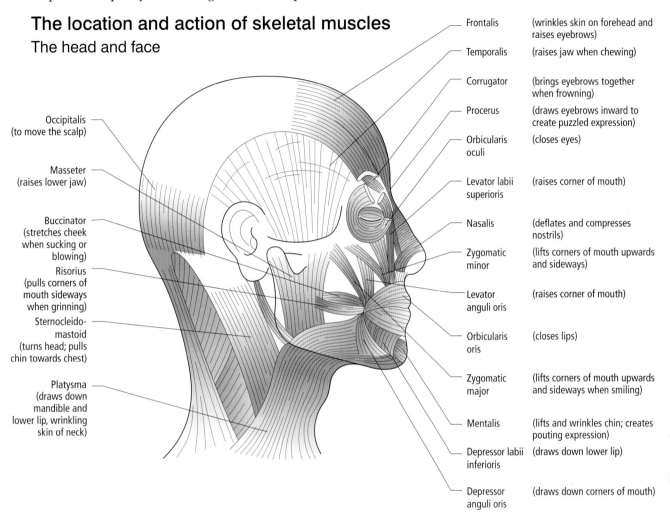

Frontalis	(wrinkles skin on forehead and raises eyebrows)
Temporalis	(raises jaw when chewing)
Corrugator	(brings eyebrows together when frowning)
Procerus	(draws eyebrows inward to create puzzled expression)
Orbicularis oculi	(closes eyes)
Levator labii superioris	(raises corner of mouth)
Nasalis	(deflates and compresses nostrils)
Zygomatic minor	(lifts corners of mouth upwards and sideways)
Levator anguli oris	(raises corner of mouth)
Orbicularis oris	(closes lips)
Zygomatic major	(lifts corners of mouth upwards and sideways when smiling)
Mentalis	(lifts and wrinkles chin; creates pouting expression)
Depressor labii inferioris	(draws down lower lip)
Depressor anguli oris	(draws down corners of mouth)

Occipitalis (to move the scalp)

Masseter (raises lower jaw)

Buccinator (stretches cheek when sucking or blowing)

Risorius (pulls corners of mouth sideways when grinning)

Sternocleido-mastoid (turns head; pulls chin towards chest)

Platysma (draws down mandible and lower lip, wrinkling skin of neck)

▲ Structure and organisation of skeletal muscles

The neck

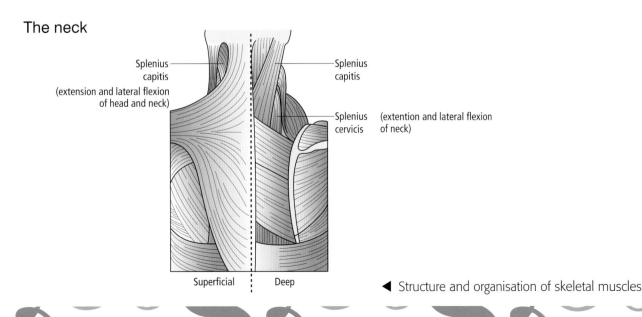

Splenius capitis (extension and lateral flexion of head and neck)

Splenius capitis

Splenius cervicis (extention and lateral flexion of neck)

Superficial   Deep

◄ Structure and organisation of skeletal muscles

The shoulders

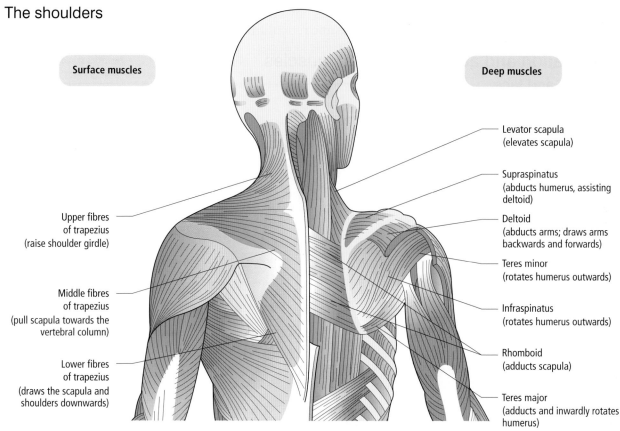

Surface muscles

Deep muscles

Upper fibres
of trapezius
(raise shoulder girdle)

Middle fibres
of trapezius
(pull scapula towards the
vertebral column)

Lower fibres
of trapezius
(draws the scapula and
shoulders downwards)

Levator scapula
(elevates scapula)

Supraspinatus
(abducts humerus, assisting
deltoid)

Deltoid
(abducts arms; draws arms
backwards and forwards)

Teres minor
(rotates humerus outwards)

Infraspinatus
(rotates humerus outwards)

Rhomboid
(adducts scapula)

Teres major
(adducts and inwardly rotates
humerus)

▲ Structure and organisation of skeletal muscles

Physical working of skeletal muscles

Antagonistic pairing

When two muscles or sets of muscles pull in opposite directions.
One muscles relaxes as the other contracts.

Contraindications associated with disorders of the muscular system

- Fibrositis
- Lumbago
- Muscular distrophy
- RSI (repetitive strain injury) variants
- Tennis/golfer's elbow
- Tendonitis
- Carpal tunnel.

The hair

The skin on the body and face are virtually covered in hair. Hair
is made up of dead skin cells which contain a protein called
keratin and pigments that are types of melanin. This determines
the hair colour.

Types of hair

There are three types of hair:

- vellus
- terminal
- lanugo.

Vellus hair

This type of hair is fine, soft and downy and covers most of the body, including the face (except the palms of the hands, soles of the feet, the lips and the nipples). The hair often has no pigment, with the base close to the skin surface. It usually does not have a medulla or a well-formed bulb. If this type of hair becomes stimulated the shallow follicle works its way downwards deeper into the skin to create a follicle that could produce terminal hair.

Terminal hair

Terminal hairs are coarse hairs which are mostly pigmented and are usually longer than vellus hairs. The follicles in which they grow are set deeper in the dermis and have well-defined bulbs. This type of hair grows on the scalp, eyebrows, eyelashes, axillae and the pubic region. It also forms male growth on the face (moustache or beard) and chest. Terminal hair may be straight, curly or wavy (this is determined by hereditary factors, ethnic origin or change due to chemical treatments such as perms).

Lanugo hair

This is fine downy hair that grows on a foetus as a normal part of gestation. This is usually shed and replaced by vellus hair at around 33 to 36 weeks into the gestation period. Lanugo hair may be present on newborn premature babies.

Hair texture

Hair may be:

- fine – this hair is more delicate and blond hair is the thinnest
- coarse – this hair tends to be strong with a rough cuticle.

The structure of the hair shaft

Terminal hair has three layers:

- Hair cuticle
- Cortex
- Medulla (where present).

The **shaft** is the part of the hair that extends above the skin surface and is made up of dead keratinised cells.

The **hair cuticle** is the outer layer that is there to protect the hair. It consists of 7–10 layers of irregular scaly bands of flat scales, which overlap each other and are made up of colourless, transparent keratin.

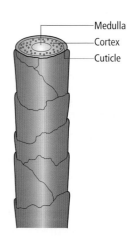

▲ Structure of the hair

The **cortex** is made up of several layers of closely packed, elongated, spindle-shaped cells that are full of hard keratin. These cells breakdown and leave behind long parallel keratin fibres which gives the cortex its strength. Granules of pigments are contained here, which give the hair its natural colour. When the pigment is no longer made, the hair colour will appear white/grey.

The **medulla** is the central core of the hair. It is a soft spongy tissue, being composed of soft keratin; occasionally some pigment granules are lodged here. If a hair is very fine, a medulla may not be present.

The hair follicle

The follicle is an indentation of the epidermis, leading into the dermis. The base of the follicle is shaped like a bulb and contains the loose connective tissue of the dermal papilla, which also contains blood vessels, melanocytes and nerve endings.

The cells of the stratum germinativum in the epidermis cover the dermal papilla and all the cells in this area are mitotically active. As these cells move up the follicle they are invaded by protein and keratin and the hair becomes a horny dead structure.

Each hair follicle has a sebaceous gland, opening into the follicle to form a pilosebaceous unit. The sebum keeps the hair in the follicle supple. The shape of hair is determined by the shape of its follicle.

The hair follicle consists of:

- the inner root sheath
- the outer root sheath
- a connective tissue sheath.

The **inner root sheath** extends around two thirds of the way up the follicle from its base. It is formed from the matrix of the hair root/papilla and it interlocks with the cuticle of the hair shaft and the sheath, which grow up together. It does not pass to the sebaceous gland level. The inner root sheath has three layers of cells:

- Henle's layer – this is one cell thick
- Huxley's layer – this is two or more cells thick
- Cuticle layer – this interlocks with the cuticle of the hair.

The **outer root sheath** forms the follicle wall as it is the continuation of the epidermis, which narrows down to the single stratum basal layer at the hair root/papilla.

A **connective tissue sheath** surrounds the follicle and the sebaceous gland, and is a continuation of the papilla. It provides a blood and sensory supply.

The **sebaceous gland** is attached to the upper parts of the follicle and produces a substance called sebum. This is secreted into the follicle and lubricates and softens the hair and the surface of the skin. It helps protect the skin against fungal and bacterial infections. The ducts of the sebaceous gland are attached directly into the hair follicle.

The **erector pili muscle** is a tiny muscle that is attached at an angle to the base of the follicle. It reacts to stimuli such as cold, fright and flight by pulling the hair upright to trap heat to keep us warm.

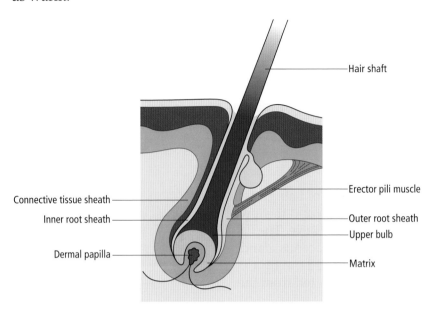

▲ Structure of hair in its follicle

The **hair root** is found below the surface of the skin and consists of two regions - the matrix and the upper bulb. At the **hair bulb**, cells are differentiated into styles of the inner root sheath, the cuticle, cortex and medulla and the hair shaft. The **germinal matrix** is the lower part of the hair bulb where the unpigmented cells actively divide by mitosis to form the hair.

The **dermal papilla** is a connective tissue sheath that is surrounded by the hair bulb. It is not part of the follicle, but is a separate small organ which serves the follicle by supplying it with blood; this is essential for the growth of the hair.

Blood supply to hair papilla

The follicle receives nourishment from blood supplied from the network vessels in the dermis.

Functions of the hair

- Protection – against cold, UV and foreign bodies or dust particles entering areas such as the nostril and the ear canal.
- Touch/sense – such as the eyelashes, which are sensitive to potentially harmful matter. They help to prevent foreign particles entering the eye. Eyebrows help stop sweat running into the eyes.

- Warmth – the erector pili muscle contracts to make the body hair stand on end to prevent heat escaping through the follicles.

Growth cycle of the hair

There are three stages of hair growth:

- Anagen
- Catagen
- Telogen.

Anagen

This is the active growing stage of the hair. The hair grows from the matrix in the hair bulb. Here it develops surrounded by the dermal papilla.

Catagen

This is known as a transitional or changing stage of hair growth. During this stage the dermal papilla breaks down and the lower end of the hair becomes loose at the base of the follicle. The follicle shortens as it moves to the base of the sebaceous gland, where it stays until it either falls out or gets pushed out by a new hair growing behind it. The hair is still being fed from the follicle wall and is often known as the club hair.

Tip We lose between 50 and 100 hairs a day from the scalp.

Telogen

This is the final stage of hair growth and is its resting stage. The follicle will rest until it is stimulated by hormones beginning the anagen phase. The club hair in the telogen stage may last for a few weeks until the new hair pushes it out. Some hairs start to produce new hair immediately and do not undergo this resting stage.

Hair growth differs depending on where on the body it grows. The rate at which hair grows may be slowed down by illness, pregnancy, the oral contraceptive pill and malnutrition.

Adverse conditions and disorders of the hair growth

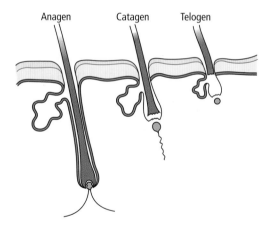

▲ Hair growth cycle

Superfluous hair

This is an excess of hair which is abnormal for the age, sex and race of the person involved.

Hypertrichosis

This is when the growth of the terminal hair is abnormal and excessive.

Hirsutism

This is terminal hair growth in a male sexual pattern. It is normally caused by a hormone imbalance by the male hormones androgens.

Topical causes

Topical causes of hair growth include plucking, shaving and tweezing the hair. The blood supply is stimulated, which results in accelerated growth. These hairs are working to form a protective barrier against further irritation and will grow coarser and deeper.

Systemic causes

Systemic causes of hair growth are triggered by the hormones that control growth, development and metabolic functions of the body. They can produce superfluous hair growth (for example in pregnancy, puberty and menopause).

Abnormal causes of hair growth include:

- Hysterectomy: this is where one or both of the ovaries are removed, which results in the oestrogen levels dropping.
- Polycystic ovaries: these are multiple cysts on the ovaries which can cause lack of menstruation, abnormal bleeding, weight gain and sometimes infertility and hirsutism.
- Anorexia Nervosa: this is more common in young women, who starve themselves to lose weight. This results in a hormone imbalance, which can produce symptoms such as cessation of periods and hirsutism.
- Stress: during times of crisis the adrenal glands produce large amounts of adrenalin, which can result in excessive hair growth.

The nails

The nails are appendages of the skin and protect the ends of your fingers and toes.

Nail plate

This is the visible portion of the nail, which rests upon the nail bed. Its function is to protect the nail bed from physical and bacterial damage. The nails become hard because of a protein called keratin.

Nail bed

The nail bed is responsible for the pinkish colour of the nail due to its blood supply. It is the part of the finger upon which the nail plate rests.

Remember...

Nails are appendages of the skin, meaning something that grows out of the skin.

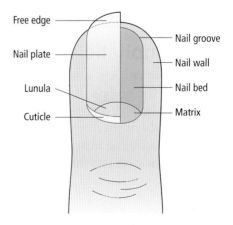

▲ Structure of the nail

Free edge

This is the hardest part of the nail and is located at the distal (top end) of the nail plate; it protects the fingertip from physical damage.

Hyponychium

Acts as a seal protecting the nail bed from infection. It is located under the free edge and forms the smile line.

Nail/side wall

These are folds of skin that help to cushion the nail from external damage and keep the nail in place, otherwise it may grow all around the finger!

Cuticle

This is dead epidermal tissue that is located at the base of the nail plate. The dead skin cells have fallen from the eponychium and attached themselves to the nail plate. It helps to protect the matrix from physical damage and invading bacteria but can be removed using manicure tools.

Eponychium

This is the extension of the cuticle at the base of the nail plate. Its function is to protect the matrix from infection.

Lunula

This is the point where the matrix and nail bed meet. The nail cells that have reproduced within the matrix are pushed forward to begin forming the nail plate. These cells are transparent at this stage and soft which gives the 'half moon' shape at the base of the nail plate.

Matrix

This is the only living part of the nail where the nail cells reproduce by a process called mitosis.

The lymphatic system

This system collects waste products from the body and is often known as the body's second circulation system. The main difference between the way that blood flows in the circulatory system and lymph flows in the lymph system is that blood is pressurised by the heart acting as a 'blood pump'. The lymph system is passive; its fluids ooze into the lymph system and get pushed by normal body and muscle motion to the lymph nodes.

The function of the lymphatic system

- Prevention of infection – collects bacteria, germs/pathogens, waste and foreign materials and carries them to the lymph glands to be filtered, to help prevent infection.
- Defence – produces lymphocytes which defend and protect the body against infection and disease.
- Drainage – drains away excess fluids to be eliminated from the body.
- Transportation – transports fats from the small intestine to the blood.

Components of the lymphatic system

- Lymph fluid
- Lymph vessels
- Lymph nodes (glands)
- Lymph capillaries
- Lymph ducts.

The cycle of the lymphatic system
Lymph

The term lymph comes from the Latin word for water: 'lympha'. Lymph is blood plasma – the liquid that makes up blood minus the red and white cells. It is a clearish liquid that bathes the cells in water and nutrients and is transported around the body through lymph vessels. Small lymph vessels collect the liquid and move it towards larger vessels so that the fluid finally arrives at the lymph nodes for processing. Once lymph has been filtered through the lymph nodes it re-enters the bloodstream.

Composition of lymph

Lymph is made up of:

- plasma
- oxygen
- carbon dioxide
- urea
- lymphocytes
- proteins
- fats
- waste products
- toxins.

Massage treatments can aid the movement of lymph fluid, helping to improve the removal of waste toxins that are transported via lymph fluid.

Lymph nodes of the face and neck

Health and Safety

Always perform drainage movements in massage towards the lymph nodes.

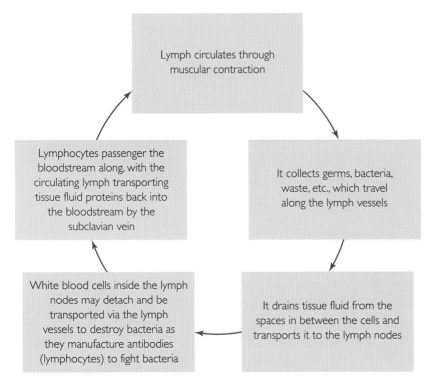

Lymph circulates through muscular contraction

It collects germs, bacteria, waste, etc., which travel along the lymph vessels

It drains tissue fluid from the spaces in between the cells and transports it to the lymph nodes

White blood cells inside the lymph nodes may detach and be transported via the lymph vessels to destroy bacteria as they manufacture antibodies (lymphocytes) to fight bacteria

Lymphocytes passenger the bloodstream along, with the circulating lymph transporting tissue fluid proteins back into the bloodstream by the subclavian vein

▲ How the system works

The diagram below shows the lymph nodes of the face and neck and where they drain lymph from.

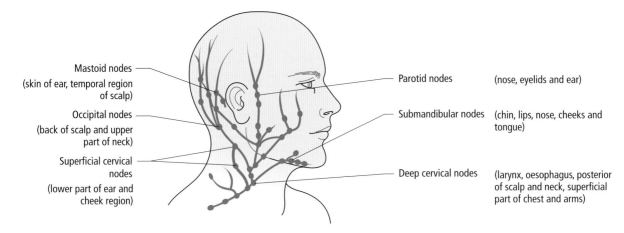

Mastoid nodes
(skin of ear, temporal region of scalp)

Occipital nodes
(back of scalp and upper part of neck)

Superficial cervical nodes
(lower part of ear and cheek region)

Parotid nodes (nose, eyelids and ear)

Submandibular nodes (chin, lips, nose, cheeks and tongue)

Deep cervical nodes (larynx, oesophagus, posterior of scalp and neck, superficial part of chest and arms)

▲ Lymph nodes of the face and neck

Lymph vessels

These are thin-walled permeable (porous) structures with valves that carry the lymphatic fluid around the body from the lymph capillaries. Usually lymph flows away from the tissues towards the lymph nodes at the right lymphatic duct or the thoracic duct (the thoracic duct is the largest lymph vessel in the body). These vessels can drain directly into the right and left subclavian vein.

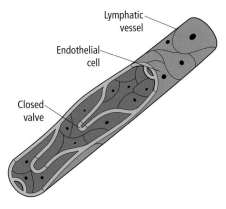

▲ Lymph vessel

Lymph nodes

These are small 'bean-shaped' structures which, in a healthy state, range from around 1mm up to 2cm. They are found all over the body but are particularly concentrated in the axillae (armpit), the neck, crease of the elbow, the groin and behind the knee.

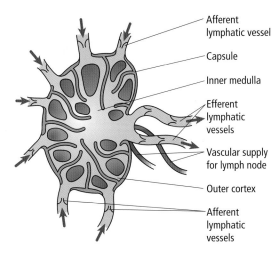

▲ Lymph node

Lymph nodes contain filtering tissue and a large number of lymph cells. When fighting certain bacterial infections, the lymph nodes swell with bacteria to the point where you can actually feel them. Swollen lymph nodes are therefore a good indication that you have an infection.

- Lymph entering the node does so through an **afferent vessel**
- Lymph leaves the node through an **efferent vessel**.

Lymph capillaries

These capillaries are concerned with the absorption of **interstitial fluid** from the tissues. Lymph capillaries are slightly larger than blood capillaries.

Lymph ducts

These are lymphatic vessels that empty lymph into one of the subclavian veins. There are two lymph ducts in the body – the right lymph duct and the thoracic duct.

The right lymph duct

This is located on the right side of the neck and ends in the right subclavian vein.

The right duct drains lymph fluid into the right subclavian vein from:

- the right arm (via the right subclavian trunk)
- the upper right section of the trunk
- the right side of the head and neck (via the right jugular trunk)
- (in some individuals) the lower lobe of the left lung.

The thoracic duct

This is the largest lymphatic vessel in the body and is given a variety of names including alimentary duct, chyliferous duct, the left lymphatic duct and Van Hoorne's canal. It drains lymph from the abdomen and lower limbs into the left subclavian vein. It collects most of the lymph in the body (except that collected from the right lymph duct).

Cisterna chyli

This is a dilated sac at the lower end of the thoracic duct in which a lymph from the intestinal trunk and two lumbar lymphatic trunks flow. It drains lymph laden with digested fats (chyle) from the intestines.

Location and function of lymphatic organs

Spleen

The spleen is located in the upper left quadrant of the abdomen. It is greyish purple in colour and makes up the largest lymphatic tissue mass in the body.

The functions of the spleen are:

- to remove old red blood cells and hold reserves of blood in case of haemorrhagic shock (this is the result of inadequate delivery of oxygen and nutrients' cellular function when there is a demand for oxygen supply, for example during the state of shock)
- to produce lymphocytes and assist in fighting infection
- to produce phagocytes to destroy worn out erythrocytes (red blood cells) and abnormal cells
- to selectively filter white cells and platelets
- to recycle iron, synthesise antibodies and remove antibody-coated bacteria and blood cells
- to assist in tissue healing.

You can live without a spleen but protection against infection may be reduced.

Thymus

The thymus is located behind the sternum (breast bone).

The functions of the thymus are:

- to process lymphocytes into active 'T' cells vital to the immune system
- to provide endocrine function (pre-puberty) in the control of growth.

Tonsils

The tonsils are located at the back of the throat. Their function is to fight infection by defending against micro-organisms entering the mouth and the nose.

Appendix

The appendix is located in the right lower section of the abdomen. Its function is currently unclear (and like the spleen, you can live without your appendix).

Peyer's patches

Peyer's patches are usually found in the lowest portion of the small intestine. They appear as oval or round lymphoid follicles (similar to lymph nodes). They play an important function in the immune surveillance of the intestine and also facilitate the generation of the immune response within the mucous membranes.

White blood cells and the immune system

White blood cells are probably the most important part of your immune system. They are a whole collection of different cells that work together to destroy bacteria and viruses. All white blood cells are known as Leucocytes. They are not like normal cells in the body; they act like independent, living single-cell organisms and are able to move and capture things on their own. Many white blood cells cannot divide and reproduce on their own, but instead have a 'factory' somewhere in the body that produces them – bone marrow.

The main types of white blood cell present inside the lymph nodes are:

- macrophages
- lymphocytes.

Macrophages

Macrophages engulf and then digest cellular debris and **pathogens** either as a stationary or a mobile cell. They also stimulate **lymphocytes** and other immune cells to respond to pathogens.

Lymphocytes

Lymphocytes identify an invader and generate specific responses that are tailored to eliminate specific pathogens or pathogen-infected cells.

There are three major types of lymphocyte: B cell, T cell and (NK) natural killer cells.

- Natural killer cells – distinguish infected cells and tumours from normal cells
- B cells – bones cells, which neutralise viruses and bacteria by producing large amounts of antibodies
- T cells – thymus cells, some of which direct the immune response, while others produce toxic granules that contain powerful enzymes to induce the death of pathogen-infected cells.

Lymphocytes start life in bone marrow but those destined to become B cells develop in the marrow before entering the bloodstream. T cells start in the marrow but migrate through the bloodstream to the thymus and mature there. T cells and B cells are often found in the bloodstream but tend to concentrate in lymph tissue such as the lymph nodes, the thymus and the spleen. There is also quite a bit of lymph tissue in the digestive system.

Once the B cells and T cells have been activated they leave antigens behind in the form of memory cells. Throughout their lifetime, these memory cells will 'remember' each specific pathogen previously encountered, and are able to deliver a strong, rapid response if the pathogen is ever detected again.

Immunisation

The theory behind immunisation is that the body is exposed to a small amount of an immunogen that the memory cells fight against and recognise in the future, to protect the body against it.

Autoimmunity

Sometimes the immune system makes a mistake and attacks the body's own tissues or organs. This is called autoimmunity. One example of an autoimmune disease is Type I diabetes.

Allergy triggers

An **allergen** is any substance that can cause an allergic reaction.

The body's response

Most humans mount significant immunoglobulin E (IgE) responses only as a defence against parasitic infections. However, some individuals mount an IgE response against common environmental antigens. This hereditary predisposition is called **atopy**. In atopic individuals, non-parasitic antigens stimulate inappropriate IgE production, leading to Type 1 hypersensitivity.

Contraindications

Diseases and disorders associated with, or linked to the lymphatic system include:

- Cancer
- HIV (and AIDS)
- Lymphoedema
- Mastitis
- Oedema.

Blood and the cardiovascular system

The cardiovascular system is a system of organs that circulates nutrients, lymph, hormones, gases and electrolytes to and from cells in the body to help fight diseases and infections, and to stabilise the body's temperature and pH to maintain homoeostasis (the body's equilibrium). Blood is a specialised bodily fluid which, through its transportation system delivers vital ingredients that cells need and removes waste products that the body does not need. Around 8 per cent of the human body weight is made up from blood (around 5 to 6 litres).

The basic structure of the cardiovascular system comprises of:

- the heart
- the blood
- the blood vessels.

The heart

The heart is composed of cardiac muscle that pumps blood around the body through a network of arteries, veins and capillaries. It is contained within a protective pericardial sac and located in the thoracic cavity, behind the sternum between the lungs. It is centrally placed but angled to the left of the midline of the body.

It is divided into two halves. Each half consists of an upper and a lower section:

- Upper section – atrium
- Lower section – ventricle.

The outside of the heart contains a network of blood vessels which are branches of the right and left coronary arteries and veins. These supply the heart muscle with blood. Blood enters the two atria of the heart through the main veins and leaves through main arteries from the two ventricles. The ventricle walls are much thicker than the walls in the atria as they need to generate the pressure to force the blood through the arteries.

There are several valves in the heart that ensure that blood only flows in one direction. These valves are flaps made of strong tissue and are attached to the muscle the ventricle walls:

- The bicuspid valve is on the left side of the heart and has two 'flaps'.
- The tricuspid valve is on the right side of the heart and has three 'flaps'.

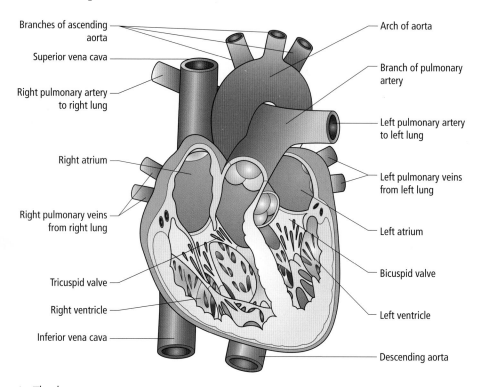

Branches of ascending aorta —
Superior vena cava —
Right pulmonary artery to right lung —
Right atrium —
Right pulmonary veins from right lung —
Tricuspid valve —
Right ventricle —
Inferior vena cava —

— Arch of aorta
— Branch of pulmonary artery
— Left pulmonary artery to left lung
— Left pulmonary veins from left lung
— Left atrium
— Bicuspid valve
— Left ventricle
— Descending aorta

▲ The heart

Right atrium

This is one of the four chambers of the heart. It receives deoxygenated blood from the inferior and superior vena cava and the coronary sinus. The blood is then pumped into the right ventricle through the tricuspid valve.

Left atrium

Another of the four chambers of the heart, this receives oxygenated blood from the pulmonary vein and pumps it into the left ventricle by the bicuspid valve.

Right ventricle

This is another of the four chambers of the heart. It receives deoxygenated blood from the right atrium through the tricuspid valve. The blood is then pumped into the pulmonary artery via the pulmonary valve and trunk. It is a triangular shape that extends from the right atrium to the apex of the heart.

Left ventricle

Again, one of the four chambers of the heart. It receives oxygenated blood from the left atrium through the bicuspid valve, which is then pumped into the aorta by the aortic valve.

Pulmonary arteries

These are the only arteries (other than umbilical arteries in the foetus) that carry deoxygenated blood, which is carried from the heart to the lungs.

Pulmonary vein

This large blood vessel carries blood from the lungs to the left atrium. There are four pulmonary veins – two from each lung, which carry oxygenated blood. This is unusual as veins usually carry deoxygenated blood.

Aorta

This is the largest artery in the body. It extends from the left ventricle of the heart down to the abdomen where it branches off into two smaller arteries known as the common iliacs. Most major arteries branch off from the aorta, with the exception of the main pulmonary artery. It distributes oxygenated blood to all arteries, which then transport the blood around the body through systemic circulation.

Blood circulation through the heart

Blood is circulated around the body via blood vessels and by the heart pumping repeatedly. There are two systems of circulation: pulmonary and systemic.

- The pulmonary circulation goes from the heart to the lungs and back again.
- The systemic circulation moves from the heart to the rest of the body's organs and back again.

Pulmonary circulation

In this system, blood travels between the lungs and the heart, producing two streams of blood circulating through the heart at the same time. Blood travels from the right ventricle to the lungs in the pulmonary artery and it returns to the left atrium of the heart in the pulmonary vein.

Systemic circulation

This refers to the circulation of the blood between the heart and all other body systems except the lungs. The blood travels from the left ventricle through the aorta and returns from the body tissues to the right atrium of the heart in the vena cava.

Portal circulation

This is part of the systemic circulation and it collects blood from the digestive organs. The hepatic portal vein contains blood which absorbs nutrients from the intestines which is then transported to the liver. The liver controls the amount of each nutrient that remains in the blood. The hepatic portal vein is the only vein in the body which does not return blood directly to the heart. It is formed by the fusion of the superior mesenteric vein from the small intestine, the inferior mesenteric vein from the large intestine and the splenic vein that comes from the spleen, stomach and pancreas.

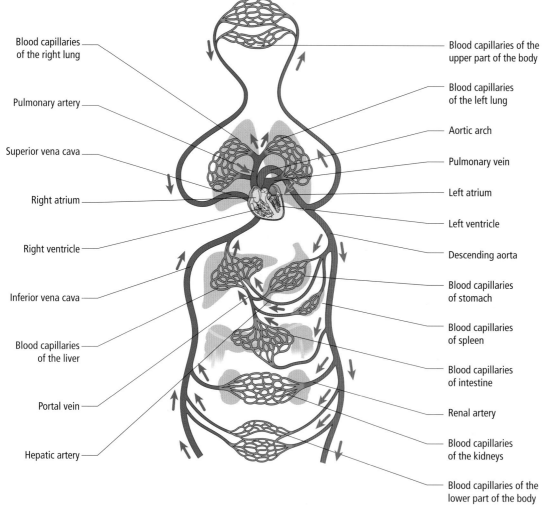

Blood capillaries of the right lung

Pulmonary artery

Superior vena cava

Right atrium

Right ventricle

Inferior vena cava

Blood capillaries of the liver

Portal vein

Hepatic artery

Blood capillaries of the upper part of the body

Blood capillaries of the left lung

Aortic arch

Pulmonary vein

Left atrium

Left ventricle

Descending aorta

Blood capillaries of stomach

Blood capillaries of spleen

Blood capillaries of intestine

Renal artery

Blood capillaries of the kidneys

Blood capillaries of the lower part of the body

▲ Circlatory system

Oxygenated and deoxygenated blood

Oxygenated blood is contained in the left side of the heart; this is brought to the heart from the lungs in the pulmonary circulation. The right side of the heart contains deoxygenated blood, which has been brought to the heart from the body tissues in the systemic circulation.

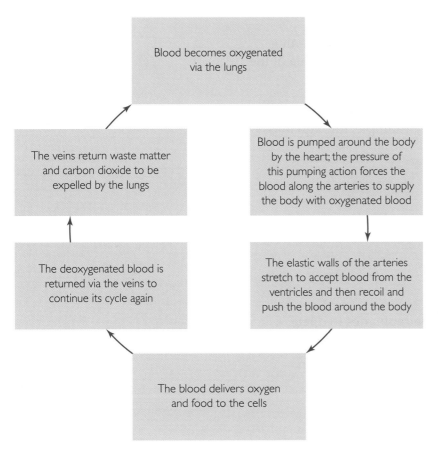

▲ Blood cycle flow chart

Blood pressure

This is the pressure exerted from the circulating blood on the walls of the blood vessels. It is considered one of the 'vital signs'. Blood pressure varies during each heartbeat and is measured between a maximum (**systolic**) and a minimum (**diastolic**). Blood pressure drops rapidly along the small arteries and arterioles and continues to decrease as the blood moves through the capillaries and back to the heart through the veins. A person's blood pressure is usually recorded with systolic pressure over diastolic. It is usually measured by wrapping a cuff around the upper arm that applies pressure at the crease of the elbow where brachial artery lies. This is the upper arm's major blood vessel that carries blood away from the heart.

What can cause changes in blood pressure?

- An increase in volume, for example fluid retention causes an increase in pressure.
- A decrease in volume, for example blood loss causes drop in pressure.
- Activity, exercise, massage, heat or excitement.

Effects of increased circulation: erythema

Erythema comes from the Greek word 'erythros' meaning red. It is a reddening of the skin caused by hyperaemia of the capillaries in the lower layers of the skin.

Causes of erythema:

- Stimulation of blood supply (for example, through massage)
- Skin injury
- Inflammation
- Infection
- Nervous blushes
- Allergic reaction
- Exercise
- Acne medication
- Sunburn
- Any treatment which causes the capillaries to dilate.

Erythema is also a common side effect of radiotherapy treatment due to the patient being exposed to ionising radiation.

Blood

Blood comprises of:

- 45 per cent blood cells
- 55 per cent plasma.

Blood cells (corpuscles)

The cells present in blood are either red blood cells (erythrocytes) or white blood cells (including leucocytes and platelets). Red blood cells transport respiratory gases around the body. White blood cells help to fight infection as part of the body's immune system.

Platelets

These are small regularly shaped clear cell fragments that have no nucleus. They are important for the process of clotting blood. The average lifespan of platelets is around five to nine days. If the number of platelets is too low excessive bleeding can occur; if the number of platelets is too high blood clots can form easily.

Plasma

Plasma is mostly made up of water (92 per cent by volume). It contains dissipated proteins such as glucose minerals, carbon dioxide, amino acids, salts, antibodies, waste products and hormones. Plasma is the main source for excretion.

Arteries, veins and capillaries

Types of blood vessel:

- Arteries
- Veins
- Capillaries.

Arteries

Arteries carry oxygenated blood (except for the pulmonary artery) that has passed through the lungs and has been pumped out of the heart. Arteries carry oxygen away from the heart to the tissues in the body at high pressure, and because of this they have thick walls. The blood carried by arteries is bright red in colour (because it is oxygenated).

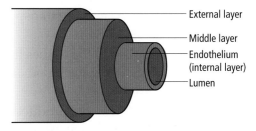

▲ Artery

Veins

Veins carry deoxygenated venous blood back to the heart and waste products such as carbon dioxide from the tissues to the lungs to be exhaled. Blood flows more slowly in the veins than in the arteries because it is being transported at a lower pressure. Veins often pass through muscles and when the muscles contract the veins are squeezed and the blood is pushed along them. Veins contain valves that stop the blood flowing backwards. The walls of veins are thinner than the walls of arteries and venous blood is a dark red colour (because it is deoxygenated).

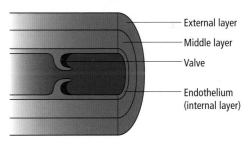

▲ Vein

Capillaries

These are smallest of the body's blood vessels. Known as microvessels, they measure around 5 to 10mm in diameter and are only one cell thick. They connect arterioles and venules.

Arterioles

These blood vessels have a small diameter and extend and branch out from an artery leading to a capillary. Arterioles are very important in the regulation of blood pressure.

Venules

These are also small blood vessels. They allow deoxygenated blood to return from the capillary beds to the veins. They measure around 8 to 100µm (micrometres) in diameter and are formed when capillaries unite. These tiny blood vessels drain blood directly from the capillary beds. When many venules unite they form a vein.

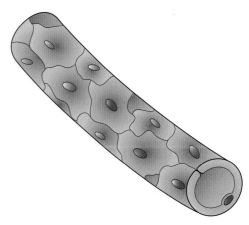

▲ Capillary

Functions of blood

- Transportation
- Regulation
- Protection.

Transportation

- Food/nutrients – such as glucose, fatty acids (dissolved in the blood) and amino acids are transported from the digestive tract to the cells.
- Oxygen – supplied to the tissues through the process of the lungs oxygenating the blood and the heart pumping it through the arteries.
- Carbon dioxide – a waste product that is removed from the cells to the lungs and then exhaled.
- Hormones – chemicals that are released by a cell or gland in one part of the body and send out messages to regulate the cells or to signal any tissue damage. These are transported around the body from the endocrine gland which secretes (releases) hormones directly into the bloodstream.
- Medication – can be transported and passed to the relevant cells.
- Waste products – transported from the cells to the kidneys and lungs to be excreted.

Regulation

Blood regulates the water content of cells, the body's core temperature and the body's pH.

Protection

Blood provides protection by circulating white blood cells to protect against infection and to coagulate blood (blood clotting), which is the body's way of repairing itself when an open wound occurs (this process also helps to prevent fluid loss).

The circulation of blood and the liver

The liver is a vital organ of the body and is necessary for survival. It is situated below the diaphragm in the abdominal pelvic region of the abdomen. It has a wide variety of high-volume biochemical reactions including the synthesis and breakdown of small complex molecules, many of which are necessary for normal vital functions. It is a reddish/pinkish brown-coloured organ with four lobes that are unequal in size and shape. It is the largest internal organ in the body (skin being the largest organ overall) and the largest gland.

Blood flow to the liver

The liver receives a dual blood supply from the hepatic arteries and the hepatic portal vein. This vein carries venous blood drained from the spleen, gastro-intestinal tracts and other organs and makes up around 75 per cent of the liver's blood supply. The hepatic arteries supply the remaining 25 per cent as arterial blood, which supplies the liver with oxygen.

Blood flows through the sinusoids and empties into the central vein of each lobule. The central veins combine into hepatic veins, which leave the liver and empty into the inferior vena cava.

Function of the liver

- Produces bile which is an alkaline to aid digestion via the emulsification of lipids
- Detoxification (removal of toxic substances from a living organism)
- Metabolism (a set of chemical reactions that help to maintain life in a living organism)
- Glycogen (glucose) storage (this molecule functions as a secondary long-term energy storage and is made primarily by the liver and the muscles)
- Hormone production and breakdown of hormones such as insulin
- Converts ammonia to urea
- Synthesises hormones that are responsible for raising blood pressure when the kidneys sense low blood pressure
- Stores iron from broken down red blood cells.

The circulation of blood and the kidneys

The kidneys have several functions and are an essential part of the urinary system. They are also responsible for the regulation of electrolytes in the body and help with the regulation of blood pressure. We have two kidneys and they are located at the rear of the abdominal cavity. They receive blood from the paired renal arteries and drain into the paired renal veins.

Function of the kidneys

- Filter the blood
- Remove wastes such as urea and ammonium that gets diverted to the bladder and is excreted via urine
- Re-absorption of water, amino acids and glucose
- Produce hormones including renin (responsible for raising blood pressure when it senses low blood pressure).

Blood supply of the head face and neck

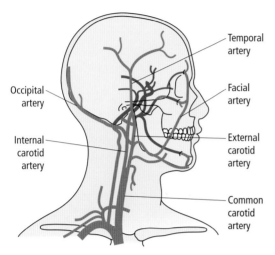

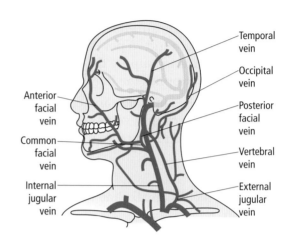

▲ Blood flow to the head and neck

The **common carotid artery** supplies the head and neck with oxygenated blood and divides in the neck to form the external and internal carotid arteries. The external carotid artery is a major artery of the head and neck and particularly supplies oxygenated blood to the neck glands, throat, tongue, face, ear, mouth and scalp. The **internal carotid artery** is another major artery of the head and neck that supplies oxygenated blood, particularly to the brain and eyes. The **external jugular vein** receives most of its blood from the exterior of the cranium and the deeper part of the face. The **internal jugular veins** collect blood from the brain and the superficial part of the face and neck.

Contraindications of the cardiovascular system

- Varicose veins
- Deep vein thrombosis
- Angina
- Hypertension
- Hypotension
- Stroke.

Varicose veins

This condition refers to veins which have become enlarged and often painful. They are commonly found on the leg but may be present elsewhere in the body. The leg muscles pump the veins to return deoxygenated blood back to the heart. They are therefore working against the effects of gravity and so veins have valves in them to protect the blood flowing backwards.

Causes

A vein becomes varicose when the valves no longer meet properly and therefore do not work. This allows the blood to flow backwards into the vein to enlarge it. This is more common in superficial veins in the legs, which are subject to high pressure with long periods of standing. Often, varicose veins may itch and scratching them can cause ulcers.

Medical treatments available

- Surgical elastic stockings can be worn to help support the veins in the legs
- Exercise
- Elevating the legs to alleviate the pressure
- Surgical treatments to strip veins, removing the affected veins from the area as the superficial veins only return about 10 per cent of the blood from the leg back to the heart. Most of the blood in the legs is returned by the deep veins; superficial ones can be removed without serious harm
- Less invasive medical treatments such as sealing the main leaking vein at the top of the thigh.

Deep vein thrombosis (DVT)

This is the formation of a blood clot within a deep vein and in medical terms this is often known as deep venous thrombosis, with the abbreviation 'DVT'. This is commonly found in the leg in the popliteal or femoral vein. It can also be found in the deep veins of the pelvis and occasionally in the veins of the arm.

In most cases the area will be swollen, red, painful and warm, and the superficial veins may be engorged with blood. However, occasionally DVT can occur without symptoms.

This is a serious condition as the blood clots could become dislodged and travel to the lungs, causing pulmonary embolism which would be a medical emergency. This condition potentially could be fatal, but is rare.

Common causes

- A decreased flow rate of blood
- Damage to the blood vessel wall
- An increased tendency for the blood to clot (hypercoagulability).

Other causes

- Physical trauma if the veins have become compressed
- Infections
- Strokes
- Heart failure

- Cancer
- Smoking
- Obesity drugs such as oestrogen
- Age
- Hereditary factors
- Pregnancy/postnatal period
- Immobilisation following surgery, wearing an orthopaedic cast, long-haul flights etc.

Medical treatment available

- Anticoagulation drugs (to thin the blood)
- An inferior vena cava filter may be used in the heart
- Graduated compression stockings may be worn.

Angina

Symptoms of this include a severe chest pain due to the lack of blood and oxygen supply to the heart muscle as the arteries narrow.

Cause

- Coronary artery disease is the main cause of angina – this is generally due to obstruction or spasm of the coronary arteries (the heart blood vessels).

Major risk factors in the cause of angina

- Smoking
- Obesity
- Lack of exercise
- Age (it is more common in men over 55 and women over 65)
- Diabetes
- Hereditary factors
- Hypertension (high blood pressure)
- Kidney disease
- Medications.

Medical treatments available

Treatments offered for this condition are often things that thin the blood:

- Beta-blocker therapy which diminishes the effects of stress hormones such as adrenaline
- Aspirin
- Intravenous nitroglycerin
- Surgical procedures.

Hypertension (high blood pressure)

This condition sees a rise in the systemic arterial pressure of blood flow. It is opposite to hypotension which is low blood pressure. Small blood vessels in the brain swell but this can be reversed if the blood pressure can be lowered.

Common symptoms

- Headache
- Drowsiness
- Visual disturbances
- Nausea
- Vomiting
- Confusion.

Causes

- Stress
- Conditions affecting the kidneys, heart, arteries or endocrine system
- Poor diet
- Smoking.

Medical treatments available

- Improved lifestyle
- Improved diet
- Medication.

Hypotension (low blood pressure)

This relates to abnormal low blood pressure and often can be associated with shock. It is the opposite of hypertension.

Symptoms

- Dizziness
- Light-headedness
- Fainting
- Seizures.

Causes

- Widening of the blood vessels
- Hormonal changes
- Shock
- Side-effects from medication
- Anaemia
- Heart problems
- Endocrine system problems.

Medical treatment available

Treatment very much depends upon the cause and this may vary from:

- adding an electrolyte solution to the diet to restore the body's balance
- either laying the sufferer down so that their head is low and their legs are raised or sitting them down with their head between their knees. Gently, but firmly, pushing their head down while they try to push their head upwards. This will encourage the blood to flow to their brain, reducing their symptoms and helping them to recover more quickly.

Stroke

A stroke is a serious medical condition that occurs when the blood supply to part of the brain is cut off.

Like all organs, the brain needs the oxygen and nutrients provided by blood to function properly. If the supply of blood is restricted or stopped, brain cells begin to die. This can lead to brain damage and possibly death.

Strokes are a medical emergency and prompt treatment is essential in order to minimise the likelihood of damage to the brain.

Symptoms (FAST is the acronym the NHS use to remember what to do in case of a stroke)

- **Face**: the face may have dropped on one side; the person may not be able to smile or their mouth or eye may have drooped
- **Arms**: the person with suspected stroke may not be able to lift one or both arms and keep them there because of arm weakness or numbness
- **Speech**: their speech may be slurred or garbled; the person may not be able to talk at all despite appearing to be awake
- **Time**: it is time to dial 999 immediately if you see any of these signs or symptoms.

Causes

There are two main causes of strokes:

- Ischaemic (accounting for over 80 per cent of all cases), where the blood supply is stopped due to a blood clot
- Haemorrhagic, where a blood vessel is weakened that supplies the brain and it bursts and causes brain damage.

There is also a related condition known as a transient ischaemic attack (TIA), where the supply of blood to the brain is temporarily interrupted, causing a 'mini-stroke'. TIAs should be treated seriously as they are often a warning sign that a stroke is coming.

Medical treatments available

Strokes can usually be treated successfully and also prevented by:

- eating a healthy diet
- taking regular exercise
- drinking alcohol in moderation
- not smoking
- lowering high blood pressure and cholesterol levels
- medication
- (in some cases) surgery.

Many people will require a long period of rehabilitation after a stroke and not all will recover fully.

Diseases and disorders

Contraindications

A contraindication is a condition that either **prevents** or **restricts** the application of treatment. The condition of the area to be worked on should be checked for any contraindications prior to carrying out any make-up treatment, to prevent the condition being spread or made worse.

Contra-actions

This is an **adverse** or **unwanted reaction** either during or after a treatment. If a contra-action occurs during the service, the treatment should be stopped immediately and the product removed with a gentle remover; a cold compress may be applied or the area could be flushed with cold water if appropriate. If the reaction persists, is uncomfortable or the client is worried they should be advised to seek medical advice.

Allergic skin reactions

An allergic reaction occurs rapidly and is a hypersensitive response of the immune system from normally harmless environmental substances known as **allergens**. These can be chemical, vegetable or animal and can enter the body via three different routes of entry, which are:

- inhalation – breathing in the allergen
- absorption – entry via the skin
- ingestion – through the mouth.

The body has some special cells that are present in most tissues known as **mast cells**. These cells are closely related to some types of white blood cell and when they are injured or irritated they identify damage to the skin and burst. This in turn releases the chemical **histamine** into the tissues. It is this histamine reaction that causes the blood vessels to dilate and create a reddening to the skin, known as an **erythema**.

Tip There are many products that are hypoallergenic that may contain less of the known irritants. These may be suitable for sensitive skins.

Allergic reaction

- **Location**: Skin.
- **Cause**: Histamine reaction to an allergen which could be animal, chemical or vegetable.
- **Description**: Swelling, irritation, red rash and itching that appears shortly after contact with product etc.
- **Contagious**: No.
- **Action**: If this occurs during treatment, remove product with a gentle remover and apply cold compress. Refer client to seek medical advice.

Eczema of the skin

- **Location**: Can be anywhere on the body.
- **Cause**: Either an external or internal irritant, for example detergents, chemical products etc.
- **Description**: Dry inflamed skin tissues; red patches; may bleed and weep. It also may itch, be very irritated and may become cracked leading to bacterial secondary infections. It may be possible to work around the area avoiding any patches of eczema, professional judgement and and caution should be used.
- **Contagious**: No.
- **Action**: Do not treat in the area if it is red, painful or there are open sores and refer client to seek medical advice if condition has never been seen before by the client or it worsens.

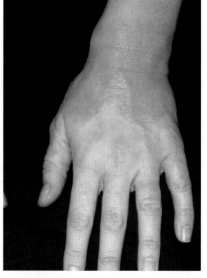

▲ Eczema

Dermatitis

- **Location**: On the skin; often found on hands but can appear on other areas such as the face.
- **Cause**: Irritants such as harsh chemicals, for example detergents etc.
- **Description**: Appears as an inflamed red rash, dry and cracked; in severe cases it can swell and blister. It also may itch.
- **Contagious**: No.
- **Action**: Do not treat in the area if it is red, painful or there are open sores. Refer client to seek medical advice if condition has never been seen before by the client or it gets worse.

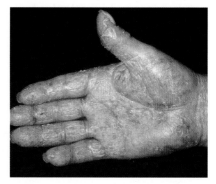

▲ Dermatitis

Viral infections

These types of infections can affect any part of the body and its tissues; sometimes several areas can be affected at one time. The viruses are thought to be parasites that need living tissue to survive. Therefore they attack healthy cells and multiply inside the cell, breaking the cell wall/membrane and allowing more parasites to attack other cells and spread infection. These types of infection cannot be treated with antibiotics and tend to be fought by the body's own immune system or antiviral drugs.

Herpes simplex (cold sore)

- **Location**: Often found around the mouth and nose area.
- **Cause**: Viral infection caused by the herpes virus.
- **Description**: Erythema or red background with tiny blisters which burst to form crusts that may itch and become irritated. Usually located around the mouth and nasal area; once this virus has entered the body it stays there and lays dormant until triggered.
- **Contagious**: Yes.
- **Action**: Do not treat in the area; many over-the-counter treatments can be purchased and the condition usually disappears within a short time. However, if condition gets much worse or persists refer client to seek medical advice.

▲ Herpes simplex

Herpes zoster (shingles)

- **Location**: Body; commonly found on trunk.
- **Cause**: Virus that attacks the sensory nerve endings. The virus can lay dormant in the body after recovery.
- **Description**: Redness of the skin occurs along the line of the affected nerve in a patch with a red rash; blisters usually develop. This condition is usually very painful.
- **Contagious**: Yes.
- **Action**: Do not treat and refer client to seek medical advice.

Verruca plantaris

- **Location**: Foot.
- **Cause**: Viral infection.
- **Description**: Also known as 'plantar wart'; usually found on the feet and tend to grows inwards. There is a circular piece of hard skin with black dots in the centre; there may be more than one verruca present at any one time.
- **Contagious**: Yes.
- **Action**: Do not treat in the area and refer client to seek medical advice.

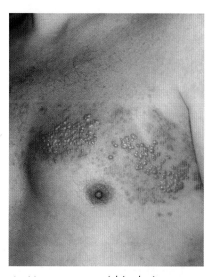

▲ Herpes zoster (shingles)

Common warts (verruca vulgaris)

- **Location**: Knees, face or hands.
- **Cause**: Viral infection.
- **Description**: Raised lumps of horny tissue, various shapes and sizes with a rough texture.
- **Contagious**: Yes.
- **Action**: Do not treat in the area and refer client to seek medical advice.

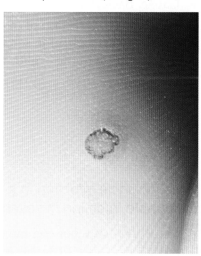

▲ Common warts (verruca vulgaris)

Bacterial infections

These are single-cell organisms that can multiply by themselves. They live inside and outside the body. Some bacteria are harmless (**non-pathogenic**) and useful in destroying some of the harmful bacteria (**pathogenic**) in our bodies. It is the pathogenic bacteria that cause diseases, which can be spread via touch, droplets and bodily fluids. The doctor will usually treat these types of infections with antibiotics.

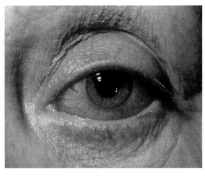

▲ Conjunctivitis

Conjunctivitis

- **Location**: Eye.
- **Cause**: Bacterial.
- **Description**: Inflammation of **conjunctiva** (membrane of the eye); red and itchy with yellow discharge.
- **Contagious**: Yes.
- **Action**: Do not treat in the area and refer client to seek medical advice.

▲ Stye

Stye

- **Location**: Eye.
- **Cause**: Bacteria.
- **Description**: Infection of the sebaceous gland at the base of the eyelash follicle; swollen, red, sore and contains pus.
- **Contagious**: Yes.
- **Action**: Do not treat in the area and refer client to seek medical advice if symptoms persist or worsen.

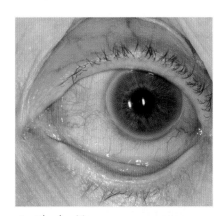

▲ Blepharitis

Blepharitis

- **Location**: Eye.
- **Cause**: Bacteria.
- **Description**: Infection of the rims of the eyelid, which may be itchy with a burning sensation; crusty, red and sore with inflammation of the eyelid. This may also be caused by a complication from a skin condition such as acne rosacea or seborrhoeic dermatitis.
- **Contagious**: No.
- **Action**: Do not treat in the area and refer client to seek medical advice.

Boils (furuncle infection in a single hair follicle or **carbuncle** infection in several hair follicles)

- **Location**: Anywhere on the skin.
- **Cause**: Bacterial infection at the base of the hair follicle.
- **Description**: Red, raised, painful, pus may be present.

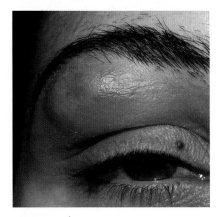

▲ Furuncle

- **Contagious**: Yes.
- **Action**: Do not treat in the area and refer client to seek medical advice if condition is painful, worsens or continues.

Impetigo

- **Location**: Skin.
- **Cause**: Staphylococci bacteria that invade the skin and cause infection.
- **Description**: Inflamed red patches with blisters, pustules and yellow/honey-coloured crusts.
- **Contagious**: Yes, highly contagious.
- **Action**: Do not treat the client and refer client to seek medical advice.

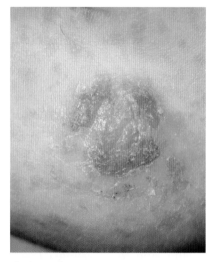

▲ Impetigo

Folliculitis

- **Location**: Skin.
- **Cause**: Bacterial infection in many hair follicles, sometimes following shaving, plucking or waxing.
- **Description**: Localised redness surrounding the hair follicle which fills with pus, turning into **pustules** and boils.
- **Contagious**: Yes.
- **Action**: Do not treat the client in that area and refer client to seek medical advice.

Acne vulgaris

- **Location**: Skin. Commonly found on the face, neck, chest and back.
- **Cause**: Often common during puberty as the **sebaceous glands** become active; stimulated by male hormone from the adrenal gland (**androgens**), which is present in both males and females. The sebaceous glands can become over active and produce excessive amounts of **sebum**, which sits in the **sebaceous ducts** as their openings become narrower, causing the skin to appear congested. **Papules** are caused by bacteria that feeds on the sebum; these bacteria leave waste and fatty acids behind which irritate the skin and cause it to become inflamed.
- **Description**: Red, inflamed papules, pustules and **comedones** that can cause scaring.
- **Contagious**: No.
- **Action**: In mild cases, a make-up treatment could be carried out with caution, perhaps using hypoallergenic products. However, in severe cases refer client to seek medical advice.

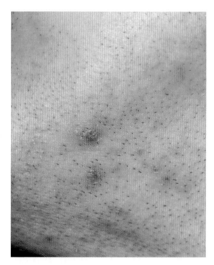

▲ Folliculitis

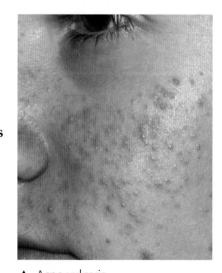

▲ Acne vulgaris

Acne rosacea

- **Location**: Skin, commonly found on the cheeks, nose and forehead and occasionally on the neck, scalp, chest and even the ears.
- **Cause**: The cause is unknown but genetic factors are thought to be one cause of this condition; over-exposure to ultraviolet rays, gastrointestinal disease (caused by Helicobacter Pylori, a bacteria that causes severe inflammation of the inner stomach lining), and even a mite occasionally found in the hair follicles. More common in adults between the ages of 30 and 50, the recorded numbers of women suffering from this are higher than men but often the condition is worse in males. Alcohol, spicy foods, stress and excessive heat are all amongst the reported possible causes.
- **Description**: Redness due to dilated capillaries (**telangiectasias**), coarse thickened skin tissues, enlarged pores, papules and pustules (containing bacteria). In severe cases **Rhinophyma** (large bulbous nose) may be present.
- **Contagious**: No.
- **Action**: In mild cases a make-up treatment could be carried out with caution, maybe using hypoallergenic products. However, in severe cases refer the client to seek medical advice.

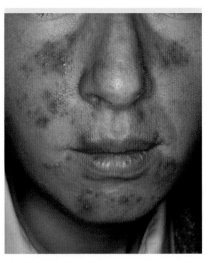

▲ Acne rosacea

Hair diseases and disorders

Alopecia areata

- **Location**: Scalp, but can affect other areas of the body.
- **Cause**: Auto-immune disorder, where the body can attack its own hair follicles. Some research points to this being a hereditary condition. It also could be triggered by stress or shock.
- **Description**: Bald patches; this can then spread to cause total baldness of the area (**alopecia totalis**). If this is just limited to the beard it is known as **alopecia bareata barbae**. If all of the body hair is lost it is called **alopecia areata universalis**.
- **Contagious**: No.
- **Action**: Refer the client to seek medical advice if the condition has never been seen before by the client or if it gets worse; they may be referred for some high frequency treatment by a qualified hairdresser.

Barber's itch (sycosis or tinea barbae – ringworm of the beard)

- **Location**: Bearded area of the face and neck.
- **Cause**: Fungal infection, possibly through shaving.

- **Description**: Swelling, crusting, small yellow spots around the follicle opening; often itchy, sometimes causing the hair to break off.
- **Contagious**: No.
- **Action**: Refer the client to seek medical advice.

Cicatricial alopecia (scarring alopecia)

- **Location**: Scalp.
- **Cause**: It is thought to be caused by external injury, such as severe infections, burns, radiation, tumours, or traction as can be seen due to repeated application of hair extensions. This may then cause inflammation at the upper part of the hair follicle where the sebaceous glands are located. If these are destroyed, there is then no possibility for regeneration of the hair follicle, and the result is permanent hair loss. This is a rare disorder.
- **Description**: Burning, redness, itching, pain or tenderness, inflammation, pustules, scaling of the skin and hair loss.
- **Contagious**: No.
- **Action**: Do not treat in the area if it is red, painful or there are open sores. Refer the client to seek medical advice if the condition has never been seen before by the client or it gets worse.

Damaged cuticle (hair)

- **Location**: Usually head.
- **Cause**: Over-processing by harsh/strong chemicals and styling.
- **Description**: Dry, rough, split hair that may sometimes cause the hair to break off.
- **Contagious**: No.
- **Action**: Reconditioning treatments by a hairdresser; avoid over-processing and protect hair during styling; may benefit from a hair cut.

Fragilitas crinium (split ends)

- **Location**: Usually hair on the head.
- **Cause**: Over-processing by harsh/strong chemicals and styling.
- **Description**: Dry, rough, split hair at the ends.
- **Contagious**: No.
- **Action**: Reconditioning treatments by a hairdresser; avoid over-processing and protect hair during styling; may benefit from a hair cut.

Hirsutism

- **Location**: Body.
- **Cause**: Can be caused by an increased level of the male hormone androgen.
- **Description**: Can affect men and women in a male pattern of body hair growth, which may grow excessively.
- **Contagious**: No.
- **Action**: Refer the client to seek medical advice if the condition has never been seen before by the client or it gets worse. Many people seek hair removal methods such as waxing, electrolysis and laser.

Male pattern baldness (androgenetic alopecia)

- **Location**: Scalp.
- **Cause**: Genetic, possibly due to the male hormone androgen.
- **Description**: Can affect males and females, where the hairline recedes and thins out. This can also be seen on the crown. This process may not occur in woman; the hair may thin out gradually all over but it is rarely turns into total baldness.
- **Contagious**: No.
- **Action**: Refer the client to seek medical advice if condition has never been seen before by the client or it gets worse. Treatment can be carried out carefully.

Monilethrix (beaded hairs)

- **Location**: Hair.
- **Cause**: Hereditary, uneven production of keratin in the follicle.
- **Description**: Short, broken, fragile hair that has a beaded appearance.
- **Contagious**: No.
- **Action**: Reconditioning treatments by a hairdresser; avoid over-processing and protect hair during styling; may benefit from a hair cut. Refer the client to seek medical advice if condition has never been seen before by the client or it gets worse.

Pityriasis simplex capillitii (dandruff)

- **Location**: Usually hair on the head.
- **Cause**: Increased cell reproduction from the epidermis and oil secretions from the sebaceous gland. Skin cells may mature and be shed in 2–7 days, as opposed to around a month in people without dandruff.
- **Description**: These dead skin cells shed in large, oily, large flakes, which appear as white or greyish patches on the scalp and flake off onto clothes. Some research cites stress as a factor in this over-production.

- **Contagious**: No.
- **Action**: Reconditioning treatments by a hairdresser; anti-dandruff shampoos. Refer the client to seek medical advice if they are concerned or if it gets worse.

Trichorrhexis nodosa

- **Location**: Usually hair on the head.
- **Cause**: Genetic or environmental factors.
- **Description**: Weak hair shaft that breaks easily, particularly close to the scalp. Split ends that may have white tips, rough, dry and damaged hair that may not grow.
- **Contagious**: No.
- **Action**: Reconditioning treatments by a hairdresser; avoid over-processing and protect hair during styling; may benefit from a hair cut. Refer client to seek medical advice if condition has never been seen before by the client or it gets worse.

End of chapter knowledge test

1. State the functions of blood.
2. State the functions of skin.
3. State the functions of lymph.
4. Name the five layers of the epidermis.
5. Where is DNA stored within a cell?
6. Describe the appearance of psoriasis of the skin.
7. Name the outer part of the hair shaft.
8. What type of infection is a wart?
9. Name the three stages of the hair growth cycle.
10. What type of hair is eyebrow hair?

CHAPTER 5

Provide eyelash and brow services

Units covered by this chapter:

VRQ Level 2: Provide eyelash and brow treatments

NVQ Level 2 Unit B5: Enhance the appearance of eyebrows and lashes

VRQ Level 3: Apply individual permanent lashes

NVQ Level 3 Unit B15: Provide single eyelash extension treatments

Chapter aims

This chapter will look at:

Levels 2 and 3

- Hygiene
- Product knowledge and ingredients
- Contraindications and contra-actions to treatment
- Consulting, planning and preparing for the treatment, including setting up of the service area, required tools, equipment and products, and preparation of client
- Maintaining safe and effective methods of working.

Level 2

- Total re-shaping of the eyebrow – sensitivity testing and eyebrow shapes
- Maintenance of the original brow shape and frequency of treatment
- Tinting of the eyebrows and lashes – colouring characteristics
- Applying and removal of artificial eyelashes – strip and individual flare lashes, using adhesives and solvents.

Level 3

- Semi-permanent eyelashes.

This chapter looks at how to enhance the appearance of the eye area, giving definition, shape and balance to the facial features, and to accentuate the eyes for a stunning look with or without make-up.

It is important that the make-up artist can perform these treatments to enhance the eyes for a variety of looks and for continuity when working as a media make-up artist. These are also popular beauty treatments that clients have done on a regular basis. Some large department stores and salons employ eyebrow technicians to be specialists in this area.

Table 5.1 Service times

Treatment	Service time
Eyebrow shaping	15 mins
Eyelash tint	20 mins
Eyebrow tint	10 mins
Apply full set of artificial lashes (flares)	20 mins
Apply full set of artificial lashes (strips)	10 mins
Apply partial set of artificial lashes (flares)	10 mins
Apply partial set of artificial lashes (strips)	10 mins

N.B. These service times are based on the NOS for working in a salon. As a make-up artist you may be working in a range of different environments so these times may not apply.

Hygiene
Cross-infection

When removing eye make-up, cleansing over the area in preparation for eye treatments or removing product after treatment, always ensure that a separate cotton pad is used per eye to avoid cross-infection.

Contra-actions

Specific contra-actions that can occur following eye treatments are:

- Watery eyes
- Red eyes
- Allergic reaction
- Swelling
- Stinging/burning sensation.

Contraindications

Specific contraindications to eye treatments are:

- Conjunctivitis
- Blepharitis
- Stye
- Bruising
- Active psoriasis or eczema
- Watery eyes
- Hay fever

Health and Safety

Remember to sterilise all metal tools before and after service.

Hygiene discussed here is specific to the eye treatments unit; general hygiene is covered in Chapter 2 Health and Safety.

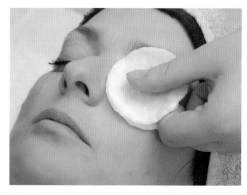

▲ Use a separate cotton wool pad over each eye when cleansing to avoid cross-infection

Anatomy and physiology

More details on these contra-actions and contraindictations can be found in Chapter 4.

- Any inflammation, redness, dry skin, cuts or abrasions in the area
- Claustrophobic clients
- A very nervous client – they may find it difficult to keep their eyes closed for a length of time.

Skin sensitivity testing for tinting, artificial eyelashes and eyelash perming

This is a method of testing skin sensitivity to a particular substance that could result in an adverse or allergic reaction. A skin sensitivity test should be carried out 24–48 hours prior to tinting, lash enhancement treatments and eyelash perming.

Many awarding organisations and professional associations recommend that this test is carried out to protect the client and the make-up artist/therapist, even if the client has the treatment on a regular basis as sensitivity can develop at any time or the product company may have added a new ingredient. The ingredients can differ between companies.

If the test is not carried out and an adverse or allergic reaction occurs then your insurance policy could be invalid.

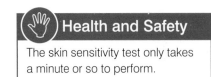

Health and Safety

The skin sensitivity test only takes a minute or so to perform.

Table 5.2 Product ingredients

Product	Ingredient
Tint	Aqua, cetearyl alcohol, p-phenylenediamine, sodium cetearyl sulphate, sodium lareth sulphate, m-aminophenol, p-aminophenol, 2,4 diaminophenoxyethanol, HCl resorcinol, 4-amino-2-hydroxytoluene (some of the later will vary due to colours)
Hydrogen peroxide	Aqua, hydrogen peroxide, triethandamine, phosphoric acid, o leth-10
Adhesive	Alkoxy-ethylcyanoacrylate and poly(methyl methacrylate)
Solvent	Gamma butyrolactone, dimethylketone, stearic acid, perfume
Sealer	Water, isopropyl alcohol, polytetrafluoroethylene

Safety precautions

- A skin sensitivity test should be carried out before use of the adhesive used for strip and individual lashes, the perm solution for eyelash perming and the tint and peroxide mixed.
- Always ensure the tint is mixed in accordance with the manufacturer's instructions. Never allow the mix to be too runny as it could seep into the client's eye during application.
- Do not overload the eyelashes with tint, adhesive or perm solution during the application as it could go into the client's eye.

- Explain the application procedure to the client prior to application so they know what will happen during the treatment.
- If any stinging or burning sensation occurs during the development time, remove the product immediately and ask the client to flush their eye with cold water or use an eye bath.

Procedure

- Record the client's test details on a record card, along with the date and gain the client's signature (this signifies the client's agreement to the test). There should be a section on the card so the results can be recorded when appropriate.

Client Record Card

Client's Name:

Date:

..../....../......

Address:..

....

Telephone Number:...............................Mobile:...........................

Sizes: 10mm ☐
6mm ☐ 12mm ☐
8mm ☐ 14mm ☐

Colours Added:
Blue ☐ Black ☐
Purple ☐ Brown ☐

Natural look ☐
Glamour look ☐
Time taken ☐

Cost....................... Infill cost........................ Removal cost.....................

Left eye   Where lash extensions applied   Right eye

Comments:

▲ Hollywood Lashes client record card

Consultation & Consent form

Client's Name:

....

Address:...

....

Telephone Number:............................Mobile:......................................

Date:

....../....../......

Please read the following information:

Hollywood Lashes are made of synthetic material, they simulate the natural lashes

Reasons of application are to create shape, depth, definition, enhance with the result of thicker and fuller eyelashes.

Treatment can take between 1 to 2 hours, depending on the look required.

The procedure is very relaxing.

Maintenance/infills will be required on a regular basis to keep the full result.

Consent for Procedure

I authorise (technician's name)... to perform the treatment of Hollywood Lash Extensions on myself

I understand that a maintenance/infill treatment will be required within a month and additional charges will apply.

Signature.......................................Date........................

▲ Hollywood Lashes consultation and consent form

- Cleanse the area where the test is to be performed.
- Mix the same colour and brand of product to be used on the client during the treatment (mix it in accordance with manufacturer's instructions and use it immediately).
- Apply a small amount of tint, adhesive or perm solution by using a brush, to either the crease of the elbow or behind the ear of the client.
- Allow the product tested to dry for a minute or two.
- Make sure the client is fully aware that the test should be left on the skin for 24 hours before it is washed off.

- Ensure the client understands that if an allergic reaction occurs during the testing process then they must wash the product off immediately and apply a cold compress. Ask them to contact you to let you know if an adverse reaction occurs as it would then not be possible to continue the treatment.

How to interpret skin sensitivity results

- *Positive result* – the client has had an adverse reaction to the test; this could be itching, irritation, swelling or redness. The treatment must not be carried out in this case and the results must be recorded on the client record card.
- *Negative result* – the client has not had a reaction to the test.

Preparing for the treatment

It is important to carry out a consultation and agree a treatment plan before you begin the treatment and complete the record card; the client's signature must be gained prior to treatment.

During the consultation it is important to find out exactly what the client wants from the treatment. You can advise them at this point whether the eyebrow shape or colour of the brows or lashes can be achieved with their natural hair growth and colour. Discuss the required look if you are applying artificial lashes: the length of time the lashes are to be worn or how much curl is required for perming are relevant. You can use a mirror to explain your treatment plan so that the client can visualise the outcome.

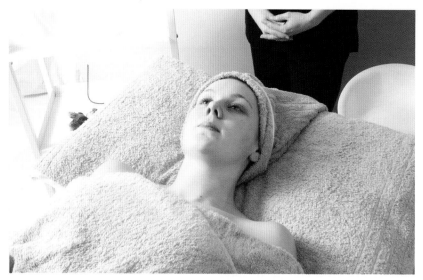

▲ Preparation of the client for treatment

Preparing the client

- Carry out the consultation and agree the treatment plan – check for contraindications and skin sensitivity test results.
- Contact lenses should be removed for any eye treatments.
- Ask the client to remove any accessories that may be in the work area, e.g. earrings.
- Position the client comfortably on the treatment couch either flat or slightly elevated.
- Gently lift and secure the client's hair off their face; use a headband or turban/towel.
- Protect the client's clothing – place a towel, cape or disposable covering over the client's chest.

Eyebrow shaping

The eyebrows follow the natural curve to the brow bone (orbital ridges) and are terminal hair. They frame the eye, giving balance and expression to the face. The shape of the eyebrow can vary and sometimes certain shapes are fashionable at that time, such as the thin, angular pencilled on look in the 1960s. Their function is to divert sweat and debris from the delicate eye area.

Benefits of eyebrow shaping

To give the eye area:

- Definition
- Shape
- Balance
- Corrective work – reshaping.

Factors to consider when deciding on eyebrow shape

- Natural shape of the eyebrow, to check what can realistically be achieved
- What will compliment the eye and face shape
- Natural hair growth pattern
- Hair colour – definition can be enhanced by tinting the eyebrows
- Client expectations

- Corrective work – not all pairs of eyebrows grow equally!
- Current fashion trends
- Client's age – a medium-shaped eyebrow is usually the most flattering as a thin shape could look too severe and a thick shape could give a hooded appearance. There may also be some coarse hair growth. These hairs could be grey or white and may need to be trimmed or removed; just ensure that removing them won't leave any bald patches.

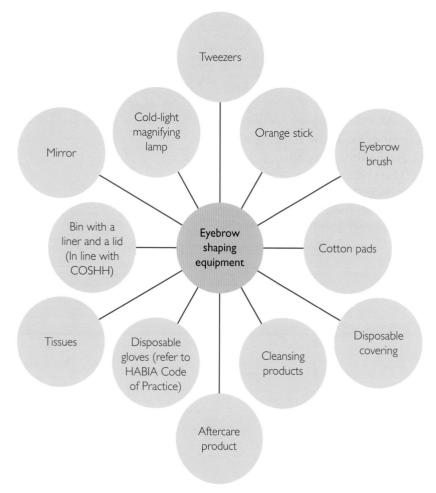

▲ Eyebrow shaping equipment

Tweezer types

There are two types of tweezers available:

1. *Manual* – these tweezers are squeezed together to grip the hair shaft and then a plucking action pulls the hair from the follicle. Tweezers with a slanted end are usually easier to use and are often used to finish the eyebrow shape.

2. *Automatic* – These are spring-loaded, so that when the sides are squeezed together it automatically closes the tweezers. These are usually used for removing the bulk of the excess hair.

▲ Automatic tweezers

▲ Manual tweezers

Selecting an eyebrow shape

Each of these shapes may be thin, medium or thick:

- *Angular* – Can help define a round face
- *Arched* – Usually very flattering to most eye and face shapes. It can help to detract attention from a large forehead, a prominent nose or large mouth by bringing balance and opening the eye by emphasising the centre of the brow bone
- *Rounded* – Can enhance large eyes by framing them by tapering down at the sides. This can also give the illusion of reducing the width of a wide forehead
- *Straight/low arched* – gives the illusion of more length. This type is particularly suitable for a client with a low or small forehead
- *Oblique* – gives the appearance of the eyes being 'lifted' in the outer corners.

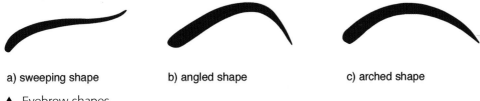

a) sweeping shape   b) angled shape   c) arched shape

▲ Eyebrow shapes

Corrective shapes

- **Wide apart eyes** – the eyebrow should begin above the inside corner of the eye to give the illusion of shortening the gap between the eyes.

- **Close together eyes** – the eyebrow should be extended past the outer corner of the eye to give the illusion of widening the eye.

▲ Eyebrows give the face and eyes definition

Measuring eyebrows

The eyebrows should be measured to decide which hairs to take out; this will aid symmetry. A new orange stick can be used for this.

Procedure

The measuring procedure is as follows:

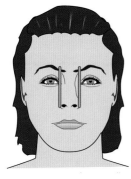 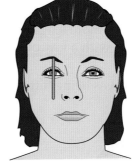 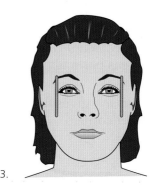

1.   2.   3.

▲ Measuring the eyebrows

1 Position an orange stick vertically at the sides of the nose to the inner corner of the eye – this is where the eyebrow should begin. Any hairs growing over the bridge of the nose in-between the brows should be removed.

2 Line the orange stick up with the outer corner of the eye – the hairs should not grow past this point.

3 Ask the client to look straight ahead. Using the orange stick vertically, measure from the pupil of the eye up over the eyebrow – this should be the highest point of the eyebrow arch.

Step-by-step guide for shaping eyebrows

The eyebrow-shaping procedure is as follows:

1. Ensure that tweezers have been sterilised prior to the treatment.

2. Cleanse the skin around the area, using the appropriate cleanser to remove make-up and clean the area (a cold-light magnifying lamp can be used for better visibility).

3. Brush the eyebrows following the natural growth and measure the eyebrows.

4. Apply warm cotton wool pads if necessary – this will relax the hair follicles and soften the tissues to aid easier removal.

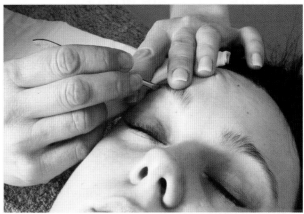

5. Start in between the eyebrows, above the bridge of the nose if hairs need removing from here as this area is slightly less sensitive and will allow the client to become accustomed to the sensation. Hold the skin taut between the index and middle finger and grasp each hair with the tweezers and pluck out following the direction of hair growth. Place the hairs on a clean tissue as you work, for hygiene.

6. Next, work towards the arch and outer corners. Keep checking the brows are even as you go along.

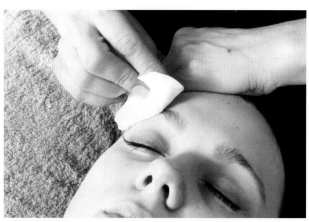

7. It is better to only remove a few hairs at first and show the client what you have done so far in the hand mirror. Remember you can always remove more hairs but you can't put them back on if you have taken too many off!

8. When the client is satisfied with the result, apply a soothing aftercare product.

When the procedure has been completed, the client should be given advice on aftercare and homecare. Waste should be disposed of in accordance with Health and Safety regulations and local by-laws.

Aftercare/homecare advice

The client should return approximately every 4–6 weeks for the eyebrows to be tidied; this will ensure that the shape lasts. If the client comes back later than this the eyebrows could possibly need re-shaping again. Therefore have a price for an eyebrow re-shape and one for an eyebrow tidy on the service menu and price list.

- The client's eyebrows will probably be red (due to **erythema**) after the treatment – a soothing/cooling aftercare product can be used.
- Ensure that make-up is not applied straight after the treatment as it can irritate already tender skin as the follicles could still be open.
- The client must not keep touching the eyebrows for at least 24 hours after the treatment as cross-infection or further irritation may occur as the follicles could still be open.
- The client must contact the make-up artist/therapist if any adverse reactions occur.
- The client can tweeze out the odd stray hair growth in between appointments if absolutely necessary.

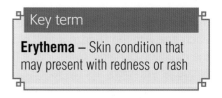

Key term

Erythema – Skin condition that may present with redness or rash

Troubleshooting

Sometimes clients have unrealistic expectations when it comes to eyebrow shaping, thinking that a thin, sparse eyebrow can instantly be transformed into a thick angular brow! Of course as a make-up artist/therapist we can enhance the appearance but ensure the client is made fully aware of what the likely outcome will be prior to beginning the treatment:

- **Sparse or patchy brows** – an eyebrow pencil can be used to draw the eyebrows on using gentle, short strokes with the direction of the hair growth. The eyebrow brush can then be used to soften and blend the pencil mark.

- **Thin eyebrows** – the same method as sparse or patchy brows can be used. A coloured powder that matches the eyebrow hair colour can be used to create the illusion of thickness. Apply the powder to the eyebrow brush and gently brush the eyebrows in the direction of hair growth to blend and shade. Eyebrow tinting can be used to help make the eyebrows look a little thicker but remember it will only work where there are hairs. Airbrush make-up can also be used to give the illusion of thicker eyebrows. There are templates available for various shapes (see Chapter 10 on airbrushing).

- **Thick eyebrows** – waxing may be a good alternative to tweezing very thick eyebrows. With this method of hair removal a large area of hair growth can be removed quickly; this must be performed by qualified therapists.

- **Long, thick, stray hairs** – these hairs can be trimmed with a small pair of scissors. Eyebrow gel or hairspray applied to an eyebrow brush can be used to help the hairs to lie flat.

- **Very sparse or no eyebrow hair present** – some medical treatments or conditions may result in the loss of hair from the eyebrow area (such as chemotherapy). In this case the eyebrows can almost be 'painted' on using alcohol-based make-up. A steady hand is required to freehand paint the eyebrow shape. A cotton bud can be used to tidy up around the shape for perfection! The alcohol-based make-up is waterproof, so it should last well throughout the day. It should be removed using an alcohol-based remover.

Advanced techniques

These techniques should only be carried out by qualified professionals:

- **Eyebrow inserts** – these are a semi-permanent option and are applied in a similar way to individual eyelashes.

- **Threading** – this is becoming a popular service and qualifications in this service are available. The hair is removed by using a piece of cotton to remove excess hair.

- **Postiche** – hand-knotted lace hair – the same type used for making moustaches and facial hair pieces (see Chapter 9).

Health and Safety

To avoid cross-infection always sharpen the eyebrow pencil when moving from one eye to the other.

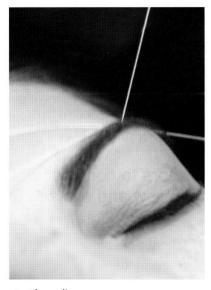
▲ Threading

- **Hair transplants** – these are now available in the USA to help thicken sparse hair growth.
- **Semi-permanent make-up** – this technique can greatly enhance and define the eyebrows and as techniques advance the eyebrows can be shaded for a softer, natural appearance. This procedure is completed by using a single-use sterile needle that lightly scratches along the layers of the skin and injects pigment.
- **High-definition eyebrows** – this is a new concept using current techniques such as tinting, tweezing, threading and waxing to sculpt a defined eyebrow shape.

Tinting eyebrows and lashes

This is a popular service to perform to enhance the eyebrows and eyelashes. It can be carried out after an eyelash perm but must be carried out before the eyebrow shape otherwise the pores will be open and the tint could get trapped in the pores and cause irritation or allergic reactions. Tinting will not lengthen or thicken the eyelashes but can give the illusion of this.

The function of the eyelashes is to protect the eye from debris.

Benefits of eyebrow tinting

- Definition
- Colours or darkens hairs; covers grey hairs
- Lasts around 4–6 weeks (fades gradually).

Benefits of eyelash tinting

- Colours and darkens – can make blonde or fair lashes appear longer
- Defines the upper and lower lashes
- Some clients don't wear mascara when the lashes are tinted but it can be worn over the top if preferred.
- It is great for holidays!
- Good for contact lens wearers – sometimes fibres from wearing mascara can irritate the eyes
- Lasts around 4–6 weeks (fades gradually).

Factors to consider when deciding on a suitable eyebrow and eyelash tint colour

- Natural hair colour
- Client preference
- Skin colour
- Type of make-up usually worn in the area of treatment.

Product types

The products available for eyelash and eyebrow tinting have been specially formulated to be much more gentle than are dyes for hair; this is because the skin tissue is very fine and more sensitive around the delicate eye area.

Tints are available in the following preparations:

- Cream
- Jelly
- Liquid.

Cream-based tints are the most popular as they have a thicker **viscosity** (denser consistency) than other types. This is best suited to the eye area as it won't easily run into the eye.

Another product is required to activate the tint: **hydrogen peroxide** (H_2O_2) 3 per cent – or 10 volume strength.

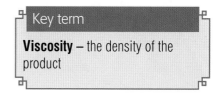

> **Key term**
>
> **Viscosity** – the density of the product

▲ Products for eyelash and brow tinting

Chemistry of tinting

The following components are used:

- **Tint** – this contains small molecules of permanent dye – **toluenediamine**. This needs to be activated in order to release its permanent colouring effects.
- **Hydrogen peroxide** – this is the **developer** that acts as a **catalyst** to encourage chemical reactions. It is an **oxidant** that contains oxygen atoms that stimulate this reaction by changing the small tint molecules into larger molecules that

absorb into the hair through the cuticle and become trapped in the cortex. Over time the colour will appear to fade as the hair replenishes itself through the growth cycle and the natural colour shows through.

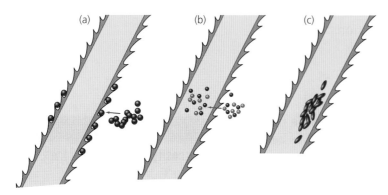

▲ Molecules in the cortex

Table 5.3 Client suitability for various tint colours

Tint colour selection	Effect considering hair colour
Black	Dark hair – a very defined look
Brown – the shade of this colour varies greatly between product companies, ranging from a natural to dark brown	Fair and red hair – a natural look
Black/brown – equal parts of black and brown can be mixed together to create the colour	Medium and red hair – a more defined look
Blue	Fair, red and medium hair – gives colour and definition (usually used on lashes)
Blue/black – equal parts of blue and black can be mixed together to create the colour but this can be bought pre-mixed	Medium and dark hair – definition and darker colour (usually used on lashes)
Grey	White or grey hair – adds a little definition and colour

Health and Safety

Only tints that have been specially formulated for eyelash and eyebrow tinting must be used around the eye area. Other hair-dyeing products are dangerous to use as they are too strong and could lead to blindness and severely damage the eye and surrounding skin tissue.

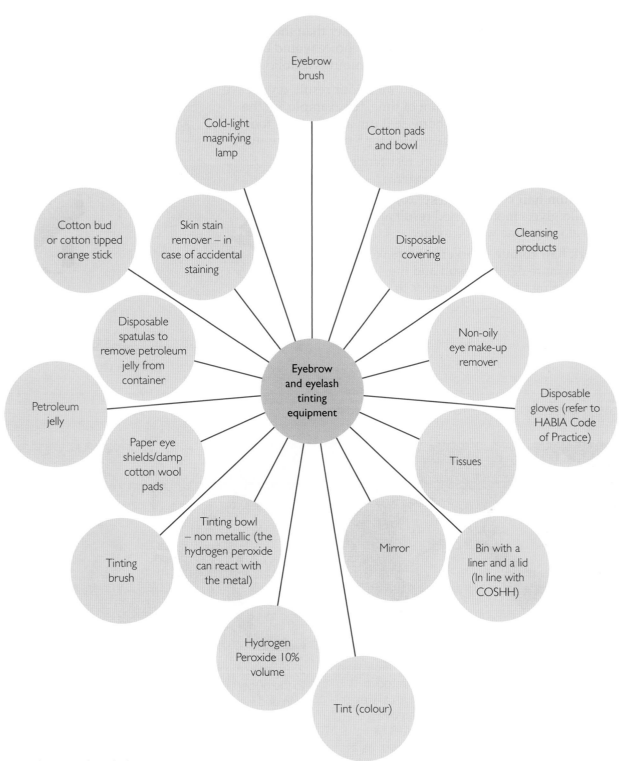

▲ Eyebrow and eyelash tinting equipment

Eyebrow and eyelash tinting development times

Take care when eyebrow tinting to ensure client satisfaction, for example if the result is too dark for the client the tint cannot be removed once it is developed! The tint may be reapplied if the client wants a darker result. Refer to manufacturers' instructions: development times may vary from 5 to 15 minutes.

The client may wish the eyelashes to be darker than the eyebrows, in which case the tint colour of choice would be left on longer. The guide depending on hair colour is as follows:

- **Very fair hair colour** – For a natural colour result, only leave the tint on for a short amount of time, for example, on the eyebrows 1–2 minutes (otherwise it can appear to be too dark). Eyelashes should be treated for 5 minutes minimum.

- **Red hair colour** – this is more resistant so the development time may be longer.

- **Medium hair colour** – darker colours would give a more defined result and the developing time will be longer.

- **Dark hair colour** – darker colours would give a more defined result and the developing time will be longer than for the other hair colours.

> ⭐ *Tip* The developing times given here are only a recommendation. The client may wish to have a very dark, defined look and would therefore need a longer development time.

▲ Eyebrow and eyelash tinting equipment

Step-by-step guide for eyelash tinting

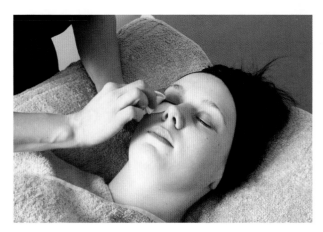

1. Cleanse the skin around the treatment area, using the appropriate cleanser to thoroughly remove make-up and clean the area. Ensure if an oily eye make-up remover has been used to remove waterproof mascara that the residue must be thoroughly removed with a non-oily remover as it would create a barrier and stop the tint from working. A mild toner can be used to wipe over the lashes to remove any last traces of the cleanser. It is best to advise the client not to use waterproof mascara prior to treatment.

> 🐞 *Remember...*
> The area must be clean and grease-free for best results.

2. Prepare the eye shields by applying petroleum jelly to the underside. This will be the part that rests on the skin and will help protect the skin from becoming stained from the tint.

> 🐞 *Remember...*
> Don't forget to do your consultaton and treatment plan prior to application.

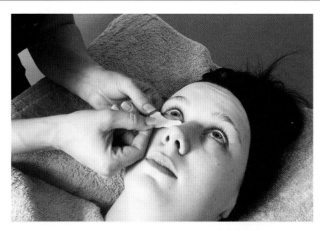

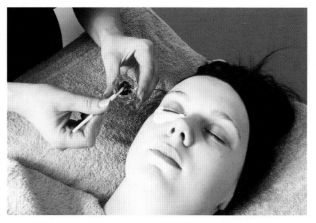

3. Remove the petroleum jelly from its container using a new disposable spatula. Using a cotton bud, disposable brush or cotton wool-tipped orange stick apply the petroleum jelly carefully around the upper and lower eyelid of one eye, ensuring it does not come into contact with the hairs as it will create a barrier and stop the tint from working. Repeat this procedure with another clean cotton bud or similar on the other eye. Ask the client to look upwards while you apply the eye shields underneath the lower eyelashes, then ask the client to close their eyes and keep them closed during the tinting procedure.

4. Mix the tint. Most tints are mixed equal parts tint to hydrogen peroxide but always mix according to manufacturers' instructions. Mix enough product to cover the area and avoid waste (around 5 mm of tint to two to three drops of hydrogen peroxide is an average guide). Mix the tint with a disposable brush until it is smooth and replace the lids onto the tint and hydrogen peroxide. The tint should be used immediately and any leftover disposed of in the COSHH bin. The tint will react with the oxygen in the atmosphere and lose its potency (oxidise); this will affect the results of the tint, weakening the colouring effects.

5. Apply the tint to the eyelashes from the base of the lash to the tip, making sure each hair is evenly covered. The bottom lashes will also be tinted as they are resting on the eye shield. Do not overload the tinting brush with tint to avoid it seeping into the eye.

6. The lashes can be covered with a piece of damp cotton wool cut in the shape of a half moon; note the time.

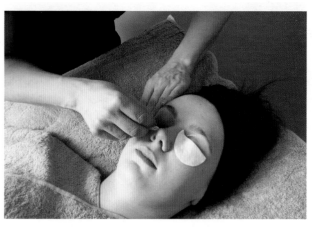

7. Once the processing time has elapsed, explain to the client that you are going to remove the tint and they must keep their eyes closed until you have finished. Remove the upper eyeshield then, using damp cotton wool, gently wipe the tint down and outwards, supporting the eye with the other hand. Then remove the eye shields and wipe thoroughly in the same manner with damp cotton wool until all tint has been removed.

8. Ask the client to open their eyes and check to ensure all the tint has been removed from the lower lashes. If any tint remains, repeat the removal procedure.

10. Advise client on aftercare and homecare.

11. Record the results on the client's record card.

12. Dispose of waste in accordance with Health and Safety, COSHH regulations and local by-laws.

9. Show the client the results with the hand mirror.

Step-by-step guide for eyebrow tinting

Eyebrow tinting must be completed before shaping the eyebrows.

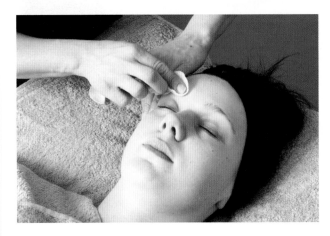

1. Cleanse the skin around the treatment area, using the appropriate cleanser to remove make-up. A cold-light magnifying lamp can be used for better visibility.

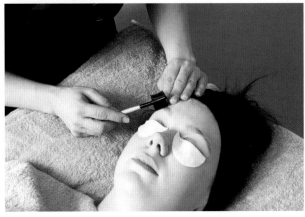

2. Brush the eyebrows following the natural growth and measure the eyebrows.

3. Apply petroleum jelly using a separate disposable brush or cotton bud/orange stick tipped with cotton wool to the skin surrounding the eyebrow to avoid skin staining.

4. Mix the tint. Most tints are mixed in equal parts tint to hydrogen peroxide but always mix according to manufacturers' instructions. Mix enough product to cover the area and avoid waste (approximately 5 mm of tint to two to three drops of hydrogen peroxide is an average guide). Mix the tint with a disposable brush until it is smooth and return the lids to the containers of tint and hydrogen peroxide.

5. Apply the tint to the eyebrows against the hair growth, from the outer corner working inwards, and brush the eyebrow hair upwards to avoid getting tint on the skin. Make sure each hair is covered evenly. Do not overload the tinting brush with tint so it does not fall off the brush and onto the skin.

6. Developing time depends on required outcome (see developing times earlier) so check the progress of the tint after a minute or two. When the developing time is up, remove the tint from the first eyebrow using damp cotton wool until all the tint has been removed.

Tip If the skin is stained during the tinting process it can be carefully removed by using a skin stain-removing product on cotton wool. Ensure the area is wiped over with damp cotton wool afterwards to remove the product.

7. Show the client the results with the hand mirror. If the client wants a darker result the tint could be reapplied if necessary.

8. Advise the client on aftercare and homecare.

9. Record the results on the client's record card.

10. Dispose of waste in accordance with Health and Safety regulations and local by-laws.

Aftercare/homecare advice

The client should return approximately every 4–6 weeks for their eyebrows and eyelashes to be re-tinted; this will ensure that the colour stays fresh looking. If the client comes back later than this the colour may have completely disappeared.

The client should contact you if any adverse reaction occurs after treatment.

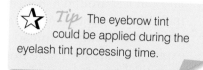

Tip The eyebrow tint could be applied during the eyelash tint processing time.

Health and Safety

Always check manufacturers' instructions as these may differ from company to company.

Artificial eyelashes

There are many types of artificial eyelashes on the market and they are all currently very popular as they enhance the appearance of their eyes.

Benefits of artificial eyelashes

- Makes the lashes look longer, fuller and thicker
- Defines the eye area
- Corrective make-up – if a client has lost their eyelashes or if they are sparse
- Enhances definition in evening, fantasy, photographic and media make-up
- Semi-permanent lashes are a great, low-maintenance option for use on holidays.

▲ Artificial lashes

Types of artificial eyelashes available

- **Individual flare** – these can last around 1–2 weeks. They are made of synthetic fibres and the lashes are secured at the base by a small bulb with a few lashes that flare outwards. These are available in different lengths so various looks can be achieved.

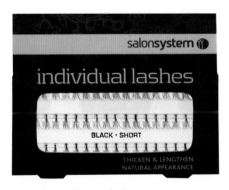

▲ Individual flare lashes

▲ Strip lashes

- **Strip** – these are synthetic fibres attached to a fine strip and secured to the base of the lashes with a special adhesive. These can be removed daily, washed and reapplied. These are available in different lengths, thicknesses, colours and fashion types such as glitter and feathers.

- **Semi-permanent** – these are also known as eyelash extensions and can last around 6–8 weeks. They can be kept on by maintenance treatments on a regular basis. The lashes are made from synthetic threads/fibres of nylon or the more expensive ones are made from human hair. 'Y' lashes split into two at the tapered end; these give the effects of double the amount of lashes and can be applied in half the normal time.

The synthetic lashes hold their curl for longer than the human hair type. They are fixed on top of the client's natural lashes individually and are available in black and brown and usually in four lengths: mini, short, medium or long and are either flared or similar to the individual lashes or single lashes. The procedure can take an hour or more, as it requires the precise placement of each individual lash.

Infills or 'touch ups'

Infills or 'touch ups' are required around every 2–3 weeks to keep the lashes looking their best. If you are having the lashes applied once for a special occasion, it is recommended that any remaining extensions should be removed after 2 or 3 weeks in order to prevent patchiness as the natural lashes adhere to their normal growth cycle. Their appearance is more natural looking than other artificial eyelash methods.

Adhesive

The adhesive provides bonding between the eyelash extensions and the natural eyelashes. When extensions are properly bonded, they last longer and do not fall off very easily. The bonding solution is essential, as it is resistant to the water, sweat and tears that would normally dissolve a regular adhesive. The proper bonding solution ensures that you can go swimming and come into contact with water, tears etc. and not worry about whether the lashes will fall off. The extensions fall off from the eyelashes themselves.

Corrective work

Lashes should be placed differently depending on the characteristics of the eyes:

- **Small eyes** – place lashes at outer corner to make eyes look larger
- **Deep-set eyes** – lashes can be applied to the upper and lower lash line. Use fine pointed lashes to give definition.
- **Close-set eyes** – place lashes on the outer third of the upper lashes to give the appearance of widening the eye.
- **Round eyes** – place the lashes from the centre of the upper lash line, working outwards with a dense application to give a thickened appearance.

Factors to consider when deciding on suitable artificial eyelashes

- Length of time the lashes are required to be worn
- Length of the client's natural lashes – this could help determine the length of lashes to be applied depending on required look
- Occasion for which they are to be worn – this may help you to determine which type of lashes would be best to apply
- Client lifestyle
- Direction of growth
- Colour of the natural eyelashes
- Any previous eyelash treatments such as tinting and perming
- Eye shape
- Client preference – check what kind of look the client is trying to achieve
- Maintenance – strip lashes can be removed easily and re-used; individual lashes need to be replaced due to natural hair loss; and semi-permanent lashes should be in-filled every 2–3 weeks
- Client's age – artificial lashes can create a defined, bold look that could be too dramatic
- Time for application – depending on the type of lashes applied.

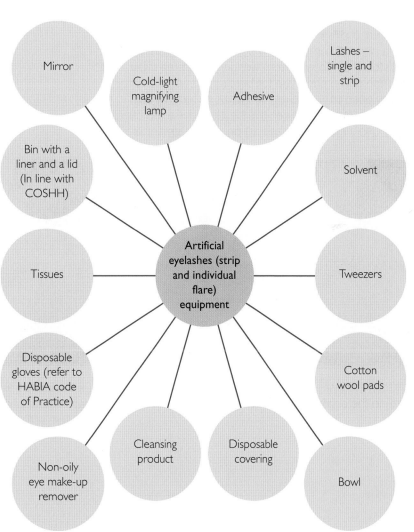

▲ Artificial lash application equipment (strip and individual flare)

Step-by-step guide for preparation and application of artificial eyelashes

1. Cleanse the skin around the area, using the appropriate cleanser to thoroughly remove make-up and clean the area. Ensure if an oily eye make-up remover has been used to remove waterproof mascara, the residue must be thoroughly removed with a non-oily remover as it would create a barrier and stop the adhesive from working. The area must be clean and grease-free for best results. A mild toner can be used to wipe over the lashes to remove any last traces of the cleanser. It is best to advise the client not to use waterproof mascara prior to treatment.

2. Ask the client to close their eyes and rest the strip lash on the client's eye to measure the strip lashes for length. Try to work from above the client and ask the client to look downwards.

3. Move the lashes away from the client's eye and cut them to the correct length.

4. If the lashes are being applied during a make-up treatment, apply them before the mascara. Hold the strip lash with the tweezers and apply a small amount of adhesive along the fine strip.

5. Still holding the strip with the tweezers, place the artificial lash gently at the base of the client's lashes, just slightly touching the skin above.

6. Using an orange stick, gently and carefully press the strip lashes into place working from the inner to outer corner.

7. Look at the lashes from the front perspective and check the fitting.

8. Ask the client to slowly open their eyes and continue the make-up application if required, with eyeliner and mascara (mascara will help to curl and seal the lashes; manual eyelash curlers can be used too).

10. Advise the client on aftercare and homecare.

11. Record the results on the client's record card.

12. Dispose of waste in accordance with Health and Safety regulations and local by-laws.

9. Show the client the results with the hand mirror.

Step-by-step guide for individual flare lashes

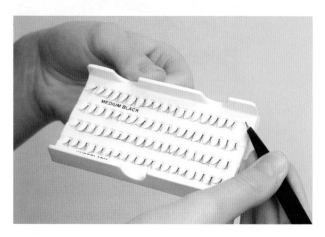

1. Ask the client to close their eyes and using tweezers remove the individual lash from the packet.

2. Stroke the bulb/root into the adhesive (do not overload it with adhesive so it does not run into the eye).

3. Try to work from above the client and ask the client to look downwards.

4. Place the bulb/root of the lash as near as possible to the client's natural lash roots. Longer lashes can be placed from the centre working towards the outer corner and shorter ones at the inner corner, and maybe one shorter flare at the very outer corner to give a softer effect. This will give an appearance of lengthening the eye area.

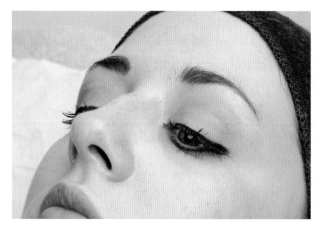

5. Ask the client to open the eye periodically to check the lashes are following the natural curve of the eyelid and are even.

6. Comb through the lashes with the lash comb when they are dry to blend the artificial lashes with the natural ones.

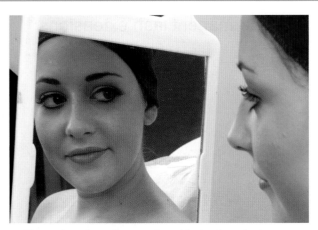

7. Show the client the results with the hand mirror.

9. Advise the client on aftercare and homecare.

10. Record the results on the client's record card.

11. Dispose of waste in accordance with Health and Safety regulations and local by-laws.

8. Apply eye make-up if required.

Aftercare and homecare advice

- Use non-oily eye make-up remover – oil-based removers will loosen and dislodge the lashes.
- Avoid overloading the lashes with mascara that may be difficult to remove as this action could loosen the lashes.
- Try to wait a few hours before allowing the eyes to come into contact with water.
- Avoid rubbing the eyes.
- Avoid extremes of temperature such as steam rooms or saunas.
- The client should contact you if any adverse reaction occurs after treatment.

Semi-permanent lash extensions

▲ Artificial lash application equipment (semi-permanent)

Step-by-step guide for semi-permanent lash extensions

You should always check manufacturers' instructions
as some may vary.

1. Try to work from above the client and ask the client
to look downwards.

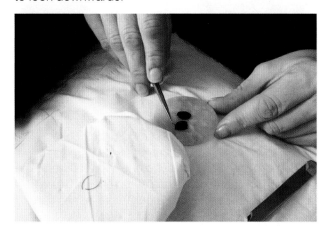

2. Place the adhesive/bonding solution or agent into
the jade stone (a cold disc that helps to keep the
adhesive at a constant temperature throughout the
treatment).

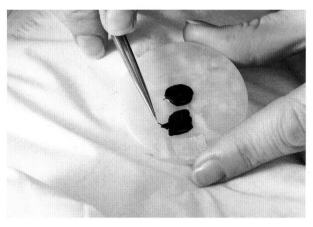

3. Ask the client to close their eyes and using
tweezers remove the lash from the packet. Stroke the
end into the adhesive/bonding solution/agent (do not
overload it, so it does not run into the eye).

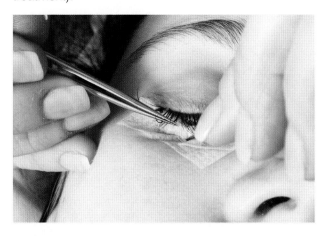

4. Place the end of the individual lash on top of the
natural eyelash in a stroking movement, releasing the
grip from the tweezers as you go.

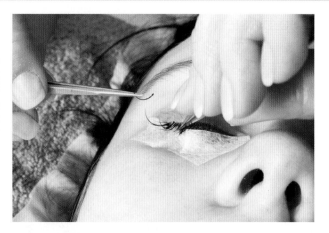

5. A very small brush may used to apply more adhesive/bonding solution/agent at the base of the lash extension if needed. It only takes a few minutes to dry and an air blower can be used to speed up the drying process.

6. Longer lashes can be placed from the centre, working towards the outer corner and shorter ones at the inner corner, with maybe one shorter flare at the very outer corner to give a softer effect. This will appear to lengthen the eye area. These lashes can also be applied to the lower lashes if required.

7. Ask the client to open the eye periodically to check that the lashes are following the natural curve of the eyelid and are even.

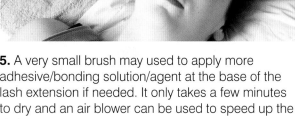

8. A sealant can be applied to the extensions after the procedure is complete. A sealant can strengthen the bond further, and it also protectively coats the extensions. This may prolong the life of your extensions (refer to manufacturers' instructions).

9. Show the client the results with the hand mirror.

10. Advise the client on aftercare and homecare.

11. Record the results on the client's record card.

12. Dispose of waste in accordance with Health and Safety regulations and local by-laws.

Maintenance of semi-permanent eyelashes

Any loose lashes can be removed with product remover. If there are any gaps, these can be filled in by following the application procedure.

Aftercare and homecare advice

The client should be told that the bond is not complete until approximately 2 hours following application, so they should:

1. Avoid water for at least 2 hours after semi-permanent eyelash extension application. This will ensure that the bond is properly formed, and will extend the life of the extensions.
2. Use non-oily eye make-up remover – oil-based removers will loosen and dislodge the lashes.
3. Avoid rubbing the eyes.
4. Avoid overloading the lashes with mascara that may be difficult to remove as this action could loosen the lashes.
5. Avoid extremes of temperature such as in steam rooms or saunas.
6. Return every 2–3 weeks for maintenance if the lashes are being kept on.
7. Contact you if any adverse reaction occurs after treatment.
8. Try to avoid waterproof mascara as it is removed with an oil-based remover.

Eyelash Extension Aftercare

- **First 2 hours:** Do not allow water to contact the eyelids.
- **First 48 hours:** Do not wash eyes or lash extensions with hot water or steam the face. Avoid sauna, jacuzzi and swimming.
- **Do not** use waterproof mascara as oil-based mascaras may damage the bond. Ask your salon about our water-based mascara.
- **Use only** oil-free products to remove mascara.
- **Do not** perm Hollywood Lashes Extensions.
- **Do not** tint over bonded area (only root area).
- **Rubbing eyes** may pull out lashes with extensions attached.
- **Do not** use heated curlers on bonded area (tips only).

Please treat your new Hollywood Lashes with care, just as you would hair extensions. Your natural lashes will shed naturally, taking extensions with them. Arrange with your salon for regular infill treatments to keep that full lash look.

▲ Hollywood lashes aftercare leaflet

Removal

The removal of various types of lashes varies depending on type:

Strip lashes

These can easily be removed by supporting the eye at the outer corner and gently and slowly releasing/pulling the lashes starting at the inner corner.

Individual lashes and semi-permanent lashes removal

1. Cleanse the eye area with appropriate eye make-up remover/cleanser.

2. Ask the client to look upwards and place a piece of damp cotton wool, cut into a half-moon shape, underneath the lower lashes. Ask the client to close their eyes.

3. Using a cotton bud soaked in eyelash solvent (but not too wet so it does not run into the eye), gently work down the lashes with a rolling action until the artificial lash detaches from the natural eyelash and place it onto a tissue.

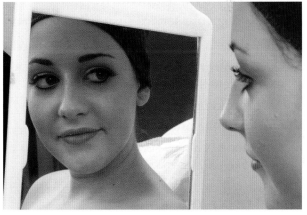

4. Show the client the results with the hand mirror.

5. Advise the client on aftercare and homecare.

6. Record the results on the client's record card.

7. Dispose of waste in accordance with Health and Safety regulations and local by-laws.

Care of strip lashes

1. Don't sleep in these lashes as the shape can be distorted.
2. Clean the lashes by using:
   - Warm soapy water – for synthetic lashes
   - Manufacturers' cleaner or alcohol 70 per cent – for human hair lashes.
3. Re-curl the lashes after cleaning by curling the lashes around a barrel-shaped object (such as a make-up brush handle) and securing them for a short time. Once re-curled, store the lashes in their original container.

Eyelash perming

Eyelash perming is a treatment that is used in the industry. It involves semi-permanently curling the eyelashes by using specially formulated perming solution and neutraliser.

The eyelashes are curled around a special rod. Perm solution is applied to break down the disulphide bonds in the air. This is removed after the correct time (refer to manufacturers' instuctions). Neutraliser is then applied to reset the bonds permanently in their new shape. This is then removed along with the rods to reveal a curled lash.

Costing of eye treatments

When costing your service ensure that you have taken into consideration:

- Cost of the products and consumables used
- Cost of the time used to complete the service – take into account how much you might pay staff to complete the service
- Level of skill required
- Quality of the products
- Whether it is a new service or brand – you may be able to charge a little more if the service has more exclusivity.

Retail products

The range of products you will need may include:

- Soothing/cooling products
- Eyebrow brush
- Eyebrow pencil
- Mascara
- Non-oily eye make-up remover
- Powder-based make-up (for brows).

End of chapter knowledge test

1. Name **one** type of tweezer available for eyebrow shaping.
2. Describe how the highest point of the eyebrow should be measured.
3. State when the skin sensitivity test should be carried out.
4. State **one** reason why the tint results may have been unsuccessful.
5. Name **one** retail product available for eyebrows.
6. State **one** consideration prior to eyelash tinting.
7. State **one** contraindication to eye treatments.
8. What product can be used to remove individual lashes?
9. Name **two** eyebrow shapes.
10. State the recommended interval between eyelash tinting.

CHAPTER 6

Skin care

Units covered by this chapter:

NVQ Level 2 Unit B4: Provide facial skin care treatment

VRQ Level 2: Provide facial skin care

Chapter aims

This chapter will look at:

- Ways to ensure good hygiene is maintained
- Skin types and characteristics, conditions, contraindications and contra-actions
- How to provide a safe and well set up treatment area
- Ways to maintain safe and effective methods of working
- Present products and theory, including retail products
- Treatments and procedures
- Provision of aftercare and homecare advice.

It is important that the make-up artist knows how to care for the skin of the client or artist they are working on to enable: 1) proper preparation of the skin prior to the application of make-up, 2) removal of make-up using the correct products and techniques and 3) ability to give aftercare and homecare advice so that the client or artist can care for their skin properly in between treatments. This will also enable the make-up artist to bring in extra revenue from the retail sales of skincare products to their clients.

Skincare treatments

- Consultation and treatment planning
- Skin analysis
- Product matching
- Cleansing the skin
- Specialised skincare treatments
- Exfoliation of dead skin cells
- Manual massage of the face, neck and shoulders
- Face mask application
- Application of specialised skincare and eyecare products
- Make-up application
- Homecare and aftercare advice
- Retail products to match skin type.

Treatment objectives

- Product matching – to suit skin type and conditions
- Advise on specialised skincare treatments – to suit skin type, conditions and client needs
- Apply professional skincare treatments – according to skin type, condition, client needs and preference
- Advice and homecare and aftercare – so the client can gain maximum benefits from the treatment and professional advice
- Retail products – to match the client's skin type, condition, needs and budget.

Hygiene

> This is specific to the skincare treatments unit; general hygiene is covered in Chapter 2 Health and safety.

Cross-infection

The following practices are effective in avoiding cross-contamination and cross-infection:

- Use a disposable spatula to remove the products from their containers.
- When removing eye make-up, always ensure that a separate cotton pad is used for each eye.
- Avoid overloading the cotton pad with remover so it does not run into the client's eye.

Contraindications

Prior to carrying out skincare treatments the make-up artist/therapist should check the condition of the client's skin for any of the following conditions and not proceed with treatment due to risk of cross-infection, pain or other effects:

- **Conjunctivitis**: Bacterial infection of membrane of the eye that prevents treatment due to risk of cross-infection
- **Bacterial infections**: E.g. impetigo – will prevent treatment from being given due to risk of cross-infection as it is a highly contagious condition that requires medical treatment
- **Fungal infections**: E.g. ringworm – will prevent treatment due to risk of cross-infection as it is a highly contagious condition that requires medical treatment
- **Viral infections**: E.g. herpes simplex or cold sores – will prevent treatment due to risk of cross-infection

> **Key term**
>
> A **contraindication** is a condition that either prevents or restricts the application of any treatment.

> **Anatomy and physiology**
> Full descriptions can be found in Chapter 4 Anatomy and physiology.

- **Bruising**: May restrict treatment due to damaged blood vessels in the area; treatment may aggravate the condition, causing pain and discomfort to client
- **Eczema or psoriasis**: May restrict treatment if inflamed, with open sores or weeping
- **Cuts and abrasions**: Will restrict treatment due to risk of cross-infection
- **Rashes, redness and inflammation**: Will restrict treatment due to risk of further adverse reaction
- **Recent scar tissue**: six months or less – Will restrict treatment due to risk damage to tissue
- **Recent sunburn**: Will contraindicate treatment due to risk of skin damage, sensitivity, client pain and discomfort
- **Hay fever**: There will be sensitivity around the eye and nose area and the client may feel uncomfortable if the condition is active
- **Claustrophobia**: Clients with this condition or very nervous clients may find it difficult to keep their eyes closed for any length of time.

Contra-actions

Specific contra-actions that can occur following skincare treatments are:

- Watery eyes
- Red eyes
- Allergic reaction
- Swelling
- Stinging or burning sensation
- Rash
- Erythema (this is a normal reaction, however if it is excessive it could indicate a sensitivity or allergic reaction to the treatment products).

Creating a relaxed atmosphere

The atmosphere must be conducive to the treatment objectives. For facial skincare treatments the atmosphere should be calm and warm, to help the client to relax and feel more comfortable. It is important to maintain a professional standard.

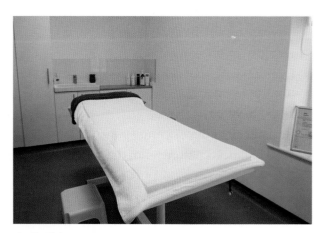

▲ Facial treatment room

Lighting

Effective lighting can be delivered in a number of ways:

- Natural lighting
- Overhead lighting or a cold-light magnifying lamp will help you to assess skin
- A dimmer switch could create a soothing and relaxing atmosphere during the massage.

Music

Music played must create the right atmosphere and be soothing, relaxing, calming and appeal to all ages.

Sound

A peaceful and relaxing environment is required for this treatment.

Identify skin types, conditions and characteristics

Skin types

There are four main skin types:

1. Normal
2. Dry
3. Oily
4. Combination.

Each of these skin types has individual characteristics and the make-up artist needs to be able to analyse the skin to determine which products to use for the appropriate skin type. Using the incorrect products can lead to adverse skin reactions.

Normal skin

Normal skin is sometimes referred to as balanced skin because it is neither too dry nor too oily and is rarely found in adults. It is recognised by the following characteristics:

- Healthy, even skin colour
- Even thickness of skin texture, soft, supple with fine/small or medium pores
- Good elasticity
- Resistance to developing spots or blemishes
- Well balanced nature – not dry, moist, dull or shiny.

Health and Safety

Remember the body cools quickly when relaxed, so when carrying out a massage treatment the room should be warm (around 70°F/21°C).

Tip To relax completely the client must feel comfortable and warm.

▲ Normal skin

Dry skin

Dry skin is lacking in moisture and sebum; it is the sebum that helps the skin to keep its moisture – the less sebum in the skin the more dry or dehydrated the skin will become. It is recognised by the following characteristics:

- Lacking in either moisture or sebum
- Pores are small and tight
- Skin texture is fine and thin with flaky patches
- Premature ageing and fine lines may occur, particularly around the eyes, mouth and neck
- Broken capillaries may be present, often around the nose and cheek areas
- Skin pigmentation may be uneven
- Milia can be located around the eyes and cheek area as the skin is so fine there
- Fine capillaries on cheek area
- Taut feel
- Often sensitive
- May be dull in appearance.

▲ Dry skin

Oily skin

Sebum is produced by the sebaceous glands, which can become extremely active during puberty, stimulated by the male hormone, androgen. This can settle down as the sebaceous gland activity decreases in a person's early 20s. With the correct use of skincare products, oily skin can stay younger looking for longer. If this overproduction of sebum continues the skin could become seborrhoeic. Oily skin is recognised by its characteristics:

- An oily film and moist feel
- Shiny in appearance
- Large open and blocked pores, blackheads and comedones, pustules and milia
- Papules, sebaceous cysts and boils may also be present
- Thickened skin tissues
- Sallow skin colour as the dead skin cells have become trapped and embedded in the sebum; this could cause uneven pigmentation
- Coarse in texture
- Sluggish blood circulation, which could give the skin a congested appearance
- Skin tone is usually good due to the protection of sebum.

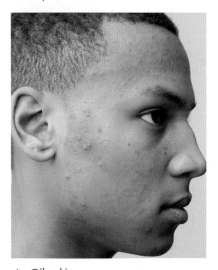

▲ Oily skin

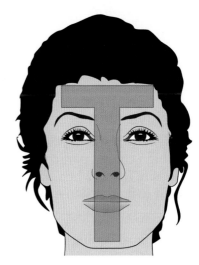

▲ The T zone

Combination skin

Combination skin is a common skin type; it is the combination of two or more skin types. It is often oily down the T zone, which is along the forehead, nose and chin and normal to dry on the cheek areas. There are more sebaceous glands concentrated along the T zone area. Combination skin is recognised by the following characteristics:

- Oily T-zone panel across forehead and down the nose and chin areas
- Shiny on T-zone panel with open pores
- Blemishes, blackheads, pustules and papules in these areas
- Cheek area is normal to dry and finer in texture than the skin in the T zone
- Occasional sensitivity, high colour and perhaps broken capillaries in the dry areas
- Occasional uneven pigmentation.

▲ Combination skin

Skin conditions

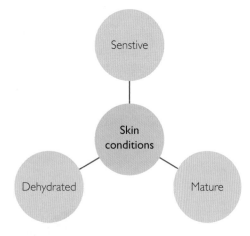

▲ Skin conditions

Sensitive skin

Dry, dehydrated and paler skins are often sensitive. There is often high colour, particularly around the cheek area and the skin easily reacts when skin care or make-up products are applied to it. The skin may also have:

- broken capillaries
- superficial flaking
- tight feel to the touch, particularly after cleansing
- warm feel to the touch.

▲ Sensitive skin

Black skin that is sensitive would react by producing a darker area rather than redness.

Mature skin

Mature skin is recognised by the following characteristics:

- Loss of elasticity
- Deep line wrinkles
- Broken capillaries
- Transparent appearance
- Hyperpigmentation
- Loose skin tissue
- Thickened epidermis.

Dehydrated skin

This skin type loses surface moisture but may still have normal sebaceous secretions. This may be a temporary condition due to the following factors:

- Environmental, i.e. central heating, air conditioning and low humidity
- Medication
- Low fluid intake
- Illness
- Drastic dieting
- Use of soap on the delicate facial skin
- Use of incorrect skin care products.

▲ Mature skin

Ethnic skin types

Skin function remains the same regardless of colour or ethnic background. The amount of pigment within various types of skin will vary due to the amount of melanin that is produced. People who originate from cooler climates tend to have lighter skin colour due to less melanin production than people from hotter climates, who produce more melanin due to the required protection from UV rays and therefore a darker skin pigment is produced.

Asian skin

Asian skin often has yellow undertones to its colouring; this is due to the increase in melanin production and can vary from a light to darker tone. Hair colour is usually dark brown to black. Hyperpigmentation may be present and the skin may scar easily; dermatosis papulosis nigra may also be a common characteristic.

▲ African-type, caucasian and Asian skin

African-type skin

In those with this skin, colour ranges from dark brown to virtually black, as it contains more melanin due to the intensity of ultraviolet light it is exposed to. The skin tone may be more prone to darker patches from blemishes and scars and from hyperpigmentation and keloid scarring; this is also due to the increased production of melanin. There may also be patches of skin that has lost pigment (vitiligo). Good foundation colour matches or camouflage make-up products can be very successful in covering skin affected by this condition to make the skin colour appear more even.

Caucasian skin

This skin type contains less melanin and thus sun damage can occur quite easily, which encourages premature ageing. The skin appears to be a paler colour than other skin types and can sometimes appear to be pink.

The condition of the skin and muscles are affected by a number of factors, including environmental and lifestyle factors.

Environmental factors

- Wind chill factor
- Air conditioning
- Central heating
- Extremes of weather
- Exposure to extremes of temperature
- Natural exposure and overexposure to ultraviolet light, which may cause dehydration, loss of moisture, damage to collagen and elastin fibres (which harden), loss of firmness to skin and muscle tone, premature ageing and pigmentation irregularities.

All of the above affect the skin tissues by leading to dehydration through loss of moisture and encourage premature ageing of the skin.

Lifestyle factors

The following lifestyle factors affect the skin:

- **Smoking**: Leads to poor circulation, congested blocked pores, lack of nutrients and skin discoloration. The action of closing the mouth around the cigarette repeatedly also has an effect on the muscle tone around the lip (the obicularis oris), causing deeper lines
- **Drinking alcohol**: Can cause the dilation of blood capillaries and can dehydrate the body and skin, depriving it of vitamin reserves, which are necessary for healthy skin
- **High caffeine intake**: Coffee, tea, fizzy drinks and energy drinks can dehydrate the body as they can have a stimulating effect on the central nervous system and have a diuretic effect upon the body. This effect increases the excretion of water from the body

- **Lack of daily skin care regime**: Leads to dehydration, skin sensitivity, broken capillaries, wrinkles and a build up of sebum
- **General health**: Affects the nutrients available to the tissues. Prolonged illness may lead to depletion of subcutaneous fat, dehydration, wrinkles, baggy skin tissues and dark circles under the eyes
- **Diet**: Poor diet leads to lack of minerals, vitamins and nutrients, which can cause dry, dehydrated skin tissues
- **Natural ageing**: Results in contours dropping, expression lines and wrinkles, a decrease in collagen and sebum production, and an increase in pigmentation irregularities and superfluous hair growth
- **Hereditary factors**: These include how muscles are attached to skin tissue and bone structure. The decline in cellular reproduction varies from person to person. Hormonal imbalances affect moisture content pigmentation and hair growth
- **Stress**: can affect skin tissues causing frown lines, wrinkles, dark circles and dry, dehydrated skin with areas of sensitivity.

> ☆ *Tip* Choose a good-quality range of products from a reputable company that will give you quality, cost effectiveness, and good service for delivery and support, including promotional materials.

Smoking and drinking alcohol also attract free radicals that have not been filtered out through the Earth's protective ozone layer; the presence of these free radicals on the skin can cause premature ageing effects. A good example of this process can be seen when slicing an apple open. Leave the cut apple for around 10 minutes and you can see it beginning to turn brown. After 30 minutes it has turned quite brown in colour; this is due to the free radicals in the atmosphere.

Skincare products

The points to consider when deciding on a suitable skincare product:

- Skin type
- Skin condition
- Client's needs
- Client's budget
- Timing
- Homecare products.

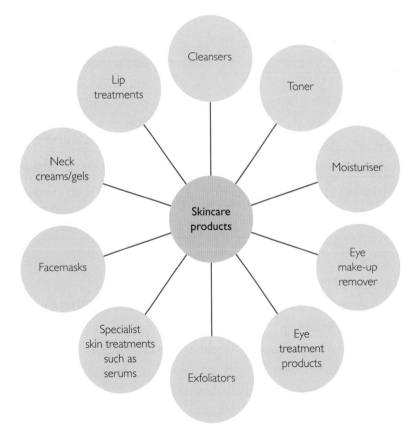

▲ Skincare products

Cleansers

Before the skin can be analysed the face will have to be cleansed and toned to allow the make-up artist to see the true picture of the skin and its conditions. The eye and lip make-up are usually removed first, followed by products on the rest of the face and neck area.

Table 6.1 Use of cleansers for varying skin types

Cleanser	Skin type
Gels	Sensitive Young person Combination Congested May be more appropriate for males who have been used to washing their face maybe with soap and water
Special cleansing creams, e.g. benzoyl peroxide cream	Oily Congested Acne
Creams	Dry Normal Mature
Milks	Normal Dry Sensitive
Bars	All skin types except sensitive
Lotions	Normal Combination Oily Young skins and/or blemished skin types
Foaming cleansers	All skin types except sensitive and dry
Eye make-up removers: non-oily	Suited to most clients Contact lens wearers Will not remove waterproof make-up products
Eye make-up removers: oil-based	Removes water-based make-up products

Benefits of cleansing

There are many benefits of cleansing the skin, including to:

- Remove make-up
- Remove dirt, pollutants, sweat and excess sebum
- Aid desquamation
- Prepare skin for further treatments
- Stimulate blood flow
- Soften and loosen blocked pores
- Relax facial muscles.

There are a variety of cleansers on the market. You will need to provide one or more from a professional and retail range to suit a variety of skin types and to be able to remove both water-soluble and non-soluble substances. Cleansers and other cosmetic preparations are often made in a combination of both water and oil. When they are mixed together, these two substances separate again. If these two substances are shaken together in a container, one substance will break up and the other one will become suspended in the other – this is known as an emulsion. However the **emulsion** needs to be stabilised by separating the two substances again and adding emulsifiers.

Cleansing gels

These vary between companies' product ranges. The gel is usually mixed with water to activate the mixture, and then rinsed.

Key ingredients

These gels have a high water content and usually contain a foaming agent similar to foaming cleansers, but have different ingredients added to suit different skin types: 1) sensitive skin and 2) young, combination, congested and male skin types. These products are not particularly suited for the removal of make-up – a cream cleanser would be better. These gels contain:

- Water
- Foaming agents
- Cleansing and wetting agents – often palm oil
- Conditioners
- Preservatives
- Colour
- Fragrance.

Special cleansing creams

Skin types and suitability

- Oily, congested and acne skin types.

Key ingredients

These are often used as topical agents for the treatment of acne (bezoyl peroxide and clindamycin). Some milder forms can be bought over the counter but some are prescription drugs. These are available in cleanser, gel and lotion form as well as in stronger prescription creams. A topical benzoyl peroxide cream can be very effective at killing bacteria and reducing sebum and an oral antibiotic such as tetracycline also fights bacteria.

Cleansing creams

Skin types and suitability

- This product contains a high percentage of oil, which makes it suitable for normal, dry and mature skin types.
- This product is also very effective for removing oil-based make-up from the skin.

Key ingredients

This specific emulsion is richer than cleansing milks and has a higher ratio of oil to water, which allows it to be gently massaged over the skin surface without tracking the skin tissue. The key ingredients are:

- Emulsion of oils, often mineral and some carrier oils
- Paraffin or beeswax
- Water
- Emulsifiers
- Preservatives
- Fragrance.

▲ Cleansing cream

Cleansing milk

This product contains a high percentage of water, which gives it a runny, fluid consistency.

Skin types and suitability

It is suitable for normal, dry and sensitive skin types.

Key ingredients

- Emulsion of oils, often mineral and some carrier oils
- Paraffin or beeswax (smaller amounts than in cleansing creams)
- Water and water-soluble ingredients (larger amounts than in creams)
- Detergent
- Emulsifiers
- Preservatives
- Fragrance.

▲ Cleansing milk

Cleansing bars

Often referred to as a 'soapless soap', these have been specifically formulated to be used on the face and are less likely to dry out the skin in comparison to soap, which has an alkaline pH.

Skin types and suitability

- This product is suitable for all skin types except sensitive.
- They are less likely to dry out the skin than soap as they have an alkaline pH; the skin is naturally acidic.

Key ingredients

This list is not exhaustive and will vary between product manufacturers:

- Emulsifiers
- Aqua
- Glycerin
- Preservative
- Artificial colourant
- Shea butter
- Glycine
- Soy oil
- Aloe vera.

Cleansing lotions

These do not usually contain oil and tend to be solutions of detergents in water. They are not particularly suitable for the removal of make-up.

Skin types and suitability

Normal, combination or oily skin types (products with a high oil content could cause further sebum production, which may aggravate an oily skin type)

- Suitable for young skins and/or blemished skin types.

Key ingredients

- Water with detergents
- Emulsifiers
- Antibacterial ingredients
- Preservatives
- Fragrance.

Foaming cleansers

These usually contain a mild detergent and a foaming agent that activates when mixed with water. These are ideal for the client who likes to 'wash' with water on their face.

Skin types and suitability

- Usually suitable for most skin types, except sensitive, very dry skin
- Not suitable as a heavy oil-based make-up remover; a cleansing cream could be used prior to this if preferable.

▲ Foaming cleanser

Key ingredients

- Water
- Cleansing and wetting agents – often palm oil
- Conditioners
- Preservatives
- Colour
- Fragrance.

Eye make-up removers

These are generally available in water- or oil-based formulae in gel, lotion or liquid types. These have been specially formulated for use around the delicate eye area, where the skin tissue is a lot finer than on the rest of the face.

Skin types and suitability

- Usually suitable for all skin types
- Oil-based and specifically designed for removal of waterproof mascara and oil-based make-up
- Water-based formulae are suited to clients who wear contact lenses

Key ingredients

These will vary between product companies and types but generally will consist of:

- Water
- Organic alcohol
- Hydrolysed wheat proteins
- Mineral oil
- Horse chestnut extract
- Vitamins (commonly vitamin E)
- Colour
- Preservative
- Fragrance.

▲ Eye make-up removers

Health and Safety

The application and removal of the cleanser will vary with each product range and manufacturers' instructions.

Method

The make-up artist/therapist will carry out a superficial cleanse prior to the skin analysis, followed by a deep cleanse once the skin type and conditions have been established.

Use a small amount of cleanser on damp skin. Using circular movements cleanse the face and neck area, then rinse off with warm water and a cleansing cloth or damp cotton wool pads.

Toners

The toner is the next step following the cleansing routine.

Table 6.2 Toner use for varying skin types

Toner	Skin type
Fresheners and tonics	Sensitive, dry, mature, combination and normal
Astringents	Oily, congested and acne – can be dabbed on pustules and papules

Benefits of using a toner

- Removes traces of cleanser
- Tightens pores
- Cools and refreshes the skin tissues
- Dissolves oil and sebum
- Hydrates the skin tissues
- May help restore pH of skin.

There are a variety of different toners on the market. Most salons tend to have one or more professional and retail ranges to suit a range of skin types.

Types of toners

Fresheners

These toners are mild and non-stimulating as they have no alcohol content.

Skin types and suitability

- Suitable for sensitive, dry and mature skin types.

Key ingredients

Usually without alcohol, the other ingredients are:

- Purified water
- Floral extracts (such as rosewater and camomile)
- Plant extracts (wheat germ)
- Fruit extracts
- Glycerine (humectant)
- Kernel oils (oat, peach)
- Essential oils
- Azulene (a soothing agent)
- Castor oil
- Preservatives
- Fragrance (sometimes).

▲ Toners

Tonics

They are stronger than fresheners as they contain a small amount of either witch hazel or alcohol, depending on the product range and are therefore slightly stimulating.

Skin types and suitability

- Suitable for combination and normal skin types.

Key ingredients

- Purified water
- Orange flower water
- Alcohol (often ethanol)
- Mild astringent (often witch hazel)
- Humectants such as glycerin
- Fruit extracts
- Plant extracts
- Essential oils
- Preservatives
- Fragrance.

 Tonic

Astringents

These have a high percentage of alcohol and therefore have a drying effect upon skin; this effect can promote healing of the skin.

Skin types and suitability

- Suitable for oily, congested and acne skin types with no sensitivity
- Can be applied on a papule or pustule.

Key ingredients

- Purified water
- Alcohol (usually ethanol)
- Astringents (such as witch hazel)
- Antiseptics (often hexachlorophene)
- Humectants
- Preservatives
- Fragrance.

Method

The application of the toner can be applied either to the skin tissues via damp cotton wool pads, working up the neck and face to remove any skin product residue. Some manufacturers provide their toners in a spray bottle, which allows them to be sprayed across the face whilst the client closes their eyes and holds their breath for a few seconds.

> **Remember . . .**
> Be careful when you spray toner. Avoid spraying it up the client's nostrils.

Toners can also be applied at the end of the facial treatment before the moisturisers, by using a fine gauze soaked in the appropriate toner and placed over the face and neck. Remember to cut a breathing hole for the nose and mouth. Damp cotton wool pads can be placed over the eyes underneath the tonic gauze. This has a cooling and refreshing effect upon the skin.

Moisturisers

Skin needs water to keep it supple and pliable; two-thirds of the body is composed of water. Moisturisers help to increase protection and hydration in the epidermal level by reducing evaporation, maintaining natural oils and locking moisture into the tissues. A basic formulation for moisturisers is an oil and water emulsion. The oil content helps to prevent moisture being lost from the surface of the epidermis; the water content helps to replace lost moisture to the surface layers of the epidermis. Sorbitol and glycerine are often used as humectants, which help to attract moisture to the skin from the atmosphere; this also prevents the moisturiser from drying out. Lighter creams usually contain humectants, therefore less oil is used in the formulation. A richer cream has a higher oil content.

Table 6.3 Use of moisturisers for various skin types

Moisturiser	Skin type
Cream	Dry, normal, mature and dehyrated skin
Milk or lotion moisturiser	Young, normal, combination and oily skin
Tinted moisturiser	Dry or mature and sensitive skins that are prone to redness, to even out the skin colour

Moisturiser should be applied for at the end of the facial treatment to protect the skin, hydrate the tissues and provide a base for foundation, allowing it to 'slip' onto the tissues evenly. Many moisturisers now have a sun protection factor to help filter out the sun's harmful rays.

Benefits of using a moisturiser

Moisturisers benefit the skin in many ways:

- Help maintain an adequate moisture level and soften the skin
- Keep the skin toned and its texture smooth and supple
- 'Plump up' the skin and reduce the appearance of fine lines
- Condition the skin
- Protect the skin against the elements, environmental pollution and dehydration

- Act as a base for make-up, creating a barrier to protect the skin
- Help prevent colour change in make-up
- May filter out ultraviolet light
- Contain additional ingredients to feed the skin tissues depending on make etc.

There are a variety of different types of moisturiser on the market. Most salons tend to have a range of professional and retail products to suit a variety of skin types. Many manufacturers include hypoallergenic moisturisers as part of their range for sensitive skin; these products do not contain common sensitising ingredients such as fragrance and lanolin – they contain soothing agents. A night cream is often a richer version of a day moisturiser.

Types of moisturisers
Cream moisturiser

This product contains 70 per cent oil and 30 per cent water depending on product range, making it thicker in texture with a dense viscosity. It is an emulsion and usually has a higher water content than oil depending on the product range, so it is more nourishing and gives the skin more moisture.

Skin types and suitability

- Suitable for dry, normal, mature and dehydrated skin.

Key ingredients

▲ Moisturisers

- Aqua and water-soluble ingredients
- Emulsions of oils and waxes (such as your jojoba, sweet almond, coconut and sunflower)
- Humectants (such as sorbitol and glycerine)
- Essential oils (such as lavender, geranium and chamomile)
- Vitamins (vitamin E is a common ingredient, but vitamins A and C can often be found)
- Plant extracts (such as aloe vera)
- Preservatives
- Colour
- Fragrance.

Milk and lotion moisturiser

This is a light, more fluid product that usually contains around 90 per cent water and 10 per cent oil depending on the product range.

Skin types/suitability

- Suitable for young, normal, combination and oily skin types.

Key ingredients

- Aqua and water-soluble ingredients
- Emulsions of oils and waxes (such as jojoba, sweet almond, coconut and sunflower)
- Humectants (such as sorbitol and glycerine)
- Essential oils (such as lavender, geranium and chamomile)
- Vitamins (vitamin E is a common ingredient, but vitamins A and C can often be found)
- Plant extracts (such as aloe vera)
- Preservatives
- Colour
- Fragrance.

Tinted moisturiser

This is a moisturiser that has a slight tint to even the skin tone. It produces a light, natural effect and is used by people who dislike foundation or who already have a suntan.

Skin types and suitability

- Suitable for dry or mature skin types
- Some product companies produce tinted moisturisers for sensitive skins that are prone to redness, to even out the skin colour.

Key ingredients

- Aqua and water-soluble ingredients
- Oil (olive)
- Essential oils (lavender, chamomile)
- Humectants (sorbitol and glycerin)
- Colour
- Preservatives.

Method

The application of the moisturiser occurs on completion of cleansing and toning, and prior to the application of the foundation.

The make-up artist/therapist removes a small amount of moisturiser from the container via a spatula, to avoid cross-infection and warms it in the hands prior to applying a light film of cream or lotion to the client's neck and face. Care should be taken to avoid the eye area and light, effleurage-type movements should be used.

In the event of applying too much moisturiser the make-up artist/therapist would blot the skin by applying a tissue to the skin and pressing gently to absorb unwanted residue. Remember to make a breathing hole in the tissue for the nose and mouth.

▲ Moisturisers

Eye treatment products

These products have been specially formulated for use on the delicate skin around the eye. They come in several forms but with many common ingredients. They form a good base for under the make-up and help with cell renewal. They have a tightening and firming effect but specific products can now be purchased for daytime or night-time application; these night eye gels have a slightly denser viscosity for a more intense treatment.

Table 6.4 Eye treatments for various skin types

Eye treatment	Skin type
Eye cream	All skin types Client preference, however a more mature skin may benefit more from a cream
Eye gel	All skin types

Eye creams

These are an oil-in-water emulsion that is easily absorbed by the skin to moisturise and tone the skin around the eye area.

Skin types and suitability

- All skin types.

Key ingredients

- Aqua
- Oil (this may vary between product companies, sweet almond is an example)
- Collagen
- Herb and plant extracts
- Essential oils
- Vitamins, such as vitamin E
- Colour
- Preservatives.

▲ Eye cream

Eye gels

These tend to feel lighter than eye creams and have cooling, soothing effects on the delicate skin around the eye. Some products may be kept in the refrigerator to maximise the effect. These products may not feel as moisturising as an eye cream for mature skin.

Skin types and suitability

- All skin types.

Key ingredients

- Aqua
- Oil (this may vary between product companies, sweet almond is an example), the oil content may be slightly less in a gel
- Collagen
- Methyl cellulose
- Azulene, cucumber and witch hazel
- Herb and plant extracts, such as arnica
- Essential oils, such as chamomile
- Vitamins – such as vitamin E
- Colour
- Preservatives.

Method

Gently apply the eye cream or gel following toner, using the ring finger with a sweeping motion or gentle patting motion and working from the outer corner inward.

▲ Eye gel

Exfoliators

These skincare products have a gentle abrasive effect on the skin that aids removal of dead epidermal cells. Cleaning the skin in this way will help to brighten and soften the skin; it will also increase the blood supply and aid cell renewal.

There are also peeling creams, fruit and marine acid peels available on the market.

Table 6.5 Exfoliator use on varying skin types

Eye treatment	Skin type
Exfoliator (abrasive variety)	All skin types
Peeling creams	Sensitive, dry and normal
Fruit and marine acid peels	All skin types, except sensitive

Exfoliator (abrasive variety)

The abrasive properties can vary from ground fruit or olive kernels or stones, oatmeal, bran, nuts, and synthetic micro-beads or poly chips, which are usually a spherical shape.

The fruit or olive kernels or stones tend to be a harsher abrasive than the other types and great care must be taken to protect the delicate facial skin as products that have larger particles may tear the top layers of the epidermis.

Skin types and suitability

- Usually all skin types. Check the manufacturers' instructions.

Key ingredients

- Aqua and water-soluble ingredients
- Ground fruit or olive kernels or stones
- Clay-based ingredients, such as kaolin
- Oils, such as palm oil, jojoba or soybean
- Essential oils
- Vitamins, such as vitamin E
- Glycerine
- Colour
- Preservatives
- Fragrance.

▲ Exfoliators

Peeling creams

These are water and oil-based emulsion, however the oil content tends to be low. They have a similar consistency to a cream-based face mask. A thin layer is applied to the skin and allowed to dry for approximately 3–5 minutes, depending on the manufacturers' instructions. This cream is gently removed by a rolling action with the fingers followed by the face mask sponges.

Skin types and suitability

- Usually aimed at sensitive, dry and normal skin types (check manufacturers' instructions).

Key ingredients

- Aqua and water-soluble ingredients
- Oil – often mineral oil
- Clay-based ingredients, such as kaolin
- Fruit and plant extracts
- Colour
- Preservatives
- Fragrance.

Fruit and marine acid peels

These products are available in lotion or mask form. They help to dissolve the dead surface epidermal skin cells whilst brightening the complexion and softening the skin, promoting cell renewal. They stimulate the blood supply and some products produce a tingling effect on the skin. Some product companies recommend light tapotement movements on the face until this tingling sensation subsides. This is not an allergic reaction but some can feel quite tingly on the delicate facial skin.

This tingling usually lasts a couple of minutes and signifies the beginning of the treatment's action. Remember to warn the client of the tingling action prior to the application of the peel.

Skin types and suitability

- All skin types, except sensitive skin (check manufacturers' instructions).

Key ingredients

- Alpha hydroxy acids (AHAs): these can be fruit acids, for example from citrus fruits and bilberries. AHAs can also be derived from sugarcane
- Marine hydroxy acids (MHAs): these are derived from seaweed
- If in a lotion format, this can be suspended in water and oil emulsion
- Preservative stabilisers
- Some companies add essential oils, colour and fragrance.

Several product companies now produce hypoallergenic products, particularly moisturisers for sensitive skin. Many of the common sensitisers, including preservatives, have been removed.

Face masks

A face mask is used at the end of the facial skin care treatment to deep cleanse, tighten and tone the skin and pores. They also have specific actions according to variety and type; many have anti-ageing properties to fight free radicals and deeply moisturise and some brighten the skin by using biological plant extracts that are good for reducing the formation of melanin, which can cause age spots. Some are pre-mixed and some need to be mixed to activate them. For combination skin types, masks may be used separately: one type along the T zone and another type on the cheek area to balance out the skin.

Setting masks

There are different types of setting masks:

- Clay
- Peel off
- Thermal.

Non-setting masks

The three types of non-setting masks are:

- Warm oil
- Cream
- Biological or natural.

Face mask preparations

Setting masks

These masks will set over a period of time according to the manufacturers' instructions. Some simply dry out and tighten, some set so they can be peeled off and some specialised masks set solid. If working on a male client or a client with excessive facial hair, these masks may cause a little discomfort during their removal, in which a different kind of mask could be used or cream could be applied underneath.

Clay mask

These usually come in powder form according to skin type and condition and need to be mixed with another product to be activated. These masks tend to be quite cost effective to use.

Table 6.6 Clay mask types, uses and effects

Mask	Skin type	Mix with	Benefits
Calamine: light pink colour	Dry, sensitive or normal skin	Rosewater, orange flower water, distilled water, almond oil and glycerol	Soothing action on surface capillaries Helps to reduce vascular appearance Gentle, calming effect
Magnesium carbonate: white colour	Dry to normal skin	Rosewater, orange flower water, witch hazel, almond oil or glycerol	Mild astringent Refines, softens and has a toning effect on skin
Kaolin: creamy white colour	Oily and congested skin	Witch hazel or distilled water, if there is any sensitivity to the oily or congested skin	Stimulating, thus improves vascular and lymphatic flow Helps remove impurities and waste products
Fullers Earth: dark green colour	Oily, congested and acne skin Must not be used on sensitive skin	Witch hazel	Stimulating and deep cleansing This mask produces a brightening effect by temporarily whitening the skin
Sulphur: a pale yellow colour	Can be used on individual blemishes, papules and pustules	Witch hazel or distilled water	Drying effect

When clay masks are mixed with another liquid ingredient, they are activated and turned into a paste. The active liquids are selected according to client skin type and mask to be used; they will help to reinforce the action of the mask.

Active liquids

- **Rosewater**: Made from rose petals, it has a mild toning effect
- **Orange flower water**: This is a natural extract from the fruit tree, it has a mild stimulating tonic effect
- **Witch hazel**: Astringent helps to shrink and contract the vessels back to normal size
- **Distilled water**: This is ordinary water that had magnesium and calcium removed from it. This can be done chemically with the use of water softeners or by boiling the water; this is used for highly sensitive skins
- **Almond oil**: This oil is obtained from the kernels of the seed of the whole almond; it can be used on dehydrated, mature or sensitive skin. The oil does not allow the face mask to dry out. Remember to check with the client for nut allergies prior to application
- **Glycerol**: a colourless, odourless liquid that helps to prevent the mask from drying out. Suitable for dry, mature skin types.

Procedure

These masks are applied at the end of the facial treatment and often feel cool as they are applied to the skin. Warn your client about this as they will feel relaxed after the facial massage treatment. Their skin temperature will be raised and you won't want to spoil the effects the massage treatment, so you should warn your client that the mask may feel cold.

- Mix the mask immediately before use with the appropriate mask and activator
- Apply the mask using a mask brush spatula from the neck upwards
- Keep in mind that these masks are to be left on for between 5 and 20 minutes; for more intense effects, leave the mask on for 20 minutes, or for those with sensitive skin leave it on for just 5 minutes
- Re-dampen these masks as they dry out, either using the mask sponges or an atomiser spray
- Remove the mask from the neck upwards with damp mask sponges; it may take a little while to completely remove all residue of the mask. A tonic gauze treatment can help with this.

Peel-off masks

These can be made from latex, gel or paraffin wax. They work by trapping perspiration on the skin's surface and forcing moisture back into the surface of the epidermis whilst increasing the skin's temperature by insulation.

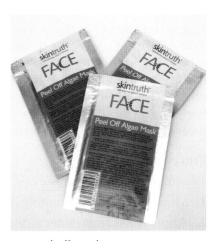

▲ Peel-off mask

Table 6.7 Peel-off mask types, uses and effects

Mask	Skin type	Mix with	Benefits
Latex	Dry, dehydrated and mature (some companies use seaweed latex masks, which are also suitable for sensitive skins)	Usually a powder is mixed with a liquid activator specially formulated for that brand	Deeply moisturising and have tightening effect
Gel	All skin types	These are usually pre-mixed	Benefits specific to brand of mask due to differing ingredients
Paraffin wax	Dry, dehydrated and mature	Pre-mixed	Deeply moisturising and stimulating action; induces perspiration to help eliminate waste toxins and stimulates blood supply
Thermal	May vary between product companies; some are deeply moisturising and may work with a latex mask and rich cream-based products underneath (for dry, dehydrated and mature skins) Some have a stimulating, deep-cleansing action and are suitable for oily, congested or normal skin types	Usually a powder is mixed with a liquid activator specially formulated for that brand	Some thermal masks are deeply moisturising and intensify other products or latex mask actions Some are deeply cleansing and stimulating, but all thermal masks are warming and relaxing

Latex mask

This is an emulsion of latex and water. The water evaporates, leaving a rubber film to form the mask. Usually the mask must be mixed from a powder with an activator into a paste; many of these types of mask use seaweed, which is known for its healing and anti-ageing properties. The seaweed is of a specific type called Spriulina, which is found deep in the sea and is rich in minerals and nutrients. These can feel very cool when applied to the skin. An alternative to latex is a synthetic polyvinyl acetate (PVA) resin. This type of mask produces a rise in skin temperature as it insulates the skin; this in turn encourages moisture to be trapped in the surface epidermal skin tissues.

Procedure

This mask is applied at the end of the facial treatment as follows:

1. Mix the mask immediately before use.
2. Apply a tissue at either side of the face and tuck it into the headband to secure the edges. Allow the tissue to lay flat so it covers the ears in case the mask runs.

3. Using a spatula, apply the mask to the neck, working upwards over the face to the forehead.

4. Timing can vary between product manufacturers' instructions, but this mask is often left on from between 10 and 20 minutes.

5. To remove the mask, gently lift it away and peel upwards.

6. Use damp cotton wool sponges to remove any residue.

Gel mask

These masks are usually ready-made and are a suspension of gums, gelatine and starches. They are easy to use as they are premixed and may be used on most skin types (check manufacturers' instructions). The mask begins to dry out once it is applied to the skin; you should be able to peel it from the face in one piece.

Procedure

Gel masks are applied at the end of the facial treatment as follows:

1. Apply the mask with either a mask brush or a spatula starting from the neck and working upwards onto the face. Finish on the forehead.

2. Timings will vary between product manufacturers but are generally between 5 and 20 minutes.

3. Use damp mask sponges to remove the mask, working from the neck upward.

Paraffin wax mask

The wax is heated up to 37°C. It is a liquid when it is applied to the skin. It begins to set on contact with the skin. This mask has a stimulating action and therefore is more suitable for dry skin types. It is unsuitable for oily or hypersensitive skin.

Procedure

This should be applied at the end of the facial treatment as follows:

1. A small amount of heated paraffin wax should be poured into a small, clean bowl that has been lined with either foil or a plastic bag to protect it.

2. Apply eye pads and begin on the neck, gently brushing the wax up towards the forehead.

3. The mask can now be gently removed as you gently loosen the sides by sliding a finger downwards to the neck area and peeling the mask backwards towards the forehead.

4. Use damp mask sponges to remove any residue.

 Health and Safety

Always check the temperature of the paraffin wax on the inside of your wrist then check on the client's own wrist before it is applied to the face. Check with the client that the product does not feel too hot when it is applied to the face.

Thermal mask

These masks set solid and are made from clay, crystals and minerals. Some companies recommend that aromatherapy oils are added to the mix for therapeutic effect. Some also recommend thermal masks be applied over the top of latex masks.

The heat is activated when the mask is mixed from a powder with a liquid activator. It is usually applied using a spatula and because it sets solid it should be applied quickly. The heat from the mask pushes the products deeper into the epidermal tissues for a deep moisturising effect.

▲ Thermal mask

Procedure

1. Mix the mask immediately before use.

2. Place damp cotton wool pads over the eyes and ask the client to open their mouth slightly; this is so they can breathe easily and to avoid them moving the mouth once the mask begins setting as it could break the mask.

3. Mask setting times vary between product manufacturers, however between 10 and 20 minutes is the average.

4. Once the mask has set it can be removed by holding it at the sides and performing a gentle rocking motion back and forth until it releases. It should come off whole.

5. Use damp mask sponges to gently remove any mask residue.

Non-setting masks

Warm-oil mask

Olive or almond oil is typically used for this type of mask treatment. The oil can be gently warmed by using a bowl floating in another bowl of hot (not boiling) water.

Table 6.8 Non-setting mask types, uses and effects

Mask	Skin type	Mix with	Benefits
Warm-oil mask	Dry, dehydrated and mature	No mixing required	Deeply moisturising and softening
Biological/natural	All skin types	Mix to a pulp and add yoghurt or honey products if required	The benefits are specific due to differing ingredients
Cream	All skin types	Pre-mixed	Deeply moisturising and softening
Collagen mask	May vary between product companies; all skin types	No mixing required	Hydrating, anti-ageing, anti-oxidant, softening, soothing, calming, cell regeneration, depending on manufacturer

Procedure

- Cleanse and tone the skin.
- Exfoliate the skin.
- Apply warm-oil mask.
- Place the oil into a bowl.
- Take a piece of gauze and cut a hole for the nose and mouth; place the gauze into the oil to soak.
- Apply eye pads then the gauze to the face, ensuring that the oil does not drip (tuck tissues underneath the headband to catch any excess oil).
- Leave for 5–10 minutes (the drier the skin, the longer the timing).
- Remove the gauze and massage the remaining oil into the skin.

Cream mask

These are pre-mixed masks that have moisturising and softening properties. The ingredients vary between product companies and often biological extracts and essential oils are added. These masks are very easy to apply and remove. They will not dry out like a clay-based mask, however they will tighten slightly as they react with the atmosphere.

Biological or natural mask

Many ingredients found in certain types of fruits, vegetables, herbs and everyday foods can have various effects when applied to the skin. Usually the ingredients are crushed to a pulp and placed in layers on the face. Biological ingredients such as natural yoghurt, honey, chocolate and egg can be applied to the face using a mask brush or a spatula.

Natural mask ingredients

These are just a few examples of ingredients that can be put into a natural mask:

- Lemon juice (good for oily skin)
- Banana
- Avocado
- Strawberry
- Cucumber
- Apple
- Peach
- Buttermilk
- Yoghurt
- Honey.

▲ Bio mask

Health and Safety

Remember clients could still be allergic to natural ingredients – nuts and wheat are good examples of this.

Collagen mask

A collagen gel-type solution can be applied using a mask brush, but many product companies use sheets of fine fabric infused with collagen and other ingredients to produce various effects that often go alongside anti-ageing properties. These masks are very easy to use and to remove.

▲ Collagen mask

Common ingredients

- Native collagen
- Collagen amino acid
- Alpha hydroxy acids (AHAs)
- Vitamins, such as A, C and E
- Seaweed
- Green tea
- Panthenol or vitamin B5.

Procedure

The collagen mask can be applied at the end of the treatment:

1. Carefully lift the fabric mask from the packet; this can be done by gently securing each side with a pair of tweezers.
2. Gently lay the mask onto the client's skin and smooth it over with a light tapping motion. This will ensure that there are no air bubbles between the mask and the client's skin.
3. The mask usually stays on for around 20 minutes and then is removed. Any residue of the active ingredient should then be massaged into the client's skin.

> ⭐ *Tip* Know the benefits and ingredients of your skincare products well, so good recommendations can be made to the client.

Specialist skin treatments and products

Many companies extend their skincare range past the basics to include specialist skin treatments to enhance and intensify basic skincare actions. These products include:

- **Serums** for the facial skin, eyes and neck: these target specific areas and needs and often contain anti-ageing properties. Serums have an almost liquid gel consistency but are often very light and fluid.
- **Ampoules**: these can be specific for the client's needs and are often hydrating, soothing, balancing or calming. They often contain essential oils and come sealed in plastic or glass vials.
- **Neck creams and gels**: these products have moisturising, nourishing hydrating, toning and tightening effects. These products are often collagen, vitamin E and elastin based and are specially formulated for the skin on the neck. The neck area can easily show signs of ageing.
- **Lip treatment**: balms, creams and lip glosses are available to hydrate and protect the delicate skin on the lips. Most of these products contain a sun protection factor.

▲ Serum

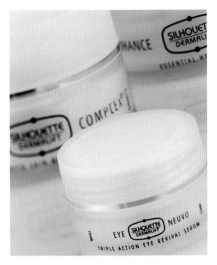

▲ Eye serum

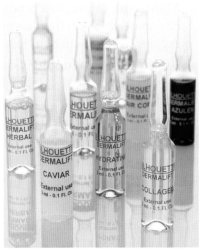

▲ Ampoules

- **Lip scrubs**: These scrubs are often made from edible ingredients! Caster sugar is commonly the abrasive in the formulation along with jojoba oil. Some of these scrubs contain mint, which stimulates the blood supply for a plumping effect.

- **Lip plumpers**: Lips may appear thinner over time due to the ageing process, when collagen and elastin production slows down. Lip plumpers have become a popular alternative to injectable lip plumpers such as collagen, which can sometimes look lumpy and uneven. Lip plumpers are applied topically and contain products such as cinnamon, pepper extracts, peppermint, camphor menthol or benzyl nicotinate, which stimulate blood flow, immediately providing a plumping effect and improving colour. They also contain hyaluronic acid (HA) and peptides that increase cell renewal and natural collagen production and moisturisers like jojoba oil and vitamin E, which help the lips feel softer.

- **Eye and lip pads**: these can be fabric or silicone-type pads infused with such properties as vitamins C and E, and collagen. These are intensive treatments that fight the signs of ageing and help to eliminate free radicals which dehydrate the skin and cause fine lines to appear. They can be used as part of the professional treatment in place of a mask but are also excellent for homecare use and can be applied after cleansing treatments.

- **Glycolic peeling AHA**: these lotions contain glycolic acid often obtained from fruit extracts such as from grapefruit or lemon; they accelerate cell division by removing the thickened horny tissue from the stratum corneum. This in turn helps to rejuvenate the production of collagen and elastin and by improving the condition of the skin help combat the signs of ageing.

- **Mattifying lotion**: this product is often oil free and helps to eliminate shine on the skin by controlling excess oil production. A common ingredient in this product is tea tree oil.
- **Blotting papers for oily skin**: these are often made from rice paper and are gently dabbed onto oily areas of the face to soak up excess oil.

There are also specialised anti-ageing creams on the market that contain muscle-relaxing properties to help soften the appearance of fine lines and smooth and firm the skin.

Specialist skincare products formulated for male skin types include:

- **Pre-shave cleansers**: These cleanse, refresh and prepare the skin before shaving
- **Shave gel**: Specially formulated for use during shaving, gel is available in normal and sensitive skin types
- **Aftershave balm**: This product helps to reduce skin irritation that can occur after shaving; it will soften the skin and make it feel soothed.

Tip There are many products on the market today made specifically for anti-ageing and for teenage and male skin.

Skin warming

Skin warming is usually performed prior to extraction and will cleanse and stimulate the skin. These methods are used to perform pre-warming skin treatments:

- **Facial steaming**: Using an electrical facial steamer filled with distilled water
- **Hot towels**: Using pre-warmed damp towels.

Facial steaming

Steaming is performed following the cleansing routine and exfoliation. An electrical vapourising unit is used that contains distilled water that is boiled to create steam. The steaming unit works just like a big kettle! Distilled water is used to help prevent the build up of limescale within the unit, which could damage it. Many models still have the facility to produce ozone at the end of the steaming treatment. Ozone is created via a high-intensity quartz mercury arc tube contained within the unit; when the oxygen from the steam passes over this, a substance called 'ozone' is produced. This substance is thought to be beneficial to congested skin as it kills bacteria, however it is thought that this could be a carcinogenic if inhaled.

Electrical facial steaming equipment

These are professional pieces of equipment that come in the following styles:

- Portable
- Table top
- Pedestal.

Contraindications

- **Hypersensitive skin**
- **Dilated capillaries**: Could make the condition worse
- **Acne rosacea**: This is a vascular skin disorder that could be made worse by extreme heat
- **Respiratory problems**: Such as severe asthma, a cold or active hay fever
- **Claustrophobia**: Could make the condition worse
- **Diabetes**: As with this condition there is usually reduced skin sensitivity. The client could gain a doctor's permission for the treatment and a thermal skin test could be performed prior to commencing treatment. Hot (not boiling) and cold water should be placed in a test tube and gently touched to the inside of the client's wrist for a few seconds. The client should be asked whether they feel hot or cold, to check their tolerance levels
- **Excessive high blood pressure**: A rise in temperature could make the client feel dizzy
- **Sunburn**: This is already a skin-sensitive condition – further heat could make it more painful and irritate the delicate skin tissues further.

Benefits

- **Opens the pores**: This will aid extraction of comedones
- **Increases circulation of blood and lymph**: Improves skin colour and assists in the elimination of waste toxins
- **Softens the surface of the epidermis**: Aids desquamation
- **Increases sebaceous gland activity**: Stimulates oil production to moisturise a dry, dehydrated and mature skin
- **Relaxing**: Due to increased warmth.

Safety precautions

- Distilled water should be used to prevent the build up of limescale on the steamer's element and possibly the nozzle, as this could cause spitting of boiling water from the steamer's jet
- As this is an electrical unit, ensure that it is been Portable Appliance Testing (PAT) tested every 12 months in line with health and safety regulations

- Do electrical checks to ensure there are no broken, loose trailing wires
- Ensure that the unit is on a stable surface or for the pedestal-style units ensure they are positioned so that they cannot be knocked during the steaming process.
- Ensure correct positioning of the unit and protection of the client
- Ensure that the steamer is at the correct height and angle it so it can be positioned for a comfortable treatment
- Ensure correct timings for steaming treatments are adhered to
- Ensure the client has removed any metal objects such as jewellery, as they could become hot and burn the client during the treatment.

Health and Safety

Always ensure work is carried out safely, especially when using electrical or heated equipment.

Skin types and timing for steaming treatments

- Dry, dehydrated and mature skin – 10 minutes
- Combination skin – 10–15 minutes
- Oily, congested skin – 10–15 minutes.

Contra-actions to steaming

- **Excessive erythema**: Exceeding the timing for that skin type or the steamer being too close to the client's face
- **Discomfort**: Steaming for too long, too close to the client's skin or with the steamer's nozzle at the incorrect angle for treatment so that the steam is blowing into the client's nostrils
- **Scalding**: This can be caused by overfilling the steamer with distilled water past its maximum capacity. The nozzle could become blocked due to poor maintenance of the steamer or it could be faulty, creating spitting from the jet.

Procedure

- Check the water levels and turn the steamer on, with the nozzle pointing away or downwards, for safety, until it is ready for use. It may take around 10 minutes for the water to heat up and be ready for steaming.
- Ensure the client is fully aware of the steaming procedure prior to treatment.
- The client should be in a semi-reclining position with a towel across the body to protect the client.
- Apply damp eye pads to the client's eyes for protection.
- Position the steamer approximately 30–45 cm away from the client's skin; for oily or congested skin the steamer can be approximately 30 cm away.
- Warn the client that they will feel gentle steam on their face and turn the nozzle carefully so it is positioned to give even coverage to the face so the steam will not go directly into the client's nostrils.

- The client may find it more comfortable to breathe through their mouth.
- Ensure that you keep checking the areas of the face, looking for any hotspots or excessive erythema. If these reactions occur, stop the steaming procedure.
- Inform the client if ozone is to be used for the last 5 minutes of the treatment.
- Once the treatment time has elapsed, inform the client that you are about to switch the steamer off. Gently turn the nozzle away from the client's skin and switch off the unit.
- Unplug the facial steamer, wrap the wire safely and move it into a position where it will not cause harm, as the unit will take some time to cool down.

> **Health and Safety**
>
> Never leave the client alone during facial steaming treatment.

Hot towels

This is a very easy, convenient and cost-effective method of pre-warming the skin. There is no special equipment needed to perform this treatment therefore it is ideal for mobile work. A small towel can be folded and placed into a clean bowl of hand-hot water for approximately 5 minutes. If electric towel heaters are available, this piece of equipment can heat several small, pre-dampened towels that are rolled up and placed in the unit.

Procedure

- If using the bowl method to heat the towel by immersing it in a bowl of hand-hot water, pour out the water before wringing out the towel so it is not too wet. If using an electric towel heater, use caution when removing the towel from the heater.
- Fold the towel in half and gently place it on the client's chin and neck area before unfolding the towel to cover the cheek and forehead areas. At this point ensure that you leave the towel loosely applied over the base of the nose so the client can breathe easily.
- Leave the towel for 2–5 minutes and then as it begins to cool, remove it from the forehead, moving downward.
- When working on skin that is oily or congested, this procedure can be repeated so that the towel stays on the skin for around 10 minutes.
- Once the treatment is complete, blot the skin dry with a soft facial tissue and and if necessary, begin extraction techniques.

Brush cleansing

This technique has a deep cleansing and stimulating effect and can be used for a deep cleanse and exfoliating effect. It can also be used to remove masks and peels from the skin. An electrical brush-cleansing unit is used for this procedure and has interchangeable heads that have various actions. This can also be used during a steaming procedure.

The ideal brush and sponge sizes are as follows:

1. Brushes (small 20 mm, medium 40 mm)
2. Brush – bristle (medium 40 mm)
3. Sponges (small 20 mm, medium 40 mm).

Skin type

1. All skin types
2. Oily and congested skin types or male clients
3. Especially good for sensitive skin.

Products

1. Foaming cleanser or facial scrub can be used (foaming cleanser may be more appropriate for sensitive skin).

Benefits

1. Deep cleansing
2. Desquamating
3. Extremely stimulating.

Contraindications

- Hypersensitive skin
- Broken capillaries
- Broken skin
- Excessively loose skin tissue
- Skin diseases and disorders
- Broken skin.

Procedure

1. Remove eye and lip make-up.
2. Carry out a superficial manual cleanse.
3. Using foaming cleanser and exfoliator matched to the client's skin type and needs, apply products either by using the hands, mask brush or brush head.
4. Select a brush head and wet it in a clean bowl of warm water. Ensure that it is not dripping when you insert the head into the machine. Switch on the machine, holding the brush head pointing downwards for safety.
5. Keep the speed control at a minimum speed.
6. Make sure the client is comfortable with the noise of the machine and make them aware that you are going to begin the procedure.
7. Place the applicator head onto the client's neck, ensuring that the speed is at an acceptable level for the client and suitable to deliver the desired action.

8. Work upward from the neck to the chin, then the cheek areas and on to the forehead. Work on each area for 5–7 minutes.

9. Avoid the delicate skin around the eyes.

10. Once the treatment has been completed, reduce the speed control, turn off the machine and lift the brush off the client's face.

11. Remove any remaining product with damp sponges.

Steaming

This is particularly suitable for the oily and congested skin types. Steaming intensifies deep cleansing while opening the pores and loosening dead skin cells in preparation for extraction.

Maintenance of brush heads

Wash brush heads in hot soapy water, then rinse and dry. They can be placed in the UV cabinet in between treatments.

Extraction

This works best following a steaming or hot towel treatment as the pores are open and the surface dead skin cells have been removed. Skin blockages such as comedones and milia can be gently removed using a comedone extractor or microlance to extract milia.

The comedone extractor should be sterilised prior to treatment.

▲ Comedone extractors

Comedone extraction procedure

1. Use the loop at the end of the extractor tool and gently place it around the comedone. Apply gentle pressure to the area and the comedone should pop up and out of the skin as the sebum plug blocking the pore is released.

2. If the comedone has not been thoroughly removed using this technique, wrap a tissue around the index fingers and place them around the comedone. Gently apply pressure at the sides until it is removed.

Contra-actions

- Do not overdo this procedure as skin bruising could occur.
- The capillaries could be damaged; if they rupture the skin damage could be permanent.

▲ Comedone extraction

Milia extraction procedure

- Using the extractor tool, ensure it is parallel to the client's skin surface and superficially pierce the epidermis carefully.
- Once the skin is opened, the trapped sebaceous matter can be removed.
- Either the comedone extractor can be used or the method of extraction using a tissue wrapped around the fingers as described earlier.
- A soothing lotion containing a mild antiseptic may be applied after extraction to help the skin to heal.

Relaxation – facial massage

Facial massage is the most relaxing and therapeutic part of the facial treatment. An effective massage requires an expert touch – gently but firmly. The massage medium used can come in several forms:

- **Creams**: These are a thick, rich emulsion that provides ample slip and is usually suitable for all skin types.
- **Oil**: These are usually carrier oils such as sweet almond, grapeseed, jojoba etc. and could include essential oils for the trained aromatherapist.
- **Specialist serums**: These suit specific skin types and conditions.

These mediums are used to help improve the skin's texture and also to provide 'slip' so the massage movements are performed smoothly and without causing discomfort. Take care not to overstimulate the skin's tissues, to avoid excessive erythema and irritation. To ensure total relaxation for your client the following points should be considered:

- Appropriate environment
- Temperature
- Lighting
- Atmosphere
- Music
- Correct positioning of the client.

Effects

- **Physical effects**: can be seen or felt on the surface of the skin.
- **Physiological effects**: occur in the body under the surface of the skin.
- **Psychological effects**: those that the client feels.

Tip Massage should always be performed in a rhythmical movement; it should flow and the hand should not leave contact with the client's skin during the treatment.

Remember...
Be very carefully when massaging over the cheekbone area and the throat – do not apply too much pressure.

Remember...
Lighting can be dimmed during the massage to help the client relax.

Tip During the treatment planning stage, explain to your client that to get the best therapeutic effect from the treatment you should not chat with them during the treatment so that they can relax.

Benefits

- Relaxation
- A sense of well being
- Increased blood circulation that warms the skin tissues and helps ease tense muscles
- Blood capillaries dilate, bringing blood to the skin surface and improving its colour
- Increased supply of oxygenated blood, improving cell renewal for the skin and muscles. The facial contours may be slightly improved as a slight toning and strengthening effect occurs
- Desquamation occurs as dead epidermal cells are loosened, thus improving the appearance of the skin
- Lymphatic circulation and drainage is improved to aid the removal of waste toxins
- Skin temperature is raised, which helps to relax the skin's pores and follicles so that it can absorb the massage product and soften the skin
- Sebaceous and sudoriferous glands are stimulated, producing sebum and sweat, and helping to maintain the skin's natural oil and moisture balance
- Sensory nerves may also be stimulated depending how large the manipulation is that is being performed.

Massage manipulations

Massage is included in the facial routine after all the cleansing, skin warming and extraction treatments have been carried out.

By the end of the massage routine your client's skin should feel slightly warm and appear clean, smooth and refreshed. Next you would remove the massage medium and tone and blot if necessary, in preparation for application of the face mask.

The stimulating effects of the massage continue for up to 48 hours after the treatment. During this time the skin 'throws off' waste and toxins, which may cause minor blemishes and blotchiness. The client should be warned in advance of these contra-actions and reassured that the skin should look at its best in 2 to 3 days after the treatment.

Some clients may arrive at the salon wearing make-up. They may also expect to leave wearing make-up. Try to advise your client that their skin would benefit more if they let it breathe for a while after the treatment. If the client wants to apply make-up afterwards they could apply a light covering of tinted moisturiser, face powder, basic eye make-up and lipstick.

Effleurage

This is a soothing, stroking, surface movement used at the beginning and end of a massage treatment. It can sometimes be used during the massage routine as a 'linking' movement between manipulations. The pressure is light and it is performed either with the palm of the hand or the padded part of the fingertips. The effects of effleurage are that it:

- Is a way of spreading the massage medium
- Is soothing and relaxing for the client
- Introduces the client to the make-up artist's/therapist's touch
- Increases circulation so the skin is nourished
- Increases lymph flow, so helping to remove waste products
- Aids desquamation and improves skin texture
- Causes an erythema, improving skin colour
- Soothes nerves
- Causes a slight increase in skin temperature.

Petrissage

These are pressure movements using either the palm of the hand or the pads of the fingers and thumbs. The hands should mould to the shape of the area being treated and movements should be slow and rhythmical. Kneading, knuckling, rolling and pinching are examples of petrissage movements; these are small, deep movements that are stimulating.

The effects of petrissage are:

- Increases circulation and lymph flow
- Aids desquamation
- Stimulates the skin. Improves the skin colour, texture and aids cellular regeneration
- Increases muscle tone and improves facial contours
- Eases away tension and relaxes muscles.

Tapotement

These are percussion movements such as tapping, which are performed lightly and briskly. The benefits of performing these movements are that it:

- Produces an erythema
- Stimulates the nerve endings, causing temporary tightening and toning of the skin
- Improves blood flow
- Helps to remove static lymph from tissues, e.g. from underneath the chin in a client with sluggish circulation.

Vibrations

Using the palms and the fingertips of the hands, place them on the area to be treated. The muscles of the make-up artist's/therapist's arms and hands are contracted and relaxed rapidly, creating fine trembling movements, which promotes relaxation.

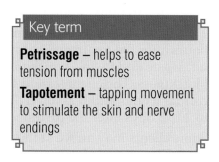

Key term

Petrissage – helps to ease tension from muscles

Tapotement – tapping movement to stimulate the skin and nerve endings

Effects of vibrations are:

- Relaxation
- Gentle stimulation of the deeper layers of the skin
- Relief from fatigue and muscular pain.

Practical facial treatments

Skin analysis

During the consultation you will have questioned the client about their homecare routine, products they use and skin characteristics. You would also listen to their needs and begin to form a treatment plan accordingly. To determine the skin type it is necessary to look more closely at the clean skin, therefore a skin analysis should be performed after the superficial cleanse.

Using a cold-light magnifying lamp to look closely at the skin, you would determine its characteristics and choose your skincare products accordingly. Open pores, comedones and blemishes will be more visible under the lamp. Gently place your ring finger on the cheek area and press lightly to test the skin's elasticity. If the skin tone is firm, the skin will bounce straight back up once the pressure is removed. Fine lines and dry, flaky patches will be more visible under the magnifying lamp than to the naked eye. Once the skin type is determined, remove the lamp, switch the light off and continue with deep cleansing using the appropriate products.

Treatment planning

Treatment planning is discussed in more detail in Chapter 2 Health and safety.

There are many things to consider when planning a facial treatment. The treatment plan may differ with each treatment the client undergoes. This may be due to the improvement in skin condition because of professional treatments received or possibly an improved homecare routine and correct retail skincare products used.

With good-quality education and vital experience, treatment planning for your client will become easier. There are so many aspects to carrying out this treatment to remember and products to learn about but it will soon become worthwhile.

Preparing for treatment

A consultation must be carried out and a treatment plan agreed prior to commencing treatment to ascertain the client needs. Before you begin the treatment the record card must be completed. Remember to get the client's signature prior to treatment.

Tip The products within a skincare product range are designed to work together in harmony.

Tip Once a good-quality skincare product has been used on the client it often sells itself as they feel the benefits from professional skincare products.

Tip It is important to educate the client about the benefits of using correct skincare products and a routine for their homecare. Spending the money on a facial skincare treatment to improve their skin is no use to them if they then go home to bad habits such as using soap and water!

Tip When planning the facial treatment you may agree with your client to book a course of several treatments to be taken over a few weeks. These treatments may vary as in the different types of mask and possibly exfoliation used; this will help to vary the treatment for the client and prevent it from becoming overfamiliar. Explain to your client that a tailor-made package will provide maximum benefit for them with their skin type and condition.

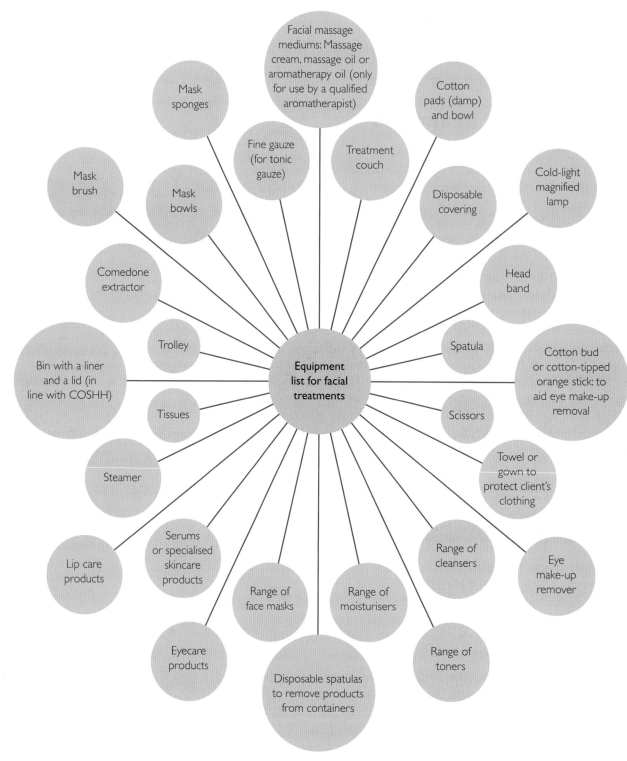

▲ Equipment for facial treatments

Set up work area

This is specific to the skin care treatments unit; see Chapter 2 Health and safety for generic set-up details.

The following should be noted:

- Place a blanket or large towel with a disposable covering where the client will lay on it.
- Place a hand towel over the back of the bed to use to wipe your hands in between product application.
- It is beneficial to complete facial treatment in an area that has a sink, to rinse mask sponges, your hands etc.

Preparing the client

- Carry out a consultation with the client and agree the treatment plan. Check for contraindications and check the results of skin sensitivity testing before commencing treatment.
- Contact lenses should be removed.
- Ask the client to remove any accessories that may be in your work area, e.g. earrings or necklace. It is very important to do this to avoid catching the jewellery during the treatment and also for health and safety if a steaming or skin-warming treatment is to be performed as metal conducts heat and this could burn the client's skin.
- Accompany the client to the treatment area and instruct them that they will need to remove any clothing from around the shoulder area as this will need to be exposed in order to perform the massage. Explain that you will leave the client to get changed and return in a few moments.
- Position the client comfortably on the treatment couch, either lying flat or with the back rest slightly elevated.
- Protect the client's clothing – wrap the client in a blanket for warmth and place a towel over the client's chest.
- Gently lift and secure the client's hair off their face – use a headband, turban or towel.

Tip A heated electric blanket can be used on the treatment couch to keep the client warm and cosy.

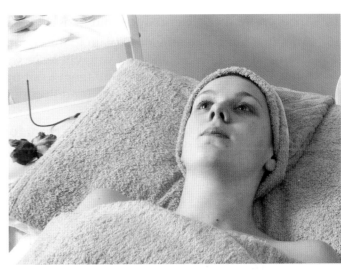

▲ Preparation of the client, bed and trolley set up

Facial procedure

1. **Sterilise equipment:** before your client comes in for the treatment you should make sure all your equipment is sterilised, disinfected and prepared, your trolley is in order and your record card and treatment plan are ready to be completed.

2. **Consultation process:** use the record card during the consultation process. Stop when you get up to the skin analysis section as this will be completed after the superficial cleanse.

3. Wash hands.

4. **Remove make-up:** remove eye and lip make-up and complete the superficial cleanse, using the appropriate cleanser.

5. **Carry out skin analysis:** record the findings from the skin analysis on the record card/treatment plan. (A cold-light magnifying lamp can be used for better visibility.)

6. Deep cleanse and tone.

7. Exfoliate.

8. Steam and extraction.

9. **Facial massage:** this massage should take approximately 10 minutes.

10. Use damp cotton wool to remove the massage medium.

11. Apply face mask and eye pads. Cover the client's exposed shoulders with a towel to keep them warm during the mask development stage.

12. Remove the mask thoroughly using damp sponges.

13. Apply tonic gauze if required.

14. Tone, apply specialist products and moisturise.

15. **Announce end of treatment:** explain to the client the treatment has finished and that you will leave the room to allow them to get dressed. Remind them to sit up slowly as massage lowers the blood pressure (and they may feel dizzy if they get up too quickly).

16. **Explain aftercare and homecare:** ask the client to take a seat whilst you explain the aftercare and homecare advice. This is the perfect time to discuss retail products and rebook the next appointment.

Health and Safety

When the practical treatment is completed and you leave the room to allow the client to get dressed, stay within earshot of the room in case the client needs any help. Explain to the client the importance of not rushing when getting dressed and trying not to bend the head downward as that may make them feel dizzy due to the lowering of the blood pressure from the massage.

Cleansing routine

Using rhythmical movements with a lighter pressure than the massage movements. This breaks down make-up, everyday dirt, pollutants, sebum and desquamates the skin to cleanse it. These movements also feel relaxing for the client and gently increase the circulation to warm the skin tissues. Remove eye and lip make-up first before proceeding to the superficial cleansing routine. If any residue from this process is left on the skin, it should be removed.

Removing eye make-up

1. Place pads under eyelashes. Ask the client to look up while you place damp cotton wool pads cut in half under the eyelashes. Ask the client to close their eyes and use the appropriate eye make-up removing product with the ring finger working in circular motions inward towards the nose.

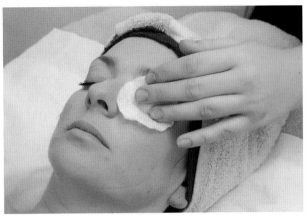

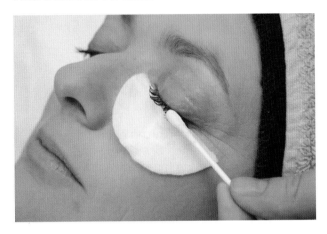

2. Use a fresh piece of damp cotton wool and gently wipe the eye, working from the outer and inner corner to remove the product and remove the piece of cotton wool from under the eye. This procedure may need to be repeated if the client is wearing a heavy eye make-up.

3. If the client is wearing waterproof mascara, repeat step 1 but take a cotton bud or a cotton-tipped orange stick dipped in oily eye make-up remover and use it in gentle circular motions on the lashes for removal. This procedure may need to be repeated until the mascara has been completely removed. You may wish to use the non-oily eye make-up remover as in step 1 to remove any oily residue.

Removing lip make-up

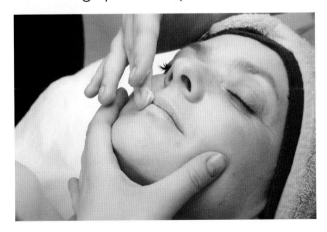

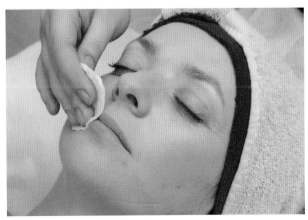

1. Ask the client to put their lips together. Using the appropriate cleansing product on your ring finger, use gentle circular motions across the lips to dissolve the make-up.

2. Using a damp piece of cotton wool, support the outer corner of the lips and gently remove the residue. This procedure may need to be repeated several times for any stubborn lip colour.

Superficial cleansing routine

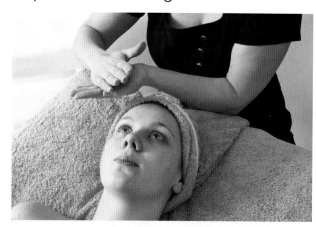

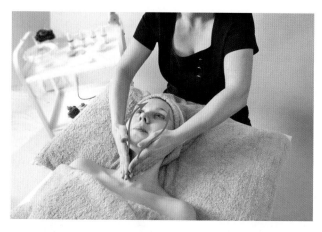

1. Remove product from its container. Use a clean spatula to remove the product if it is in a container and gently warm in your hands by rubbing the palms together for a few seconds.

2. Apply the products beginning at the neck with effleurage-style movements. Move up and over the cheek area and onto the forehead, applying gentle pressure while sliding the palms down on either side of the face and back to the neck area. Repeat three times.

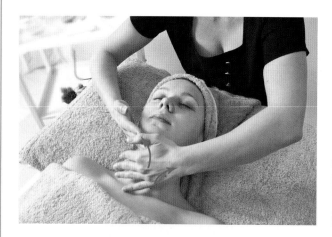

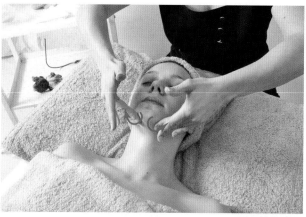

3. Place the hands on the lower neck on the right-hand side. Using the palm of the hands in an upward rolling movement towards the lower jaw, work across to the left side and then back again to the right. Repeat this three times.

4. Place the middle two fingers of both hands on the jaw line to the centre of the chin. Gently slide the fingers out towards the end of the jaw line and back to the start. Repeat this three times.

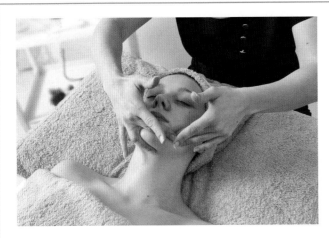

5. Separate the middle two fingers and place them on the left side of the chin, resting them on the jaw. Gently sweep across to the right-hand side of the chin so that the middle finger is on the chin and the ring finger rests just below it. As you reach the right side with the left hand, begin the same procedure from right to left with one continual movement. Repeat three times.

6. Place the middle two fingers of both hands on the right-hand side of the chin. Keep the left hand still as the right-hand gently slides outwards towards the ear. Repeat this procedure, working to the zygomatic bone, and gently slide the hands back to the starting point. Repeat three times. Use the same procedure on the left-hand side of the face. The left hand will be the working hand.

7. Place the fingertips on the chin and gently slide the hands upward, to the forehead.

8. Place the middle two fingers just above the centre of the eyebrows and gently slide them outward, towards the hairline. Use gentle pressure to return to just above the starting point and repeat, moving upwards each time until you reach the hairline. Then begin again in between the centre of the eyebrows. Repeat the whole movement three times.

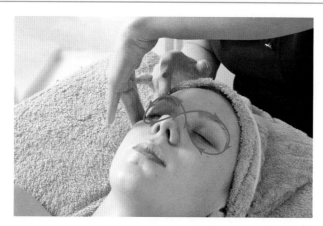

9. Gently rest the middle two fingers of the right hand just above the outer corner of the right eyebrow with the middle two fingers of the left hand just below it. Use the middle two fingers of the left hand to gently slide down under the right eye towards the nose up, over the left eyebrow and round the lower part of the left eye, and up over the nose across the upper right eyebrow in a figure-of-eight movement. Gently slide both hands to the left eyebrow using the fingertips and rest them just above the outer corner. Repeat the figure-of-eight movements. The right hand becomes the working hand. Repeat this three times with each hand.

10. Slide the fingertips down either side of the face, applying very gentle pressure just below either side of the jaw line.

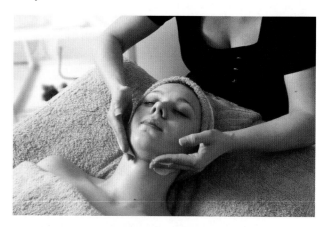

11. Remove the cleanser using damp cotton wool pads.

Deep cleansing routine

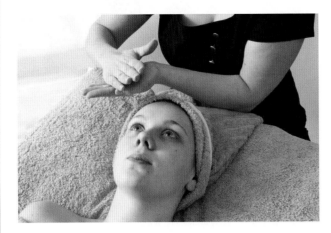

1. Remove the product from its container. Use a clean spatula to remove the product from its container and gently warm it in your hands by rubbing the palms together for a few seconds.

2. Apply the products beginning at the neck with effleurage-style movements. Move up and over the cheek area and onto the forehead, applying gentle pressure while sliding the palms down either side of the face back and to the neck area. Repeat three times.

3. Place the hands on the right-hand side of the lower neck. Using the palm of the hands in an upward rolling movement towards the lower jaw, work across to the left side and then back again to the right. Repeat this three times.

4. Place the middle two fingers of both hands on the jaw line, to the centre of the chin. Using a small circular motion, move the fingers out towards to the end of the jaw line and with very light pressure slide them back to the start. Repeat this three times.

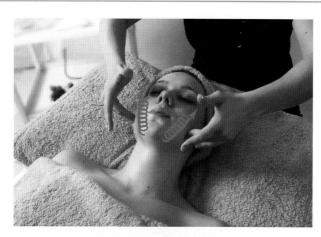

5. Place the middle two fingers of both hands on the centre of the chin. Keep both hands moving in a circular motion over the chin and outwards towards the ear. Repeat this procedure working to the zygomatic bone and gently slide the hands back to the starting point. Repeat three times.

6. Place the fingertips on the chin and gently slide the hands upwards towards the forehead.

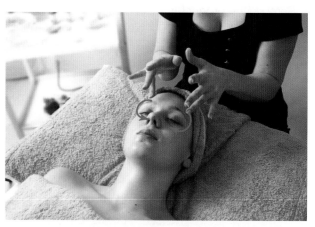

8. Place the ring finger of both hands on the upper, outer portion of the eyebrows and with one continual movement, circle gently around the eye area. Repeat three times.

7. Place the middle two fingers just above the centre of the eyebrows and gently use finger circles outwards toward the hairline. Use gentle pressure to return to just above the starting point and repeat, moving upwards each time until you reach the hairline. Begin again in between the centre of the eyebrows and repeat the whole movement three times.

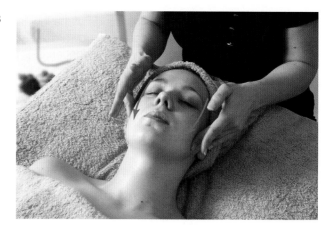

9. Slide the fingertips down either side of the face, applying very gentle pressure just below either side of the jaw line.

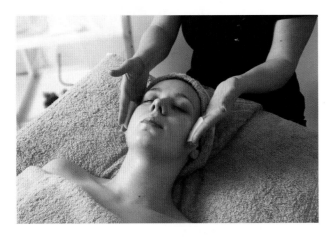

10. Remove the cleanser using damp cotton wool pads.

N.B.: When using abrasive exfoliators, follow the superficial cleansing routine. Follow with damp mask sponges and steaming/hot towels.

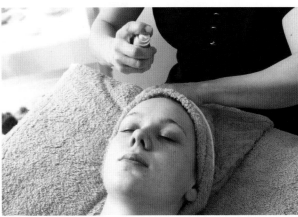

11. Follow with the appropriate toner on damp cotton wool pads. Begin on the neck and work upward onto the chin, over the cheek area and onto the forehead. Avoid the delicate eye area. If a spritz-style product is to be used, stand behind the client, tell them you are about to spray and ask them to close their eyes, take a deep breath and hold it for a few seconds whilst you spray the product and allow it to dry.

Facial massage movements

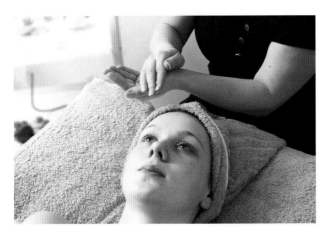

1. Remove the massage medium from the container using a clean spatula and warm it by rubbing the palms together for a few seconds.

2. Apply the massage medium with sweeping effleurage movements beginning on the shoulders, then the neck and upward onto the face. Repeat three times.

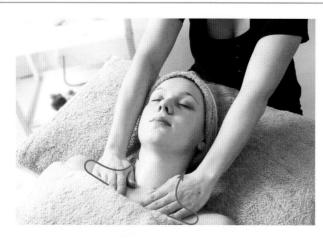

3. Place both hands on the sternum. Use effleurage movements across the shoulders, around the back and up along the back of the neck. Return to the starting position. Repeat three times, slowly and rhythmically.

4. With both hands on the sternum and using the pads of the fingers, make small circular movements three times, then move outwards to the front of the shoulder just above the axillae and circle three times. Move around to the back of the shoulders, keeping contact at all times with the client skin, and circle three times. Then move in circles on the trapezius muscle at the back of the neck three times. Move back to the sternum and repeat the whole procedure three times.

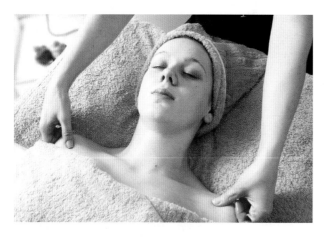

5. Repeat Step 4 using thumb circles.

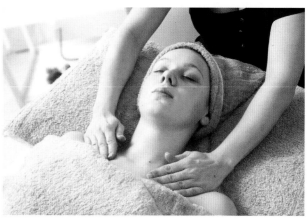

6. Repeat Step 4 using palm circles.

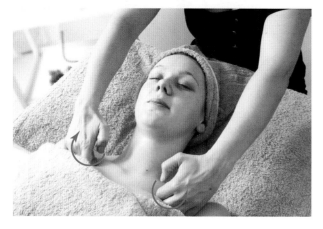

7. Repeat Step 4 while gently using the knuckles (don't use this movement if the client has prominent bone structure as it could feel uncomfortable).

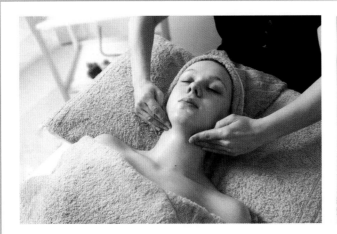

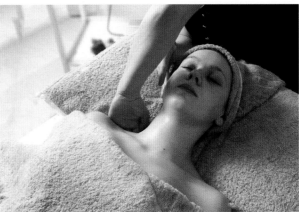

8. Move the hands in imaginary petal shapes (petaling), starting from the sternum and working from one side to the other. Place the hands side-by-side and using the middle two fingers, gently slide upward just before the jaw bone and gently back down to the starting position.

9. Perform a full neck and shoulder brace three times from side to side. Gently place the middle two fingers of the left-hand on the right side of the jaw. Using the right hand and sweeping effleurage movements, move down the back of the neck and along the trapezius towards the deltoid, on to the shoulder, and across towards the sternum. Work towards the other shoulder and up along the left side of the neck. Reverse this movement by placing the right middle two fingers on the left side of the jaw. The left-hand becomes the working hand.

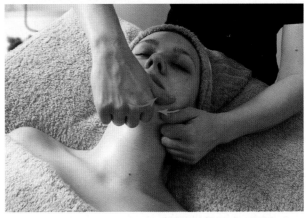

10. Perform finger rolling from side to side on the neck and working upward. Using the middle of the fingers with light pressure, particularly over the throat, work from right to left and begin on the lower part of the neck working upwards towards the jaw. The hands continually move in an upward rolling motion.

11. Knead from side to side on the jaw line with the finger and thumb. Do this three times. Using the outer edge of the index finger and thumb, gently knead, keeping both hands moving across the jaw line from side to side.

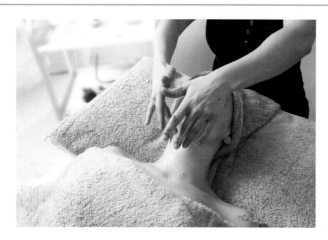

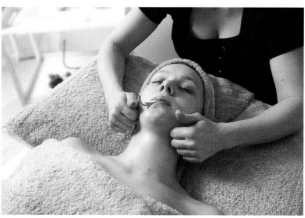

12. Carry out tapotement along the jaw line using two taps, then one tap working from side to side three times. Use the pads of the middle two fingers to perform a rhythmical but gentle tapping motion.

13. Begin thumb flicks gently along the laughter lines. Using the outer side of the thumbs and beginning on the chin in line with the corners of the mouth, gently flick the skin in an upward motion. Keep the movements going to the top of the smile lines just at the sides of the nostrils. Gently slide the thumbs back to the starting point.

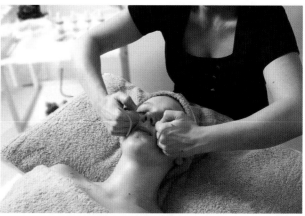

14. Gently pinch the skin three times along the laughter lines, working upward. Using the outer sides of the thumb and index finger, very gently squeeze the skin, working from the chin in line with the corners of the mouth and upward towards the nostrils. Let your fingers gently slide back down to the starting point.

15. Gently roll the fist three times up and down along the laughter lines. Begin on the chin in line with the corners of the mouth, working upward towards the nostrils and gently sliding back down. (Note that this movement must be performed with very gentle pressure.)

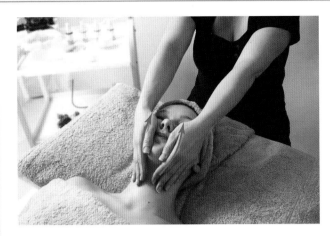

16. Using the whole hand, place both hands on the lower neck. Let the heel of the hand lead the movement and gently pull upward, taking care over the facial contours and to not apply too much pressure. Work upward over the cheeks, avoiding the nose and pressure on the eyes, and then upward over the forehead to the hairline. Gently slide down either side of the face using the pads of the fingers and place both hands on the jaw on the right side for the next movement. Do this only once.

17. Finger roll upward along the cheeks, moving across three times and working from the sides of the nose out towards the ears. Repeat this on the other side. The whole procedure should be done three times in total (these are the same movements as performed on the neck as in Step 10.

19. Repeat this once as in Step 16.

20. Finger roll from side to side, working on the forehead. Do this three times, as in Steps 10 and 17.

21. Perform finger friction on forehead as in Step 18.

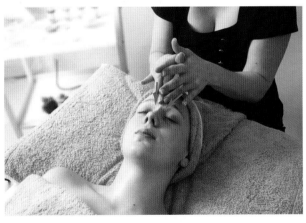

18. Perform finger frictions. Use the middle two fingers inside each other and work from the jaw upward to the cheekbone and gently sliding back down to the jaw. (Ensure the pressure is gentle on the cheekbone.)

22. Using the pads of the ring finger, perform single-finger friction on the middle of the forehead. Only work from in between the eyebrows and towards the hairline, sliding gently back down to begin the next movement.

23. Gently place the middle and ring fingers on the top and bottom of the eyebrow, with the tips of the fingers pointing inward. Begin at the centre, working outward and gently slide the fingers outward to the outer end of the eyebrow. Then place the pads of all four fingers on the underside of the eyebrow. Work back to the centre of the eyebrows using a lifting motion – a walking action with the fingers.

24. Start at the centre of the eyebrows. Using the outer portion of the index finger and thumb, gently pinch and squeezing and working outwards along the eyebrows. Place the finger and thumb so the eyebrows are between them. Slide back to the centre starting position. Repeat three times.

26. Perform this once as in Steps 16 and 19.

27. Using effleurage movements, sweep along the shoulders and neck, as in Step 2.

25. Using the middle two fingers, place the left-hand on the chin side of the right jaw. Move outward over the cheeks with T-strokes. The left hand works upwards and simultaneously the right hand strokes outwards towards the ear. This is a lymphatic drainage movement.

28. Prayers, along jaw line, working outwards. Place the heels of hands on the centre the jaw with the hands together. With the heels of the hands leading the movement, the hands separate to slide along the jaw line to its outer side and then with little pressure, gently slide back to the starting position. Repeat three times.

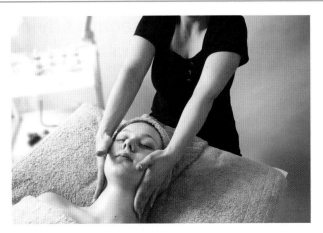

29. Raindrops on the face, working from the jaw upward to the forehead and down the sides of the face back to the beginning. Using the pads of all four fingers individually, move in a tapping motion.

30. Place the palms of the hands on either side of the jaw. Tense the arms to give a gentle vibrating motion.

31. Perform this once as in Steps 16, 19 and 26.

32. Begin just above the centre of the eyebrows and stroke along the forehead, working upward. The heel of the hand leads the gentle backward movement to the hairline. Keep one hand moving at all times. Repeat three times.

33. Carry out finger rolling three times, then apply gentle pressure onto the hairline and slowly release it (as in Steps 10, 17 and 20).

N.B.:All massage movements should be carried out three times unless otherwise stated.

Tip Applying light pressure to the hairline after the final movement of the massage is complete will signify to the client that the massage has come to an end. If the client falls asleep during the massage and does not awaken at this point, gently place your hand on their shoulder and quietly inform them that the massage has come to an end and you are about to apply the face mask. Otherwise, if you apply the face mask without taking this step it could make the client jump, as the mask may be cool and not knowing it is coming could spoil the therapeutic, relaxing benefits of the treatment.

Aftercare and homecare advice

During the consultation you will have gained information on the client's current skincare products and needs. It would be more sensible to try to retail products to the client that they are either running low on at home or don't currently have; they may be more inclined to purchase the products in this case.

This time will also enable you to advise the client and recap regarding the products that have been used during the treatment. This can also act as a sales tool as the client now knows how the products feel and may be more inclined to purchase them. It is also a good time to give the client some free samples of the products to try at home, also encouraging them to purchase the products in the future. Inform your client that most product ranges are compatible with each other and work best together.

This is also an excellent time to rebook the client's next skincare treatment appointment.

Purpose of giving aftercare and homecare advice

This can be very useful to both you and the client as you can:

- Advise on the suitability of homecare products for specific skincare needs and budgets; this will enable the client to get the maximum benefit from the treatment
- Advise on what products have been used during the facial skincare treatment and the benefits of those products
- Advise on further treatments
- Advise on frequency of treatments
- Ensure that the client knows the dos and don'ts for following the treatment
- Ensure that if the client purchases any retail products or is given any samples by you that they understand how to use them at home. Remember to record any purchases on the record card for future reference
- Epilation (hair removal) should not be carried out after facial skincare treatment.

Specific aftercare advice

It should be explained to the client that this advice should be followed 24–48 hours after the treatment given:

- The client should contact you if any adverse reaction occurs after the treatment
- Avoid heat treatments for 24–48 hours
- Avoid UV exposure for at least 24–48 hours following the treatment
- Try not to keep touching the area treated to avoid cross-contamination.

Specific homecare advice

This advice should be adhered to in between professional skincare appointments to get maximum benefit:

- Use the retail products regularly as recommended by the professional
- Follow the recommended skin care routine for homecare.

It is a good idea to give the client an aftercare and homecare advice leaflet, so they don't forget the advice that you have given them. This is also a good place to record the recommended retail products for the client and is therefore also an aid to selling.

Retail products

Retail products can be classified as follows:

- Cleansers
- Toners
- Moisturisers
- Eye treatment products
- Specialist skin treatments such as serums, night creams, exfoliators etc.
- Face masks
- Face washing cloths.

Health and Safety

Always check the manufacturers' instructions; these may vary between different product companies.

▲ Facial retail products

End of chapter knowledge test

1. Name three classifications of massage movements.
2. What type of movement do we start our massage routine with and why?
3. List three benefits of a facial massage.
4. Name two massage mediums.
5. Can you explain what a physical, physiological and psychological effect is?
6. Name three skin types.
7. Name two characteristics of a dry skin type.
8. What is meant by the term exfoliation?
9. Name three benefits of facial steaming.
10. Name three contraindications to a facial treatment.
11. Name two different types of cleanser.
12. Why do we use a toning lotion?
13. What type of water do we use in the steamer and why?
14. Name two types of face mask?

CHAPTER 7

Applying make-up

Units covered by this chapter:

NVQ Level 2 Unit B8: Provide make-up services

NVQ Level 2 Unit B9: Instruct clients in the application of skin care products and make-up

VRQ Level 2: Apply make-up

Chapter aims

This chapter will look at:

- A range of skills and techniques for make-up application for day, evening and special occasion
- Product information
- Colour theory.

This chapter will help you to understand and develop skills to enhance, define and even alter the features of the face with make-up. It is up to you to decide what degree you want to enhance or define your client's or artist's features. This chapter will give you useful advice on working on those with different skin tones and types.

Make-up application is an amazing art. You can create so many different looks and when make-up is applied well, it boosts the wearer's confidence, helps them to play different characters, and also helps to cover birthmarks, scars and imperfections. Make-up can create special effects, make 'monsters' look real and much more.

Wherever we go we see the effects of make-up application – in TV, films, books, magazines, billboards, on buses and in newspapers; we are surrounded by it in images that people want to aspire to. Role models or people who we like may influence the way we decide to present ourselves and often create trends with hair and make-up.

History of make-up application

The history of make-up is fantastic and goes back many years to the ancient Egyptians and Greeks, the medieval, Elizabethan and eighteenth-century time periods and many more. It is fascinating to look back and see that people were so concerned about image and fashion way back then. Vintage styles are currently very much back in fashion.

Make-up use today

Make-up has become so advanced now and is a part of many people's everyday lives. As a nation, we spend millions of pounds on make-up products.

Equipment list

The following list is a general guide to the things you will need to have on hand if providing a make-up application service:

- Towels, robe or a shawl (to protect clothing)
- Hair pins and head bands to remove hair from the face
- Client record cards and face charts
- Hand sanitiser
- Cotton wool
- Make-up remover or facial wipes
- Cleanser, toner and moisturiser
- Cotton buds and tissues
- Make-up brushes
- Sponges or make-up wedges
- Powder puffs
- Spatulas
- Palette
- Sharpener
- Disposable mascara wands (you must sanitise reusable wands after each use)
- Comb and brush
- Foundation (with a good selection and variety of products to suit all skin types and skin tones)
- Concealer and corrective make-up palette
- Highlighters and shaders
- Translucent powders
- Eye shadows
- Eyeliners (pencil, liquid and gel)
- Mascaras (regular, waterproof, clear, brown and black)
- Individual and strip lashes
- Eye lash glue
- Blushers
- Lip liners
- Lipsticks and lip balms
- Lip gloss
- Brush cleaner
- Mirror.

 Remember . . .

Check that you have the right equipment needed to perform each job. Ensure you are set up correctly and you have everything to hand. If you are mobile, or a freelance make-up artist, it is very wise to check whether the location you will work in has a make-up mirror and if not, hire a portable make-up mirror).

Make-up and products
Foundation

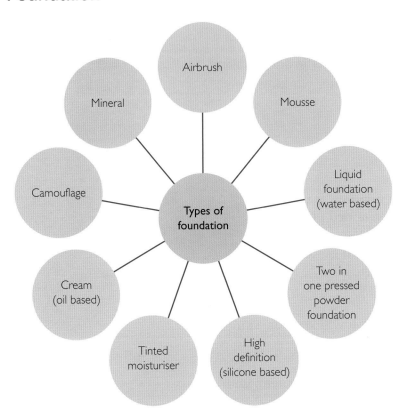

▲ Types of foundation

Camouflage

- **Skin type**: Suitable for all skin types
- **Coverage/texture**: Provides excellent full coverage without looking like a heavy, thick application
- **Ingredients**: High pigment content in make-up
- **Important notes to remember**: This product is water resistant and excellent for covering hyperpigmentation, hypopigmentation, erythema, bruising, scars, birthmarks and tattoos. This product is available on the NHS.

▲ Camouflage make-up

Liquid foundation (oil and water)

- **Skin type**: Suitable for normal or combination skin. Matte/ medicated foundations are available for oily or greasy skin types
- **Coverage/texture**: Light coverage semi-matte finish (this produces a light, natural look in photos and on screen)
- **Ingredients**: Pigment, minerals, wax, titanium dioxide, cerasin
- **Important notes to remember**: It has a shorter working time on application than cream foundation.

Tinted moisturiser

- **Skin type**: Suitable for all skin types
- **Coverage/texture**: Natural coverage
- **Ingredients**: The same as liquid foundation, as well as moisturise humectants, oil and water, added pigments
- **Important notes to remember**: It is very useful for light coverage and gives a very natural effect. It is especially good for use on children and men.

▲ Liquid foundation

Cream make-up (water in oil)

- **Skin type**: Suitable for most skin types. It will keep the skin extra-moisturised
- **Coverage/texture**: Medium coverage
- **Ingredients**: This make-up contains a higher oil content, with pigment, minerals, wax, titanium dioxide and cerasin
- **Important notes to remember**: It is available in compact and pan stick forms. It is long lasting when used with setting products such a translucent powder.

Tinted gel

- **Skin type**: Suitable for most skin types. This is not a full coverage foundation so works better on unblemished skins
- **Coverage/texture**: Provides very light, transparent coverage
- **Ingredients**: Pigments in a water-based gel
- **Important notes to remember**: It is light, transparent coverage and very good for giving a sun-kissed look and healthy glow (gels can be drying).

Bronzer

- **Skin type**: Suitable for most skin types.
- **Coverage/texture**: Gives very light, sheer coverage
- **Ingredients**: Pigments in a water-based gel
- **Important notes to remember**: It is generally used for giving a tanned glow. Working time is very short which products it can go sticky on application. When applied correctly it will give a very natural, sun-kissed glow to the skin. It is good for use on both males and females.

Mousse

- **Skin type**: Suitable for all skin types
- **Coverage/texture**: This gives light, sheer coverage and is very natural looking
- **Ingredients**: Pigment, minerals, wax, titanium dioxide and cerasin. Available in either oil or water base

Two-in-one foundation

- **Skin type**: Suitable for oily skin type (because of its very high powder content – it helps to absorb oils)
- **Coverage/texture**: Medium to heavy coverage with a matte finish
- **Ingredients**: Contains power producers or a small amount of mineral oil, talc and kaolin pigments
- **Important notes to remember**: Make-up is very durable and lasts a long time on the skin.

High definition

See Chapter 14 for more information on high definition make-up.

- **Skin type**: Suitable for normal, combination or dry skin types (oily skin types will need to be powdered well)
- **Coverage/texture**: Full coverage. Provides a light, very natural finish
- **Ingredients**: Silicone and strong pigment
- **Important notes to remember**: Provides full coverage very similar to that of an airbrush – a very natural finish.

Airbrush

For information on this type of make-up, see Chapter 10.

Concealers

To camouflage dark circles under the eyes, broken capilliaries, blemishes, rosacea and minor inperfections (for example, birthmarks and minor scars) and uneven pigmentation. Various shades are available.

▲ Corrective make-up palette

Highlighter and shaders

For highlighting, shading and contouring the face to enhance features. Available in a variety of shades to suit all skin types.

Powder

A lightweight powder for setting make-up and controlling shine.

Eyeshadow

Eyeshadows are available in a wide range of colours and are used to enhance the eyes. They come in a variety of forms including powder, liquid and cream. Depending on the type, they can give a sheer, matte or shimmery finish.

Eyeliner

Used for highlighting and defining the eyes. They come in a variety of forms, including pencil, liquid and gel or cream.

▲ Highlighters and shaders

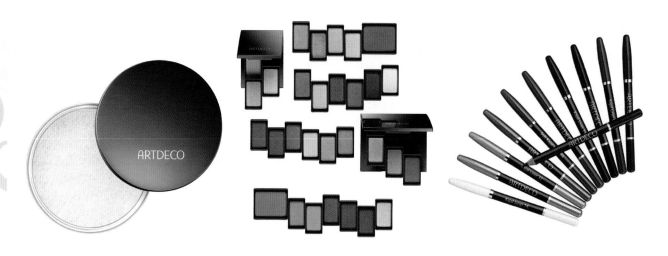

▲ Translucent powder   ▲ Eye shadows   ▲ Eyeliners

Mascara

Mascaras are used to enhance the eyes. They can darken, thicken or lengthen the eyelashes, depending on the type used. Mascaras come in liquid, cake and cream form. Some mascaras are waterproof and water-resistant – these have formulas that repel water and minimise smudging and running. An oil-based remover is required to remove these types of mascara. Thickening mascaras have wax and silicone polymers that coat the lashes and add volume. Lengthening mascaras have plastic polymers that cling to the lashes to extend them.

▲ Mascara

Blusher

These are available in powder, cream and gel or liquid form and are used to enhance the cheeks and emphasise the cheekbones. Powder blush is the densest type and is particularly suitable for oily skins. Cream blushes offer the most intense shade. Their moisturising ingredients make them particularly suitable for dry skins. Liquid or gel blushes give a sheer glow and are good for normal to oily skin.

Lip liner

Used to outline and define the lips. Lip liners are available in pencil form and in a variety of colours to match your lip colour.

Lip colour

Lip colours can include lipsticks and glosses. They come in a wide variety of shades and can give complete coverage or a hint of colour, depending on the product chosen. Finishes can be shimmery, glittery or matte. Common ingredients include wax, oil and pigments, as well as fragrance, alcohol and preservatives. New forms of lip colour include lip injection, which stimulates the lips to create plumpness and natural colour.

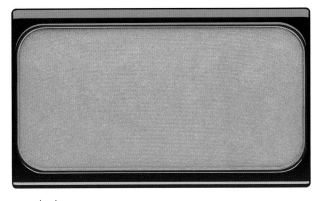

▲ Blusher

▲ Lip liner   ▲ Lipstick   ▲ Lip gloss

Make-up Brushes

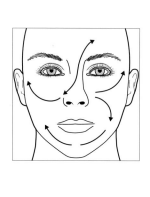

▲ Foundation brush: To apply and blend liquid or cream foundation flawlessly without absorbing excess product.

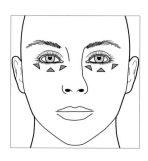

▲ Concealer brush: A smooth, firm brush to apply liquid or cream concealer under the eyes or to small spots on the face.

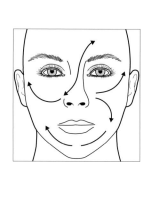

▲ Powder brush: An extra large paddle-shaped brush with a softly rounded top for smooth application of powder to the face.

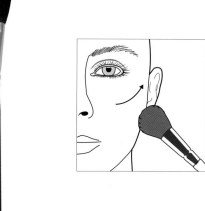

▲ Blusher brush: Gently pointed tip allows easy and precise blush application.

▲ Eye shader brush: For all over eye shadow application; the shape holds and distributes colour smoothly and evenly.

▲ Smudger: Firmer hair makes this brush ideal for smudging colours together.

▲ Pencil crease: To apply precision eye colour and gently blend at the crease.

▲ Brow and lash comb: To comb clumps out of the lashes and brush brows into shape.

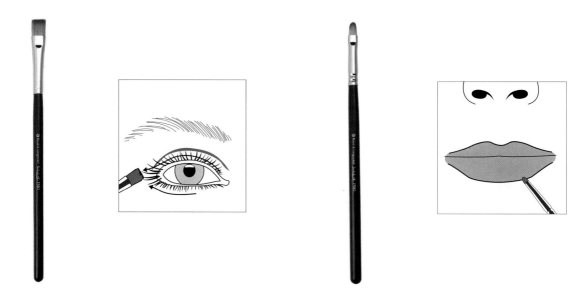

▲ Eyeliner brush: Firm brush to add instant definition to the eyes.

▲ Lip brush: Firm, gently pointed brush for precision application of lipstick, also ideal as a lip liner.

▲ Eyebrow brush: Small angular brush easily adds colour to brows; also ideal for creating a dramatic line at base of lash.

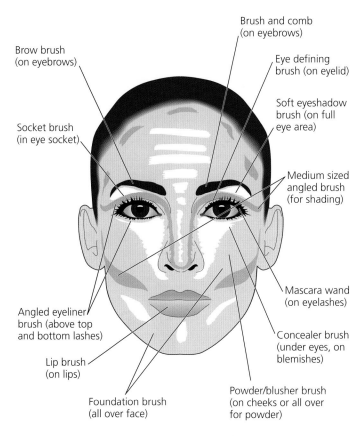

Brush and comb
(on eyebrows)

Brow brush
(on eyebrows)

Eye defining
brush (on eyelid)

Soft eyeshadow
brush (on full
eye area)

Socket brush
(in eye socket)

Medium sized
angled brush
(for shading)

Angled eyeliner
brush (above top
and bottom lashes)

Mascara wand
(on eyelashes)

Concealer brush
(under eyes, on
blemishes)

Lip brush
(on lips)

Foundation brush
(all over face)

Powder/blusher brush
(on cheeks or all over
for powder)

▲ Where on the face each brush is used

Brush cleaning

Use gently shampoo and lukewarm water. Reshape and lie flat to dry completely for best results.

Skin types

For more details on different skin types please refer to Chapter 6 Skin care

Face shapes

It is very important that you know your face shapes as well as possible. Take time to study the subject's face shape without any make-up on; you can do this by observing visually or by touch. It is important that you have a good idea of what you are working with, because it becomes easier to enhance the overall appearance.

Assessing clients' face shapes

Take time to study the shape of each face and assess the following:

- Size
- Shape
- Bone structure
- Areas of excess tissue
- Muscle tone.

In order to make the best assessment of the face:

- Pull hair back from forehead
- Look at jaw line
- Look at cheekbones
- Look at the fullness of the cheeks.

These shapes should help you determine corrective work needed:

Oval shape

The oval shape is often referred to as the most perfect shape because of its balanced features. Corrective make-up applied normally tries to recreate this shape. You can draw attention to cheekbones by shading below the cheekbone and highlighting above the cheekbone. Blusher should be applied along the cheekbone, blended upwards to the temples.

Square shape

Those with square-shaped faces have a broad forehead and a broad, angular jaw line.

- **Corrective make-up method**: Using a darker colour apply to the jawbone and blend up towards the cheekbone. Ensure blusher is applied in a circular pattern on the cheekbones and take it up and out towards the temples.

Heart shape

Heart-shaped faces have a wide forehead, with the face tapering to a narrow.

- **Corrective make-up method**: Lighten the angles of the jawbone. Darken the point of the chin, temples and side of the forehead. Apply blusher in an upward and outward direction towards the temples.

Diamond shape

This face shape is characterised by a narrow forehead with wide cheekbones tapering to a narrow chin.

- **Corrective make-up method**: Apply a darker colour to the tip of the chin and the forehead to reduce length. Use a lighter colour for the sides of the temple and lower jaw. Apply blusher to the fullness of the cheekbones to draw attention to the centre of the face.

▲ Oval face shape

▲ Square face shape

▲ Heart face shape

▲ Diamond face shape

Circle shape

The circle-shaped face is usually wider than the oval-shaped face, with fuller cheeks and often a non-prominent or a rounded chin. A round-shaped face tends to have that baby-face look.

- **Method for corrective make-up**: Couture under the cheekbones, the temples and under the jaw line to give the illusion of a more defined bone structure.

Triangle shape

Those with a triangle-shaped face type have a dominant jaw line that narrows at the cheekbones and forehead.

- **Method for corrective make-up**: Countering under the cheekbones will help to add some width to the face.

Oblong shape

This corrective make-up should reduce the length of the face.

- **Method for corrective make-up**: you can achieve this by applying shader to the tip of the chin and and narrowest part of the forehead. Apply highlighter to the temples and lower jaw and cheeks to add fullness.

▲ Round face shape

▲ Triangle face shape

Principles of colour

- The colours we see depend on the colour of the light source, the colours of any filters used and the colours of the objects that reflect in the light.
- In the retina at the back of the eye, there are two kinds of cells; these respond to light focused on them by the lens of the eye.
- One sort is for colourless vision in dim light and the other for colour perception in bright light.
- The colour wheel or colour circle is used by artists and decorators for distinguishing colours and can also be applied to the colours of make-up, which include paints for the face as follows:
  1. **Primary paint colours: red, blue and yellow**; when mixed with equal proportions, this will produce **grey**
  2. **Secondary paint colours: orange, green and violet**; these are each made by mixing two adjacent primary colours
  3. **In-between colours**: made by mixing more of one colour than the other colour, for example, **bluish green** and **greenish blue**
  4. **Tints**: made by adding **white** – this can produce colours such as **opal**
  5. **Shades**: made by adding **black** – this can produce colours such as **emerald**
  6. **Hue**: pure colour

▲ Oblong face shape

7. **Tint**: ranging from any hue white
8. **Shades**: ranging from any pure hue to black
9. **Tones**: ranging from any pure hue to grey.

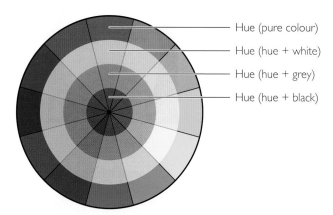

Hue (pure colour)
Hue (hue + white)
Hue (hue + grey)
Hue (hue + black)

▲ Classifying colour wheel

Classifying colour

Grey scale

The principles of greyscale are as follows:

- Brightness represents the range from light to dark.
- From any light colour to any dark colour there is a brightness scale.
- The scale of greys is simply because there are no hues.
- The darkness or the lightness of a colour – its position on the range – is called its **value**.
- A light colour has a high value while a dark colour has a low value.

▲ The greyscale

Intensity

Intensity is the range from any pure hue to a point of the greyscale. A grey blue, for example, has a blue hue yet is different from the pure blue on the colour wheel. Although it is of the same hue (blue), it is of lower intensity; it is nearer to the centre of the wheel, and more grey. The colours on the outside of the wheel are brilliant; those nearer the centre of the wheel are less brilliant and known as tones.

The principles of colour are as follows:

- White light is a mixture of many different wavelengths.
- If you shine a beam of white light through a glass prism, the rays are a multicoloured spectrum.
- The spectrum can be seen if something is placed in its path.
- The order of the colours is always the same as the order as seen in a rainbow: violet, indigo, blue, green, yellow, orange and red.

Primary colours

The mixing of primary colours is as follows:

Yellow + Blue = Green
Red + Yellow = Orange
Blue + Red = Violet

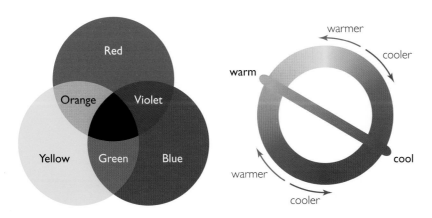

▲ Mixing colours   ▲ Warm and cool colours

Colour harmony when using colour pigments

The colour wheel explains the principle of colour harmony. One colour changes to another by the process of mixing colours, which can be combined in many ways. All make-up artists need to understand the mixing of colours. Pigments are unlike light; they are not pure, so mixing the same colour again is difficult. There is usually some trial and error involved. When you buy a colour with the same name from different manufacturers, the colour will never be the same.

Colour interaction

Colours advance and recede

Brighter colours make an area seem larger. For example, putting a brighter colour in the inner corner of the eye opens the eye out, making it seem larger. Darker colours close a space in.

Colours reflect other colours

When putting colours near other colours they reflect. For example, when you are wearing a bright colour your skin appears brighter and reflects that colour.

Colour will steal colour

A darker colour will steal the light from a lighter colour when placed next to each other, making the brighter colour stand out more than the lighter or paler colour.

Colour has temperature

Colours can be warm or cool depending on their lightness or darkness. For example, yellow and orange on the colour wheel are brighter and appear to stand out more; they appear further forward. Darker colours like blue will appear further away, which makes them cooler as they appear less intense.

Colour reacts with other colour

A colour can be changed depending on what it is placed next to. For example, a warmer colour such as yellow or red would appear warm next to one colour and cold next to another. This is because the hues are individual and therefore separately affected by the colours around them.

Colour is affected by light

Natural daylight will give off a bluish tone and artificial lighting will give off a yellowish tone. Fluorescent light gives off a green tone. The colour is changed by the colour of the surroundings it is placed in or near to.

Make-up application

Contraindications

Contraindications to the application of make-up include:

- Conjuctivitis
- Blepharitis
- Stye
- Bruising
- Active psoriasis or eczema
- Watery eye.

> **Anatomy and physiology**
> For further details of these contraindications please refer to Chapter 4 Anatomy and physiology.

Contra-actions

Contra-actions of the application of make-up include:

- Erythema
- Irritation and soreness of skin
- Eye irritation
- Blocked pores and pustules
- Allergic reactions
- Cracking of foundation.

Preparing for make-up application

When preparing your client or artist for application of make-up, you can use the following techniques:

- Use consultation techniques, e.g. open and closed questioning by observing their body language.
- Make notes by recording treatment details on a client record card or face chart.
- Record what the client or artist has agreed so that expectations are met.
- Take into consideration your subject's skin type and lifestyle so you can decide what type foundation would be best.
- Look at the underlying colours in the skin, skin type and tone to find the best colour match for your subject.
- Record the client's skin type and chosen colour.

The visual assessment figures show things that should be considered before applying make-up.

Anatomy and physiology
For further details of these contra-actions please refer to Chapter 4 Anatomy and physiology.

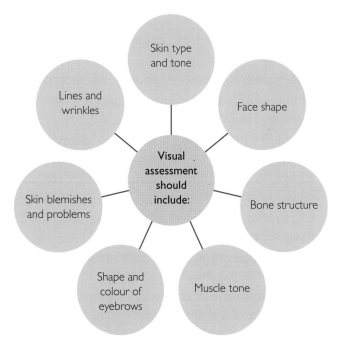

▲ Things to consider when applying make-up

Colour matching

After you have completed your consultation with your client or artist you will have observed the skin tone and it is time to do a colour match. You can do this by placing a small amount of the shade or tone of the make-up you have chosen onto the side of the subject's jaw line. Blend the make-up into the jaw line and work downwards into the neck. Work the make-up into the skin (if you are not happy with your choice you may need to mix a few colours together to achieve a perfect match or pick another

 Remember . . .

Make sure that you always look professional and smart, with your hair tied back and excellent personal hygiene. Oral hygiene is very important as you will be working very closely with people so it is wise to always have a toothbrush, toothpaste and mouthwash in your kit bag.

colour that is better matched to the skin tone. Repeat this until you find the perfect colour match. You should match the colour so it blends into the skin completely. When you are happy with the colour match you can start your application to the face and work on balancing out the skin tone.

Ask your client questions to identify whether they have any contraindications to skincare and make-up product use. Record accurately the client's response to the questions before ensuring:

- The client is seated comfortably
- The client has a good view of the mirror
- Accessories are removed and clothing and hair are effectively protected
- Skin is clean, moisturised and toned prior to application of make-up
- Skin type and condition, and age are recorded accurately
- Client is encouraged to ask questions so you can clarify treatment information
- Necessary information is gained to identify contraindications
- Client is given advice without reference to a medical condition and without causing alarm or concern
- Skincare and make-up instructions are clear (and understood) and that realistic expectations are agreed with the client prior to application
- Prior to application that agreement is reached about the service and acceptable outcomes to meet the client's needs
- Prior to application ensure objectivity is clear for make-up and skincare and are realistic and agreed to be suitable for the client's tone, condition, age-group and the occasion
- A suitable range of skincare and make-up products are available that suit the client's skin tone type and condition
- Necessary tools and equipment are available and at hand
- Face charts and client record cards are used to make accurate notes.

 Remember . . .

Do not forget to pay attention to personal hygiene, including no smoking.

 Remember . . .

Remember a make-up artist will dress differently to a beauty therapist, who may wear a very tidy and smart uniform. A make-up artist will tend to wear all black, be very smartly dressed and wearing sensible shoes.

 Health and Safety

Make sure you follow all safe working practices and legislation (see Chapter 2).

 *Remember . . .*

Ensure minors have consent from parent or guardian prior to using your service. Ensure that the parent or guardian is present throughout the service for minors under the age of 16.

 Health and Safety

Check your working area complies with health and safety regulations, for example; correct lighting and ventilation, correct height of chair and make-up station.

 Health and Safety

Dispose of waste responsibly. Most single-use items can be disposed of in a pedal bin with liners. Hazardous waste must be disposed of in line with current safety legislation.

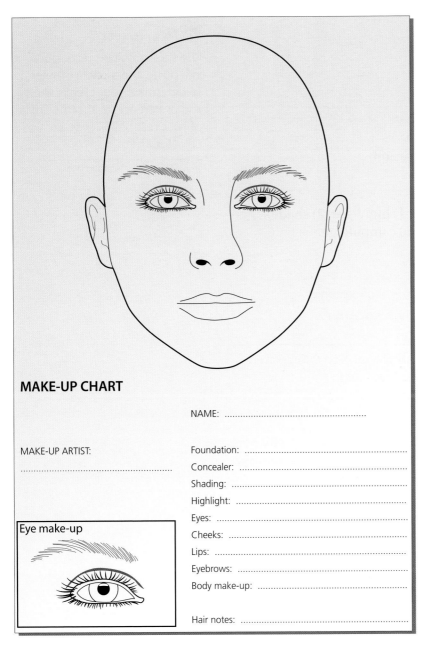

MAKE-UP CHART

MAKE-UP ARTIST:

....

Eye make-up

NAME: ....

Foundation: ....

Concealer: ....

Shading: ....

Highlight: ....

Eyes: ....

Cheeks: ....

Lips: ....

Eyebrows: ....

Body make-up: ....

Hair notes: ....

▲ Face chart

Hygiene techniques and procedures

- Sanitise tools and equipment
- Wash brushes in isopropyl alcohol (IPA) or antibacterial liquid soap. Allow to dry and place in a UV cabinet.
- Disinfect work surfaces
- Cover cuts and abrasions.

 Health and Safety

In practising excellent hygiene, remember to sanitise your hands with gels and sprays before and after make-up application, products are dispensed with a spatula, pump or spray and use disposable products whenever possible.

 Health and Safety

Avoid overexposure when using chemicals by replacing lids on uncapped bottles and pots.

Health and Safety

Check the end date (use-by date) for any products and store them away from heat, damp and direct sunlight.

 Health and Safety

Make sure all your equipment is sanitised and all items are labelled clearly.

Corrective make-up

Use corrective make-up to:

- enhance facial features
- soften a problem area
- draw out the best features
- make features bigger or smaller
- prepare the face for a specific occasion.

Correction methods

Correction make-up can be used to: 1) highlight, 2) shade, 3) blush, 4) contour, 5) conceal and 6) camouflage.

Correction methods for different skin types

High colour **Green** colour corrector or Yellow	Yellow undertones **Lilac concealer**
Ashy Asian skin **Blue** neutraliser	Dark shadows on Asian skin Orange/coral

Forehead shapes

- **Forehead is prominent**: Apply a darker colour centrally over the prominent area, blending outwards, towards the temples.
- **Forehead is shallow**: Apply a lighter colour in a narrow band beneath the hairline.
- **Forehead is deep**: Apply a darker colour in a narrow band beneath the hairline.

Lip shapes

- **Thick lips**: Select natural colours and darker shades. Avoid bright and glossy colours. Blend foundation over the lips to disguise the natural lip line. Apply a darker lip liner inside the natural lip line to create a new line.
- **Thin lips**: Apply brighter, pearlised colours. Avoid darker colours, which make the mouth appear smaller. Apply neutral lip liner just outside natural lip line.
- **Uneven lips**: Use a lip liner to draw in a new lip line that balances the lips out evenly. Apply lipstick to the lips, filling in the area where you have balanced the lips.

> *Remember...*
>
> Use the consultant techniques in a polite and friendly manner to determine your client's needs and preferences within the limits of your responsibility as a make-up artist.

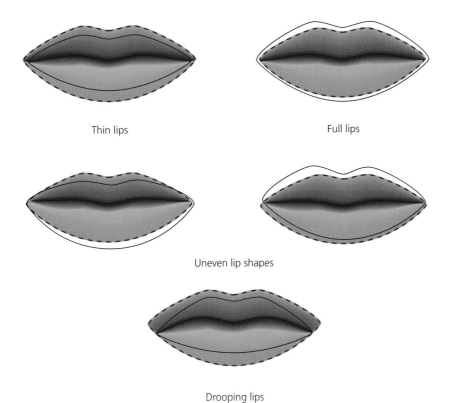

Thin lips

Full lips

Uneven lip shapes

Drooping lips

▲ Lip shapes

Nose shapes

- **Broad nose**: Apply a darker colour (about two shades darker than the foundation) to the sides; this will make the nose appear to be thinner.
- **Short nose**: Apply a lighter colour (two shades lighter than the foundation) in a thin band from the bridge to the tip; this will help to make the nose appear longer.
- **Long nose**: Apply a darker colour to the tip of nose and blend it in; this will appear shorten the nose.
- **Bump on the nose**: Apply a darker colour over the area and blend it in; this will create a shadow. Remember that shading creates a reducing effect.
- **Crooked nose**: Apply darker colour over the crooked side to balance out the nose, and blend it in.
- **Hollow along bridge of the nose**: Apply a lighter colour to the hollow area; remember highlighting will bring it out.

Chin shapes

- **Jaw line too wide**: Apply a darker colour from beneath the cheeks and along the side of the jaw line. Blend the make-up into the neck.
- **Double chin**: Apply a darker colour to the chin area, blending outwards along the jaw bone and under the chin.
- **Prominent chin**: Apply a highlighter to centre of the chin area and blend it in.
- **Long chin**: Apply a darker colour to the prominent area of the chin and blend it in.
- **Receding chin**: Apply a lighter colour along the jaw line and at the centre of the chin and blend it in.

Eye shapes

Make-up is applied to the eyes to give definition to the shape of the eyes. Enhance the eye area by highlighting and shading, and adding contouring to the socket lines to give a deep, open-eyes look. This technique should also be used to balance out the eyes, complimenting the natural eye colour.

- **Dark circles**: Apply concealer. Some make-up artists put this on before foundation and some choose to apply it after – this is optional. If you tip the head slightly down and look into your make-up mirror, it will make the dark circles stand out more and will help you to establish and see the areas that need to be corrected.
- **Round shape**: Apply a darker colour to the central upper lid. To elongate the shape, apply an eyeliner to the outer upper and lower corners.
- **Narrow eyes**: Apply a lighter colour in the centre of the eyelid to make the eye appear more open.
- **Overhanging lids**: Apply a lighter colour to the middle of the eyelid. Apply a darker colour to outer corners.

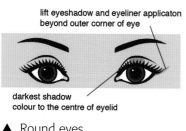

lift eyeshadow and eyeliner applicaton beyond outer corner of eye

darkest shadow colour to the centre of eyelid

▲ Round eyes

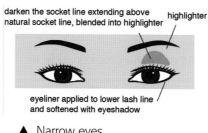

darken the socket line extending above natural socket line, blended into highlighter

highlighter

eyeliner applied to lower lash line and softened with eyeshadow

▲ Narrow eyes

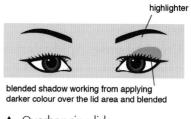

highlighter

blended shadow working from applying darker colour over the lid area and blended

▲ Overhanging lids

Day-look make-up

N.B. These techniques reflect those used by a make-up artist working in the industry rather than a beauty therapist working in a salon.

1. Apply make-up using a damp sponge/make-up wedge or foundation brush (this will be the preferred choice of the make-up artist), using firm strokes and patting and rolling techniques. Work the make-up into the skin and work your way round the face, balancing out the skin tone. Be very careful not to get a build up of make-up in the hairline.

 Remember . . .

Be sure to work and blend the foundation down the neck.

 Remember . . .

Ensure you choose a perfect base by successfully colour matching the skin: white, brown, black, fair, medium and dark skins all require a different base.

2. Apply the concealer under the eyes, if required. Use a concealer brush to do this, as a foundation brush will be too large to get into the smaller, more delicate areas. At this point if your foundation has not covered over problem areas, you can also apply corrective make-up, if necessary, e.g. to cover blemishes, scars, broken skin, rosacea and capillaries.

 Remember . . .

Always choose the correct colour and product for best results as if it is too white, pink, greasy, dry, chalky, pale or dark it may emphasise the flaws you are trying to hide.

 Remember . . .

Be sure to work and blend the foundation down the neck.

3. Highlighting and shading can really make a difference to the contouring of the face under lighting in photo shoots, film, TV and theatre. Dark colours shade and make areas appear reduced, for instance the hollows of the cheeks, temples, under the chin, and sides of the nose. Light colours highlight and make things come forward: the apples of the cheeks, under the eyes, the brow bone and middle of the chin. Apply this make-up with a firm brush or damp sponge. While blending, concentrate on keeping the product in the general area where it is being applied, but use blending techniques to eliminate any obvious line.

 Remember . . .

Highlighter = emphasise. Light colour tones should match skin type and be used to enhance cheekbones. When highlighting use two shades lighter than the base colour. Highlighting the eyes can appear to give width to the face.

 Remember . . .

Corrector = hide. When using shading, dark colour tones minimise and soften facial features, and appear to make them smaller.

4. Use a large powder brush to apply a light dusting of translucent powder over the face to set the make-up. When using translucent powder, be careful about: 1) which colours you applied to the make-up, 2) choosing a powder that matches the foundation applied. Colourless powder is a good option as this will not change the colour as the wrong colour powder does, giving the wearer an unnatural look. Place a generous amount of translucent powder under the eyes; this protects the make-up that you have already applied, stopping any darker eye shadow dropping onto the face and excess dust from the eye shadow dropping onto the translucent powder.

5. Use a powder-based eyebrow shaper, such as eye shadow or eyebrow pencil, to sharpen up the appearance of the eyebrows by filling in any gaps where the brow hair is missing. It may be necessary to darken the eyebrows if the brow hair is very light and you should sharpen the area under the brow to give it a nice, tidy appearance. It may be advisable to get your client or artist to have their eyebrows shaped or waxed prior to the appointment. Work from one side to the other so that you can balance out the brows; this will help to keep the eyebrows even.

 Tip If powder is used, any dark eye shadow droplets will be prevented from spoiling the look as they can simply be dusted away, leaving no trace or damage to the foundation underneath. A large domed brush should be used to dust away the powder.

If the make-up under the eye area is damaged from fallen droplets of eye shadow or mascara, use a damp cotton wool bud to gently remove them. Then correct the make-up, using a little foundation or concealer on your concealing brush to repair the damaged area and set the make-up with a small amount of translucent dusting powder.

Health and Safety

Sanitise you lip liners and eye pencils and thoroughly sharpen them after each use.

6. Apply eye shadow. When applying the eye shadows, remember lighter colours bring things forward and under a flash will highlight areas. When put in the right places and used with the correct shading, eye shadow will help to recapture the face and can have great effects. A good make-up artist can create fantastic optical illusions if they know how to highlight, shade and understand lighting. This is a very important part of a make-up artist's job. Let's face it, we all want to hold on to our youth for as long as we can so if you as a make-up artist can master these techniques, you are sure to be a big hit. Using a blending brush, apply a base colour to the eye under the brow and over the lid. Work on one eye and then swap over to the other. It is important to even up the eyes as you go along; this will help to balance the eyes out and to use an even amount of product. Apply a soft wash of colour on the eyelid and under the eyebrow.

Remember...

When correcting eyes, determine their shape and decide what needs to be bigger, smaller, opened and made closer.

7. Apply make-up to socket line. Remember, using a darker colour will make the socket line look deeper set. Choosing a darker colour and using a blending brush, start to blend your chosen colour into the socket line of the eye; this is found under the brow bone where the eyeball actually fits into the socket. If you get your client or artist and close their eyes or look slightly down, you will see where the brow bone ends and the eyeball fits into the socket line. In putting darker colours here, you will deepen the socket and therefore open the eye out more and enhance the features of the eyes. The eyes will appear to be deeply set.

8. Use a thumb to hold the eyebrow firmly and get the client or artist to look down and then up – this helps determine where to start applying the make-up. Apply the make-up into the socket line using a circling motion from left to right for blending. Also use a technique whereby you sculpt your brush under the brow bone, blending again and circling and blending underneath the eyebrow.

Remember...

If you wish to achieve a more dramatic look you should continue applying eye shadow in the socket line by repeating this technique to build the depth of colour you wish to achieve.

9. Apply eyeliner. You can use a few different techniques to apply eyeliner: a kohl pencil, eye shadow with an angled brush or liquid eyeliner can be used. To apply liner with a pencil, support the eye by using a thumb on the eyebrow to hold the skin of the eye area firmly so the eye does not wrinkle, causing gaps in the application. Hold the pencil on its side to get a nice, soft look, and this helps to steady the hand. The use of short strokes of the pencil across the top of the upper eyelid and lashes will come when changing to the other eye. This will help to achieve balance, so the application comes out even.

10. Use a disposable mascara wand to apply mascara. There are also reusable mascara wands that must be sanitised after every use. These should be cleaned in the same way as you would clean your make-up brushes. Wash them in hot water with a sanitising liquid soap. Get the subject to close their eyes and gently apply the mascara to the roots of the lashes. Place a thumb on the eyebrow and with a gentle lifting technique, lift the brow slightly; this will gently raise the lid, allowing you to work on the underside of the lashes. You should be able to work the mascara into the underside of the lashes and this should keep the subject relaxed. On some subjects you may be able to reach the bottom lashes while their eyes are closed. For people who have very short eyelashes you may have to ask them to open their eyes and look up when you are applying mascara to the bottom lashes. When applying mascara to eyes when they are open, always get the client to look up. Work alternately on the eyes, and use the mascara wand to lift and separate the lashes with a zigzagging movement.

> ⭐ *Tip* It you do get spotting of mascara onto the skin above or under the eye, use a damp cotton bud to gently remove it, then retouch the area with the required make-up.

> ⭐ *Tip* Heated eyelash curlers are great for adding lift to the base of the eyelashes once mascara has been applied.

11. Use a blusher brush to apply blusher to the apples of the cheeks in a small, circular motion and stroking up towards the cheekbone. Get your subject to smile – this will help you to establish the position of the apples of the cheeks. It is always best to be sparing with the blusher; you can always build the colour up gradually. You can also use cream or gel blusher, which you can apply with the fingertips. Again apply these products to the apples of the cheeks and use the fingertips to work the make-up into the area desired. Build the colour up gradually.

12. Use a lipliner to sharpen the appearance of the lips. Make sure it is freshly sharpened and make short strokes across the lips. Always have the client's lips in a natural position for best results – if you have them stretched wide open then the line will appear very uneven when the lips are relaxed. If the client/artist has uneven lips you may need to balance them out, or they may like you to draw ouside the natural lip line to make the lips look larger or inside the lip line to make them smaller.

13. Apply lipstick with a lip brush to get a nice, even coverage. Use short, firm strokes to balance the lips.

14. The completed look.

Evening-look make-up

N.B. These techniques reflect those used by a make-up artist working in the industry rather than a beauty therapist working in a salon.

1. Repeat steps 1–5 from day-look make-up.

2. Apply a light beige matte eye shadow as a base.

3. Create the socket line. You should build up your socket line very gradually.

> **Remember...**
> When working on mature skin you must take into consideration that the skin around the eye may have lost its elasticity and therefore be looser, making it harder to create a socket line.

4. Using an angled brush, mix some brown and black eye shadow and apply it along the top lid close to the lash line. This will give the eye a 'lift'. Try turning your line up at the corner. If you would like a stronger look, wet the eye shadow and this will give a more defined line. This line will be softer than liquid liner, with a more matte finish.

5. Using a soft light brown eyeliner, apply liner under the eye and gently smudge it to soften the line.

6. Apply mascara. (See step 10 of the day-look make-up look for details on how to do this.)

7. Apply a warm peachy-pink blusher. Depending on the occasion you may require a stronger colour of blusher.

8. Apply a warm-toned lip liner.

☆ *Tip* By applying individual lashes after the mascara you will find that they sit better into the natural lashes. You may loosen them or pull them off with the mascara wand. When you have applied the lashes you may feel it necessary to go over the join of the lashes and eye lid with your eyeliner just to blend them in.

9. Apply a lip gloss.

10. The finished look.

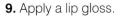 *Tip* When working with a very dark colour such as black, some professional make-up artists will apply the foundation after the eyes are completed.

 *Remember...*

When working on mature skin, be sure to pick the right foundation to match the skin type. Mature skin is quite often dehydrated and will need a foundation with moisturisers and vitamins. Most foundations also have a sun protection factor (SPF 15). Your client may have very oily skin and therefore need to use an oil-based foundation. Matte colours work well on mature skin but glittery, shimmery colours will enhance wrinkles and have an ageing effect.

Special occasion make up

N.B. These techniques reflect those used by a make-up artist working in the industry rather than a beauty therapist working in a salon.

1. Repeat steps 1–5 from day-look make-up.

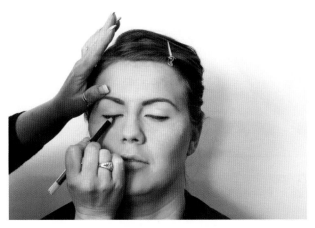

2. Apply eyeliner. Draw a semi-thick line of black eyeliner as close as possible to the top lashes.

3. Over the eyeliner, apply black powder eye shadow using a sponge-tipped applicator. Soften further with a small shadow brush.

4. Taking the shadow brush from the corner of the eye, draw an arc into the crease of the eyelid, emphasising the shadow on the outer third of the eye. Dust away any powder under the cheeks.

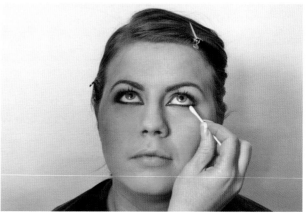

5. Apply mascara as for day-look make-up step 10.

6. A winged effect is accomplished by drawing the shadow from the outer corner and outward into the direction of the temple. Always make sure to soften the look by blending with your shadow brush sponge. Cotton buds are also good for softening and blending. Using a small angled brush, mix black and brown eye shadow and apply a soft line under the eyes.

7. Apply the final finishing touches by highlighting the brow bone area.

8. Use light beige powder eye shadow applied with a soft blending brush. Applying a pale powder eye shadow last can help to reduce hard edges.

9. See day-look make-up step 11 for application of blusher. Apply warm, pink-coloured blusher. Depending on the occasion you may require a stronger coloured blusher.

10. See day-look make-up step 12 for application of lip liner. Apply a natural-coloured lip liner.

11. See day-look make-up step 13 for application of lipstick. Apply a soft, natural-tinted lipstick.

12. The finished look.

Bridal make-up

▲ Bridal make-up

See Chapter 11 Art of fashion and photographic make-up for more information on bridal make-up.

Weddings

It is important to get payments for weddings upfront as you have to book another make-up artist to help you. If people do not turn up, you will still have to pay the make-up artist you have booked. For wedding make-up it is advisable to take a deposit for a make-up rehearsal, and then upon completion of the rehearsal, and if the client is completely satisfied, the full payment for the wedding is taken.

Payments should be made non-refundable in case of cancellation as you may have to book a team of make-up artists to come out to help you to do a job. You must cover yourself as you may not get another booking to fill that slot. You may also have to pay other members of staff for loss of earnings. If you get the client to fill out a contract for the job, this can be in print at the bottom and you can explain this to them at the make-up rehearsal, get it signed and understood by the client.

▲ Bridal make-up

Aftercare advice

It is important to ensure that the finished results of the make-up are to the client's satisfaction. This is the opportunity to allow time for the client to ask any questions with regard to the make-up products used.

Use a make-up record cards to record details of the products used and face charts to show how you achieved the make-up look. A make-up chart can be given to clients to reinforce the decisions that have taken place all throughout the make-up treatments process; this will also be a useful tool for the client if they wish in future to purchase any of the cosmetics used.

You will need to tell your client how to remove the make-up applied. Prepare an aftercare sheet your client can take away with them. This sheet should provide information on how to remove the make-up safely as recommended by professional manufacturer guidelines.

▲ Prom make-up

Costing and budget

The cost and budgeting should be planned out at the very beginning of every job (at the planning stage). It is important to plan beforehand so you have time to order any make-up required to do the job. It is also important that you fulfil your client's expectations and stay within the budget originally agreed.

With some products you will find that you do not use a whole bottle so you can estimate how many applications you would get out of a bottle, for example of foundation. You would never use a whole bottle of foundation on a face for a bridal make-up session and so therefore estimation would be practical. Most of the big make-up companies will give an approximate number of applications per container for each product and you will find that you gradually build your kit up by purchasing products gradually and estimating the costs involved.

End of chapter knowledge test

1. Which one of the following will contra-indicate a make-up treatment?
   a) Oily skin
   b) Broken capillaries
   c) Milia
   d) Conjunctivitis
2. What skin tone would benefit from a green concealer?
3. What types of foundation would be most suitable for a dry, mature skin?
4. Why should lipstick be applied with a lip brush?
5. What skin type is a cream blusher most suited to?
6. When choosing a foundation colour for a client what must you take into consideration?
7. Why is it important to have your client positioned correctly during a make-up service?
8. Name the main ingredient commonly found in face powder.
9. Why should a moisturiser be applied prior to the application of foundation?
10. Name the most appropriate method for cleaning make-up brushes.

CHAPTER 8

Create an image based on a theme within the hair and beauty sector

Units covered by this chapter:

VRQ Level 2: Create an image based on a theme within the hair and beauty sector (VRQ)

Chapter aims

This chapter will look at:

- ☞ Researching a theme
- ☞ Planning an image
- ☞ Preparing and presenting a mood board
- ☞ Designing and developing an image
- ☞ Evaluating the finished look.

Image is of the upmost importance in the hair and beauty industry. As a hair or make-up artist you will need to be able to generate creative ideas, research them, plan them, adapt them where necessary and then put your ideas into practice effectively. This is as much about research and planning skills as it is about the creative idea itself. We have written this chapter as if someone is going through the process of researching, planning and creating an image. The theme that we have chosen to explore is 'burlesque'.

Theme: Burlesque

Burlesque started in the music halls and theatres in the 1800s, turning the art of the tease into an evocative *strip* tease!

Burlesque glamour is all about being a lady. Make-up and hair should always be immaculate as the burlesque look is all about elegance. Don't be afraid to stand out – a burlesque performer should stand with confidence. The striptease involved a flash of a tastefully jewelled stocking, elegant corsets, and possibly the glimpse of a thigh, but it also involved imagination. Comedy and dance were important, and, as any burlesque dancer will tell you, the attitude is as important as the glamour and extravagance.

The research for this theme was undertaken using the internet, period books and newspapers, and books about fashions in hair and make-up.

Mood board

Presenting burlesque-themed photos on a mood board helps to develop and plan the hair and make-up designs, and provides a visual guide for the look and feel of the final image. Here research has been done and images included of the clothing to complete and capture unique glamorous looks.

> **Key term**
>
> **Burlesque** – Variety show, especially with striptease

> ☆ *Tip* There is a huge range of resources available to you to research your chosen theme and identify the image you want to create – use the internet, TV, films, books, photos and magazines to inspire you.

> ☆ *Tip* You may have to present your mood board and ideas to an audience. Think about how you might effectively do this both formally and informally in a professional manner as well as the tools you could use (e.g. audio-visual equipment, props and prompt cards).

▲ Burlesque mood board

You should include lots of photos of burlesque dancers on a mood board. The photos do not necessarily have to be of famous people, though a burlesque film poster would be good to include if you can find one.

Tip Remember that your mood board needs to clearly communicate your ideas to other people (e.g. tutors, fellow students, photographers and TV crews).

 Remember . . .
Do not breach copyright restrictions when using photos and images.

Make-up and hair face chart

Using a face chart helps to plan the make-up and hair products,
colours, shapes and designs to be used to complete the final image.
It also helps to estimate the costs for the products being used.

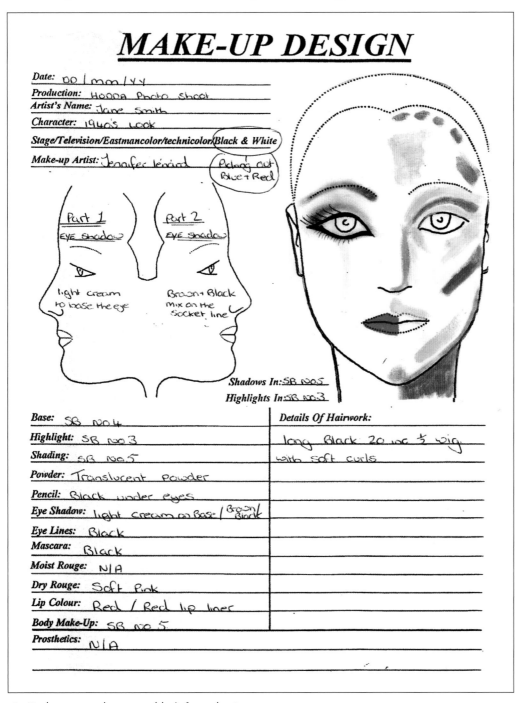

▲ Burlesque make-up and hair face chart

Research and planning notes

Create a plan of everything you will need to consider for your look.

Hair

This image will need the following:

- Hair pins
- Hairspray
- Patience (lots of it!).

The hair part will be the most complicated as it is a very fiddly task. Movie stars and burlesque performers of the day used rollers to create curls and pile their hair on top of their heads in elaborate styles that literally took hours of hard work to achieve. Women wore very tight waves made from using rollers: the World War II pin-ups set and styled their hair in ringlets at the front of their heads or created one big roll with all their hair.

Make-up and look

The burlesque look is very glamorous. The elements that really make this look so iconic are:

- Strong eyebrows
- Big smoky eyes
- Eyeliner flicks at the outer corners of the eyes
- Red lipstick
- Painted nails.

Find out what your model looks like to help you with the final design. For instance you need to take into account the length of their hair to decide if you need to use a wig, hair pieces or extensions. Find out their eye colour to make sure the final look you want will be effective.

Clothing

Burlesque clothing is very beautiful, elegant, glamorous and very well made. It is also to be worn perfectly by stunning, confident ladies! The ensemble consists of:

- Corset
- Lace knickers
- Long gloves
- Seamed tights
- High-waisted fitted pencil skirt
- Jewellery
- Heels
- Hats
- Hair accessories.

> **✋ Health and Safety**
>
> You must always find out if your model has any allergies to any of the products you intend to use.

The complete look

You will be using a number of skills in the completion of your look so be sure to refer to the relevant hair and make-up chapters within this book to make certain you are demonstrating the required technical skills. As well as hair and make-up you may be called on to provide or assist with nail art as part of the completion of an image. Opposite is an illustration of the types of nail art techniques that can be used.

▲ Nail art

▲ Finished look

Evaluation

After completion of your final look it is important for you to evaluate the look and the process. Think about what worked well and what didn't work well and take any lessons on board that will improve your speed, efficiency and skills for your next look.

Enjoy creating your ideas!

End of chapter knowledge test

1. What resources can you use to give you inspiration for your mood board?
2. Why would you use a make-up, hair and face chart?
3. How can you present a design plan to a client?
4. Why is it important to evaluate the final look and the process?
5. Why is it important to find out what your model looks like when planning the image?
6. Why is it important to communicate ideas accurately?
7. Why is it important to prepare products and equipment before applying the make-up?
8. Why is it important to agree a budget prior to completing the job?

CHAPTER 9

The art of hairdressing design

Units covered by this chapter:

The core of this chapter covers:

VRQ Level 2: Make and style a hair addition

VRQ Level 3: Style and fit postiche

Other units that this chapter addresses:

VRQ Level 2: The art of colouring hair

VRQ Level 2: The art of dressing hair

VRQ Level 3: Creative hairdressing design skills

VRQ Level 3: Provide hair extension services

VRQ Level 3: Style and dress hair using a variety of techniques

Chapter aims

- To provide background knowledge about the tools, equipment, products and techniques you will need to know about when working as a hair designer. For more detail about specific colouring and styling skills, you will need to refer to another textbook, for example *Hairdressing Level 2* by Rachel Gould and Martin Wady (Hodder Education, 2010).

- To give you the knowledge and skills you will need to succeed in industry.

This chapter is intended to show hairdressing skills used in the context of make-up artistry. These skills can ensure the make-up artist is more employable, especially when working on a production for any length of time. It helps with continuity on live shows such as theatre and TV dancing shows, where quick changes of styles are needed. As a make-up artist you will not be expected to cut or permanently colour hair.

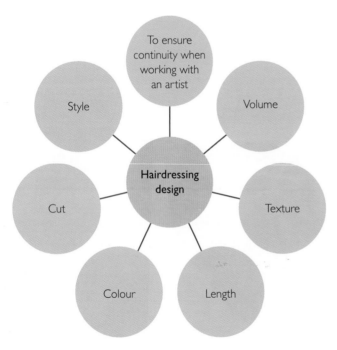

▲ Hairdressing design

Hairdressing design services

- Colouring
- Perming
- Cutting
- Styling, dressing and finishing
- Adding hair
- Shaving.

Tools, equipment and products used in styling and dressing hair

- Hand-held dryer
- Hood dryer
- Diffuser
- Nozzle
- Round brushes
- Flat brushes
- Rollers secured with pins
- Pin curl clips
- Straighteners
- Curling tongs
- Heated rollers
- Combs
- Hair brushes
- T-pins
- Rollers
- Postiche pins/hair grips
- Added hair (padding)
- Section clips
- Hair net
- Wig cap
- Crepe hair
- Malleable block and polythene covering, clamp
- Postiche oven/hood drier.

▲ Tools, equipment and products used in styling and dressing hair

 Health and Safety

Always ensure that brushes and combs are free from stray hairs and access products and are cleaned and disinfected with an appropriate product.

 Remember . . .

When blow-drying the hair, different nozzles can be added to the end of the hair dryer to create a smoother finish. Ensure the nozzle directs the air flow with the direction of the brush otherwise a smooth finish will not be achieved.

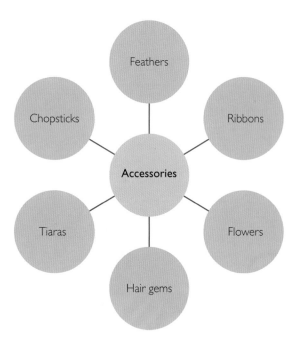

▲ Hair accessories

Products

Conditioning spray

- **Purpose**: This is a leave-in conditioner, particularly suitable for dry hair. Many of these products have a UV filter and may be particularly suitable for use on holidays.
- **How to use**: Refer to manufacturers' instructions. They may be sprayed on wet or dry hair accordingly.

Setting lotion

- **Purpose**: For volume, styling and hold
- **How to use**: Apply to wet or dry hair depending on the products, manufacturers' instructions and whether they are to be used in a wet or dry setting. Some setting lotions may also be coloured; ensure that these are applied to wet hair and that the client's clothing is suitably protected to avoid staining. Ensure you are wearing gloves and an apron as personal protective equipment (PPE). The setting lotion can be sprinkled evenly and directly onto the client's hair with caution; ask the client to lean their head back slightly to avoid the product running onto their face. If the lotion does not have a nozzle, place your finger over half of the opening when sprinkling the product.

Thermal setting lotions may be applied to dry hair and are activated by the use of heat.

Health and Safety

The more often heat styling is used the more risk of damage to the hair however, there are many thermal or heat-styling products that help to protect during this process.

Finishing spray

- **Purpose**: check the manufacturers' instructions for specific uses. Most finishing sprays are used after dressing to hold the style in place and to protect the hair from atmospheric moisture. They come in different strengths chosen according to requirements.
- **How to use**: Spray directly onto the hair, ensuring that the product does not go into the client's face.

Gel

- **Purpose**: For sculpting hair with a firm styling hold
- **How to use**: Those in a container are of a thicker viscosity and those in a spray form are more fluid. Gels can be used on wet or dry hair depending on styling requirements. Always check the manufacturers' instructions.

Dressing cream

- **Purpose**: Reduces static, gives control and smoothes stray hairs
- **How to use**: Apply a small amount with the fingertips and work it through the hair, paying particular attention to the ends.

Mousse

- **Purpose**: For volume and texture
- **How to use**: Apply a bead of mousse approximately the size of a golf ball from the roots to the ends of towel-dried hair and then comb through it with a large-tooth comb. Apply coloured products in the same manner, ensuring that the client's clothing is well protected and you are wearing gloves and an apron as PPE.

Mousse can be applied to dry hair when dry setting in the same manner as mentioned earlier.

Heat protector

- **Purpose**: To protect the hair from intense heat when using heat styling equipment
- **How to use**: Refer to manufacturers' instructions with individual products. These often come in spray form and should be applied directly to the hair before heat styling.

Waxes

- **Purpose**: Definition, smoothing and hold. Refer to manufacturers' instructions but many waxes can be used for setting, blow drying or as a finishing product.
- **How to use**: Use small amounts and work it into the hair using the fingertips and paying particular attention to the ends.

Serum

- **Purpose**: Adds smoothness and add shine. Refer to manufacturers' instructions as this can be used for setting, blow-drying or as a finishing product.

 Health and Safety

Any styling tools or equipment should come with setting controls so that the user can differentiate heat settings accordingly. Health and safety is of course a factor when deciding on a temperature; it must be comfortable for the client so no injury from burning occurs on the scalp or skin. Excessive heat could also cause damage to the hair.

- **How to use**: Apply a small amount with the fingertips, paying particular attention to the ends of the hair. Apply according to manufacturers' instructions as this may be applied to wet or dry hair.

Oil
- **Purpose**: To add extra shine to dry hair as a finishing product
- **How to use**: Refer to manufacturers' instructions; oils often come in a spray form.

Adhesive and solvent
- **Purpose**: To stick in hair weave
- **How to use**: Section the hair. Create a line around the perimeter with a tail comb and pin. Add adhesive to the weave and place carefully along the sectioned piece. Allow to dry.

Tools and equipment for colouring hair
- Brush and bowl
- Applicator bottle
- Highlighting cap
- Colour packages (foils/wraps)
- Steamer
- Drying equipment.

Products for colouring hair
- Semi-permanent
- Quasi-permanent
- Permanent, bleach
- Lightening products
- High street retail products – many professional product manufacturers have now developed a range available on the high street
- Professional salon products – professional product ranges are usually of a higher quality in comparison to high-street brands. There are many retail products available for the client to buy.

Science of styling hair (structural changes)

The cortex is the part of the hair that gives it strength and elasticity. It is here where the changes take place that allow the hair to be permanently and temporarily styled. The cortex is structured from bundles of fibres that run parallel and are made up of smaller fibres. Minute chains of molecules (polypeptide chains) hold

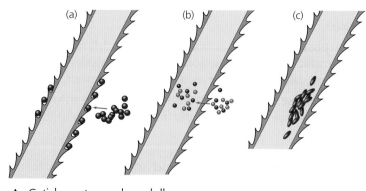

▲ Cuticle cortex and medulla

the cortex together and are made up of amino acids that are held together by two types of cross-linkages or bonds known as hydrogen and disulphide bonds:

- Hydrogen bonds are broken by water
- Disulphide bonds are unaffected by water.

When hair is soaked in water it can be stretched to up to 1.5 times its normal length:

- Alpha-keratin (or α-keratin) – hair in its un-stretched state
- Beta-keratin (or β-keratin) – hair in its stretched state.

The change from alpha- to beta-keratin is referred to as the alpha–beta transformation. Care must be taken not to overstretch the hair when styling as this would cause breakage. The higher the water content on the hair the greater the hair will be stretched.

Check the condition of the hair prior to styling to allow the treatment plan to be formed and the correct products to be chosen to suit the client's needs. The condition of the hair can be further checked once it is wet by taking a few strands of wet hair between the fingers and thumb and gently pulling the hair. The hair should stretch slightly but quickly return to its original length. If this does not happen or it snaps, this indicates that the hair is in poor condition and will be prone to overstretching and possibly breaking during the styling process.

Preparing for designing and styling hair

There are many things you need to take into account before you begin to design and style a client's or artist's hair.

Appearance of hair

Hair is classified as follows:

- **Virgin hair** – hair that has never been chemically treated
- **Healthy and undamaged** – hair that is in good condition. Good health and diet and a good hair care regime will help to maintain healthy hair.
- **Damaged** – Hair that is damaged has a rough cuticle that allows light rays to scatter as they hit the hair shaft, giving it its dull appearance. The rougher the cuticle the more porous the hair. Hair that is repeatedly chemically processed or overprocessed can be physically damaged. Hair can also be damaged by excessive heat styling without use of hair care products to help to protect the hair. Rough handling of the hair and environmental factors such as damage from UV rays and ill health could be factors that cause the hair to appear unhealthy.

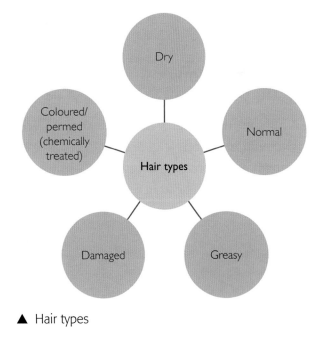

▲ Hair types

Factors to consider when designing and styling hair

Determine whether the hair is:

- Wet
- Dry
- Curly
- Straight.

The following should also be taken into account:

- Client requirements
- Hair texture
- Length
- Density
- Head and face shapes and features
- Client lifestyle
- Contraindications
- Body shape
- Hair growth patterns
- Hair type
- Hair elasticity
- Fashion trends
- Haircut
- Image
- Occasion.

Contraindications

Contraindications to the styling of hair include:

- Viral infections (e.g. warts, cold sores, folliculitis)
- Bacterial infections (e.g. impetigo, sycosis)
- Fungal infections (e.g. ringworm)
- Infestations (e.g. head lice, scabies)
- Skin disorders (e.g. psoriasis, seborrhoea, eczema).

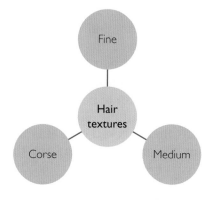

▲ Hair textures

Health and Safety

You must ensure that any electrical equipment you are going to use has been safety checked.

Remember...

Check client comfort in positioning and when using heat-styling tools and equipment.

Anatomy and physiology

For further details of these contraindications please refer to Chapter 4 Anatomy and physiology.

Styling techniques used in hairdressing design

There are a wide variety of styling techniques that you should be aware of, including:

- Blow-drying
- Finger-drying
- Setting (brick wind, directional wind)
- Curling (point to root, root to point)
- Waving
- Pin curling
- Finger waving
- Smoothing
- Straightening
- Twisting, knotting, plaiting, weaving and incorporation of temporary hair extensions (wefts, pin curls, ringlets, switches, wiglets), accessories and ornamentation.

▲ Setting the hair

For further detail of these skills you should refer to *Hairdressing Level 2* by Rachel Gould and Martyn Wady (Hodder Education, 2010) or a similar hairdressing text.

Dressing techniques used in hairdressing design

The dressing techniques used in hairdressing design that you should be aware of are:

- Backcombing
- Backbrushing
- Shaping
- Moulding
- Rolls
- Knots
- Twists
- Plaits
- Curls
- Woven effects.

Hair-up styles

- Plaiting
- Braiding
- Twists
- Knots
- Barrel curls
- Weaving
- Woven effects
- Frames
- Marcel waves.

Long-hair looks

- Scalp plait
- Vertical roll
- Twists.

Tip Backcombing and backbrushing are effective ways of shaping and securing hair as well as increasing the duration of the style.

Remember . . .

Explain the importance of controlling and securing long hair effectively.

Explain the importance of considering tension in hair-up styles.

Describe the methods used to secure ornamentation in hair-up styles.

Procedure for a vertical roll

1. Prepare the client.

2. Set the hair using heated rollers.

3. Backcomb the hair.

4. Determine the height of the crown area and secure with grips.

5. Through the back section, comb the hair over to one side using a bristle brush and secure by criss-crossing kirby grips.

6. Roll the hair over the criss-crossed kirby grips and secure. For longer hair, divide into smaller sections to roll.

7. Bring the sides into the back area and secure.

8. The finished look.

Procedure for a scalp plait

1. Prepare the client.

2. Take a small section from the recession area back to the crown.

3. Split the top section into three equal pieces.

4. Cross an outer piece over the centre.

5. Repeat, crossing each outer piece over the centre.

6. Incorporate a section of hair from each side into the plait. Continue to do this as you work down the hair.

7. Secure with a band.

8. The finished look.

Procedure for a bun

1. Use a paddle or bristle brush to smoothe the hair. Secure in a band in a low ponytail at the back of the neck.

2. Backcomb the hair using a comb.

3. With a bristle brush smooth the outer ponytail.

4. Take the ponytail, twist and wrap the hair around your thumb in a circular direction. Tuck in and smooth the hair as you go.

5. When all the hair is tucked in, cup the hair to hold securely and pin using geisha pins to anchor and hold firmly.

6. Use the end of your comb to tuck in any stray or wispy hairs.

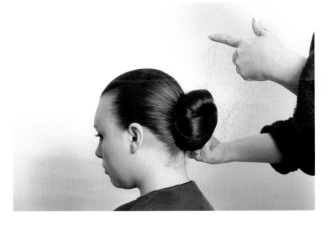

7. Place a hairnet over a bun.

8. Secure so the bun is neat and tidy.

9. Complete by adding hair accessories of your choice.

Creative hairdressing design skills

There are interesting and varied opportunities within this sector for hairdressing design skills, including hairdressing competition work, hair shows and photographic sessions.

"Hair design is used within hairdressing and is often expected of a make-up artist. Being capable of both is key to becoming successful in the industry. This lead me to begin training in media make-up. The course has unleashed my creativity once again. Planning photo shoots and shows, whilst being able to consider possibilities with the hair and the make-up is fantastic. It not only helps me to create a whole vision, it also gives me an understanding of how important the connection between hair design and make-up really is."

Ellenora Dean

 Remember . . .

Try to anticipate any problems when you are planning your design; these could be:
1) Availability of models,
2) Space limitations, 3) Venue restrictions, 4) Budget,
5) Availability of resources.

▲ Hair design by Ellenora Dean

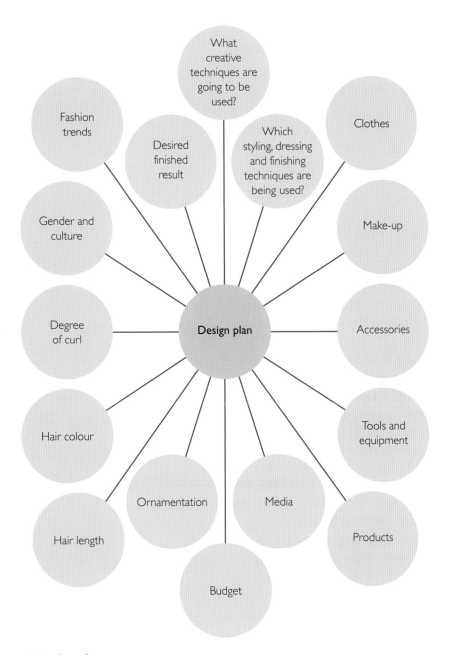

▲ Design plan

Styling and fitting wigs, postiche and hair extensions

Postiche and hair extensions play a vital role in the art of hairdressing design. This chapter now looks at this in greater detail. This section will also provide you with the knowledge and understanding you need to maintain wigs and hair pieces. You should be able to:

- Recognise various wig types and evaluate the uses of each
- Take measurements of the head

Key term

Postiche – Pre-made hair pieces to be added to natural hair, including false buns, small curls and wiglets.

- Complete a course
- Prepare a malleable block, and block on a wig in preparation for washing, setting or dressing
- Set interest wig according to design requirements
- Protect wigs
- Fit a lace wig to a model
- Remove the lace wig from the model
- Clean various types of wigs safely and efficiently.

A history of wig use

The ancient Egyptians wore wigs made from hair or wool if they were rich or papyarus if they were poor. These were placed on top of their natural hair, using beeswax and resin to keep the wigs in place and cones of scented wax on top, which would melt down and make them more fragrant. People of other ancient cultures also wore wigs, including the Romans, Greeks, Phoenicians and Assyrians.

In 1665 a wigmakers' guild was established in France; this development was then copied elsewhere in Europe. A wigmaker's job in this period was a very skilled one as wigs in the seventeenth century were extremely and extraordinarily elaborate; they covered the wearer's back and shoulders with locks of hair that flowed down the chest. As you can imagine, these wigs were also very heavy and often very uncomfortable to wear. These wigs were very expensive to produce and the best wigs were made from natural human hair. The hair from horses and goats was often used as a cheaper alternative.

Queen Elizabeth I increasingly wore wigs as she got older, as the leaded make-up she wore made her bald. King Charles became known for the periwig he wore, which had side and back panels made of a ladder-type construction. These were very expensive items at the time and commonly stolen or left in wills. The tops of these wigs could be dressed quite high, and this was echoed in women by the 'fontage'. As times increased in opulence, so did the wigs.

Men's wigs in the eighteenth century were powdered in order to give them their distinctive light or white colouring.

Pomard would be used for styling and helping the white powder to stick (this was probably pretty smelly and could make a wig burn like a candle if the wearer got too close to a chandelier). Cloth bags were sometimes used by men to cover the ponytail of their wigs, to stop the powder ruining the back of their jackets. Powdering wigs became outlawed when the Corn Laws were passed as it was a waste of flour.

In the early 1800s things became a bit more naturalistic, with the exception of Apollo knots – these were elaborate pieces worn on the top of the head. As Victoria came to the throne, this naturalism continued but as her reign went on hair became more elaborate and incorporated hairpieces to give extra plaits and coils.

In the early 1900s these styles became tighter and pieces would be used, for example, on the front of the head and these would be dressed into curls. In the Edwardian era, styles were more voluminous (Gibson girls) and with the advent of better curling methods, hair was dressed more through the wars. In the 19550s and increasingly in the 1960s, wig wearing and the use of pieces such as wire clusters, was very common.

More recently there has been a massive surge in the wearing of extensions, and wigs are often worn by African-Caribbean ladies, although many would still prefer to have their own hair braided and extensions (weaves) sewn in. Increasingly they are using lace fronts, which will be attached separately or they will use lace front wigs.

The quality of wigs available for private users differs greatly, from those made entirely of acrylic weft, to those that are hand-tied (knotted) in hair or fibre and have mono tops (which give the impression of the hair growing from the head).

While there are wig companies and theatre companies who have staff for wigmaking, a lot of people are 'out knotters' (freelance/self-employed people who will work from home for various companies).

When creating a hair addition it is important to consider the client's budget, what the addition will be used for (for example, theatre, TV, film or private use) and what style is required. This will affect how the foundation is made and how the hair is knotted in.

In the nineteenth century the wearing of wigs became a symbol of social status – the taller the wig put you higher up the social status ladder. During the late nineteenth and early twentieth century the hairdressers in France and England did good business supplying postiches, or pre-made, false buns, small curls, and wiglets, to be incorporated into the style of the natural hair.

Postiches were very popular in the decade between 1910 and 1920, but they went out of fashion during the 1920s, when women started having their hair cut into a bob style and setting and styling their hair in finger waves.

Wig use today

A number of celebrities wear wigs for their jobs in film, theatre and television. In fact, a lot of celebrities wear them as part of their everyday life.

The history of wig use was contributed by Jackie Sweeney of Wigs Up North. Jackie studied at the London College of Fashion and went on to work for The London and New York Wig Company and as a make-up artist at Granada TV before becoming freelance. She has worked for various companies, including the BBC, Sky, Living TV and S4C, and her theatre work includes Phantom of the Opera, Les Misérables and Jesus Christ Superstar. Wigs Up North was launched in Manchester in June 2004 to fill a gap in the theatrical wig-making market. It makes or hires wigs and facial hair to professional theatres, TV and amateur groups throughout the UK.

Visit their website for more information: www.wigsupnorth.co.uk.

Special wigs are also worn by judges and barristers, and certain parliamentary and municipal representatives as a symbol of the office they hold. The wearing of wigs is a normal part of court dress.

Wigs are worn by some people on an occasional or daily basis in everyday life; this is sometimes for reasons of convenience or by individuals who are experiencing hair loss due to medical reasons. One of the most common groups of people who wear wigs are cancer patients who are undergoing chemotherapy or those who are suffering from alopecia areata.

Wigs are also worn by men who cross-dress. They use different styles of wigs to help create a more feminine look.

Jewish married women are required to cover their hair for reasons of modesty. **Sheitel** is Yiddish for 'wig' and women are required to wear this. Orthodox and Modern Orthodox Jewish women will often wear human-hair wigs. Most Hasidic Jewish women wear synthetic wigs covered partly by a hat.

▲ Judges wig

Types of wigs

Weft wigs

Weft wigs are made as a mass-produced item. Different types of wigs will vary in price and quality but tend to be a lot cheaper than a hand-knotted lace wig.

Machine-made wig foundations are often made from a flesh-coloured plastic on the top to give them the illusion of natural hair growth on the partings, for a more realistic look. The hair used in these wigs is usually made from synthetic fibres, but preset and styled human-hair wigs are also available. After washing these wigs they will need to be shook out and left to dry naturally. They cannot be restyled with tools with heated elements as they are not as durable as a custom handmade knotted lace wig.

> **Key term**
>
> **Weft** – Weaving the root ends of the hair onto a warp of three silk threads.

Real hair

Real-hair wigs are the most expensive form of all the wigs that you can get; they can cost considerably more than £1000. This type of wig can be styled as it is made from real hair. These wigs do require regular maintenance such as needing to be styled on regular basis. You can use a straightener, curling iron, heated rollers, hair dryer and styling products with this type of wig. Real-hair wigs feel and look the most like your own hair and can be ordered in many shades of hair colours.

Synthetic

There are two major types of synthetic wigs: 1) mono-filament and 2) classic machine-made wigs. Both of these wigs are very good wigs but you will find that the texture and look of both wigs is very different. Synthetic wigs must not be around intense heat, so you must not use strainers, heated rollers, curling irons or hair dryers on these wigs. You also need to be very careful when you are near an oven or dishwasher as the intense heat could singe your synthetic wig. Synthetic wigs are already prestyled so you don't have to style them every day.

Monofilament top wigs

Mono wigs are highly recommend monofilament wigs for customers who require the ultimate in luxury and realism. These wigs are also very popular for those seeking the best wigs due to medical conditions causing hair-loss such as with chemotherapy treatment for cancer or alopecia.

▲ Equipment for wigs and postiche

Monofilament top wigs have been specially designed with a translucent material on top that shows your actual hair colour along the roots of the hair. This special translucent material that has been placed along the partings of the wigs creates the illusion of your skin at the roots of the hair along the front hairline or top of the wig.

Monofilament wigs are more expensive than synthetic machine-made wigs as the translucent material part of the wig has the hair hand knotted (one to two hairs at a time, to give the effect of the monofilament). This is a more expensive wig, typically with prices ranging from £100 and up, but the price you pay is well worth it for the quality of wig you get. The wig has been designed to look as though the hair is growing from your scalp. The fine netting on the scalp is softer and eases any itchiness.

When it comes to synthetic wigs, the monofilament wigs look the most like real hair.

Handmade lace-knotted wigs

There are two methods of attaching hair to wigs: the oldest is to weave the root ends of the hair onto a warp of three silk threads to create a 'weft'. The wefts are then sewn onto a foundation net or another material. The other method is to use wigs or hairpieces. It is possible to combine the two techniques using weft for the main part of the wig, and then having the fine wig lace put onto the front and along the parting of the wig (this is known as a lace-front wig). Sometimes theatres request that their wigs are made in this way.

> ⭐ *Tip* A **two-strand flat weave weft** is one of the oldest techniques of attaching hair and one you will be assessed on.

Foundation

A foundation is made up of wig lace; it looks a bit like net. Different sizes and textures of wig lace are used for different parts of the wig, starting with the thicker lace, where the wig needs stronger support, then gradually working with finer lace as you come to the front and sides of the wig. The lace is finer at the front and sides so it will appear to be very inconspicuous and allows the hair to look as if it is coming directly from the skin underneath when it is placed on the skin on the forehead and on the side of the face. These wigs are usually referred to as 'lace-front wigs' when placed on the skin on the forehead and on the side of the face.

The edges of the front lace might be trimmed and can fray so you will need to ensure that frayed edges do not appear; you can reinforce it on the edges with a narrow ribbon called a 'galloon'. Sometimes synthetic material or flesh-coloured silk is applied where it will show through the hair at the crown and partings. Elastic or small bones are inserted to help make the wig fit more securely.

▲ Hackle

Hair types used on wigs and preparation

Natural human hair is very commonly used but the fur from animals such as the goat and yak are also used. All hair must be sorted carefully so that the direction of growth is maintained, root to root and point to point. This is because of the scale-like structure of the cortex of a hair shaft: if some hairs were to get turned in the wrong way, they will ride up backwards against their neighboring shafts and cause tangles and matting.

Some types of hair will cost a lot more depending on the quality and colour of the hair. The highest quality hair has never been bleached or coloured (virgin hair), and has been carefully sorted to ensure that the direction is correct.

For less expensive wigs, the sorting process is substituted for by processing the hair. The hair is treated with a strong base solution that will partially dissolve the cortex, leaving the strands smooth. The hair is then bleached and dyed to the required shade and is then given a synthetic resin finish, which will partially restore the strength to the now damaged hair.

Synthetic fibre is manufactured in the required colours and has no direction (root to point). The wigmaker will choose the type, colours and length of hair that is required.

Mixing hair colours in a hackle

Wigs are made by pulling the hair through the upright teeth of a very sharp-nailed brush-like tool called a 'hackle'. This is a very useful tool for mixing the hair and also makes it possible to remove tangles and any broken or short strands. The tips on the hackle are very sharp so you must be very careful when using one.

The hair is placed on one of a pair of short metal-bristled brushes like matts, called 'drawing matts'. The root end of the hair placed over one edge label of the drawing matt, putting root

Health and Safety

When working with a hackle be cautious as the nails are very sharp.

Key term

Hackle – A sharp metal tool with a similar appearance to a bed of nails used in wig making.

on one of the corners. This will help you to not get the root and point mixed up.

Place your hand on the drawing matt and press down on top of it so that you can pull a few strands of hair at a time. Leave the rest of the hair you are not using undisturbed until it is needed.

How to take measurements for a custom-made lace wig

The figure shows how to take the measurements needed before work on a custom-made lace wig can begin. Make sure you record this information on the order form.

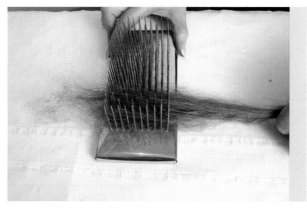

▲ Place crepe hair into the hackle and draw through to blend the hair and mix the colours

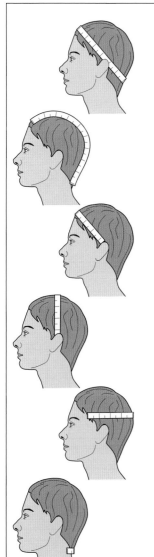

1. Measuring the circumference of the head. Measure all the way around the head. Position the tape measure so that the edge follows the natural hairline around the head and nape of the neck. (The average measurement size is 22 inches.)

2. Measuring from the forehead to the nape of the neck. Measure from the natural hairline at the centre of the forehead, continue with the measuring tape straight back over crown to centre of hairline add carry on to the nape of neck. (Remember that your front lace of the wig, is glued to the outside perimeter of skin just beyond the natural hairline, so you must allow about a ½ inch for this.) (The average measurement is 14.5 inches.)

3. Measuring ear to ear across the front hairline. Measure from the front of the ear, placing a measuring tape from the hairline at the bottom of the sideburn, bringing the measuring tape up across the hairline along the forehead to same point in front of the other ear on the posit side. (The average measurement is 12 inches.)

4. Measuring from ear to ear over the top of the head. Measure from the hairline directly above the ear, and then continue across the top of the head to the hairline directly above the other ear on the opposite side. (The average measurement is 13 inches.)

5. Measuring from point to point. Measure from temple to temple around the back of the head. (The average measurement is 14.5 inches.) Remember to place the tape measure about ½ inch in front of your natural hairline at the temple-to-temple point on each side of the head, as the wig lace also has to be glued to the outside perimeter of the skin in front of your natural hairline in this area as well.

6. Measuring the nape of the neck. Measure the width of the hairline around the nape of the neck. (The average measurement is 5 inches.)

▲ Taking measurements for a custom-made lace wig

Wig Order Form Part 1

THE BIZ

Client's name ....

Address ....

.... Postcode ....

Telephone: Home .... Work ....

Order 1 Wig ☐   2 Wigs ☐   Hand-made ☐   Acrylic ☐   Hair-lace front ☐   Toupee ☐   Half wig ☐

Measurements	Notes
Circumference (1cm back centre front)	
Measurements with cling film mould	
Front to nape	
Ear to ear (front)	
Ear to ear (top)	
Temple to temple (Back)	
Nape of neck (width of nape)	
Parting: Left ☐ Centre ☐ Right ☐	
Parting distance from centre	
Natural break: Left ☐ Centre ☐ Right ☐ Crown ☐	
Abnormalities: Scalp ☐ Bumps ☐ Other ☐	

Details of hair
A Length of hair

Front	Temples	Crown	Nape

B Exact Colour: Pattern ....
Enclosed samples
C Sraight ☐   Waved ☐   Curly ☐   Loose ☐   Medium ☐   Strong ☐
D Full fringe
E Weight of wig: Light ☐   Normal ☐   Heavy ☐

Wig Order Form Part 2

THE BIZ

	Date of completion	Date	Time	Signature on completion
Measurements taken		(Client's first visit)		
Hair ordered				
Fit and check base				
Second fitting and meeting with the hair dresser		(+6 weeks)		
Client satisfaction check		(+8 weeks)		
Cost				
Deposit	NHS purchase order	NHS purchase order number		
Client's signature on deposit		Date of client's signature on deposit		
Wig dressed by				
Wig made by				
Completion date				
Client signature on completion		Date of Client signature on completion		

▲ Example order form for a custom-made wig

Measuring with cling film

1. Measure around head. Bring the hair back off the perimeter of the natural hairline using gel or soap. The method of measurement depends on the length of the natural hair. If the hair is long you can warp it flat as you measure around the head, getting the best shape of the subject's head. Or you can 'pin curler' the hair flat to enable you to get the best result.

2. Stretch the cling film tight and pull firmly around the head to get an accurate measurement.

3. Trim the cling film to size to get an accurate fit. Use the transparent adhesive tape to mould the shape of the head.

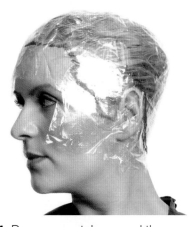

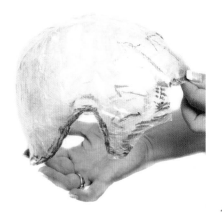

4. Draw accurately around the hairline. Seal the marker using tape.

5. Trim around the client's ear to release from the head. Trim around the mark of the hairline. Return to the client's head to check the fit.

Adding hair to a lace-front wig

Hand-knotting

- Hand-knotted wigs will have the hair knotted directly into the foundation, a few strands at a time, while the foundation is fastened to a wooden block. With the hair folded over the finger, the wigmaker pulls a loop of hair under the lace mesh.

Single knotting

- Move the hook forward to catch both sides of the loop. The ends are then pulled through the loop. The knot is then tightened – this is known as a 'single knot'.

Double knot

- A second loop is pulled through the first before casting off and finishing – this is more secure. Double knotting is used over the majority of the wig in the less obvious parts; single knotting is used more around the edges and parting areas. The wigmaker will take into consideration the number of strands of hair that will be used and the direction of each knot to give the most natural, realistic effect. The wigmaker will also use differently sized knotting hooks to achieve this.

Styling the wig

- When the wig is finished it will need to be cut into the required style and then set and styled by a professional stylist.

Block the wig

- This type of wig will need to be blocked on with blocking-in ribbon and blocking-on pins, onto a malleable block. Lace wigs are very delicate so you must block them properly before dressing the lace wig. If the lace is ripped at the front of the wig it can be very expensive to have it refronted – it will cost hundreds of pounds!

▲ Block on the wig

Blocking on and dressing a lace-front wig

You will need:

- Wig clamp or wig stand
- Blocking-on ribbon
- T-pins

- Blocking-on pins
- Malleable block
- Lace-front wig.

1. You will need to block one lace wig correctly onto a malleable block.

2. When you are happy with the position in which you have placed the wig you will need to secure it onto the malleable block using pins. Place a few T-pins in the centre point to ensure the wig stays central on the block. Pin the wig down using blocking-on pins at the back of the wig and at the sides behind the ears. Take the ribbon and lay it flat onto the front wig lace. Use the blocking-on pins in the staggered pattern shown. This will secure the front wig lace. This is done to distribute the pressure put on the very delicate front lace of the wig while it is being styled. You will need to do this all the way round the front part of the lace of the wig then tie the remainder of the ribbon into a neat bow so it does not get in the way while you are styling the wig.

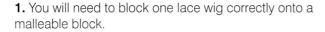

3. Depending on the hair design brief you are following to style the wig, you may need to set your wig with heated rollers, hot sticks, or other heated elements. You may also like to use setting lotion to help to set your style; this will make the curls nice, crisp and strong, and help the style to last longer. Set the wig using rollers or hot sticks. When you have done this you must let the heated elements cool down so they are cold before removing them.

4. When rollers/hot sticks cool down completely, remove them from the hair. Remember to take them out very carefully, placing the cold hair back into the position it was in. At this point if you are adding any kind of padding to build out the hair, you will need to pin-curl the hair where you are going to place the padding.

5. You may need crepe hair to help you to achieve your desired style. Crepe hair can be bought by the metre and it will be plaited very tightly together. You will need to pull some out of the plait by stretching it out and cutting off the amount that you need. You will need to pull the hair apart and fluff it up to create padding for shaping the hair, using a hairnet that matches the colour of your crepe hair. Fill the net with the desired amount of crepe hair.

6. Place the padding that you have created with the hairnet and crepe hair onto the area that you have prepared with the pin curls (use long pins to secure this – geisha pins are very good for this). Secure the padding to the pin curls. Now you are ready to dress the hair according to your design brief. Use fine pins to create your style and make sure that you hide the pins. Hairpins are available in blonde, brown and black; you can also get the pins with a matte colour coating – this helps stop them from shining when the light catches them. Continue dressing the hair and make sure that you distribute the hair evenly so it covers the padding.

7. Taking small sections, backcomb to cover the padding. Bring the hair over the top of the padding and smooth.

8. Once smooth, you can dress the curls around the padding.

9. Dress the sides of the hair into the back of the wig.

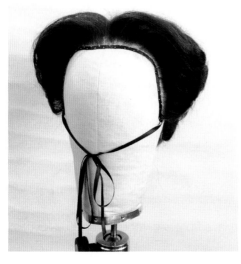

10. The completed look

 Remember . . .

When you are ready to use the wig, you will need to block the wig. Never pull the ribbon with all the pins holding it out by dragging this ribbon as it can seriously damage the wig lace. Each of these pins must be removed individually; you may as well leave a large wig pin at the top of the lace wig to secure it on the malleable block until you apply the lace-front wig. If you use a T-pin, be careful that the little bend on this pin does not get hooked into the hair you have styled as they are difficult to get out if hair gets caught in the small loop of the T-pin.

Synthetic wigs

- These wigs are more restricting – most of these wigs have been designed to stay in one particular design. You can put non-heated rollers in these wigs and use steam to create the style.

Applying wigs (hard front and lace front)

1. Wrap the hair and soap the hairline back as for measuring for a wig. Place a wig cap on the client/ artist's head to keep the hair as flat as possible and to absorb perspiration and prevent sweating on to the wig.

2. Get the artisit to hold the front of the wig by their hairline. Draw the wig back over the hair, tucking the back of the hair in.

3. Pin and secure the wig. You can also do this using toupee grips sewn inside the wig.

4. For a lace front wig, repeat step 1 as for hard front wigs.

5. Line the wig up against the hairline perfectly and put on the wig.

6. When you're happy that the wig is perfectly in position, use hairpins to secure the wig. Trim away any remaining superfluous wig lace. Use adhesive (spirit gum) to stick the wig against the bald part of the skin by the natural hairline.

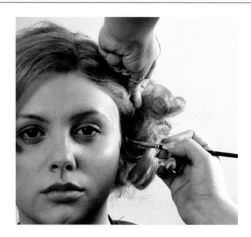

7. Stick down the lace around the hairline using matt spirit gum in the area needed. Tap on the spirit gum very gently with your finger to feel whether it is tacky as needed.

8. When the spirit gum is tacky you can press the wig lace into the spirit gum using a piece of silk material. A press and rolling technique works well. (This type of spirit gum will not shine through the wig lace.) When you are happy that the wig is secured and the front lace has been successfully stuck down, so you cannot see the wig lace. Do any finishing touches to the hair styling to achieve the desired look You may experience a situation in which the spirit gum will not stick down the lace very well. There are a few reasons for this – it could be that the client has alcohol in their system; this will have an effect on the spirit gum. We use alcohol to clean and remove postiche so as you can imagine, if it is coming out of the pores of the skin of the wearer, it will dissolve the spirit gum. Medication may have an effect as well.

9. The finished look.

Remember . . .

Bring the spirit gum onto the set with you. On some occasions, when the wearer has had the wig on for a long time, you may need to re-stick the lace down.

Removing a lace-front wig

1. Set up your equipment.
2. Remove hair pins.
3. Pour spirit gum remover/surgical spirit into a bowl. Apply using a brush to the edges of the wig, to release the adhesive. Use a brush underneath the lace.
4. Gently lift the wig off from the font and place it on a malleable block.

Remember...
When removing a wig, be sure to use spirit gum remover or surgical spirit.

Health and Safety
Never pull lace wigs off. It can be painful for the client and damage wig's lace front. Lace-front wigs can be expensive.

Health and Safety
Give the client a tissue to place over their eyes so the remover doesn't splash into them.

Cleaning wigs and postiche

1. Lay the postiche on a piece of tissue on a flat surface.

2. Use a firm bristle brush to apply IPA or surgical spirit, tapping the lace gently to dissolve the glue.

3. The same method can be used to clean lace-front wigs. Again, make sure you use a gentle tapping method as the lace is delicate.

Styling postiche

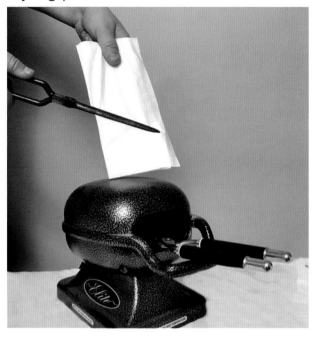

1. Heat tongs in oven and test temperature by placing tongs on tissue. If they are too hot they will turn the tissue brown and would therefore melt the hair.

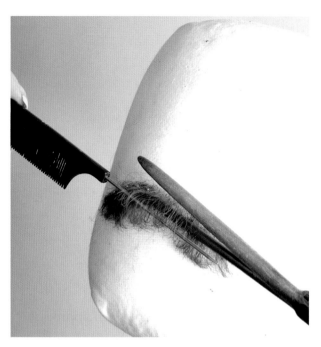

2. Using a tailcomb, take small section and tong the hair.

3. Trim with scissors before and after application

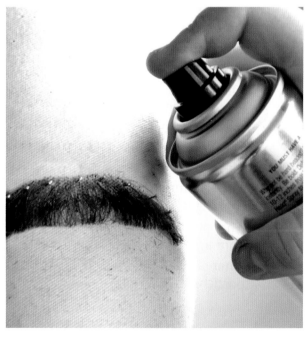

4. Use moustache wax or hairspray to help maintain the style, especially in damp weather.

How to evaluate results
Methods
- Visual
- Verbal
- Written feedback
- Repeat business
- Photographs.

Costing of service

When costing any hair service the following should be taken into consideration:

- Time it will take
- Products needed
- Equipment needed
- Skill level
- Time needed to design image, if appropriate.

End of chapter knowledge test

1. Name two accessories that can be used in hair design.
2. State the purpose of using a serum.
3. Name the outer layer of the hair.
4. Give two examples of an infestation of the hair and scalp.
5. What is meant by the term postiche?
6. Name two types of hair used in wigs.
7. What tool can be used for mixing hair during the wig-making process?
8. Why is it important to block a lace front wig before dressing it?
9. What product could be used to remove spirit gum from a wig?
10. What product can be used for the application of a postiche moustache?

CHAPTER 10

Apply airbrush make-up

Units covered by this chapter:

NVQ Level 3: Plan and provide airbrush make-up

VRQ Level 3: Apply airbrush make-up to the face

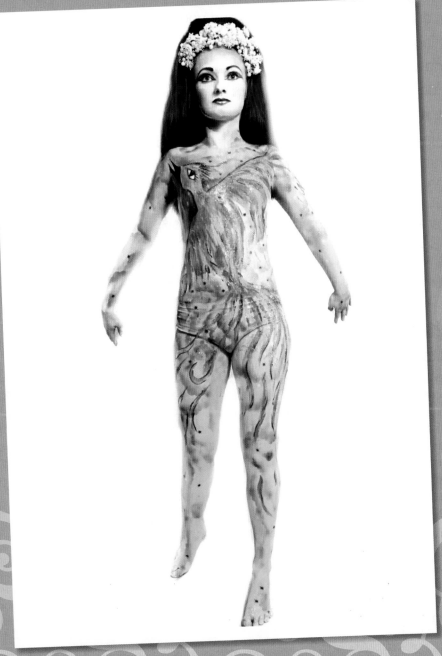

Chapter aims

This chapter will look at:

- Safe working practice (see Chapter 2 for full details)
- Tools, equipment and products for applying airbrush make-up
- Setting up the service area and preparing the client
- Getting started and troubleshooting
- Airbrushing techniques, including freehand, stencilling and masking
- Applying airbrush make up to the face and body
- Highlighting and shading
- Stencilling tattoos
- Fantasy designs
- Aftercare and homecare advice

Airbrush make-up has been specially formulated to spray evenly with an airbrush – an appliance that is about the size of a pen. The make-up is applied very quickly and evenly. Tiny molecules of water, alcohol, polymer or silicone-based foundation are sprayed through a fine- to medium-sized airbrush nozzle onto the skin. This type of make-up is a favourite for celebrities and models as it gives a flawless and very natural look.

Using airbrush make-up

Ingredients

The ingredients for airbrush make-up are straightforward. Like most liquid cosmetic formulations, the ingredients comprise of pigments, resins, solvents and additives. Pigments, which are often natural and mineral based, don't dissolve. They are a fine colour powder suspended in the solvent liquid. Solvents can be alcohol, water or oil based. The solvents help to get pigments and resins through the airbrush applicator and begin to evaporate as cosmetic film is laid down on the skin. **Resins**, also known as 'film formers', are the agent that binds the pigments to the skin surface.

You will find that manufacturers have their own specific recipes that include proprietary ingredients distinguishing their particular brands. Professional make-up artists have very specific criteria, especially for their work on high-definition TV, film sets, theatrical stage or long photo shoots, working in different climates, under water and much more. In most cases

---

Health and Safety

Be able to use and prepare for airbrush make-up:

- Set up your make-up station safely so no leads or wires are sticking out
- Ensure kit is clean and safe to use (PAT tested) and everything is to hand
- Store products as per manufacturers' guidelines
- Follow safe working practice and legislation.

make-up artists are looking for long-lasting make-up, make-up that is resistant to sweat or something special for airbrush make-up, tanning and body art. Today many manufacturers offer a wide range of products to meet both personal and professional use.

Range

While this make-up comes in a wide range of tones, the stock colours have additives that allow the pros to blend them perfectly.

Airbrush make-up manufacturers have made great advances over recent years. Improved manufacturing in pigments and foundations means greater ease of use and choices for personal daily wear. It is no longer just for use by celebrities and models. While many of the ingredients in airbrush make-up are generic, such as water or oil, all manufacturers in the beauty industry have to meet high standards. Reputable companies usually stand out by offering make-up that is hypoallergenic and made of high-quality, natural mineral pigments. This is not only great for daily wear, but especially beneficial for people with skin problems such as acne, rosacea, vitiligo or general facial discoloration.

Benefits

Airbrush make-up works very well for high-definition TV. It is very natural looking and long lasting.

Hygiene techniques and procedures

It is very important that you undertake the following to ensure excellent hygiene standards are maintained:

- Sanitise tools and equipment
- Clean brushes in isopropyl alcohol (IPA)
- Disinfect work surfaces
- Cover cuts and abrasions
- Sanitise your hands before and after make-up application
- Sanitise with gels and sprays
- Put dirty towels in a covered bin
- Dispense products with a spatula, pump or spray
- Use disposable products whenever possible
- Use chemicals correctly
- Avoid overexposure to chemicals
- Maintain excellent personal hygiene
- Follow manufacturers' instructions
- Enforce a no smoking rule
- Replace lids on uncapped bottles and pots
- Check product end dates and dispose of those out of date
- Store products away from heat, damp and direct sunlight.

 Health and Safety

Manual handling
Airbrush equipment can be very heavy. You may have a long way to travel to your make-up station and therefore a strong trolley is recommended as part of your kit.

 Health and Safety

Use personal protective equipment (PPE) including face masks when required. Health and Safety at Work Regulations and Provision and Use of Work Equipment Regulations must be followed.

 Remember . . .

You must have up-to-date public liability insurance – it is a must to cover yourself against anything that may go wrong.

 Health and Safety

All employers must be covered with employer's liability insurance under the Health and Safety at Work Act 1974.

Types of airbrush make-up

- **Silicone based**: Silicone-based formulations can help fill in pores and fine lines. It is a favourite among make-up artists, actors and models. Silicone has a natural glow that renders a dewy finish to this type of make-up. Silicone-based products can also be set with powder, which cannot be done with many water-based products.

- **Water based**: A water-based product is often oil and alcohol free, which makes it safe for clients of all skin conditions and ages. This type of formulation is now readily available from manufacturers who produce make-up for personal daily wear. Most manufacturers also offer SPF protection in their products.

- **Alcohol based**: Alcohol-based airbrush make-up is, for the most part, non-transferable, meaning that slight rubbing or brushing against clothing will not cause any wearing away or smudging.

- **Other formulations**: Airbrush make-up can be made to be resistant to sweat and have a long durability so that it does not need to be retouched for many hours. In such cases, polymer additives or alcohol-based additives have to be used.

While airbrush make-up comes in a wide variety of skin tones, stock colours have additives that allow the pros to blend them perfectly. Alcohol-based make-up is not generally used for the face but is a firm favourite for body work and prosthetics.

To apply airbrush make-up you will need:

- Compressor
- Airbrush
- Air hose
- Face make-up in a range of colours and body paints
- Stencils, sticky backed or non-sticky backed
- Adhesive
- Airbrush cleaning fluid, proprietary to the brand of make-up you are using
- Tissues, wet wipes, cotton buds, make-up remover
- Soft foundation brush
- Concealer and brush
- Mylar or acetate shapes for shaping and blocking out
- Frisket for masking off
- A well-ventilated work area
- Good lighting
- Make-up station and chair at correct height.

> "I founded Impet2us Limited in 2003 to supply Temptu products to the UK. At the time airbrushing make-up was still relatively new idea and considered by many as a gimmick and a passing fad. Over the past few years the finish airbrush make-up gives and the flexibility of the tool have been widely documented, so much so that actors, models, presenters etc are asking to be airbrushed. The art of airbrushing is now a prerequisite for any make-up artist and an essential skill to master."
>
> **Alison Wolstenholme**, make-up artist and body painter

Remember . . .

Only mix the same bases together, i.e. silicone with silicone, alcohol with alcohol, water base with water base. If you do mix the different types of make-up together you will find they will react against each other and cause a blockage in your airbrush.

▲ Airbrush equipment

How to troubleshoot

Spitting

- This is an unsteady stream of make-up that occurs when you start with make-up before air, or if you release too suddenly instead of gradually.

Flooding

- This is a solid messy stream from the airbrush that occurs when the make-up is not shaken or too much is applied without enough air.

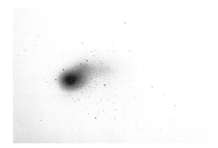

▲ Splattering

Spidering

- This is a blob of make-up that forms similar to a spider. It occurs when working too close to the face. Spray with less make-up and more air.

Clogging

When make-up does not flow through the airbrush. This occurs when:

- make-up is left in the cup for a long period of time
- the airbrush is not cleaned after each use
- make-up consistency is too thick.

To fix clogs, clean the nozzle and clean the needle.

To clean the nozzle:

- pour cleaning solution into the fluid cap
- depress and pull back the main lever while repeatedly replacing and removing your forefinger over the needle cap to produce back spray in the paint passage. This will dislodge residue from the nozzle and passage.
- increase the air pressure up to 40 psi and spray several fluid cups of cleaning solution through the airbrush. Return to the desired working pressure before continuing. Pressure cleaning by this method will thoroughly clean the paint passage, nozzle and needle.
- pressure cleaning at the end of each session will keep your airbrush maintenance-free.

▲ Spidering

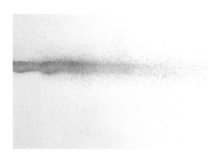

▲ Flooding

To clean the needle:

- loosen the needle chucking nut and slowly pull it out
- wipe residue off the needle by gently rotating it in a soft cloth or tissue.

Before each session, retract, rotate and reseat the fluid needle in another position to ensure consistent wear on the nozzle and needle. For smooth trigger action, grease the needle periodically with petroleum jelly. Do not use machine oil for lubrication.

Disassembling the airbrush for cleaning

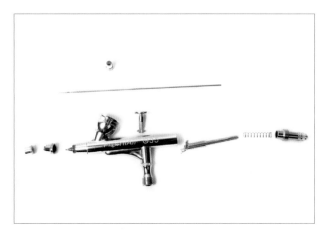

1. Always use white paper towels or cloths when disassembling the airbrush so you can see all the parts clearly and avoid losing any.

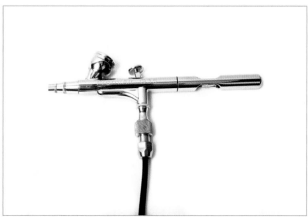

2. This is what an airbrush looks like when it is fully assembled and ready to use.

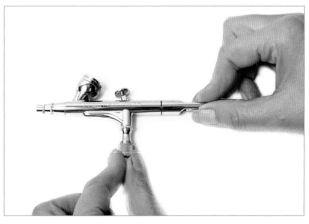

3. With the compressor turned off, remove the air hose from the airbrush unit by unscrewing the base.

4. Unscrew the handle.

5. Unscrew the chucking nut.

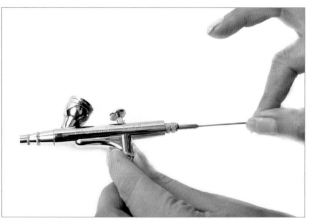

6. Carefully remove the needle (remember that the needles are extremely delicate).

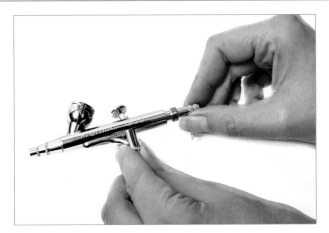

7. Unscrew the spring guide.

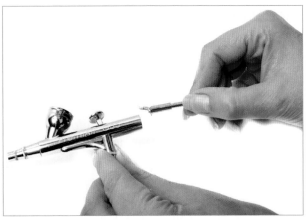

8. Remove the chucking nut, guide and needle spring. The chucking net, guide and needle spring must be removed simultaneously.

9. Remove the trigger and auxiliary lever. Hold the airbrush upside down and remove the trigger and auxiliary lever. Very gently shake the components onto white paper towel or cloth.

10. Unscrew and remove the head cap.

11. To keep your airbrush in good working order it is recommended that you thoroughly clean your airbrush after every use. Submerge all the parts in IPA. If your airbrush is severely clogged you can soak it for approximately 30 minutes. Always use the appropriate cleaning solution for recommended make-up. Clean the feeding cup.

12. Clean the nozzle and needle.

Airbrushing techniques

1. **Even colour washing**: This is the technique of applying an even colour to the body or face. The skill of the artist is important here. With a dual action airbrush it is important to keep the trigger in the same place and keep the airbrush at the same distance from the body. Any variation can cause an uneven effect. When applying an even colour wash over the body, consider using a single-action bottle-fed airbrush for speed.

2. **Back bubbling**: This is the technique of mixing two colours together to create a new colour in the airbrush itself. You must only do this with the same product type from the same manufacturer. Put the two colours you want to mix into the airbrush. Block off the front of the airbrush with a piece of tissue against your finger (this stops the air coming out of the airbrush). Depress the trigger and pull back – you will now see the colours bubbling and mixing in the cup.

3. **Colour fading**: This is fading two or more colours into each other, forming a seamless transition from one colour to another. To do this it is normally easiest to start with the lightest colour first and then build up from there.

4. **Blending**: Getting a perfect colour match to the model's skin can be easily achieved with back bubbling. When matching the foundation exactly to the model it is easier to blend the colour to those areas that may not have make-up applied, e.g. the neck, the décolletage etc. Blending the colour is an important job of the make-up artist.

5. **Stencilling**: Most people think of tattoos when we talk about stencilling but actually stencils can produce so much more. A wavy edge can produce sea foam, fish net tights can produce reptile or fish scales, and a straight edge of a stencil can create

▲ Stencilling

▲ Even colour washing

▲ Colour fading

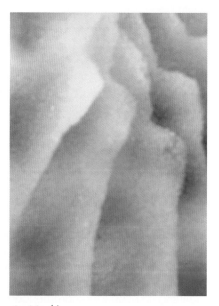

▲ Masking

interesting 'long eye' effects – the possibilities are endless. The art of good stencilling lies in getting the stencil as close to the skin as possible for a sharp outline.

6. **Masking**: This is similar to stencilling but instead of spraying through the stencil, masking involves blocking out or masking off, such as when using frisket for areas excluded from colour application.

7. **Freehand**: The technique of applying make-up or body paint to the model without any form of stencil or mask. The natural fine mist of the airbrush means this technique is best for when a sharp edge is not required such as in bending.

8. **Pulsing**: This is an important technique to learn but one that most people need a little time to master. Pulsing involves short, sharp movements on the trigger to produce a circle or dot (depending on how far away you are from the subject) without breaking the airflow.

▲ Freehand

Contraindications

It is important to recognise when a contraindication is present and not proceed with the application of airbrush make-up:

- Asthma
- Open or broken cuts, open wounds or infected skin
- If your client has a recent scar from an operation or an accident, in which case a doctor's letter is required to confirm it is safe to carry out the treatment.

Anatomy and physiology
See Chapter 4 for more information on contraindications.

Preparations

It is imperative to prepare and develop your airbrush design make-up plan before application can begin. You should make sure of the following:

- Look professional and be prepared to do the job – it gives the client confidence in your ability to provide them with the outcome they desire.
- Establish how long it will take you to apply the make-up.
- Work out the cost of the make-up, type of make-up (water, silicone or alcohol based) you will need and amount of product you will need to achieve the design.
- Know if you will need to modify the treatment.

Preparing your working area for yourself and your client

The following are essential for good working practice:

- Working station and chair set to correct height in a work area set up and prepared with everything to hand
- Protective clothing where necessary, including face/eye masks
- Products clearly labelled and chemicals stored correctly to comply with appropriate health and safety regulations.

Environmental conditions

- Good lighting
- Good ventilation.

Consultation techniques for effective objective setting

The following can be used before treatment to ensure treatment is delivered as required:

- Open questions
- Closed questions
- Consultation sheet, face chart and body chart
- Hand-written notes
- Eye contact
- Body language
- Nodding.

It is important of carry out a detailed skin analysis and relevant skin testing to establish whether your client or artist has any allergies and to prevent contra-actions and contraindications.

▲ Hard masking

Selecting products, tools and equipment

- Use detailed notes, face charts, design briefs and scripts to establish the design required.
- Establish what tools, make-up and equipment you will need to successfully meet the design.
- Consult with the client or artist, make detailed notes, and carry out a skin test (ensure you date and record skin test results on the face chart or client record card).

▲ Hard masking

Modification of service

There are many reasons why you may need to modify your airbrushing service depending on where and which part of the body you are working on. Good ventilation will be a key factor, especially if you are working on a full-body make-up. Take into consideration the comfort of your clients and adapt the treatment accordingly. In general you should note the following:

- Your treatment area should be clean and tidy, to reduce the risk of cross-infection.
- The area should be well ventilated with good lighting, and you may want to use relaxing music.
- Dehydrated skin can be recognised by flaking and tightness.
- Open pores can be recognised by stretched ducts or hair follicles.
- To create bold lines use the hard masking technique.

▲ Thick line

Airbrushing – getting started

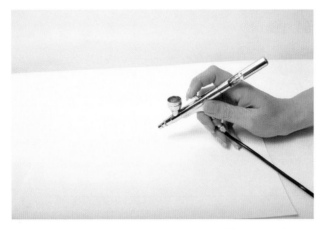

1. Grip the airbrush using your second finger and thumb; use your index finger to operate the trigger.

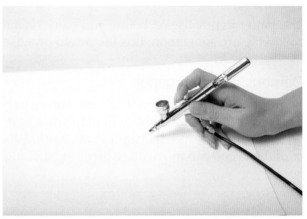

2. Press down the trigger so the air blows out.

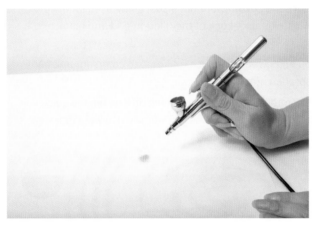

3. Pulling back the trigger releases the colour. Pull trigger further. Pulling the trigger further allows more colour to come through; the further back it goes the more colour comes out. Assess how much colour and coverage you need and adjust the spray accordingly.

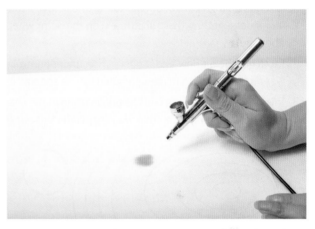

4. Push the trigger forward to stop the flow of a colour.

5. Take your finger off the trigger and this will stop the flow of air. Always remember to turn on the air first and turn off the air last.

6. Push down trigger to let out a small blast of air to blow away any residue.

Practising techniques on paper

Freehand

Use paper to practise on before you work on a model. The
following are some more tips for you to practise.

Demonstration on paper

Draw shapes and fill them in. Draw crosses to practise your aim.
Try writing your name; this will help you to get good control
with the air flow and distribution of colour. When you feel
confident, you can move on to blending techniques.

Activity

To start practising your techniques on paper, here are some exercises to complete:

1. Practise on a grid sheet similar to the one below. Aim to do a series of different dot sizes, going from small to larger dots, getting them accurately on the point where you are aiming. Look at the filled-in grid and blank grid sheet below.

2. Try to get the air flow and trigger action under control – you don't want too much make-up to come out and be wet on the skin. The make-up should dry as soon as it is sprayed onto the skin.

3. This worksheet requires you to work on filling in the shapes, controlling the colour and keeping it within the guide line. Keep good, consistent air flow working in different directions, using the airbrush as you would if you were drawing.

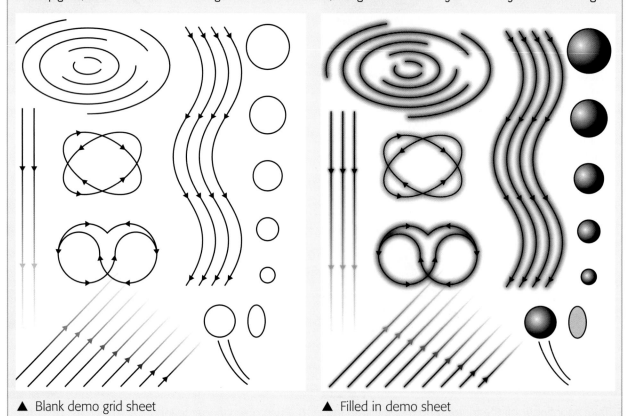

▲ Blank demo grid sheet   ▲ Filled in demo sheet

Blending techniques

Use masking tape to make small windows to work in. Try the activities opposite.

Stencilling

Some stencils have a sticky backing to help secure the stencil in place and stop the colour from seeping through. You can also get a special spray adhesive to spray onto the stencil, which can be cleaned off with IPA. These stencils should be cleaned after every use for hygiene purposes.

Activity

1. On paper, do a nice, even wash of colour.
2. Colour fade halfway down a window, for example from red to white (the colour of the paper).
3. Fade two colours into each other.
4. Fade three colours into each other.
5. Use the torn edge of a piece of paper or a stencil and spray part onto the paper. Hold the paper down nice and firm so the colour does not seep.

Airbrushing full straight make-up

N.B. These techniques reflect those used by a make-up artist working in the industry rather than a therapist working in a salon.

1. Set up your work station.

2. Sanitise your hands and prepare your model.

3. Protect your model's hair and clothing.

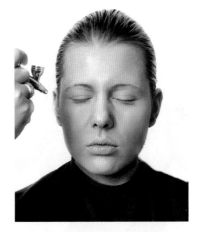

4. Use concealer and brush under eye area. There are limitations on application of make-up by the eye area – it is not safe to spray make-up under the eyes when the eyes are open and eye liner and mascara must be applied with make-up brushes and mascara wands. You will also need to use a foundation brush to work the foundation into areas such as open pores around the nose and under the eyes.

5. Choose the make-up and colour best suited to your model's skin type and tone. Set the psi (pounds per square inch) to the correct recommended pressure for the area you are working on: for the face it should be between 4 and 15 psi. Put a few drops of make-up into the airbrush and press the trigger down to let the air flow. The closer you are working toward the eyes, nose and mouth the lower you will have to set the psi. Working from the outer part of the face, work your way inward and adjust the psi accordingly. You will need to add a lighter colour (about two shades lighter) to add highlighting to the face.

6. Move in a small circular direction and with an even flow of make-up. At first when you are applying the make-up you may think it is not coming out, but it is such a fine mist and you will see it start to appear. It will build up gradually and you can control the amount of make-up coming out by pulling back and forth on the trigger as needed.

7. When your model and you are happy with the application you can move on to highlighting and shading. Put a few drops of your chosen shading colour (about two shades darker) into the airbrush and apply. Use a foundation brush to work make-up into the skin around the nose, eyes and skin area where there is any soft down hair.

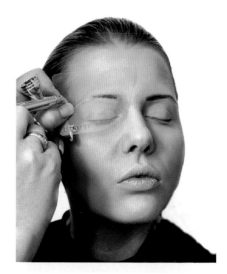

8. Apply powder. At this point on a regular make-up session you would set the make-up with translucent powder. With airbrush make-up, especially silicone based, your client or artist may like the glow that it has on the skin, so this is optional.

9. You can use a stencil to draw on the eyebrows in the same way as for tattoos, or you can use a specially designed acetate shape to achieve this by holding it safely in place and designing your own shape of eyebrow. First change the psi to a lower setting as you are working near the eyes. Remember to flush your airbrush out to get the darker colour out.

10. Change the psi to a lower setting. Use a light base colour for the eyes and a small brush to work the make-up into the skin using a patting and rolling technique. Flush out the airbrush with cleaning fluid.

11. Pick out the colours for the eye shadow socket lines. Put a few drops of the eye shade colour into the airbrush cup. Instruct the model to keep their eyes closed then softly move the spray in a circular, left-to-right half movement to contour the eye socket line. You can add a few drops of a darker colour (use the back bubbling technique to mix the colours together to add depth to the colour). You can then add a bit more depth to the socket line. Always work alternately from one eye to the other as this will help you to balance the colours evenly.

12. Apply the eye liner under the eyes and then apply the mascara. It is important that you do the under-eye liner with an eye liner pencil or an eye liner brush, and eye liner or eye shadow. The mascara will have to be done in the usual way. There are limitations to applying make-up with an airbrush – you cannot apply airbrush make-up under the eyes when they are open. Remember to clean out the airbrush with some cleaning fluid.

13. Apply cheek colour. When you have chosen your cheek colour, put a few drops into the cup of the airbrush. Make sure the psi is correct for the area you are working on. Get your subject to close their eyes. If you get them to smile, the apples of the cheeks become prominent and this will help you to place the blusher in the correct place. Use a fine mist and build up the colour gradually until you achieve the desired look. Remember to flush out the airbrush.

14. Apply lip colour. You must make sure the mouth is closed. It is easiest to use lip liner and lipstick for the simple reason that if you are on a set or a photo shoot it is more practical to use a lipstick than to have to carry a compressor around with you. You can get rechargeable airbrushes but if you have to get another artist to look after your model this is an easier option.

15. The finished look.

Airbrushing tattoos using stencils

1. Set up your work station.

2. Sanitise your hands and prepare your model.

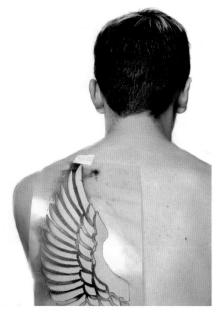

4. Alcohol-based make-up with a setting powder is good for creating tattoos. It is waterproof and will last longer than other types of make-up. It will not rub off onto clothing and can last up to 5 or 6 days. If you need it to come off sooner, use a recommended remover.

3. Place and secure the stencil. Choose the stencil type. Remember you can apply a self-adhesive stencil. Peel off the backing and place the sticky side of the stencil onto the desired area. Alternatively a spray adhesive can be applied to the back of the stencil.

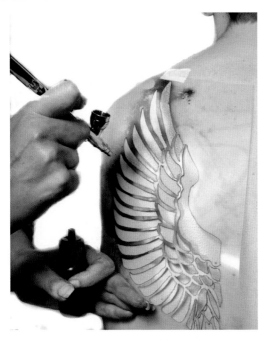

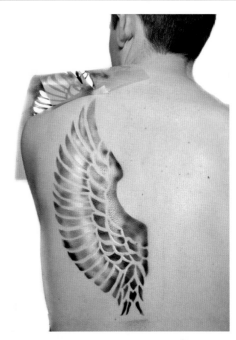

5. When the stencil is secure and in place, spray your chosen colour onto the inside edge of the stencil. Repeat this until the area inside and up to the edge of the stencil is coloured in evenly. When applying the make-up, make sure the applied make-up is not wet on the skin – it should be dry as it is a fine mist. If you find the make-up is too wet, you are either pulling the trigger back too much and letting out too much make-up or your psi/bar setting may be too high.

6. When you are happy with the coverage of make-up within the tattoo area, peel off the stencil. The edges should be nice, sharp and cleanly finished. If you have a smudge you can use a cotton bud dipped in remover and gently remove the smudged area. Use the dry end of the cotton bud to remove any excess remover.

7. Place some setting powder onto a clean tissue and apply it to the tattoo with a powder brush. The setting powder will give the tattoo an aged look.

8. The finished tattoo.

Airbrushing body art

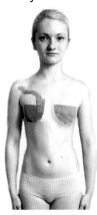

1. Prepare your model. When doing body art you need to put your model in flesh-coloured seamless knickers. It is optional what you put on top – you could use a seamless bra or nipple covers. Here we have chosen to use cut-out shapes of Lycra™ stuck on with Pros-Aide®. A sponge stippled with Pros-Aide® has been used around the edges and a setting powder has been used to make a softer edge to blend into the skin.

Draw the outline of your design using a white eyeliner and then start to fill in your design with the main colours.

2. Following the guide of your design drawn on with eyeliner, use a freehand technique with the airbrush to start to fill in your design. Use an even colour wash and blending technique. Sponges and brushes can be used to add detail and to outline your design.

4. Use the same techniques to add more detail, definition and dimension to your design.

3. Continue to use freehand techniques with the airbrush. Use even colour wash and blending techniques as well as sponges and brushes to completely cover your body and fill in your outline design.

 Remember...

Take into consideration the comfort of your model at all times.

 Remember...

Always work in a well-ventilated area when airbrushing.

5. Use stencils or cut-out shapes to enhance and intensify the effect of your design. We have used a cloud shape to create grey clouds.

6. At this point you can put in your final detail by adding any outline highlighting, shading or contouring and adding any additional media such as glitter gems.

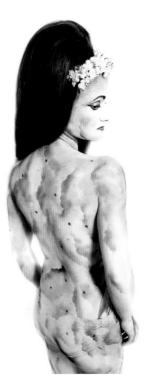

7. Stars have been airbrushed on all over the body using a stencil.

The eyebrows have been airbrushed on using an eyebrow stencil.

Black has been airbrushed into the eye sockets and extended out to make the eyes look larger. To do this, ask the artist to close their eyes and use a stencil to block out the air flow going into the eye. Use the outer part of the stencil as a guide for the top eyeliner.

The under eyes have been completed using a powder eye shadow and an angled brush. (There are limitations on where you can use an airbrush: it would be very dangerous to use when the eyes are open.) The traditional method has also been used to apply mascara.

The airbrush and a freehand technique have been used to apply blusher.

The lips have been outlined with a lip liner and a lipstick has been applied with a lip brush. A shimmer has been added to the middle of the bottom lip to give a frosting effect.

8. Different colour glitter has been added to the front and back to complete the design.

Remember . . .
Remember to turn the psi lower when working won the face, eyes and nose.

9. The finished look.

Additional media

You can also use additional media to achieve lots of different effects. Here are some for you to try:

- Lace
- Fishnet tights
- Feathers
- Different shapes
- Microspore tape to mask shapes.

Contra-actions

- redness, itching or swelling
- burning or stinging
- blistering
- rash

Remove make-up immediately with suitable remover and clean the area with water if any of these occur seek medical advice.

Aftercare and homecare advice

- **Suitable removal technique**: The removal of make-up will depend on the make-up used. Check with the manufacturer for the recommended removal method, e.g. 70 per cent IPA to remove alcohol-based make-up.

- **Make-up longevity**: Again, this depends on the make-up used. Some alcohol-based body paints, for example, can last a week if they are not removed! Good-quality airbrush make-up will last a minimum of 12 hours.

Remember . . .

It is important to avoid swimming and strenuous activity while wearing airbrushed make-up. The type of make-up applied will depend on the occasion or activity for which it is intended. Some types of make-up last longer than others and some, like alcohol-based make-up, are waterproof. Find out from your client what they wish to achieve from the make-up and choose the most suitable.

 Anatomy and physiology

Refer to Chapter 4 for more information.

End of chapter knowledge test

1. What type of PPE can the make-up artist wear to protect themselves when performing airbrush treatments?
2. Why is it important to complete airbrush make-up services in a commercially acceptable time?
3. Why is it important to have adequate ventilation when carrying out airbrush make-up services?
4. Why is it important to check for contraindications before completing an airbrushing service?
5. Why must you position the client correctly when carrying out airbrush make-up treatments on the face?
6. Why is it important to run cleaning fluid through the airbrush after use?
7. How can overspray be removed from the client's skin after completing a temporary tattoo?
8. What is the best method of removing alcohol-based airbrush make-up products from the skin?
9. What is the maximum PSI for airbrush make-up on the face?
10. How often should the airbrush compressor be serviced?

CHAPTER 11

Art of fashion and photographic make-up

Units covered by this chapter:

VRQ Level 2: The art of photographic make-up

VRQ Level 3: Fashion and photographic make-up

NVQ Level 3 Unit B11: Design and create fashion and photographic make-up

Chapter aims

This chapter will look at:

- Types of lighting
- Make-up products for fashion and photographic make-up
- Period looks
- Fantasy make-up
- Catwalk fashion
- Bridal make-up
- Commercial photographic make-up
- Make-up products
- Venue research.

What is fashion and beauty? It is hard to escape seeing beautiful images of men and women in magazines, showing off their amazing looks. This encourages us to go and seek a better look for ourselves, to look and feel good. Fashion and trends show off personality and individuality.

These images are plastered all over magazines and billboards for everyone to see. It is common knowledge that many people aspire to look like their idols, so fashion photographic images show the general public products, clothing and accessories that they want them to desire. Famous celebrities and models who are associated with a product or clothing line are a commercial asset for the companies to help sell their goods. Make-up artists play a big part in working as a team within the fashion, make-up and hair industry.

Photographic make-up

When applying make-up for photographic purposes, it is important to consider the effect that has to be created; this should be planned in advance with the photographer prior to the application of make-up.

You will need to take into consideration the brightness of the lighting being used. The brighter the lighting is the lighter the make-up pigment will appear. Therefore the make-up will need to be applied more strongly. The lighting can get very hot and may affect the make-up application by making the make-up melt, especially with oil-based make-up. Therefore it is best to avoid oily make-up and apply powder regularly to remove shine.

Remember . . .

Remember to keep the skin as cool as possible during application of make-up. Grease on the face will produce an unattractive shine and emphasise creases and open pores. Choose powder-based products to help achieve a matte finish.

The pearliest make-up products look attractive on photographs because they reflect light, but they can also cause glare. These products look more attractive when kept to a minimum and they should be contrasted with matte-finish products.

You may need to use body make-up or corrective make-up to balance out any high colour or blemishes. You will need to be careful and protect the clothing, especially when applying make-up around the collar and neckline, and the body by placing tissues in and around vulnerable areas of the clothing so you can work without causing make-up damage to the clothing. Remember to remove these tissues prior to the photographic session.

Photographic lighting wipes out the natural highlights and shadows created by the facial contour. Make-up artists use highlighting and shading techniques to define the bone structure and to balance the features. Hard lines are emphasised more on camera. All make-up products must be blended in well to ensure that there are no hard demarcation lines; this is particularly important when applying contour cosmetics and blending foundations under the jawline and into the hairline.

The camera will pick-up patches of discoloration and natural shadows created by skin folds. All you need to even out the skin colour and light in areas such as under the eyes and creases at the side of the nostrils, is highlighting and shading the face to sharpen and bring out its contours and soften areas where needed.

Tip Redness from blemishes shows up easily so great care should be taken to apply a clean, even base.

Tip Make sure to powder over the ears as they can look red in colour photographs.

Tip To help to keep body temperature down for your artist and model, you will need a chamois leather cloth and a bottle of cologne. Spray the cologne onto the cloth to make it damp but not wringing wet. Hold the damp cloth at arm's length and swing it in a circular motion. You will need to do this fairly fast for a few seconds, then stop. The cloth becomes icy cold and you can put it on the back of your artist's or model's neck to help cool them down; it is also very refreshing. This is a must for a make-up artist's kit box.

Lighting

One of the hardest things to get right in photography is the lighting. Too much light, too little or a combination of the two can ruin an otherwise perfect photo. Luckily this problem can be solved if you understand the type of lighting, the effect on your camera and what you can do to use the effect to your advantage.

Back lighting

Back lighting is just as it sounds: light that comes from behind your subject. This type of lighting can make a beautiful photo or turn what could be a beautiful photo into a complete disaster.

Back lighting is what turns palm trees into silhouettes against the sunset. In this case it is a good thing and adds to a photograph but the same thing can happen if you want to take a photograph of a person who has this strong back light behind them such as the Sun, sky or bright lights. The camera reads the brightness, including the light behind the main subject and causes its internal meter to compensate for the extra light in the shot. This causes underexposure of your subject and as a result will usually turn them into silhouettes.

▲ Photographic make-up

Side lighting

Side lighting can also have a very dramatic effect on your photos, but unlike back lighting, its brightness comes from the right or the left of your subject. One side tends to be cast into total darkness, while the other is put in the spotlight. This is a wonderful way to get a mysterious, dramatic portrait photo. Pose your subject in front of a window, with one of their shoulders close to the window. Your camera will expose properly for the bright side and will usually cast the other side of the face in complete darkness. If, on the other hand, you want a natural portrait you can use something to reflect light onto the darkened side of the face. A white post or other light-reflective surfaces can bounce enough light back onto your subjects to soften the effect of the side lighting. Side lighting is wonderful for showing texture and adding depth to the photo.

▲ Bright lighting

▲ Moonlighting: lighting affects the make-up colours

For more on lighting see Chapter 14.

Diffused lighting

Sometimes lighting from any direction is just too harsh. Diffused lighting can be used when you want to soften the incoming light, to take away some of the contrast for a more pleasing photograph. Bright sunlight at midday is the worst kind of light for a photographer – it makes colours appear washed out and contrasting shadows too dark. To avoid this, wait for the sun to go behind a cloud or if your subjects are mobile, put them in the shade of a tree or a building and take the photo. The light will be much more natural here and will result in a better photo. If it is not possible to move your subject and there is no cloud in sight, you can sometimes make your own shade with an umbrella or some similar object, or come back in the morning or evening when the sun is lower in the sky.

Artificial lighting

Artificial lighting comes in all shapes and sizes, from a built-in flash on your camera to expensive lights in studios. All of these sources of artificial lighting have their strengths and weaknesses.

On-camera flashes are simple and easy to use, but sometimes cause the awful red eye effect so common in snapshots. The further the flash is away from the lens the less likely this is to happen. Another problem with on-camera flash is the harsh light it casts onto the subject. If you have an off-camera flash you can bounce the light to soften the effect.

One last thing to remember about artificial light is that unless you are using black and white film, regular indoor lights will give your photos a yellow cast. These lights are not the equivalent of flash bulb lights and therefore will not give you the same result.

Knowing the simple tips about lighting will help you to go out and make the most of all your photo opportunities. With practice, your photography will open up new opportunities for you.

Cross lighting

Cross lighting is used in photos taken with a mixture of flash, man-made sources and outdoor or natural lighting. It is very similar to flash and strobe lighting, but it is a must that these photos be taken outdoors and are affected by natural light, either at a main or fill source.

This is a light source from more than one direction, i.e. daylight and lamp, or two studio lamps.

Colour

Strong, bright tones on coloured photos look fantastic but foundations need to be of good coverage and not thick and heavy. Good foundations with strong pigment are recommended as they provide very good coverage without giving a heavy made-up outlook. High-definition foundation works well.

▲ Colour photography

Monochrome

Monochrome is the incorporating of black and white into the application of make-up. The make-up base has to be very clean but can be of a heavier consistency than when using colour film. Eye shadows and lipsticks have to be chosen for their depth upon appearance rather than the colour. Remember to choose products that contain enough depth to show up on film.

Remember that darker colours will appear darker when photographed, therefore it may be necessary to apply a lighter shade in preference to a darker one. For example, a dark shade of cheek colour would create a dark shadow. Lip gloss should be avoided unless you wish the lips to appear to be fuller.

Make-up products
Make-up: Camouflage

- **Skin type**: Suitable for all skin types
- **Coverage/texture**: Provides excellent full coverage without looking like a heavy, thick application
- **Ingredients**: High pigment content in make-up
- **Important notes to remember**: This product is water resistant and excellent for covering hyperpigmentation, hypopigmentation, erythema, bruising, scars, birthmarks and tattoos. This product is available on the NHS for some conditions.

▲ Monochrome photography

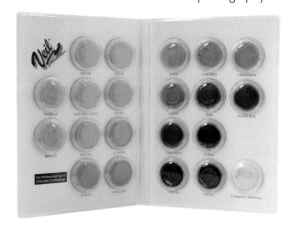
▲ Camouflage make-up

For more information on camouflage make-up, see Chapter 13.

Make-up: Liquid foundation (oil or water)

- **Skin type**: Suitable for normal or combination skin. Matte/medicated foundations are available for oily or greasy skin types
- **Coverage/texture**: Light coverage semi-matte finish (this produces a light, natural look in photos and on screen)
- **Ingredients**: Pigment, minerals, wax titanium dioxide cerasin
- **Important notes to remember**: It has a shorter working time on application than cream foundation.

Make-up: Tinted moisturiser

- **Skin type**: Suitable for all skin types
- **Coverage/texture**: Natural coverage
- **Ingredients**: As for liquid foundation, as well as moisturise humectants, oil and water, added pigments
- **Important notes to remember**: It is very useful for light coverage and gives a very natural effect. It is especially good for use on children and men.

Make-up: Cream make-up (water in oil)

- **Skin type**: Suitable for most skin types. It will keep the skin extra-moisturised
- **Coverage/texture**: Medium coverage
- **Ingredients**: This make-up contains a higher oil content, with pigment, minerals, wax, titanium and dioxide cerasin
- **Important notes to remember**: It is available in compact and pan stick forms. It is long lasting when used with setting products such a translucent powder.

Make-up: Tinted gel

- **Skin type**: Suitable for all skin types
- **Coverage/texture**: Provides very light, transparent coverage
- **Ingredients**: Water, alcohol, pigment and titanium dioxide
- **Important notes to remember**: It is light, transparent coverage and very good for giving a sun-kissed look and healthy glow (gels can be drying).

Make-up: Tinted self tan

- **Skin type**: Suitable for all skin types
- **Coverage/texture**: Gives very light, sheer coverage
- **Ingredients**: Pigments in a water-based gel
- **Important notes to remember**: It is generally used for giving a tanned glow. Working time is very short. When applied correctly it will give a very natural, sun-kissed glow to the skin. It is good for use on both males and females.

Make-up: Mousse

- **Skin type**: Suitable for all skin types
- **Coverage/texture**: This gives light, sheer coverage and is very natural looking
- **Ingredients**: Pigment, minerals, wax, titanium, dioxide cerasin. Available in either oil or water base

Make-up: Two-in-one foundation

- **Skin type**: Suitable for oily skin type (because of its very high powder content – it helps to absorb oils)
- **Coverage/texture**: Medium and heavy coverage with a matte finish
- **Ingredients**: Contains powder producers or a small amount of mineral oil, talc and kaolin pigments
- **Important notes to remember**: Make-up is very durable and lasts a long time on the skin.

Make-up: High definition

- **Skin type**: Suitable for normal, combination or dry skin types (oily skin types will need to be powdered well)
- **Coverage/texture**: Full coverage. Provides a light, very natural finish
- **Ingredients**: Silicone and strong pigment
- **Important notes to remember**: Provides full coverage very similar to that of an airbrush – a very natural finish.

Make-up: Airbrush (silicone based)

- **Skin type**: Suitable for all skin types.
- **Coverage/texture**: Provides full coverage and a light, very natural finish
- **Important notes to remember**: Used to fill in pores and fine lines.

Make-up: Airbrush (alcohol based)

- **Skin type**: For use on the body rather than the face
- **Coverage/texture**: Highly pigmented for full long-lasting coverage
- **Important notes to remember**: This is non-transferable so will not smudge when rubbed slightly.

Venue research

Before booking a venue, you should find out:

- If the group organiser has conducted a risk assessment and ask to see it. If this is not the case, you should carry out your own risk assessment and health and safety inspection

- If first aid facilities are available
- Whether security and parking are available
- About the ventilation system
- If there is hot and cold water
- What type of lighting is available
- Where the electrical sockets are
- Where the fire exits are and the building evacuation procedures
- What the maximum number of people is in accordance to the fire certificate
- The number of chairs and tables available
- Whether there will be disabled clients and whether they have disabled facilities
- If make-up mirrors are available and if the make-up chair will be at a good height
- Who the first aider is.

Fashion and photographic make-up
Period looks

It is essential to know about and understand how lifestyle, position in society, and social history have affected fashion in different countries of the world.

You should also know about historical characters such as those from the following locations and time periods: 1) ancient Greece, 2) Egypt, 3) Medieval, 4) Elizabethan, 5) eighteenth century, 6) Victorian, 7) Edwardian, 8) 1920s, 9) 1930s, 10) 1940s, 11) burlesque, 12) 1950s, 13) 1960s, 14) 1970s, 15) 1980s etc.

It is important to research these properly so that you get the period look correct. Sometimes going to stately homes, museums and art galleries is very helpful as you can look at original portraits and delve into the archives of different generations of families and staff who lived within the establishment.

Different people dress differently according to their place in society. You could be very wealthy and have your own servants to look after your family or you could be working class (very poor and be working in the work house).

Washing facilities weren't what we are used to, oral hygiene was not good and people's teeth may have looked yellow, rotten, or were even missing. In some periods working class people would look quite grubby.

Remember . . .

Prepare yourself by making sure that you are suitably dressed, equipment is sanitised and you have good oral hygiene.

Health and Safety

Patch testing should be carried out at least 24 hours before you use the products on the client or artist, i.e. eyelash glue, spirit gum etc.

Remember . . .

If you are working freelance, you must turn up on time for the job as make-up call times are given to fit in with those of all the other crew members. Make-up and wardrobe are the first ones in so if you arrive late you put out all of the other timings for the rest of the day and there will be other crew members sitting around waiting. Remember time is money and you will have some producers and members of the crew who will be very cross as they have very early starts and work long hours.

Remember . . .

Select the right products, tools and equipment within the budget to suit the make-up design.

Health and Safety

Follow health and safety working practice. Refer to Chapter 2 for details.

Inspirational looks

Fantasy make-up

Creating a fantasy make-up look can let your imagination run free; things can be larger than life, dramatic and colourful. With this style:

- There is no right or wrong
- Your ideas are individual
- Your thoughts are your own
- How one sees, another may miss
- All passions are different
- All experiences are different
- We all have personal memories
- You can think outside the box.

Fantasy make-up

N.B. These techniques reflect those used by a make-up artist working in the industry rather than a beauty therapist working in a salon.

1. Repeat steps 1–5 from the day look in Chapter 7. Use pigment with water to create a thick creamy texture of make-up.

2. Apply different colours and consistencies in a similar way to how an artist would use oil paints.

3. Continue adding liquid face paint on top of this to create other dimensions and to add texture.

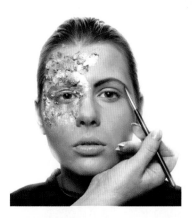

4. Use an angled brush and black eyeshadow to define the eyebrow.

5. Add black to the eyelid and a strong socket line on the left eye.

6. Add liquid eyeliner to build up a stronger and sharper effect.

7. Add dark mauve lipliner and shimmery gloss lipstick.

8. The finished look. The inspiration for the look is an artist's palette.

Catwalk fashion

Fashion make-up may be for catwalk shows, fashion shoots or private clients. Catwalk shows are used for designers to display their forthcoming collections. Collections are usually launched twice a year: Spring/Summer and Autumn/Winter. Design is usually worked on a season in advance.

Catwalk shows are live events viewed by an audience or televised, therefore make-up has to be strong enough to be seen from a distance and it also has to complement and work well with the lighting. Lots of famous people normally turn up to fashion shows.

The make-up designs will be dictated by the designers so the make-up and hair is working to complement the designs within the clothing collection shown at the fashion show.

Make-up tends to be more avant-garde and eye-catching. For the runway most catwalks are organised by the Pacific PR groups, who work with teams of hair and make-up artists. Designers can be quite demanding in their aspirations to create certain emotions through images. Working in this field of make-up tends to be created and many of the designs are described as 'fantasy'.

The strong artificial lighting that floods this stage can make a lot of colours look less vibrant and the make-up has to be compensated for with warmer shades of foundation and bolder colours for eyes and lips.

Stage lighting also produces a lot of heat, particularly if spotlights are being used. Make-up application will make the face perspire even more and the foundation will melt. If this does occur, there is a big risk of the clothing becoming damaged, causing costume changes.

The make-up will appear less obvious to people sitting at the back of the large venue, so extra definition is required when contouring the face with make-up for eyes, eyebrows and lips. A greater contrast is needed between highlighters and shaders.

You must look after your models during the show, helping them to keep cool so that the make-up is not spoiled or ruined. Use a fine mist of water spray over their face, pressed powder or blot powders to remove any shine. It is important that you check your models regularly to maintain their make-up throughout the show. You may be required to do hair and make-up changes during the performance and you must be organised and aware of when they need to happen so that they are all done on time.

▲ Fashion make-up

▲ Fashion make-up

 Remember...

When working on a fashion show it is very important to see the area where your artists will be. Check the lighting and distance that the subject will be from the stage or catwalk; this is important because the distance will determine how strong the make-up needs to be and what kind of make-up to use for the best results.

A running order of the show is essential. Usually you will have a make-up and hair designer who will organise this for you as a guide on the make-up and hair changes. This guide will show when, where and who will be responsible for dealing with the changes.

It may help to get blot papers to remove oils from the chin and T-zones.

Generally fashion make-up gives the make-up artist a chance to be very creative. It is an opportunity to try new products, such as seasonal colours, and new techniques.

▲ Catwalk look 1

▲ Catwalk look 2

▲ Catwalk look 3

Bridal make-up

Bridal make-ups have such a wide range of looks, including traditional, cultural and a themed wedding look. The following should be noted:

- A trial run should be carried out before the wedding day to discuss the client's needs and requirements.
- The trial will give the make-up artist a chance to collect as much information as possible and to ensure the bride is confident and happy with the make-up.
- It is always a good idea to make a note on a face chart of the client record card of all of the chosen products ready for the actual makeover.
- If you are not doing the hair, it is important to arrange times for applying make-up in conjunction with the hair stylist. Consider how the hair will be worn: straight or curly, up or down, a tiara, headdress or veil?

- The main aim for most bridal make-up is to create a very natural look that enhances the bride's features as many brides do not usually wear make-up but want to make a special effort on their wedding day. It is a good idea not to dramatically change a bride's make-up for her wedding day as she will not feel comfortable or confident, and could give the groom a shock!

- The colouring of the bride's hair, eyes and skin should be considered as with any other makeover.

- The colour and style of the dress is a major factor when deciding on make-up choice. Not all brides wear white or ivory. There are so many different designs, styles and colour choices on the market including extremes such as pink, black, red and purple worn by the bride. People often follow current make-up and fashion trends and some will dare to look very different on their wedding day.

- The type of wedding and location, e.g. registry office, church, castle, office, boat etc. will also give the make-up artist an idea of the bride and her personality, and will also set the tone for the make-up choice.

▲ Bridal look

- Weddings often have a chosen theme and colours. Sometimes a colour theme will be the only factor to consider but themes can be as eccentric as medieval, period, cultural, or with oriental designs, or seasonal themes (Christmas, summer etc.). Flower designs will need to be considered.

- How the make-up will last throughout the day is an important consideration. Waterproof mascara is essential and a long-lasting lipstick is advisable. It is advisable to encourage the bride to buy lipstick or lip gloss to top up throughout the day. Some make-up artists will include lipstick or lip gloss within the price of the wedding makeover.

The bride may want her bridesmaids and mother to be made over also. Consider charging for trials and work out a price for a package whenever possible. Sometimes deals can be made to cover the cost of all of the makeovers.

There are many interpretations on bridal make-up and it is very individual and personal. The make-up style requested may be:

- Traditional
- Themed wedding
- Period look
- Cultural.

Male make-up

Male make-up is becoming increasingly popular.

Commercial photographic make-up

Colour

Make-up used for commercial purposes can be used to promote a wide variety of products including:

- A product, which may be perfume, make-up or clothing
- Hair products
- A product such as furniture
- Workout videos
- Book covers
- Magazine covers

There are several things to consider when doing a photo shoot for commercial purposes. The number one priority is to show all the potential of the product. For example, if the company has brought out a new range of lipstick, your job as a make-up artist will be to show off this product to its best potential. If the lipstick is a bright red colour, the make-up should not overpower and draw the attention to the lashes on the model. If the eyes are beautiful and more simply made up then the strong red lips will stand out more. In this way the focal point has become the stunning model and those amazing red lips. Remember it is about showing off that new shade of red lipstick.

▲ Male make-up ("guyliner")

▲

▲

Commercial make-up

N.B. These techniques reflect those used by a make-up artist working in the industry rather than a therapist working in a salon

1. Repeat steps 1 to 5 of the day make-up procedure in Chapter 7. This includes applying foundation, concealer, highlighting and shading and adding powder.

2. Cover the whole eye with shimmer cream shade and fill the socket area with soft taupe shade.

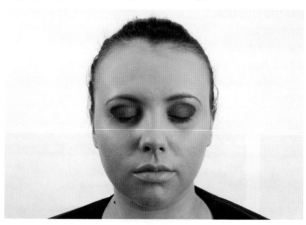

3. Focus on the outer corners of the socket and define across the lash line and slightly above the natural socket line using a darker taupe brown shade.

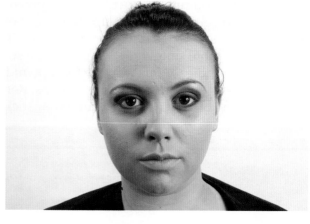

4. Soften harsh lines using the soft taupe shade. Outline under the eye using the darker taupe shade to define.

5. Use liquid eye liner. Apply as close to the lash as possible and add a slight flick to the outer edge. Add a fine line underneath the eye, finishing just over half way.

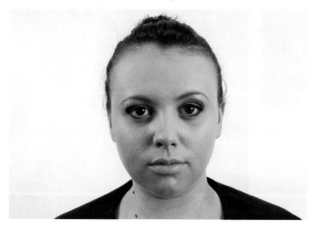

6. Apply a generous coat of black mascara to the top and bottom lashes. Once dry apply a set of strip lashes.

7. Add warmth to the contours of the cheeks using a soft red powder-based blusher.

8. Using a sharp lip pencil, outline the natural lip with a true red shade.

9. Fill in the full lip shape using a strong red lip shade.

10. Gloss the centre of the lips and shade above the lip line to add extra definition.

11. Style the hair, clothes and nails for the finished look. This look has been created to promote a new lipstick.

Black and white

When working with black-and-white photography you need to take into consideration the colours that the subject will be wearing. Some colours will not come up under the lighting and you must be aware of this.

Remember...

Application of foundation

When choosing colours to match your model's skin tone for still photos or on-screen make-up it is best to match the foundation to the model's natural skin tone.

▲ Black-and-white photography

End of chapter knowledge test

1. Why is effective communication important when designing fashion and photographic make-up?

2. How can you move the discussion forward when agreeing ideas when planning and designing an image for fashion and photographic make-up?

3. Why is it important to check for contraindications prior to performing a make-up service?

4. Why is correct positioning of the client important when carrying out a make-up treatment on the face?

5. How can a health and safety risk be reduced when working backstage at a fashion show?

6. Explain why communication with the hair and fashion designers is important when designing make-up for a photo shoot.

7. Explain the importance of knowing what lighting is being used when designing make-up for a fashion show.

8. Explain why evaluating the results of the make-up after completing it is important.

9. Why is gaining feedback from the client when designing make-up for a photographic shoot important?

10. Why must you ensure that the costing of your photographic image is correct prior to the photo shoot?

CHAPTER 12

Design and apply face and body art

Units covered by this chapter:

VRQ Level 2: Body art design

VRQ Level 3: Design and apply face and body art

Chapter aims

This chapter will look at:

- Cultural and historical influences
- Modern body painting
- Body painting in the commercial arena
- Materials and equipment
- Researching and planning your design
- Face and body art techniques
- Correcting mistakes
- Removal of face and body make-up.

Body painting is a form of body art. Unlike tattoos and other forms of body art, body painting is temporary and can be removed with remover recommended by the professional make-up manufacturers. Body painting consists of paint applied to the human skin, which can last for several hours depending on the type of make-up used. Alcohol-based make-up can last for a few days (for example temporary tattoos) or at most (in the case of the henna or Mehndi tattoo) this can last a couple of weeks.

Body painting that is limited only to the face is known as 'face painting'. It is common to see face painting being done at football matches, parties, fun fairs, school bazaars and fêtes.

Smaller or more detailed body-painting work is generally referred to as 'temporary tattoo' whilst full-body painting is more commonly referred to as 'body painting'.

Cultural and historical influences

Body painting with pigments, clay and other natural materials is part of most, if not all, tribalist cultures. Henna and Mehndi semi-permanent tattoos using henna dyes (commonly known as henna tattoos) are often traditionally designed and still worn during ceremonies among the indigenous people of Africa, New Zealand, Australia and some parts of the Pacific Islands. Since the late 1990s semi-permanent henna and Mehndi tattoos have become very popular and fashionable among young women in the western world, Middle East and India. These tattoos are especially popular with brides who want to wear them for their wedding ceremonies.

▲ Henna and Mehndi designs

For centuries actors and clowns all over the world have been painting their faces and bodies and this practice is still very much popular today. Face paints are used in the military by soldiers to camouflage their faces so as to blend into the background in forests, deserts and other locations.

Modern body painting

In the 1960s hippies used face painting and body art to show their support for what they called 'flower power'. They painted flowers and art on their bodies and those of other people. Since the 1960s there has been a revival of body painting in western society.

Body painting takes place at carnivals and festivals, and by amateurs and professionals for competitions all over the world. There are also body-painting festivals held annually at international locations. One of the most famous festivals is The World Body Painting Festival held in Seeboden, Austria. There are also body-painting festivals held in the USA in Orlando, Florida and Las Vegas, Nevada.

Body painting is not always carried out on fully nude bodies – it can be on small displayed areas or otherwise partially clothed bodies.

▲ Face and body painting designs

Body painting in the commercial arena

Body painting has a significant presence in the promotional and media sector. Many professional body-painting artists work on commercials and their work is seen regularly in television, commercials, magazines and books. Keep a look out for professional examples to inspire you.

Materials and equipment
Body paints

Always use water-based make-up that is hypoallergenic and non-toxic. Water-based face and body paints are made according to stringent guidelines from Registration, Evaluation, Authorisation and restriction of CHemicals (REACH). Paints manufactured in line with this guidance are non-toxic, usually non-allergenic, and can be washed away easily.

Body paints can be applied by hand, synthetic sponges, a paint brush, a natural sea sponge or with an airbrush.

Very recently, 'glitter tattoos' have become popular. These tattoos are made by applying a stencil and setting the tattoo with glitter instead of powder. This type of tattoo can also be created by painting a design freehand. All brands of face paint will work and you will find the ones with more pigment and brighter, stronger colours may work exceptionally well but may be harder to wash off.

 Health and Safety

Products that are not intended for use on skin can cause a variety of health issues ranging from discomfort to severe allergic reaction. Acrylic and craft paints are not meant for use on the skin, nor are watercolour pencils or markers. If a product is marked 'non-toxic' that does not mean it is safe for use on the skin.

Split-cake paint

Split-cake make-up has both the dark and light shades of a colour. Some will be made of one-half UV re-active (black light) paint. The idea of split-cake paint is to provide more colour choices in a smaller kit, enabling the mixing of colours whilst achieving maximum coverage and the brightest colours.

Brushes

The following are some of the brushes used for body painting:

- Small synthetic rounds
- Stiff-bristle brushes with sharp points: help you to achieve fine lines.
- Sponge stippler
- Chisel blender
- Short shader
- Angular
- Curve
- Liner
- Glaze wash
- Comb brush
- Wisp.

It should be noted that the bigger brush size you work with, the less control you will have. All brushes can be found in most arts and crafts shops or make-up shops.

Disposable applicators

You can also use disposable applicators to apply body paint.

- Cotton buds
- Cotton pads
- Firm sponges with rounded edges
- Pottery sponges (cut to different sizes)
- Disposable brushes
- Large car-cleaning sponges cut into pieces are good for covering larger areas with paint. These sponges can be cut into small pieces and are good for getting paint into delicate areas.

Face painting kit set up

Face-painting kits are unique to the individual artist. The following guidelines should be observed:

- Use one sponge per colour
- Each client must have their own set of sponges that are disposed of at the end of application
- If you use natural sponges and powder puffs, they need to be put on a boil wash to sanitise them after use
- Always use a palette to mix your make-up, face paint and body art colours, to prevent contamination.

Contraindications

Contraindications to the application of face and body art include:

- Conjuctivitis and eye infections
- Blepharitis
- Stye
- Severe bruising
- Active psoriasis or eczema
- Watery eye
- Cuts and abrasions.

Paint allergies

As with other types of make-up, if the skin shows any sign of reaction to the paint, you should stop using it immediately.

Researching and planning your design

It is important for you to think about research and plan your design carefully before you set about applying it. There are lots of resources you can use to find inspiration – magazines, TV, film, theatre, fashion, cartoons and art, to name but a few. Once you have an idea for a design, create a mood board that includes images that have inspired your ideas.

See Chapter 8 for further details on researching ideas and creating mood boards.

Don't forget to use your knowledge of colour theory to help you develop a well-coordinated design.

Refer to Chapter 7 for details about colour theory and the colour wheel.

▲ Face painting

 Anatomy and physiology

For further details of these contraindications please refer to Chapter 4 Anatomy and Physiology.

✋ Health and Safety

Before using face and body paints on a client you should always ask if they have had their face or body panted before. You should also ask if they have had any reaction to the make-up. Fill out a client record card. You may need to do a patch test and should record this on your client record card.

Applying transfers

1. Set-up work station.

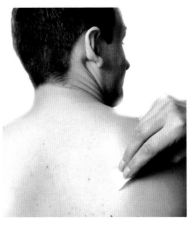

2. Clean transfer site.

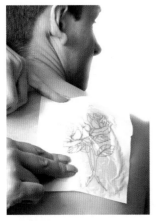

3. Apply and then remove the transfer.

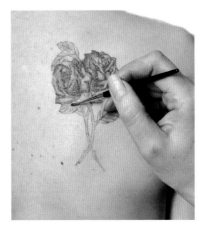

4. Add paint.

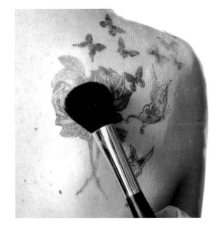

5. Set the transfer.

6. The finished look.

Sponge techniques and designs

- Wet the very tip of the sponge.
- The amount of water determines how much paint there will be to work with.
- If you wipe a sponge across the cake make-up a few times, the consistency of the make-up will be thin, watery and transparent.
- By working the sponges into the make-up many times, the make-up will become more creamy, thicker and opaque.

▲ Stippling

Stippling

This is one of the most useful sponge techniques. Stippling is very good for blending colour, adding texture and highlighting facial hair such as stubble. To get the best results use the following step-by-step guide for sponge techniques.

Drawing lines with a sponge

Use the edge of the sponge to place line strokes on the skin.

Stubble

Use greasepaint. Choose the colour you will be using for your stubble. Using a palette knife, take some of the greasepaint and put it onto a palette. With the stipple sponge take a small amount from your palette, put it onto the sponge and test this on your (clean) hand to see if the amount you have on your sponge is satisfactory. With very gentle tapping and rolling techniques apply the paint to the desired area. Repeat this until the look is complete.

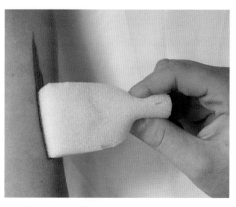

▲ Drawing a line with a sponge

Health and Safety

Don't forget to sanitise your hands.

Circular strokes

Circular strokes can be used in cheek art and to section off parts of the face. A round sponge is good for this. To make circular strokes, apply the make-up onto the sponge you have used for your palette test on your hand. With the rounded sponge, apply the end of the sponge to the face, spin the sponge and lift it away.

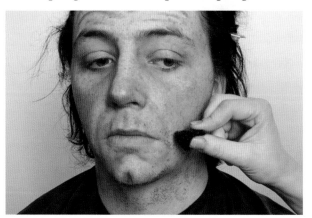

▲ Stippling stubble: use a stipple sponge and lightly tap on to the skin

Animal fur

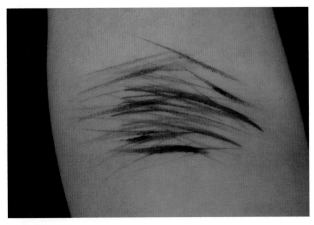

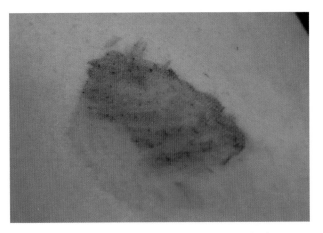

1. Load paint onto sponge. Fill your sponge with your first colour of face paint, then pull the sponge in a downward direction across the face. Rub the same sponge into a second colour and lightly drag your sponge over the base coat to create the look of fur.

2. Drag sponge with a second colour over the base coat.

Glitter

To apply glitter with a sponge, use the following as a guide:

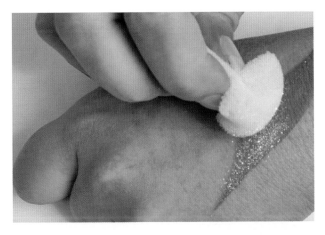

1. Put glitter onto palette. Press sponge into glitter and apply to desired area. Repeat until complete.

Brush techniques

Hold your brush like a pencil and close to the end for more control. Sometimes it helps to use your little finger to help steady your hand.

Thin to thick line

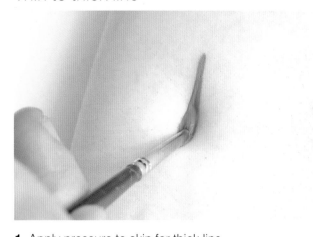

1. Apply pressure to skin for thick line.
When creating a thin to thick line, the wrist movement is very important. Using a constant speed throughout this technique, draw the wrist back and gently, with a flowing action, start by applying light pressure on the skin and progress to heavier pressure to create a thicker line.

2. Lighter pressure on skin creates a thin line. Using this technique you will need to reverse these actions and with a constant flow of speed apply heavier pressure at the start on contact with the skin, which will create the thicker part of the line. To create a thinner line, start to release pressure gradually and draw the brush away from the skin.

Swirls and curls

To create swirls and curls, use the following technique:

1. Press your brush down onto the area you are working on, with harder pressure to make the thicker part of a swirl. To achieve a thinner line apply less pressure onto the area you are working on.

2. To create a swirl, hold your brush lightly and use smooth firm strokes, maintaining a steady speed.

Raindrops/teardrops

To create raindrops and teardrops use the thinnest point of the brush. Apply light pressure to tip of your thinnest brush. Flatten your brush to apply more pressure and create the thicker part of the raindrop.

Stars

If you are painting a five-pointed star or a starburst, you can create the perfect shape – it is all in the movement in the wrist. Flick your brush very lightly, with a smooth stroke action, to create your design.

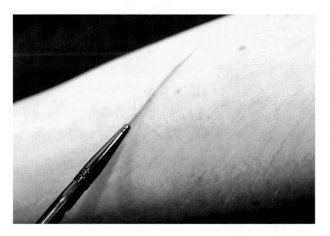

1. Position your brush to create the centre point. Flick your brush outwards accurately in the point at the start of your design.

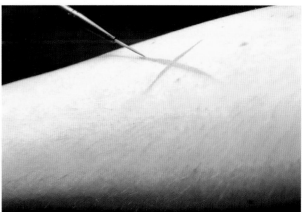

2. Everybody is individual in the way that they work, so choose either the clockwise or anti-clockwise direction to work in – whichever is more comfortable for you. Flick your strokes with firm action with your brush to create the section of your star design that you are working on.

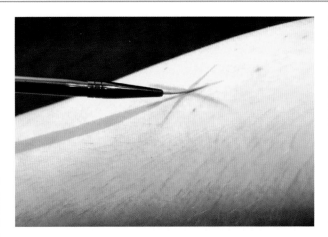

3. Work through each section of star. Rotate evenly to the next section of your star design and repeat this technique. Be aware of keeping the balance throughout your design.

4. Finish basic star shape. You will need to repeat this method to create the rest of the star until you get your desired look.

5. Add detail to star. As you are working and developing your star with more detail you will begin see your star develop more dimension and be more dynamic. With highlighting and shading techniques you will be able to make the star look more three dimensional.

6. Stars can also be created by using the airbrush.

More important techniques

Flicking

Flicking in different directions, creating growth patterns and using different shades and colours creates this effect. Use lighter and darker shades to create different textures and dimension to your design. Again, use the same technique by applying heavier to lighter pressure where needed to achieve the desired look. Brush strokes made with differently sized brushes, made randomly and in specific directions around the hair or beard lines can simulate natural growth of hair. They are made with lighter and fainter strokes on contact with the skin. For an animal fur look you will need to build lots of colours to create a more full and textured look.

▲ Flicking

Spattering

Spattering techniques can be used to add texture on rocks, to enhance star bursts, to create freckles, or to simulate blood splattering in a casualty simulation in special-effects make-up design. Using a brush with very loose bristles, firmly flick paint using one hand as a firm point of contact as you flick, to create a controlled splatter action. Repeat this until you achieve your desired look.

▲ Flicking skin illustrators on to the face to create liver spots and freckles

Mottling and camouflaging for natural and dramatic skin textures

Painting random squiggles and splatters to break up a smooth paint job is known as 'mottling'. This technique is used a lot for skin textures and character designs such as monsters and zombies, and for prosthetics, to blend in lines and joins. Use of this technique adds texture, dimension and detail.

Use a regular paint brush with bristles that have been cut down short. Load your brush with the desired colour before flicking it onto the area you are working on. Use a sponge when you have done this to smudge and work the make-up into the skin. Use different textures of paint consistency to build texture (both transparent and more solid colours). You can add a wiggly stroke to other mottling texture but use a thinner consistency of paint to do this.

> **Key term**
>
> **Mottling** – Painting random squiggles and splatters on a smooth paint job

Applying a wash

Place a dab of paint onto your make-up palette, then water it down to create the consistency you desire. Washes of colour work well when they are used beneath objects. This technique enhances designs by giving them a popping or lifting effect, giving your design dimension.

Applying glitter

Dip the end of a paint brush into the glitter and use the same technique as for splattering, tapping gently in a more random fashion to create a more shimmering, even, glowing look. To get a more detailed look use a fine brush to apply glitter into smaller, detailed areas more accurately.

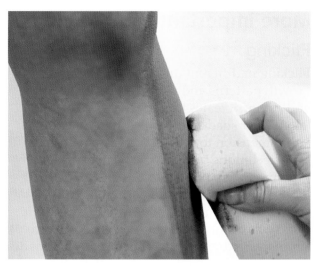

▲ Applying a wash

Painting eyes

Standard eye

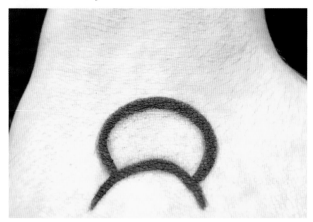

1. Draw a small arch (the cheek), with a large arch above (eye outline).

2. Add a thicker half-arch inside the eye (the iris).

3. Add thick and thin strokes at corner of eye to create eye lashes. To finish, add white highlights to cheek and whites of eye.

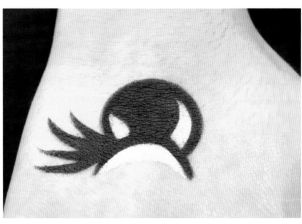

Evil eye

1. Start painting eyebrows in a sideways S-shape.

2. Create an eye shape: paint an almond shape below the sideways S-shape (the eyebrow).

3. Shade the eyebrows by using blending and shading techniques under eyes.

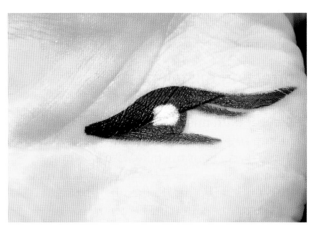

4. Use white to fill in centre of eye.

Cotton bud techniques

Apply lipstick/face paint to lips

Using a cotton bud on the lips is another way of applying lipstick.
After the lips are painted you can throw away the cotton bud.

▲ Applying lipstick/facepaint to lips

▲ Applying lipstick/facepaint to lips

Correcting mistakes

1. Roll wet cotton bud over mistake
2. Repeat until mistake disappears. Use a
   damp cotton bud in the area where you
   have made your mistake. Use a rolling
   technique to remove the mistake and repeat
   this until it is gone. Remember to use a
   clean, damp cotton bud each time.

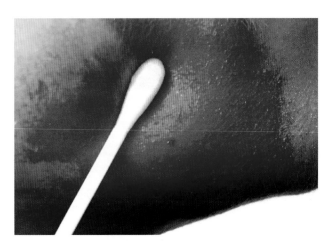

▲ Correcting mistakes

Drawing dots

With paint on cotton bud, apply to skin.

Dots made with cotton buds tend to be more
consistently accurate for example, making
freckles or beauty spots, or multiple dots that
need to be the same size.

Dip the cotton bud into the desired colour that
you wish to use, then place the cotton bud
onto the skin where you would like to make
the dot. Gently place and slightly rotate the
cotton bud before removing it from the skin.
Repeat as required.

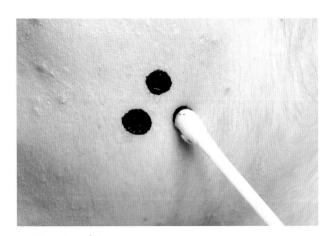

▲ Drawing dots

3D designs

1. Draw basic shape. This is a basic skill to make your face and body art look three-dimensional (3D). Establish the basic shape and apply the base coat in the shape of the object you wish to portray.

2. Highlight basic shape. To add highlight to your object, for dimension, apply the highlight more thickly in one small spot. Then stipple the colour out from the bright centre, overlapping the highlight.

3. Create depth with shadows. Leave a little line of the mid-tone to represent reflected colour. Then apply white to the very centre of the highlight and add a white highlight on the reflected colour at the bottom of the sphere.

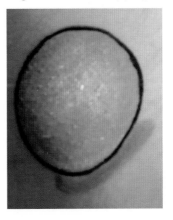

4. Outline the shape. Outline the shape using a brush. When outlining, don't look at the tip of your brush; rather, look at the object you are outlining and let your eye trace the outside. Your brush will automatically follow your eye. When you finish a stroke but need to keep the outline going, don't start a new stroke at the end of the finished stroke. Instead, overlap the strokes so the line is consistent. Adding a dark shadow underneath the sphere makes it appear to be resting on a surface.

Fantasy body art

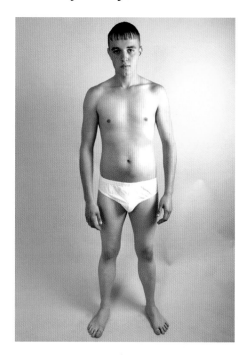

1. Prepare your client/artist.

2. Apply prosthetic adhesive to the prosthetic. Make sure it is dry (it will be clear when dry) and then place on the skin, blending the edges. For a stronger hold apply the adhesive to both the prosthetic and the skin.

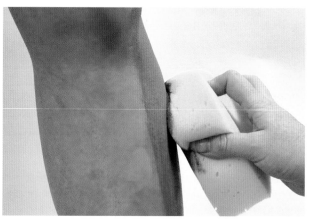

4. Apply an even colour wash. Using a large sponge will speed up application time when covering large areas.

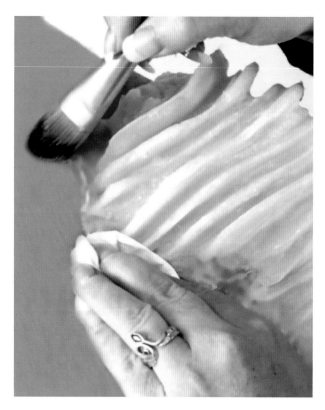

3. Apply the prosthetic to the shoulders and the chest, blending the edges down using acetone, soft brushes and cotton buds.

5. Use stencils and airbrush techniques to add dimension to the design.

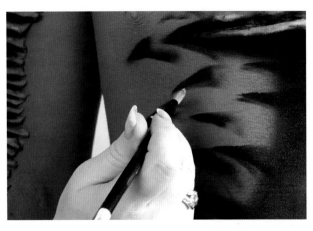

6. Use freehand brush techniques to add more detail.

7. Use these freehand techniques to create three dimensions.

8. We have added a 1/2 face prosthetic, teeth and a wig to complete the design.

▲ The finished look

Removal of face and body make-up

Always remove products as directed by the manufacturer. To remove face and body paints, use the following:

- Cold cream
- Lotion
- Baby oil
- Wet wipes
- Shampoo (to remove hair colour)
- Recommended remover for alcohol-based make-up
- For full-body make-ups it is best to shower and use a shower gel
- Choose one of the above for the appropriate make-up then wash off immediately. Use make-up remover to remove eye make-up.

End of chapter knowledge test

1. What type of product can be used for face and body paint?
2. What guidelines do face and body paints need to be manufactured in accordance with?
3. Name two pieces of equipment that body paints can be applied with.
4. What is painting random squiggles and splatters to break up a smooth paint job known as?
5. How can you prepare a colour wash?
6. How can you correct a mistake when face or body painting?
7. What is the best method of removing a full body make-up?
8. Why is it important to understand colour theory as a make-up artist?

CHAPTER 13

Camouflage make-up

Units covered by this chapter:

VRQ Level 3: Camouflage make-up

NVQ Level 2 Unit B10: Enhance appearance using skin camouflage

NVQ Level 3: Provide specialist skin camouflage services

Chapter aims

This chapter will look at:

- Types of conditions requiring cosmetic camouflage
- Client consultation with a sensitive approach
- Product knowledge
- Contraindications
- Tools and equipment for applying camouflage products
- Camouflage application techniques
- Step-by-step guides to covering tattoos
- Transgender make-up
- Aftercare and homecare advice
- Contra-actions
- Retailing
- Evaluation.

Cosmetic camouflage is a very specialised form of make-up artistry used to correct or conceal areas the client wishes to disguise. It uses a particular kind of make-up that is waterproof, making it last longer. In this chapter you will learn how to correct or conceal according to your client's wishes, including covering tattoos, erythema and hyper- and hypopigmentation. You will also learn how to advise and instruct the client on products and techniques of application for use at home. Some conditions can be very distressing to the client and so becoming skilled in this area can help you to make a real difference to their confidence.

Anatomy and physiology

It is very important to have a good understanding of the structure and function of the skin for successful application of camouflage products. It is imperative to achieve successful results.

The better quality the skin the better the results achieved. Different skin types will have different lasting power due to the oil secretions on the surface of the skin. An oily skin type may need careful powdering throughout the day to ensure the durability, whilst a dryer skin type may hold the products, enhancing a flaky texture.

Providing excellent homecare advice to clients is important, to keep the skin in optimum condition and this will help them or the make-up artist to achieve professional results with lasting power throughout the day.

Conditions that can be covered

Camouflage products are used to 'correct' or conceal skin disorders, disfigurements or discolorations, whether they are accidental, dermatological, surgical or of congenital origin.

Hypopigmentation

Hypopigmentation is a loss of skin colour. It is caused by the melanocytes in the basal layer of the skin being unable to produce melanin.

Vitiligo

Vitiligo is a hypopigmentation disorder resulting in lighter patches on the skin. There is very little or no pigmentation present on the skin in these areas.

Hyperpigmentation

Hyperpigmentation is a darkening of the skin. It is caused by an increase in melanin levels.

Chloasma

Chloasma is a hyperpigmentation disorder causing areas of increased pigmentation in the skin. Darker patches of skin will be visible on the skin surface.

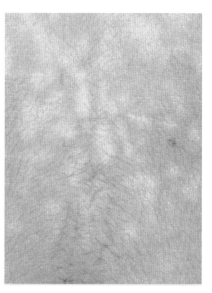

▲ Hypopigmentation

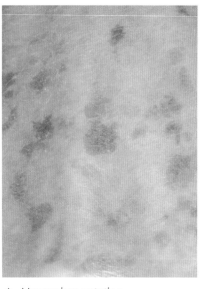

▲ Hyperpigmentation

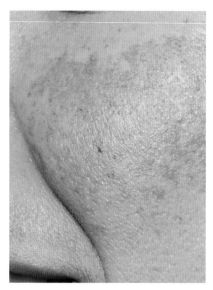

▲ Chloasma

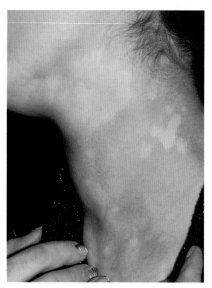

▲ Vitiligo

Erythema

Erythema is a temporary reddening of the skin, caused by the blood vessels dilating. This condition is caused by extra stimulation on the skin due to heat or maybe massage techniques or product application.

Telangiectasia

Telangiectasia is the name used for dilated or broken capillaries. These thread veins appear as small red veins on the surface of the skin.

Birthmarks

Birthmarks appear as darker pigmented patches on the skin. Examples are strawberry naevus and capillary naevus (port wine stain).

Scar tissue

Scar tissue is connective tissue formed over a wound through skin, muscle or internal organs. As damaged areas cannot return to their original state, a fibrous tissue replaces them: the scar. Scar tissue does not have various qualities of the original, undamaged skin, i.e. the ability to produce sweat.

The process of wound healing is complex and scars differ much in appearance from person to person, and even on one person depending on damage site and injury type.

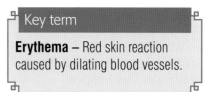

Key term

Erythema – Red skin reaction caused by dilating blood vessels.

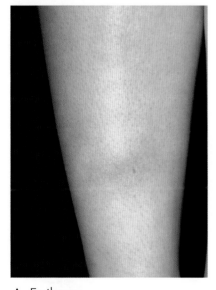

▲ Erythema

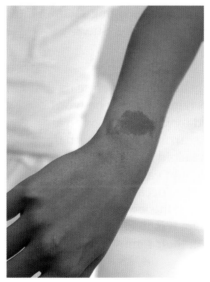

▲ Birthmarks

▲ Telangiectasia

Atrophic scars

Atrophic scars are sunken, areas of scar tissue. This sort of scar tends to form as the result of acne or chickenpox.

Normal scars

A wound healed under optimum conditions will form scar tissue that is almost the same colour and thickness as the skin. The body tries to form scars that mimic the tissue around them. Initially scars may be red or purple, but over time they will fade from pink to white, leaving a very subtle effect.

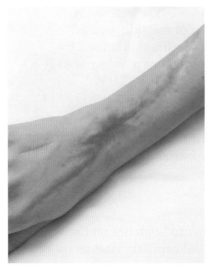

▲ Atrophic scar tissue

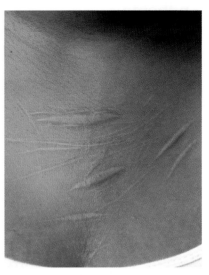

▲ Hypertrophic scar tissue

Hypertrophic scars

Hypertrophic scars are raised scars that do not extend beyond the border of the wound. They are formed when the rate of collagen production in a wound exceeds the rate of collagen breakdown. The scar takes the form of a raised red lump.

Hypertrophic scars sometimes form next to piercings, especially on the ear. They often fade in colour and become less raised over time. Wearing good quality jewellery and massaging vitamin E oil into the skin can help reduce hypertrophic scar tissue.

Keloid scars

Keloid scars are large, raised and generally uneven scars that extend beyond the border of the original injury. The word 'keloid' is very commonly misused by individuals who are actually referring to hypertrophic scarring. People with dark skin are much more likely to form keloid scar tissue, especially on the back, shoulders, upper arms and earlobes. Keloid scars tend to increase in size over time. They occasionally form next to piercings, and while removing the jewellery and rubbing with vitamin E oil may help, it is likely that a medical professional will have to assist with their removal, either by steroid injection or surgically.

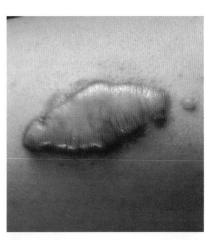

▲ Keloid

Tattoos

Tattoos may be all black or contain a variety of colour pigment. Different application techniques will be required to conceal the tattoo.

▲ Tattoo

Sensitive approach to client care

A client requiring cosmetic camouflage may suffer from psychological problems. This often leads to loss of self-esteem, resulting in a withdrawal from social and working lifestyles. The use of camouflage techniques can be very successful in restoring a sense of confidence and acceptance within the community. As a camouflage practitioner you need to be aware of the varying needs of the individual client and this is best achieved through the consultation process.

Techniques for a successful consultation

It is important to allow plenty of time for the initial consultation. The client may be a little nervous or feel slightly embarrassed about the condition they will be discussing with you. You must ensure that a professional and relaxed atmosphere is created to ensure that the client feels comfortable. Try to provide a private location for the consultation and treatment.

Points to consider:

- Is the client undergoing any medical treatment at present?
- Are there any contraindications present?
- Does the condition need a doctor's consent before treatment?
- The client's lifestyle
- Daily routine, including skincare and products used
- Sports or hobbies they participate in
- Have they used cosmetic camouflage products before?
- What other make-up products they may be using.

Cosmetic camouflage tools, equipment and products

Products required

- Client record card
- Skin cleanser (oil free)
- Hand sanitiser
- Toning lotion
- Cotton wool
- Tissues
- Sponges
- Brushes
- Couch roll
- Palette
- Bowl
- Spatula
- Powder puffs

▲ Cosmetic camouflage products

- Dusting brush
- Headbands/clips
- Towels
- Mirror
- Camouflage creams (range of colours)
- Camouflage powder
- Setting products/fixing spray
- Colour wheel
- Brush cleaner
- Mirror.

Remember . . .

Always ensure all products are stored and used correctly, following COSHH regulations and manufacturers' instructions. Where possible always use disposable brushes or sponges and keep the work area, clean, tidy and sterile.

Traditional make-up only contains 10–15 per cent of concealing pigment. To fully cover skin defects an ordinary concealer or foundation won't be completely effective. To cover skin defects you will need to use professional concealing cosmetics that contain between 50 and 54 per cent pigment. These products can be used to successfully cover pigmentation spots, scars, birthmarks and tattoos. Camouflage cosmetics should last up to 36 hours, and should be able to withstand high temperatures and water if applied correctly.

Desirable qualities of a camouflage product

- Hypoallergenic
- Contains a sun protection factor (SPF)
- Highly pigmented
- Perfume-free
- Maximum coverage
- Flawless finish
- Water resistant
- Perfect colour match
- Non-comedogenic
- Non-acnegenic.

The desired coverage will be down to the individual and specific concern. Many companies advertise and promote 'excellent coverage products, with long-lasting results'.

Some cosmetic camouflage products are available on the National Health Service via prescription for coverage of large birthmarks, port wine stains, pigmentation etc.

Brands of available camouflage products

All of the following camouflage products vary in their coverage and staying power:

- Dermacolor
- Covermark
- Veil

- Ben Nye – media pro concealers
- Grimas camouflage make-up – tatoo cover kits
- Keromask
- Cinema Secrets – CS foundations
- Screenface – blemish treatment concealer
- MAC Studio Finish Concealer SPFs. Select cover up
- Estée Lauder Maximum Cover make-up
- Clinique Continuous Coverage make-up.

Contraindications

- Hypersensitive skin
- Cuts and abrasions
- Recent scar tissue
- Severe bruising
- Broken skin
- Weeping acne
- Severe skin conditions such as eczema, psoriasis or dermatitis
- Eye infections such as conjunctivitis
- Eye diseases and disorders such as watery eyes, styes or blepharitis
- Skin disorders or diseases
- Bacterial infections
- Undiagnosed lumps
- Swelling or inflammation of the skin.

Restrictions to camouflage application

- Facial piercings
- Minor bruising
- Minor inflammation.

Preparation of client/working area

- Ensure the working area is sterile, neat and tidy at all times throughout the treatment.
- Ensure all products are available with a variety of different colour shades.
- Complete the consultation process in a sensitive manner, ensuring all personal details are gathered and the objective of the treatment is confirmed with the client.
- Take a before-photograph of the area to be concealed.
- Protect the client's clothing and remove hair from the face if required.
- Remember to photograph your finished results.

Anatomy and physiology
For more information on contraindications refer to Chapter 4.

Tip Before the treatment commences ensure the working area is of a comfortable working temperature, with as much daylight as possible. The client must be seated in a comfortable position. Always take into account your posture, to prevent back problems.

Application of camouflage products

Sequence of make-up application for pigmentation

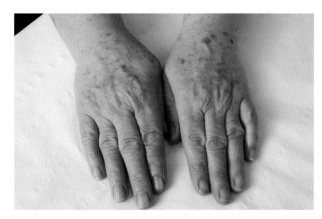

1. Prepare the skin. Ensure the skin has been prepared with a suitable cleaning product to suit the client's skin type/condition.

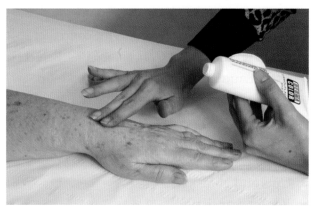

2. Apply a suitable moisturiser base, for example, an anti-shine product, skin-firming product or eye gel. (Some products work better without a moisturising base.)

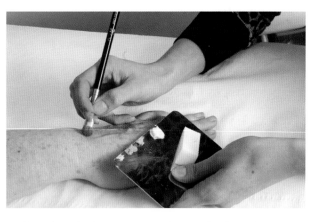

3. If a primer/colour corrector is required apply it prior to applying the foundation.

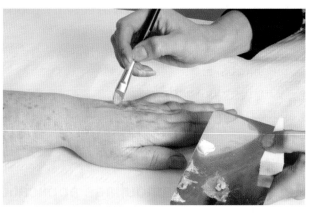

4. Select a colour that best matches the skin tone and apply. Colours can be mixed on a palette. A sponge can be used to blend the make-up. Build up thin layers to ensure complete coverage.

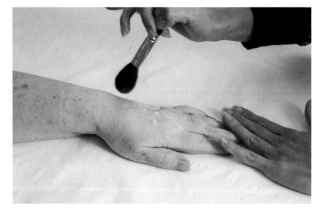

5. Set the make-up with fixing powder.

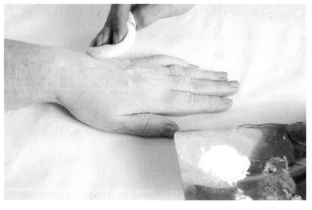

6. Brush off excess powder with a brush.

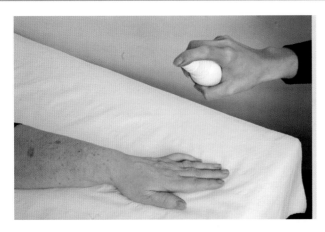

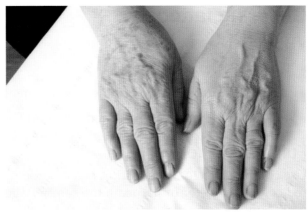

7. A fixing spray may also be required at this stage. Ensure spray is a reasonable distance away from the skin.

8. Fill out client record card. Record products selected and application techniques on the client record card.

9. Ensure homecare advice is given, including personal application, colour choice, skincare advice and product removal.

Colour pigment concealer

Green: helps to counteract high colouring and to conceal dilated capillaries

Lilac: counteracts a sallow skin colour and disguises dark circles

Orange-based undertone, if used correctly, will lift dark circles under the eyes on Asian skin tones.

Blue-based neutraliser will lift the shallowness of an Asian skin.

Covering tattoos

- Prepare the working area as above

- Complete the consultation process

- Analyse the tattoo to determine the treatment process.

- Ensure the skin is fully prepared using oil-free products.

Full black tattoo

Use colour corrector if needed. A black tattoo may require a red colour corrector underneath the camouflage cream; this will counteract the black pigment in the skin. An excellent product for this process is Dermacolour D32 colour corrector camouflage cream.

Apply powder. The colour corrector will require a fine layer of powder. It is recommended that this is left on the skin for approximately 10 minutes before the excess is dusted off with a soft brush.

Colour match camouflage make-up. Determine the colour choice of cosmetic camouflage cream. It is very important to match the colour as close to the client's skin colour as possible. More than one colour may be required to create the perfect match.

Apply product. Carefully stipple the product onto the client's skin. Take great care to ensure the product is not pulled or rubbed as the colour corrector will appear through.

Apply setting powder. Apply a fine layer of setting powder. Again leave the powder on the skin for approximately 10 minutes before dusting off the excess. A second layer of camouflage cream may be applied if required. Ensure layers are kept very thin. Set with powder as before. Fixing spray may be used for extra lasting power. Hold the spray a reasonable distance away and spray a fine mist onto the concealed area.

Covering a coloured tattoo

1. Prepare the working area and skin as for full black tattoo removal.

2. Complete the consultation process.

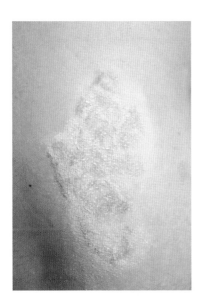

3. Analyse the tattoo to determine the treatment process. For successful coverage of a coloured tattoo an understanding of colour therapy is required. It is useful to have a colour wheel at the work station for this process (see colour wheel on page 378).

4. Carefully choose the complementary/opposite colour from the colour wheel. For example a red heart tattoo will require green colour corrector or a blue flower will require orange colour corrector. This process will help to counteract the colour pigments with the tattoo before camouflage cream is applied.

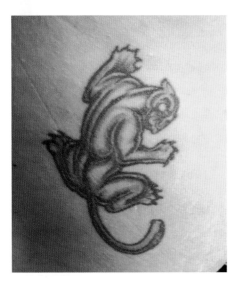

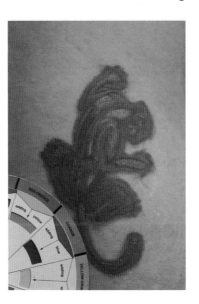

5. The colour corrector will require a fine layer of powder. It is recommended that this is left on the skin for approximately 10 minutes before the excess is dusted off with a soft brush.

6. Determine the colour choice of cosmetic camouflage cream. It is very important to match the colour as close to the client's skin colour as possible. More than one colour may be required to create the perfect match.

7. Carefully stipple the product onto the client's skin. Take great care to ensure the product is not pulled or rubbed as the colour corrector will appear through.

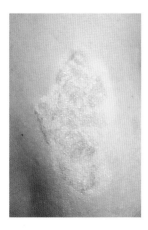

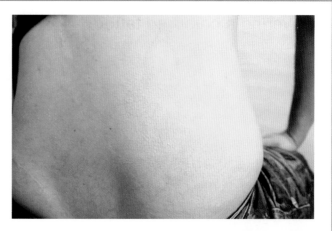

8. Apply a fine layer of setting powder. Again leave the powder on the skin for approximately 10 minutes before the excess is dusted off. Apply a second layer of cosmetic camouflage cream if required. Powder as before.

9. Fixing spray may be used for extra lasting power. Hold the spray a reasonable distance away, spraying a fine mist on the concealed area.

Understanding colour theory

1. *Primary colours:* Red, blue and yellow. These colours cannot be made with any other colour.

2. *Secondary colours:* Green, orange and purple. These colours are formed by mixing primary colours together.

> ☆ *Tip* Black and white are not colours but purely tones used to create light, dark shade and depth.

> More information on colour theory can be found in Chapter 7.

Transgender make-up

A client who has or is going through transgender treatment would greatly benefit from the use of cosmetic camouflage products. A complete consultation is required with a sensitive approach. Other beauty treatments would be very beneficial to some clients, including laser, electrolysis, waxing, tinting and tanning. The excellent coverage and lasting power of cosmetic camouflage products prove to be a good camouflage for the shadow of a beard.

Ensure not to over build the products. Excessive use of powder will draw attention to the area rather than conceal. It may also be beneficial to conceal heavy eyebrows using brow wax and sealer prior to make-up application.

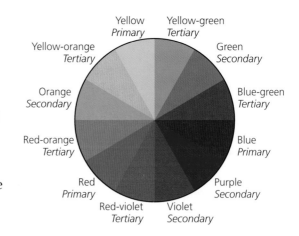

Yellow *Primary*

Yellow-green *Tertiary*

Yellow-orange *Tertiary*

Green *Secondary*

Orange *Secondary*

Blue-green *Tertiary*

Red-orange *Tertiary*

Blue *Primary*

Red *Primary*

Purple *Secondary*

Red-violet *Tertiary*

Violet *Secondary*

▲ Colour wheel

Contra-actions

Remember a contra-action can appear during or after a treatment. The most likely reaction may be an allergic reaction to a product used in the treatment and may be in the form of itching, swelling, sensitivity or erythema in the treatment area. Reactions are very rare as most cosmetic products are hypoallergenic and allergy tested. If a reaction does occur, remove the product from the client's skin immediately, soothe the area with cool water and stop the treatment process. If a severe reaction occurs, advise the client to seek medical advice. Always note any reaction on the client's record card.

Aftercare and homecare advice

It is very important to give thorough aftercare advice after treatment to ensure the client knows how to look after the camouflage application and gains the best results from the treatment. The following should be noted:

- If possible the client should avoid activities that make them perspire, such as sports and sunbathing. Great care should be taken whilst swimming.
- The cosmetic camouflage make-up must be thoroughly removed using the appropriate cleansers and toners to suit the client's skin type. Camouflage make-up manufacturers normally specify their own brands for use in removal and these are often oily, in order to help remove the waterproof make-up effectively.
- Ensure the area does not become wet. Advise the client to gently pat the area dry with a soft towel.
- Make sure the products are removed every evening as they may clog the skin and cause irritation and spots.
- The area should be treated with care in order to keep it looking effective. Rubbing may remove or smudge it, e.g. from clothes or straps.
- Wearing loose clothing is recommended.
- Avoid oily products such as body lotions, creams or oils as this will affect the make-up application.
- It is recommended that a homecare plan be devised for the client. A good homecare routine will help with application of camouflage products and maintain the durability of application.
- An SPF may need to be recommended on a daily basis for a client suffering from pigmentation disorders.

Additional advice

Airbrushing

Airbrushing techniques may also be very successful for cosmetic camouflage. Fine layers of product can be used to create excellent results. Always consult manufacturers for the best choice of products.

For more information on this, see Chapter 10.

Retailing

For successful cosmetic camouflage and client satisfaction retailing is a very important part of the treatment. Make-up lessons can be offered to show your clients the correct sequence of application. If samples are available it is always beneficial for a client to try a product before they buy it. Always keep it simple and allow the client to perform the procedure under your professional eye before trying it at home.

Evaluation

The evaluation of the cosmetic camouflage treatment process is very important. Is the client happy? Have the results discussed in the consultation been achieved? Can the client recreate the procedure at home if required? It may be advisable to invite the client back to discuss the results.

Useful organisations and websites

- British Red Cross www.redcross.org.uk
- British Association of Skin Camouflage (BASC) www.skin-camouflage.net
- Vitiligo society www.vitiligosocietyweb.org.uk
- Birthmark Support Group www.birthmarksupportgroup. co.uk
- Skin Camouflage Network www.skincamouflagenetwork.org.uk
- Skin Cancer Screening Clinic www.themoleclinic.co.uk
- Scar information service www.equip.nhs.uk/Links/id/423/details.aspx
- Let's Face It (facial disfigurement) www.letsfaceit.force9.co.uk
- RAFT (Restoration of Appearance and Function Trust) www.raft.ac.uk
- Changing Faces (psychology of facial disfigurement) www.changingfaces.org.uk
- National Lichen Sclerosis support group www.lichensclerosis.org
- Cica-Care (treatment for scars) www.dressings.org/Dressings/cica-care.html

End of chapter knowledge test

1. Why is sensitivity required in a cosmetic camouflage make-up consultation?
2. Why is it important to use a colour corrector concealer prior to skin colour application?
3. Describe contra-actions that may occur during to cosmetic camouflage application.
4. List **three** possible contraindications that would prevent camouflage application.
5. What conditions may require camouflage application?
6. A darker patch on the skin would be known as?
   a. Hypopigmentation
   b. Hyperpigmentation
   c. Port wine stain
   d. Vitiligo
7. Which description would be the best homecare advice to be given to a client?
   a. Avoid sports that cause perspiration, heat and remove
   b. Leave the products on as long as possible
   c. Rub the skin well if it becomes damp
   d. Tight clothing is recommended for lasting power
8. What is the best way to colour match a cosmetic camouflage cream?
   a. Pick which colour looks nearest to the client's skin colour
   b. Try a variety of shades on the area to be concealed
   c. Use the one with the most pink tone
   d. Try the cream on the inner wrist
9. When would it be recommended for the setting powder to be used?
   a. At the beginning to prepare the skin
   b. Only at the end of the treatment
   c. After each layer of the camouflage cream
   d. Once the fixing spray is dry
10. Why is it important to give homecare advice and what would this be?

CHAPTER 14

Media and theatrical make-up

Units covered by this chapter:

Level 3 VRQ: Media make-up

Level 3 VRQ: Apply prosthetic pieces and bald caps

Level 3 VRQ: Create and cast small prosthetic pieces and bald caps

Chapter aims

This chapter will look at:

- ☞ The tools and processes in the film and TV industry
- ☞ Theatrical and film crew and their roles
- ☞ The pre-production stage
- ☞ Continuity for film and television
- ☞ Working on set
- ☞ Working on location
- ☞ Using suitable products and skin compatibility
- ☞ Treatment planning
- ☞ Applying and making prosthetics
- ☞ Bald caps
- ☞ Various looks for media and theatrical make-up.

As a media make-up artist you will need to have an understanding of the products, tools and equipment used to create a range of theatre and media make-up techniques. This chapter gives some general background information on working in the media and theatre industries, and examines some of the techniques used in theatrical and media make-up.

Understanding the tools and processes in the film and TV industry

When working in the film and TV industry it is important to have an understanding of the different types of film and lighting used.

Types of camera film

It is important that the make-up artist is familiar with the types of camera film the director will be shooting in. Whatever type of job you're working on, it is good practice to check your make-up application on the monitor in order to view how the final effect will look on film. You can then make any necessary adjustments before filming begins. It is better to make changes now as mistakes cannot usually be rectified once filming has begun due to continuity, time constraints and budgets.

Some of the types of camera film you may work with are:

- Electronic
- 8mm
- 16mm
- Super 16mm
- 35mm
- High definition.

Electronic

This is basically videotape. It is much cheaper than film and produces a hard clinical look. Lighting, camera lens and filters can alter the effect. It has been widely used in television for soap operas, documentaries, sport, game shows, news and studio-based work and many series and productions.

Also in this category are home video and more recently digital camcorders.

8mm

This is almost obsolete. It has been used in recent years for 'special effects' as it produces an old home movie effect.

16mm

This isn't really used much any more as the 'super 16mm' has taken its place.

Super 16mm

This is fairly standard in the industry and widely used for 'better quality' projects. It is more expensive than shooting on video and tends to be used on the 'top end' high quality drama series and for commercials.

35mm

This is very high quality, used for movies and many American produced series, especially those aiming for worldwide sales. It produces a much more flattering effect on the performer by picking up more detail and being less harsh on skin tones.

High definition

Many films and American series are now being filmed in the new HD format. It has outstanding clarity and sharpness. The UK media are also starting to work with HD and 'red camera', for some of the higher end productions. Due to the sharpness and clarity of the picture viewed on screen the make-up industry has had to step up its skills as HD shows any imperfections in the make-up application. It is now imperative that the make-up artist is fully equipped to address this by being trained in the use of airbrush make-up techniques when the role demands a perfect make-up, for example, on TV presenters.

Green and blue screen are used for shots where the background needs to be separated from the subject and then another background added in. The make-up artist should try to avoid using blue and green make-up colours for better separation.

The effects of lighting on stage and in film/TV

A lit-up make-up mirror is essential as the make-up artist needs to see the model clearly, to view their work; this is a frontal light source. The light is usually created by a daylight bulb which

Remember . . .
Cameras are an ever-changing technology and it is important to consider this when doing make-up. The majority of films are filmed in either HD or IMAX. IMAX uses a bigger roll of film, therefore allowing bigger scenes to be created at a better quality than HD.

Remember . . .
Remember that for character make-up you may not want a 'perfect' or 'flawless' look.

is often a florescent bulb, but can also be a standard light bulb. This type of lighting is usually used during a production so the make-up artist can judge the colour. However, there are many different types of florescent bulbs, so the bulb should be carefully chosen. Most give out a yellow-green colour cast as there is very little red in the colour spectrum. The exception are those with a CRI (colour rendering index) of 100, which is the colour of daylight and therefore ideal for colour matching.

Frontal lighting

Frontal lighting may be hard or soft, and is the illumination of the model from the front.

Cross lighting

Cross lighting brings up texture more heavily on the skin. It illuminates the model with two light sources coming in from opposite angles but at equal distance.

Side lighting

Side lighting is when one side of the model is lit up and the other is left in shadow.

Under lighting

Under lighting is when the light is coming from underneath the model, which can create unnatural shadows and effect.

Overhead lighting

Overhead lighting is when the light comes from above the model and is shone down onto the model. Shadows are created around the eyes, under the cheekbones and under the mouth and the jaw line. This is not lighting for make-up application as the model's face is not lit clearly and poor make-up application could result.

Rim lighting

Rim lighting outlines the profile of the model as the light comes from behind the model.

Colour effects on a make-up filter

- Peach warms up the skin without altering colours in the make-up.
- Blue changes tones such as red, showing them darker. Blue and green shades show lighter, and the colour cools down the skin tone.
- Red shows the face as lighter and blue and green tones show darker. Blue appears greyer.
- Green shows darker, including red. Greens show lighter and blue appears darker, purples becoming very dark.

Balloon lights

Balloon lights are lights that are contained within a fabric balloon. They are being used more and more commonly within the film and TV industries because they are more effective in producing a soft, even light and filling more space with that light than more traditional lighting methods. As a result they are more efficient than traditional lights and are therefore cheaper to use. They are also popular because they provide a more natural daylight effect with no hotspots or flares, which would need to be considered if providing make-up for a film or TV production using this type of lighting.

Theatrical crew and their roles

Stage manager

The stage manager communicates with technical crew and calls all of the cues for lighting and sound effects, as well as coordinating the crew for any scene changes that need to take place throughout the production. The stage manager assists with the production from the very start and should be present at every stage rehearsal and music rehearsal. During rehearsal, the stage manager records blocking notes for the stage director and maintains order in the cast. The stage manager may also deal with various administrative tasks relating to the cast and any discipline problems within the cast.

Technical director

The technical director's responsibilities include making sure that all technical aspects of a show are carried out on time. This job includes coordinating the set design, set construction lighting, along with the handling of any technical details needed during performances.

Set designer

The set designer will take direction from the stage director and produces very detailed designs. He or she must work closely with the master carpenter and lighting designer so that a feasible design is produced. The design must include colour choices, but it is not necessary to go into more construction detail than simple elevations and suggested ideas for construction. The set designer will meet with the director in order to make sure that the design is consistent with the director's artistic concepts and will accommodate any technical needs. On some occasions the set designer will have an assistant set designer, who may provide additional skills or expertise where needed; this could be an opportunity to shadow the set designer for work experience.

Master carpenter

The master carpenter will turn the set designs into reality, by making the set pieces needed for the show. He or she should not only know how to use the tools and materials of the set but also to shop properly and safely, and to organise the crew. The master carpenter is also expected to teach others, to make sure that everything is built within the time given. The set crew assist the master carpenter in constructing and installing the set pieces and maintaining them throughout production. At the end of the production they will then have to dismantle and pack out of the theatre.

Lighting designer

The lighting designer creates a lighting plan based on the script and the set design. He or she is responsible for the deployment and coordination of lighting instruments, working with the master electrician. Along with the technical aspects of the show, the lighting should be designed to be consistent with the direction.

Master electrician

The master electrician makes the lighting plans happen according to plan. He or she is responsible for organising the light hanging crew to get all the lights hung from the lighting grid, gelled, focused and connected to the dimmer board. The lighting crew assists the master electrician in installing lighting instruments and cabling.

Light board operator

The light board operator controls the lights during the show. He or she is normally part of the lighting crew that helps the master electrician to hang the lights on the run up to production week. During performances, he or she will take cues from the stage manager to make any lighting changes, so they happen at the right times.

Costume designer

The costume designer buys, makes, finds or hires costumes for the cast. He or she works with the technical director but will also communicate with the director to make sure that the costumes match the requirements of the design. Costume designing is a very big job that involving a lot of work, including creating and sourcing looks to create the characters. The costume designer may also be called upon to provide make-up assistance. For some shows, the costume designer may select costumes from stock; others may be borrowed or rented from other community theatre groups. Usually a few costumes must be made from scratch. The costume crew will assist the master tailor or seamstress in making the costumes for the show.

Make-up artist/wigs

The make-up artist will be responsible for making sure that the proper wigs are ordered and dressed in character to the script and

 *Remember . . .*

Lighting is a key point of any media or stage production as it helps to create the scene and atmosphere. Lighting should compliment make-up to help get the point of the scene across. The make-up artist should not use make-up that will run under heat as when the lights heat up and if the make-up is applied incorrectly it can run and smudge.

 Remember . . .

Costumes are of utmost importance in planning the stages of make-up and the make-up artist needs to take costume into consideration when deciding on what make-up to use and do. For example, an innocent, happy clown would have an outrageous costume full of bright colours so the make-up artist would need to use bright, happy colours. An evil clown would have an outfit of dark colours and you would use a gothic make-up techique to match.

the correct amount of make-up needed for the show is available for the cast. They are also responsible for ensuring that all of the cast know how to use it and remove it safely. The make-up artist will usually apply any special make-up effects and wigs, but will show the cast members how to do their own basic make-up. Make-up artists are also responsible for dressing, setting the wigs and doing any make-up or wig changes during the performance.

Choreographer

The choreographer designs dance routines and teaches them to the cast. The choreographer's responsibility is to make the director's vision happen on stage.

Props manager

The props manager is responsible for locating anything to be used by actors on stage. This may include wands, weapons, teapots, bottles, luggage etc. Many props can be found in a theatre's own props store or borrowed from other theatre groups. Sometimes props will need to be made or built.

Run crew

The run crew are involved with the set changes and any other tasks necessary during the show (for example setting up, resetting, packing out).

Orchestra manager

The orchestra manager is to recruit all the players for the orchestra and ensure that all aspects of the show involving the orchestra run smoothly. He or she should work very closely with the music director. The orchestra manager is also responsible for organising the scheduling and rehearsal of the orchestra.

Publicity manager

The publicity manager's role is to advertise the show. This is a process that will start long before opening night. The publicity manager must gather all relevant information from the producer and directors and find a graphic designer for flyers and posters, as well as having to handle mailings and public announcements. The publicity crew will assist the publicity manager in deploying the publicity materials.

Programme designer

The programme designer is in charge of putting together the programme that will be sold to all audience members that wish to buy it. He or she must collect all the information from the cast, orchestra members and crew. The programme designer also manages the sale of the programme, decides on its layout and overall design, as well as arranging any adverts for inclusion. They also arrange for the completed design to be professionally printed.

Remember . . .
Props help the actor to get his or her point across. Make-up should not be able to run off on to the prop as the scene will lose its atmosphere if spotted.

House manager

The house manager will handle all aspects of the show regarding the audience. This includes the sale of tickets, any seating issues and refreshments. The house manager will be answerable to the producer and receives support from the ticket manager.

Ticket manager

The ticket manager makes sure that tickets are available to be sold. He or she will also take responsibility for handling online ticket reservations.

Film crew and their roles

The number of people involved in the making of a film or TV production is vast, and as a hair and make-up artist you will be working with people in many different roles. The film/TV industry generally consists of five distinct areas:

- Development – writing scripts for the production and sourcing finance.
- Production – organising the process of setting up and shooting all the scenes that are going to be shot.
- Post-production – this is where all shots are edited and assembled, treated and mixed into the final finished product.
- Distribution – this is the selling of the product to the audiences, via the rental firms, retailers and cinemas.
- Exhibition – cinemas that screen the films for the general public. There are hundreds of different jobs in the film industry, each one requiring unique specialist skills.

The hair and make-up department

The hair and make-up department is a key component in the overall design of a film. It is responsible for the design and applying of make-up, dressing hair and applying wigs (where necessary) in accordance with the design and script, and maintaining continuity of hair and make-up during the production stage.

The work within the department will range from creating modern everyday looks, high fashion looks or period designs and styles to transforming an actor's face and/or body using prosthetics or creating more character-based looks.

Chief make-up artist

A chief make-up artist is responsible for the design of the make-up on the production. Other responsibilities include script breakdown, maintaining continuity, sourcing, ordering and controlling stock, getting wigs made or renting them, booking the make-up crew (including the main team and dailies). (On some films the department may be divided into a separate hair team and a make-up team.)

 Remember...
Working in TV and film is by no means a regular 9–5 job – the hours can be very unsociable (it becomes a lifestyle).

 Tip This is a contacts business so if you want to stay in work you will always need to be networking. You will meet lots of different people in different departments and spend a lot of time with them – people will recommend you if they seen and liked your work.

Remember...
You have to get along and fit in with a lot of people when you're working on a TV or film production. Hair and make-up is a very important part of the process – but remember it is only a part; good interpersonal skills are needed, and you must be good at working as a team.

Prosthetics artist

Prosthetics make-up artists work on all types of productions, from feature films and television productions to commercials and pop promos. They are responsible for applying prosthetics (which are made of silicone gelatine or any other material that is safe to use on the skin) to an actor's face or body in order to change their features, shape and appearance.

Make-up artist

Make-up artists work with the chief make-up Artist and are often required to create a variety of looks.

Assistant make-up artist

An assistant make-up artist's responsibilities will vary depending on the production they are working on.

Make-up and hair designer

Make-up and hair designers are often required to work on feature films and high-budget television dramas. They must be very skilled in both make-up and hair techniques as well as being good at creating characters (for example from different periods in time, fantasy, different social classes).

Make-up and hair assistant

Make-up and hair assistants work with a make-up and hair designer and are often used on smaller productions such as feature television films, commercials, pop promos, corporate productions, light entertainment programmes, documentaries and dramas. They too must are skilled in both make-up and hair techniques.

Make-up and hair artist

As above.

Make-up and hair trainee

Make-up and hair trainees are recruited onto productions to help with general things and gain valuable work experience. Initial responsibilities can range from sorting and passing hair pins to cleaning brushes and making tea!

Chief hairdresser

Chief hairdressers are responsible for the design of hair styling on feature films. If there are separate hair and make-up teams on the production they are in charge of the hairdressing team. As well as styling and dressing performers' natural hair, dressing and applying all wigs and hairpieces, they also design and create different styles.

Remember . . .

As a trainee the jobs you are given may not seem important, but they are crucial to the smooth running of a hair and/or make-up department, especially on a busy day. Just by being there and seeing how it all runs is an incredibly valuable experience, and one that you won't get in the classroom. It also provides valuable networking time!

Hairdresser

Hairdressers work with chief hairdressers, most usually on feature films, pop promos and commercials. They will liaise with colleagues in the hair, make-up and costume departments, as well as with directors and work closely with the actors and extras.

Assistant hairdresser – film

Assistant hairdressers most usually work on feature films. Their responsibilities vary depending on the size of the production, but they will always need to carry out the hair designs and use their hairdressing skills as required by the Chief Hairdresser.

Working with other film and TV departments

As a make-up artist you will need to work with a range of other departments on set. Below you will find details of some of the other departments and people you can expect to work with.

Costume

Hair and make-up departments need to work closely as a team with costume departments, to ensure that each actor's look complements the Director's vision and the script.

The costume department are responsible for the design, purchase, fitting, manufacture, hire, continuity and care of all costume items. They are also responsible for cleaning and dirtying down (e.g. putting on blood) when necessary. You will find the following roles in this department: costume designer, costume supervisor, wardrobe supervisor, costume maker, costume daily, costume design assistant, costume assistant.

Camera

Cinematography involves the creation of a beautiful arrangement of images on screen. When shot well it can help to portray the character and surroundings and to capture the viewer in that moment.

The director of photography will create the film's unique photographic signature by manipulating light and shade. A great deal of thought, preparation and hard work is involved in operating moving cameras, to enhance but not detract from what is happening on screen. Camera crews work with delicate and expensive equipment and are amongst the most highly skilled members of a film crew. Roles include script supervisor, first assistant camera, camera trainee, aerial director of photography, aerial camera assistant, grip, video assist operator, director of photography, camera operator, second assistant camera, steadicam operator, aerial camera pilot, marine and diving camera crew, crane operator.

Casting

Good casting is important to the filming industry. Good casting directors will need a very good knowledge of a wide range of actors and have an understanding of their abilities. The casting director is supported by casting assistants and casting associates.

Direction

This is probably the best known role on a production. The director is the person who is responsible for the overall style and creative vision of a film. They are the driving force in a film's production, motivating and inspiring the passion that is required and providing the link between the production, technical and creative teams.

The Director is supported by a number of assistant directors, who help to ensure that the director's artistic ambitions are achieved in the filming process by providing organisational and management support.

Lighting

The lighting department plays a very important role in most film crews. Although a lot of productions may make use of natural daylight, for the most part it is necessary to use artificial light to achieve the visual image required to set the scene for the film. They set up a wide range of lighting equipment to achieve a wide variety of effects, moods and atmospheres. Hair and make-up artists need to be aware of the effects of the lighting on the hair and make-up they are using to ensure that the performers look right for their roles. Roles within the lighting department include: gaffer, lighting technician, practical lighting technician, apprentice lighting technician, director of photography, best boy, moving light operator, console operator, genny operator.

Script

The script development process may be a screenplay for sale to a production company, a screenwriter writing a 'spec' or a producer commissioning the screenwriter to write a screenplay based on a particular concept. Roles include screenwriter, script editor, development executive and script reader.

Production sound

Recording all sound on set or location is the role of the production sound crew. Although film is a visual medium, much of the storytelling and emotional resonance of the script is conveyed through dialogue. Ensuring dialogue is recorded and is clear is a complex job as sets often have unwanted noises to deal with. Roles within the production sound crew include production sound mixers, boom operator, sound assistants and sound trainees.

Art department

Creating a visual setting for a film is the role of the art department. A lot of work and imagination goes into creating fabulous backdrops to any story. The look of sets or locations sets the scene and brings the audience into the time, place or fantasy story; it is therefore important to make the scene convincing. The art depart employs a large number of people, which may include an art director, standby art director, set director and assistant set director, production buyer, special researcher, storyboard artist, art department coordinator, production designer, supervising art director, assistant art director, assistant production buyer, concept artist, graphic artist, draughtsman and junior draughtsman and an art department assistant.

Props

The props department are responsible for any moveable items used within the production, including dressing and setting props, hand props, stunt props, hero props or mechanical props. Roles within the department include prop maker, greensman, prop master, armourer, props storeman.

Editing and post-production

The process of post-production takes the raw material shot by the camera, production and sound crews and edits into the completed film. Post-production can include picture editing, sound editing, composing and recording the score music, adding visual and special effects and adding audio.

Performance

Hair and make-up artists have to work closely with and need to be able to work well with all performers on a production, from the principal actors through to supporting actors, stunt performers and extras. They need to be aware of and sensitive to the responsibilities of every performer. A performer's responsibility is to work with the director to create believable characters. They must learn their lines very quickly. They have to know their fellow actors' lines so that they can respond to them. They often need to repeat the same scene many times over as scenes are shot from lots of different angles. This means that as a hair and make-up artist you may be making-up or re-touching the same performer over and over again.

Other roles

There are a range of other departments that are equally important to the success of a production. These include accounts, catering, construction, health and safety, location and transport, exhibition and publicity.

Key term

Mise en scène is a term used by the media industry to describe the surroundings and props used in a scene. Mise en scène and the media make-up artist have to coincide with each other for a film or production to work. The make-up artist has to consider lighting, props, scenery, costumes and cameras to be able to do this.

Remember...

It is important to consider scenery while doing make-up for a production. Certain films, for example, are filmed in a particular style and the make-up has to reflect this. Horror films tend to have a quite dark scenery and feel to them, so the make-up artist would need to consider this and incorporate the scenery into their make-up to make the scene realistic.

The pre-production stage

When a make-up designer is asked to work on a production the first real piece of information they will receive is the script. This will then need to be broken down, marking any areas which will affect make-up and hair. The designer will also receive a character list to include background artistes and a shooting schedule.

A meeting will then take place with the producer, director and costume designer. The budget will be discussed and the design specification agreed for the production. The make-up and hair design will then need to be researched and presented on the Continuity Character Sheet with a brief written explanation for each design; photos will be added as the shoot progresses to ensure continuity.

Test shots

These can be carried out to ensure make-up and hair is going to work on screen. The director must approve the overall appearance.

Pre-production make-up

Pre-production make-up is carried out on the main performers; this is especially important when the script calls for more complicated looks, including prosthetics, wigs, hairpieces and casualty effects. Pre-production meetings will be held with the production crew and director usually months in advance. The make-up designer will have input on the look of the characters and in which order shooting should take place. Usually the more complicated or longer scenes will be shot first; this would also take into account the most complex make-up applications. Wigs and prosthetics will need to be pre-ordered.

Continuity for film and television

This is a very important part of film and television; if you are unprepared this can be detrimental to the whole production. At the beginning of a new production or episode scripts are distributed, each department will read the scripts thoroughly making detailed notes.

Each department is responsible for their continuity.

The make-up designer will prepare a 'make-up bible' with very detailed notes.

- The make-up bible is put together, using the script, containing very detailed notes on make-up and hair looks. The script is placed in a large file with clear sheets to hold photos (six per page/double sided). The photos will have the scene number, the characters name and may have make-up notes on the back of the photo, for example, day look/evening look/work look.

- If the artist requires special effects make-up you will need to make detailed notes of this and take lots of photos. It could be a cut and a bruising; as you know, a recent cut will have

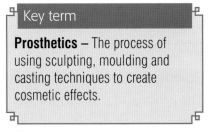

Key term

Prosthetics – The process of using sculpting, moulding and casting techniques to create cosmetic effects.

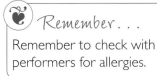

Remember...

Remember to check with performers for allergies.

runny blood and the bruising will be very red. If the artist is seen a few days later, the colour will be at the day two stage, it will look different to when it was first done – you will need to do your research.

- When we start filming and the first time each artist is seen, an all round photo is taken, this is the establishing shot.

- Filming is not always done in the order of the script. The reason for this is that it takes time to set up and breakdown equipment; so the order of filming is worked out well in advance. For example, if we are shooting interior shots in a building, the call sheet is designed to show us the order of set ups for that day, scene shooting will be out of sync, it can be day 1/day 2/day 3, and jump to day 5. So you may need to do make-up changes on set.

- Make-up, hair and costume changes will be carried out either at the unit base, studio, or an area set up at the location; the details of this will be on your call sheet.

- The call sheet has a two-day advance schedule on it, so you can work things out well ahead of time. Stand by scenes are also put on the sheet and whether cover is required, it is all planned and organised (see example of a Call Sheet below).

- The bible will build up a bank of continuity information. As a make-up department you must be very disciplined, ensuring all photos are put in the bible at the end of each days shoot, even something seemingly insignificant as long hair over one shoulder is very important. Another make-up artist may have to take over from you; if this was on a master shot, continuity could be compromised and the position of the hair will appear to be moving around.

- The master shot is the establishing shot. For example, if there are four artists in the scene, a wider shot is taken of everyone in the shot. At the end of the take the establishing photos are taken (all round photos of each artist). These are the master shots. After which the camera team will then move the cameras and do a POV (point of view) of each artist. This has to match the master shot, by this we mean the hair, special effects make-up etc., may need to be reapplied. This may require a few takes. You will sit by a monitor and watch the rehearsal. You will be told when they are going for a take, they will call out 'checks', then all departments go in and ensure everything is in place for the take.

- On some occasions you may be working with more than one camera at a time, this will speed up the time of filming. They can shoot the whole scene straight off from all directions.

- The key to maintaining good continuity is to be well prepared; keep detailed notes and take continuity photos. Always put them in order in the continuity bible. Have a good, responsible and reliable team working with you.

Remember . . .

Remember each day they are seen is a different look, they may even have a day look/ evening look/a work look, you are responsible for having them in the right look at the right time; getting this wrong could be detrimental. This is very important.

The right personal qualities are over 50 per cent of being a successful make-up artist and the main ones are reliability, good timekeeping, discretion and listening, as the days can be very long. On film sets 15 and 16-hour days are quite normal, sometimes for six days a week. A real passion for what you do and an understanding group of family and friends are a necessity.

Louise Young, Make-up artist

Tip You will need a set chair to sit on, this can double up as a set bag.

Good Boys
Starlight Productions
338 Oakwood Rd
London
N1 3BH

Call Sheet No. 1

Date: Wednesday 13 July 2011
Crew call: 1000–1200
Costumes/Make-up: 0900
Breakfast: 0915
Lunch: 1500–1600
Sunrise: 0401
Sunset: 2109
Weather: Dry sunny day. Dry night. 19–25°C. Winds 5–10mph

Location:

1. Resturant
    Gold Star
    14 High Street
    London E12

Scences in shooting order:

SCENE	PGS	TIME	SET	CHARACTERS	SYNOPSIS
13/44 (location 1)		2230	INT. Resturant	Rob, Jasmin, Theo	Rob and Jasmin finish conversation while Theo picks up bill
13/50 (location 1)		2230	EXT. Resturant	Rob, Jasmin, Kyle, Lisa	Rob and Jasmin meet Kyle and Lisa while leaving resturant
13/32 (location 1)		2102	INT. Resturant	Theo	Theo clears table

ARTISTE	NUMBER	CHARACTER	PICK UP	MAKE-UP	COSTUME	LINE UP	ON SET
James Green	4	Rob Gordon	0745	0930	0915	1000	1015
Nisha Young	5	Jasmin Koli	0745	0945	0915	1000	1015
Karl Saunders	3	Theo Brooks	0845	1000	0945	1000	1015
Lawrence Church	7	Kyle McAdams	0830	0900	1015	1000	1100
Natalie Withington	7	Lisa Jennings	0830	0900	1015	1000	1100

EXTRAS	SCENES	CALL	ON SET
2 x waiters	13/44	0900	1015
1 x maitre'd	13/44	0900	1015
4 x bar staff	13/44	0900	1015
12 x diners	13/44, 13/32	0900	1015
7 x passers by	13/05	0900	1100

Transport

VEHICLE	TIME	ARTISTE	FROM	TO
George		James Greer	Home	Location 1
Helen		Nisha Young	Home	Location 1
Helen		Karl Saunders	Home	Location 1
George		Lawrence Church	Home	Location 1
George		Natlie Withington	Home	Location 1

PROPS

Sc. 13/44
14 x plates
14 x knives
14 x forks
14 x wine glasses
2 x jugs of water
7 x bottles of wine

CREW

1 x Director
2 x make-up artist
1 x camera assistant
1 x sound assistant
1 x steadicam & op
Camera equipment (2 x 9" monitors)
1 x induction loop system
2 x time coded DAT tapes

CATERING

0915 Breakfast
1500 Lunch
1900 Hot snack

For directions and movement order see separate sheets

▲ Example call sheet

On set

Before turning up on a job you must check where you are likely to be filming, you can then decide what kit you are likely to need (see the example of a Call Sheet). You must be prepared for every eventuality, so careful planning is essential. You may be working in a small interior fixed television studio set or on a huge film set; it could be cold in the morning and very hot in the afternoon. The performers could end up perspiring under the make-up you have applied.

On location

Alternatively, you may be working on location inside or outside. When working on location it is important that you dress sensibly. You should wear layers of clothes that you can add or remove as the need arises.

When choosing your kit for location work you need to take several things into consideration:

- Will you have access to electricity?
- What type of make-up do you need to use, i.e. waterproof?
- Do you have access to water?

▲ Make-up artist working on location

Set bag

You will need this when going on set, ensuring everything you need is to hand. It is a good idea to have a clear bag so you don't have to keep searching for items. You may not have access to an electric supply so it is a good idea to carry some 'non-electrical' appliances with you in your set bag such as:

- Camera
- Portable heated curlers/roller
- Gas filled heated straighteners, tongs and hot brush
- Battery powered fan
- Battery powered baby bottle warmer – to heat glycerine so it's more workable.

Set bag products

- Make-up kit
- Derma pallet
- Pressed powder is better for on set in case of spillage – MAC and Givenchy are excellent
- Anti-bacterial hand gel
- Antiseptic wipes

- Anti-shine papers
- Anti-shine cream – 'Body Shop' does a great version but be careful, as it can show white on HD screen. 'Lancôme Anti-shine' and 'Grimas' products are really good
- Blood – should be in a dropper bottle on set
- Tear stick
- Mouth freshener – 'Gold Spot'
- Glycerine – for sweat this can be quite sticky, KY Jelly can be used as an alternative
- High factor sunscreen – if outside
- Insect repellent
- Bite cream
- Antiseptic cream
- 'Compead' cold sore cover up
- 'Nu Skin' – 'Germalene' or 'TCP' spray on plaster
- Lip balm – you may want to source a matt version for males
- Moisturiser – actors often ask for 'Elizabeth Arden 8 hour cream'
- Hand cream
- Nail polish remover
- Dental floss
- Wipes
- Hair serum
- Shine spray
- Eye drops – can also be mixed with glycerine and used for slow tears
- Hair mascara – 'Kyrolan' is a good product can be used with a mascara wand, toothbrush or comb
- Acetone
- Clean dirt
- Spray olive oil – good for making greasy hair. ('Sally's' – 'Thirsty Hairspray')
- A and B Compound
- Hair wax – (Dax Wax is good)
- Gelatine – supermarket
- Flocking – this can be put in the gelatine
- Charcoal dust
- Gafquat
- Silicone pieces.

Equipment/sundries

- Script
- Make-up design plan
- Make-up brushes in portable make-up pouch
- Make-up sponges
- Water sprays
- Tissues
- Hair brushes in portable brush pouch
- Tail comb
- Scissors
- Cotton
- Cotton wool
- Cotton buds
- Compact mirror for actor/actress to check hair/make-up
- Plasters
- Compressed air
- Syringe and tube – for blood squirting effects
- Water bombs – for blood bags
- Cling film
- Sandwich bags
- Dentist gun
- Toothpicks
- Mirror
- Rain bonnets
- Umbrella
- Hairgrips
- 'Snag free' hair elastics
- Nail file.

This list is intended as a guide but you must always be well prepared. It is the make-up artist's responsibility to ensure continuity; therefore you are responsible for carrying items such as sun cream to prevent the actor getting sunburned whilst out on location.

Skin compatibility tests

Skin compatibility tests are of utmost importance when carrying out special effects make-up. Performers are much more likely to react to chemicals in these products and their removers. Materials such as adhesives, solvents and latex are often used in special effects make-up.

Carry out these tests 24 hours before application on an area of skin, preferably close to the area where you are planning to use the product. Behind the ear is a good place as it is hidden by the hair if a reaction does occur. Never test products on the face in case the performer has an adverse reaction; if the filming schedule is disrupted it can be costly and affect your professional reputation. The test results should be noted on your record cards.

If a contra-action occurs such as excessive redness, a rash, itching, burning or stinging, the make-up should be removed carefully and immediately. Advise your client to seek medical advice if the condition worsens and make a note of the reaction on your record cards.

NOTE: The skin will appear slightly red after the removal of latex, Collodian and wax such as Derma Wax. You must inform your performer of this so they don't panic.

Suitability to skin, environment and durability

When designing make-up for a performer, the make-up artist needs to consider the durability of the products they have chosen to use. If for example you have been asked to apply an old scar to your performers face, latex would be the natural choice, however if the scar has to stay on for a 12 hour day Collodian would be more durable as latex may peel off more easily. The scar may need to be reapplied throughout the day especially if it is near joints or creases. Ensure you have continuity records and photographs.

There tends to be more adverse reactions to Collodian, so skin testing is a major consideration when deciding what products are suitable for your performer.

What points should be considered when deciding on a suitable products and design?

- Skin type
- Skin condition
- Results of any skin compatibility tests if appropriate
- Client's/artist's needs
- Client's budget
- Timing
- Set conditions – filming location, weather conditions, underwater etc.
- Running order
- Continuity
- Script.

Treatment objectives

- Product matching – to suit skin type, client requirements and set conditions
- Apply professional media make-up – according to skin type, condition, client/artist need and preference
- Safe removal of media make-up
- Advice on aftercare – for professionalism and in case of contra-actions.

Cross-infection

To lessen the risks of cross infection:

- Remove make-up from pallets
- Brush care – refer to Chapter 7 Apply Make-up
- Avoid cross contamination of products by using a disposable spatula to remove the products from their containers
- When removing eye make-up, always ensure that a separate cotton pad is used for each eye to avoid cross-infection
- Avoid overloading the cotton pad with remover to prevent it running into the client's eye.

Contraindications

Prior to carrying out any skin-care treatments the make-up artist should check the condition of the client's skin for any of the following conditions to avoid cross infection:

Anatomy and physiology

This list of contraindications is specific to the chapter but the full descriptions can be found in Chapter 4 Anatomy and physiology.

- Conjunctivitis – bacterial infection of membrane of eye which prevents skincare treatment due to risk of cross-infection
- Bacterial infections – for example impetigo, will prevent skincare treatment due to risk of cross-infection, a highly contagious condition that requires medical treatment
- Fungal infections – for example ringworm, will prevent skincare treatment due to risk of cross-infection, a highly contagious condition that requires medical treatment
- Viral infections – for example herpes simplex or cold sores, will prevent skincare treatment due to risk of cross-infection
- Bruising – may restrict skincare treatment due to damaged blood vessels in area, treatment may aggravate condition causing pain and discomfort to client
- Eczema or psoriasis – may restrict treatment if inflamed with open sores or weeping
- Cuts and abrasions – will restrict skincare treatment due to risk of cross-infection
- Rashes, redness and inflammation – will restrict skincare treatment due to risk of further adverse reaction

- Recent scar tissue – 6 months or less – will restrict treatment due to risk damage to tissue
- Recent sunburn – will contraindicate treatment due to risk of skin damage, sensitivity, client pain and discomfort
- Hay fever – sensitive around the eye and nose area and the client may feel uncomfortable if the condition is active
- Claustrophobic clients or very nervous clients may find it difficult to keep the eyes closed for a length of time.

Contra-actions

Specific contra-actions that can occur following make-up treatments are:

- Watery eyes
- Red eyes
- Allergic reaction
- Swelling
- Stinging/burning sensation
- Rash
- Erythema (this is a normal reaction, however if it is excessive it could indicate a sensitivity or allergic reaction to the treatment of products).

Equipment list

- Make-up chair
- Set chair – for the make-up artist when filming is in progress, to sit by the monitor to keep a check of the make-up when final checks are called
- Set bag
- Cotton pads (damp) and bowl
- Disposable covering
- Tissues
- Bin with a liner and a lid (in line with COSHH)
- Disposable spatulas to remove products from container
- Cotton bud or cotton tipped orange stick – to aid eye make-up removal
- Cape or gown to protect client/artist clothing
- Eye care products
- Facial skincare products
- Lip care products
- Make-up products
- Spatula
- Scissors.

Treatment planning

This is discussed in more detail in Chapter 2 Health and safety.

Lots of things should be considered when planning a make-up service/treatment. Your design plan may differ with each make-up service according to the remit.

With good education and vital experience treatment planning for your client will become easier. When you first begin this unit there are so many aspects to remember and products to learn but it will become easier and is worthwhile.

Preparing for the treatment

A consultation must be carried out and a treatment plan agreed prior to treatment to ascertain the client needs. Before you begin the treatment the record card must be completed and the client's signature must be gained.

Set up of work area

This is specific to this chapter – see Chapter 2 Health and safety for generic set up.

- Blanket, large towel, the client will lay on disposable covering
- Place a hand towel over the back of the make-up chair to wipe your hands in between product application
- It is beneficial to complete facial treatment in an area that has a sink to rinse mask sponges and your hands etc.
- Carry out consultation and agree treatment plan – check for contraindications and skin sensitivity test results
- Contact lenses should be removed
- Ask client to remove any accessories that may be in the area your working – e.g. earrings or necklace, this is to avoid catching the jewellery during the service/treatment
- Accompany the client to the treatment area, instruct them that they will need to remove any clothing from relevant areas; remember to protect client's clothing and their modesty
- Position client comfortably on the make-up chair
- Gently lift and secure client's hair off their face if appropriate using clips.

> ⭐ *Tip* A blanket can be used on the treatment chair to keep the client warm and cosy.

Aftercare/homecare advice

It is important that the artist/model is aware that contra-actions such as redness or allergic reaction may occur after using products such as latex, Collidon etc. Follow this aftercare advice for 24–48 hours after make-up service:

- No heat treatments
- No sunbathing or UV exposure
- Avoid hair removal treatments
- If a slight redness is still present following the use of latex, collidon, solvents and adhesive type products, apply cold compress to reduce redness. If stinging, itching, excessive redness, rash or swelling/inflammation occurs seek medical advice straight away
- If redness gets worse or other symptoms occur seek medical advice
- The artist/model should contact you if any adverse reaction occurs after treatment
- Try not to keep touching the area treated to avoid cross contamination or making the skin more sensitive.

Specific homecare advice (this should continue between professional skincare appointments)

- Regularly use the retail products recommended by the professional
- Advice on skincare routine for homecare.

Applying and making prosthetics

Direct applied wounds

This means that the wound is applied and moulded onto the skin using products such as Derma Wax, gelatine and sculpt gels (silicone).

Products for use with prosthetics

When applying prosthetics you may need to use some of the products and techniques listed below.

Blood

- Film blood – this tends to be a runny substance and comes in bright red for arterial blood or dark red venous blood.

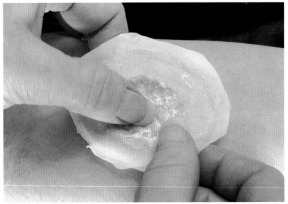

▲ Applying prosthetics: Cleanse the area to remove excess oils so adhesive will stick. Place the prosthetic on the skin and measure the area that spirit gum/prosthetic adhesive needs to be applied

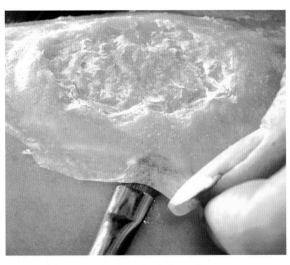

▲ Applying prosthetics: Seal the edges using a brush and spirit gum/prosthetic adhesive

- Fresh scab or scratch – this is a thick sticky type of product that is excellent for use with a stipple sponge to create scratches, scabs, or to fill in a wound.
- Congealed blood – this is a thick gooey product that is excellent to add to a wound to make it look as though the blood is starting to dry out before it forms a scab.
- Wound filler – this is similar to congealed blood but may be a little more textured.
- Eye blood – this comes in a bottle with a dropper and can be gently dropped into an artist's eyes to give the appearance of blood in the eyes. The artist will be able to see the red colour, so they should be warned about this in advance. This only lasts for a few minutes.

From time to time you may need to make your own blood, particularly on low-budget films. Sometimes blood has to be stored in the mouth and although there are blood capsules available for this, a blood mix can be made very easily and cheaply and can be stored in the fridge for a couple of days. To make a blood mix you will need:

- hot water
- golden syrup
- treacle
- red, green and blue food colouring
- cornflour (optional for thickening)

Remember that a lot of blood mix uses food colouring, which can often stain.

Wound filler

This can be purchased ready-made or you can create your own. Use the blood recipe with not too much hot water so it is thicker. Place the Bran flakes in a small food bag and crush; this can be mixed in with the blood recipe to create texture. Mashed banana is an excellent substitute fatty tissue and can be mixed into a wound if appropriate.

Bruising

This can come in the form of a cream-based make-up, which moves very easily to create the different shades of bruising. Sometimes this does not last for a long time and may be easily smudged. As an alternative, Bruce gels are available on the market that dry out rapidly and last very well. They can be removed easily with the appropriate cleanser.

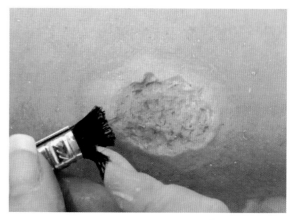

▲ Applying prosthetics: Use a cotton bud soaked in witch hazel or acetone to blend the edges for a seamless finish

▲ Applying prosthetics: Use a standard paint brush cut short and flat to flick alcohol-based skin illustrator on to the prosthetic, building up layers of different shades

Tears and perspiration

Glycerine creates excellent sweat and tears (there are other products available on the market but this is the base ingredient for most). These products are very easily removed and have an almost oily feel, that could interfere with the make-up.

- **Perspiration** – very easy to apply by dipping a stipple sponge into the glycerine and dabbing it on to the skin.

- **Tears** – apply from the corner of the eye using an eye dropper, being careful not to drop into the eye itself. It will run quite quickly. Artificial tears can be purchased in a bottle that usually comes with the dropper.

- **Tear sticks** – usually contain menthol and sometimes camphor and can be placed near the artist's eye to induce their own tears.

Slit throat (using sculpt gel/silicone)

- Check for contraindications and allergies
- Ensure that the skin is clean
- Add bruising, cuts, scratches, etc.
- Mix parts A, B and C of the sculpt gels together. (C is the deadener that gives elasticity. The more deadener used, the more subtle the finished texture.)
- Add flocking to the mixture to create dimension in the skin texture (use sparingly).
- Use a spatula to apply to the area and create laceration.
- Fill inside the wound using grease/cream make-up with fine brush with black or dark red colours (always use darker colour first)
- Blue veins can be lightly painted on the wound using grease/cream make-up and fine brush if desired or using airbrush make-up. Bruising can be added around edges of wound and spot bruising with stipple sponge

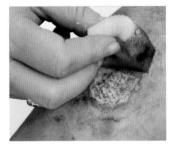
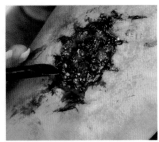

▲ Apply prosthetics: Colour using a sponge, cream-based make-up and alcohol-based skin illustrator. Add congealed blood, wound filler and fresh scratch

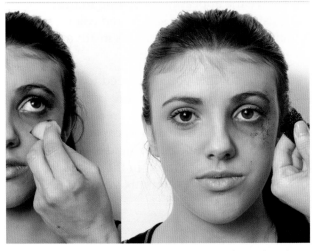

▲ Slit throat: Apply bruising using cream-based make-up and sponge. Spot bruising using strippled sponge

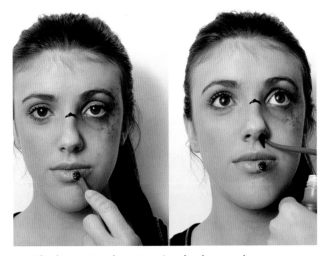

▲ Slit throat: Apply cuts using fresh scratch

- Add thick blood or 'wound filler' inside the wound and on edges of 'flesh' with modelling tool
- Use 'pro-blood' or 'film blood' (these are the runny bloods!); use this with a brush or modelling tool and apply to centre of wound and 'spill' or 'splatter' over onto wrist if desired
- Check with wardrobe for continuity
- Also check with wardrobe if the performer will have any changes of clothes whilst wearing the wound as it may come off and blood may go onto costume
- Take a photo for continuity.

> ⭐ *Tip* Blood bags (or bladders) filled with film blood can be attached to the body under the artist's clothing. When pierced they will leak blood and are great for stab-wound scenes!

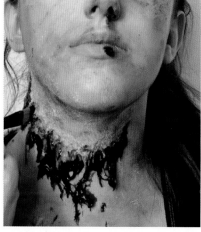

▲ Slit throat: Apply sculpt gel, working downwards to create a flap of skin

▲ Slit throat: Add fresh scratch, wound filler and film blood

▲ Slit throat: final result

Wound removal

A little warm water (for gelatine) or recommended professional remover products on a small brush can be used around edges, then gently lift edges up to dissolve the bond between the skin and the product.

Procedure for creating a severed finger

Products

- Skin cleanser
- Derma wax
- Cream based make-up
- Blood – congealed and film
- Bones.

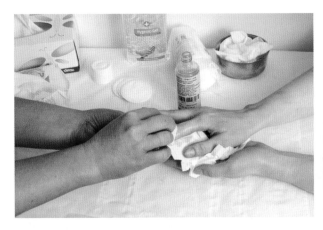

1. Cleanse finger.

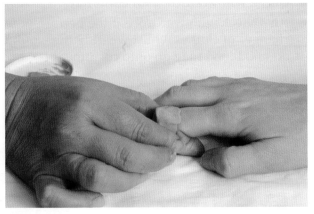

2. Soften Derma Wax and roll into cylinder.

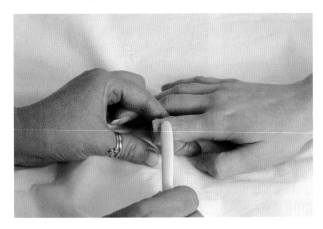

3. Bend client's finger and apply wax to knuckle.

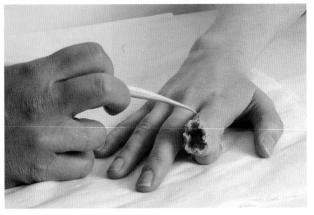

4. Make edges of Derma Wax jagged so skin looks torn.

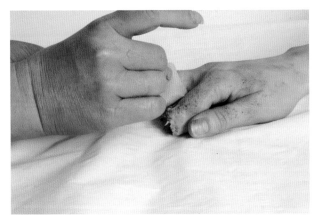

5. Carve in crease lines on knuckles.

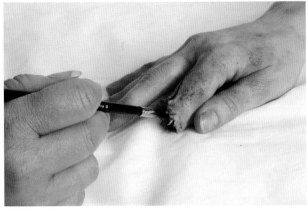

6. Paint inside the creases with reddish/brown cream based make-up.

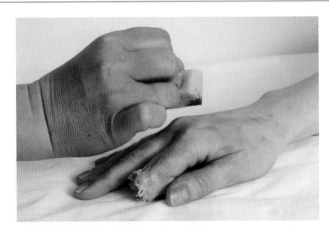

7. Using sponge apply red and blue tones down the finger using cream based make-up.

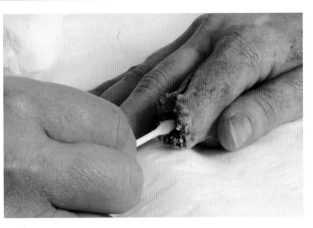

8. If desired attach a small piece of pre made bone on centre of wound with Derma Wax.

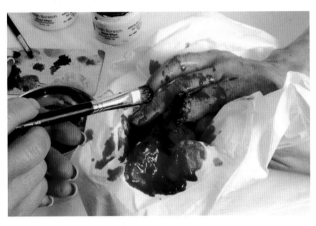

9. Add congealed and film blood.

10. Add a little mashed banana if required.

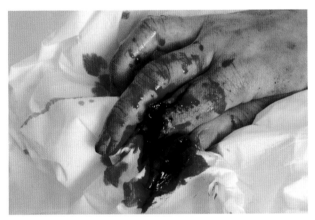

11. The finished look.

Bullet wounds

- The size depends whether it's an entry or exit hole
- An entry wound would leave a smaller hole than an exit wound
- When the bullet leaves the body it takes flesh and blood with it or if it is in the head it also takes skull and brain tissue

Also consider:

- The size of the bullet
- The calibre/how powerful the weapon is
- The range at which it was shot
- The angle at which is shot
- How visible/close up is it going to be filmed?

Entrance bullet hole

- Roll Derma Wax into a ball and apply to skin
- Smooth edges
- Make a hole in the wax
- Fray the edges of the wax using modelling tool
- Cream based make-up – apply black to the base of the hole
- Apply dark reds to frayed edges
- Red and blue shades around surrounding skin
- Apply congealed blood then film blood
- Dark grey/black eye shadow or charcoal dust can be sprinkled around the wound to look like gunpowder.

Exit bullet hole

- Melt gelatine by submerging the bottle in hot water
- Pour gelatine into a mixing bowl – check the temperature on your own wrist before applying to the client/artist
- Apply to the area in layers, building it up and moving a palette knife around to create texture and dimension
- Colour as usual and apply blood
- Pale or yellow/death cream can be applied if required
- Powder can be used around the wound if you don't want a fresh appearance.

Concrete burn

- Liquid latex
- Cream based make-up
- Brushes
- Modelling tool/spatula
- Film blood
- Cleanse area
- Apply a thin layer of latex and a tissue split to 1 ply and dry with hairdryer (cool setting)

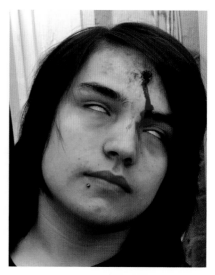

▲ Bullet wounds (entry)

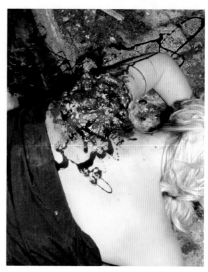

▲ Bullet wounds (exit)

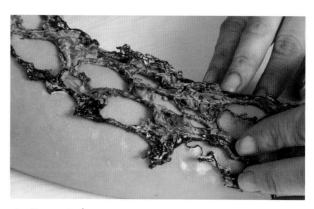

▲ Concrete burns

- Apply 2–3 layers of latex and dry each layer with hairdryer (cool setting)
- Apply cream based make-up (darkest colour first)
- Bruise/colour surrounding area
- Using spatula fill wound with film blood.

Removal

- Cleanse carefully with acetone on cotton wool, add oil and gently lift edges of latex
- Cleanse area with cream cleanser
- There may be a slight erythema where the latex has been removed from.

▲ Zombie: Apply crushed cereal with latex (spirit gum)

Zombie

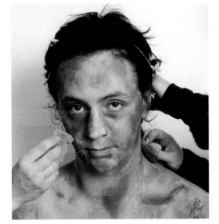

▲ Zombie: Colour up using grease, paint and body art products

▲ Zombie: Tear latex skin carefully

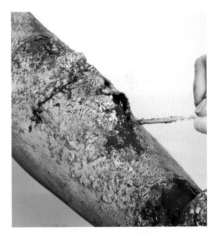

▲ Zombie: Apply fresh scratch into open wound

- Cleanser and moisturiser
- Cream based make-up
- Sponges and brushes
- Tissues
- Mastix or spirit gum
- Liquid latex
- Liquid foundation (if required)
- Derma Wax
- Clean dirt, fresh scab and film blood
- Check you have all the materials you need
- Ensure you have checked for allergies and carried out a skin sensitivity test if appropriate

▲ Zombie: Finished look

- Ensure the model's skin is clean and free of grease
- Protect model's clothes with a gown
- Apply Derma Wax for wound
- Slit wax with spatula and mould into shape
- Smooth edges using a little moisturiser to help blend them away.

Latex

- Apply small pieces of tissue to the cheek using mastix or spirit gum
- Allow this to set for a minute or so
- Apply a thin layer of liquid latex over the tissue and help the setting process by using a hairdryer on a cool setting
- Using spatula pull the latex before it's completely set to give the illusion of melted skin
- Build up layers of latex until desired effect is achieved
- Apply white cream based make-up to the face using a make-up sponge
- Apply bruising around cut using cream based colours (darkest first)
- Colour inside the wound using cream based colour (darkest first)
- Apply dark circles around the eyes with cream based make-up and sponge
- Using a fine make-up brush apply dark red along the lower lash line
- Using stipple sponge cream based make-up and 'fresh scab' blood to apply grazes
- Fill in latex wound with cream based red colour where appropriate
- Fill the latex with congealed blood using spatula, so the blood is 'oozing' out of the wound
- Apply red or a dark colour to the lips
- Using shades of cream based reds and a make-up sponge apply shading around the mouth and latex wound
- Apply 'film' blood to the wounds and allow it to run.

Dirtying down

- If appropriate tear the clothing
- Apply 'clean dirt' to clothing and hands
- Apply 'film' blood to clothing hands and neck.

▲ Theatrical ageing: shade in the natural smile line with a darker colour to age the skin

▲ Theatrical ageing: creating eye bags

▲ Theatrical ageing: emphasising lines in the forehead

▲ Dirtying down

Use latex to create the ageing effect

▲ Cleanse skin and gently stretch to apply latex with sponge

▲ Keeping the skin stretched, dry the latex using a hairdryer on a cool setting until transparent

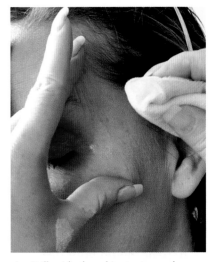

▲ Still with the skin taut, apply powder over the latex. Release the tension and manipulate to form wrinkles. To achieve deeper wrinkles apply more layers of latex, powdering in between each application.

Equipment list

- Hairdryer
- Loose powder
- Latex
- Sponge
- Powder brush.

Top tips for ageing

- Do not put too much latex on your sponge
- Keep latex away from the eyes, hair and clothing
- Have everything to hand on your make-up station
- You may get your artiste to assist you by holding parts of the skin tight while you apply the latex, they quite often will pull the skin tighter than what you can
- The tighter you can stretch the skin the better the effect you will achieve
- You will need to stretch the skin in the area which you are ageing and keep it stretched when applying latex with a sponge
- Next you must keep the area still stretched and dry it thoroughly with the hairdryer on a cool temperature
- When the latex is dry you must keep the area still stretched, and then apply loose powder with a powder brush
- Do not release the pressure on the skin until the latex is completely covered with the loose powder
- When you are completely satisfied that you have covered the latex with the loose powder you may release the skin
- As the skin settles you will see it will start to form into wrinkles

▲ Using skin illustrator to create liver spots and freckles

▲ The finished look

- To age the skin more you will need to repeat this method a few times to get your desired look
- The more layers you apply the older the skin will appear
- You can also use green marble and a small amount of Attagel® mixed together.

Scar tray

You will need: a small sheet of reinforced glass, sculpting tools, non-drying modelling clay Plasterline, petroleum jelly, Crystacal R plaster.

Method

- Take some non-drying modelling clay Plasterline; how much you need will depend on the size of your scar.
- Roll into a ball or a long sausage shape; this will vary depending on your design.
- Place modelling clay on to the sheet of reinforced glass; press your shape of modelling clay on to the glass and smooth the edges down so they become as flat to the glass as you can get it. This will make your skin addition become invisible when you apply it to the skin.

- When you are happy with your edges, then you can start to sculpt your desired design.
- When you are happy with your design you can smooth over with petroleum jelly and then put in skin texture, you can do this by stippling with sponges or using dried out orange peel.

- You will need to make a wall around your design with modelling clay, you must smooth the wall modelling clay to the reinforced glass. Make sure your wall is high enough so moulds are not too thin.

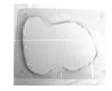

- When you are happy that the wall of modelling clay is sealed to the reinforced glass, spray all over the designs and the inside of the scar tray to release them from the plaster. Mix up Crystacal R plaster. Work out how much you will need for your design and mix Crystacal R plaster with cold water, not hot as this will make it set faster. You should also consider the temperature in the room you are working as this can also have an effect on how fast the plaster will set.

- Use a small cheap brush to put your plaster on to your design to get all the detail, when you have done that, you can then fill your design with plaster on a flat level table.

- You will need to let the plaster set for whatever the recommended time is.
- When your cast is set, remove all the modelling clay, being careful not to damage the scar tray. Use a small pin for any difficult bits.

- You are now ready to make skin additions with latex, gelatine or silicone.

Bald caps

Equipment needed:

- Gel or wax
- Cling film
- Sticky tape
- Scissors
- Black marker pen
- Head block
- Petroleum jelly
- Wax
- White soft eyeliner
- Coarse nail file
- Powder
- Powder puff
- Liquid cap plastic or glatzan
- Cap plastic application brush/a good paint brush
- T-pin
- Tissues
- Hair dryer

Creating and applying a bald cap

1. Gel or wax the hair back off the face, away from the hairline to create a flat surface.

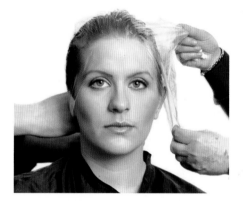

2. Place cling film around the head, wrapping it over the ears. Make sure that the cling film covers well over the hairline.

3. Cut lengths of sticky tape and place them over the edge of the cling film and over all the cling film; use the sticky tape to tighten the cling film to the shape of the head. The cap should be stiff when all the cling film is covered with sticky tape.

4. Using the marker pen, draw on the outline of the hairline, keeping the hairline long at the back and around the base of the ear. Also draw the shape of the ear in, which will help to line the cap up on the head block.

5. Cut slits through the middle of the ear shape, which will help to lift the cap off the model's head.

6. Cut around the outline you drew but do not cut out the ear shape.

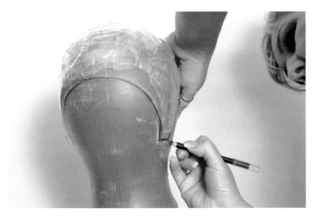

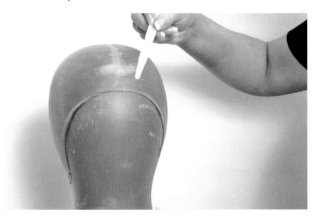

7. Put the cap on the head block. Leaving a width of 2cm, draw a line around the cap, keeping the line long at the back, so when the cap is stuck down it isn't to the nape of the hair. The slits you cut in the ear shape should be stuck together again as this could show an incorrect shape of the hairline. Then remove the cap from the head block.

8. File down any rough edges on the head block, applying wax over anything uneven and blend the edges out. Apply petroleum jelly within the pattern and dab off any excess – this acts as a releasing agent.

9. Pour some cap plastic into a bowl and apply thinly to the head block. Working within the pattern, work from the centre of the front hairline to the nape, applying in one direction. Work quickly and try not to overlap your strokes. Overload your brush and make sure there are no loose hairs that will ruin the final result. When the first layer is applied, dry with a hair dryer.

10. After the cap plastic has dried generously powder all over the cap with a powder puff. This will help to set the cap plastic.

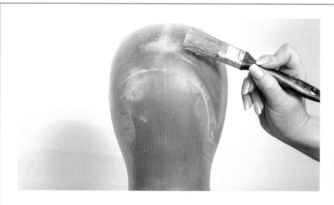

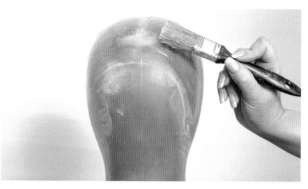

11. Apply the second layer using the same technique but working from side to side, which will increase the strength of the bald cap and cover any areas that might not be covered already. Dry again with a hair dryer and powder generously.

12. Apply the third layer, applying the cap plastic around 3cm inside of the front hairline. This creates a thin edge which can be blended with the skin more easily, creating a more realistic application. Dry with a hair dryer and generously powder.

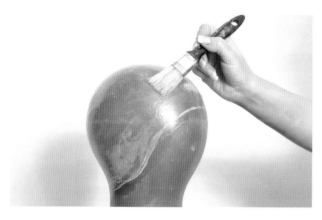

13. Apply the fourth layer in the same way as the second. Apply, starting 3–4cm inside the pattern line. Dry with the hair dryer and powder generously. Continue 5–8 times depending on how thick you want the layers to be. The last layer should cover the crown of the head for strength. Leave until completely dry. It is best to make the cap the day before you need to use it. Clean your brush immediately with acetone.

14. Using a T-pin carefully lift the edges of the cap, powdering generously underneath the cap as its been lifted.

15. When the cap is fully removed, powder generously inside and outside the bald cap. Pack out with tissues and store in a safe place.

Equipment needed:

- Cap plastic bald cap
- Water spray
- Hair gel
- Hairbrush
- Scissors
- Skin adhesive
- Lint-free cloth or damp powder puff
- Acetone
- Tissues or towel
- Cottons buds
- Make-up of your choice

Fitting a plastic bald cap on a model

For details of how to measure the head, refer to the section on fitting wigs in Chapter 9.

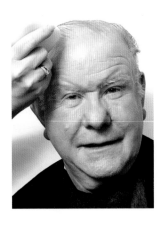  

1. Cleanse, tone and moisturise the face so you start clean. Gel back the hair or scalp the hairline as you did when making the cling film cap. Shorter hair is easier but long hair should be sectioned into parts and wrapped in different directions around the head, creating a surface as flat as possible. Never use hair grips as they can pierce the cap. Ask the model to hold the cap at the front while you stretch the cap over the back of the head and into position. The cap should be smooth with no wrinkles. Stretch the bald cap over the head and line up over the ears.

2. Cut around the ear hole just inside the edge so the cap can be tucked behind the ears. Take time as you're using scissors so close to your model.

3. Apply the skin adhesive to the centre of the forehead first. Make sure you using the skin adhesive sparingly. Stick the cap down, sticking the sides and behind the ear down in the same way. Use a damp cloth to help put the cap in position. Before gluing the back, ensure the model's head is level to prevent wrinkles.

4. Ask you model to cover their face with a tissue to protect them from dripping acetone. Dip a cotton bud in acetone. Do not overload the cotton bud too much as this will result in excess dripping. Work the cotton bud on the edge of the bald cap, keeping off the skin as best as you can, blending the edge into the skin.

5. You can now apply the make-up of your choice, using a pink (rose) base before a natural colour matching to the skin tone. This colour takes away any colour showing through from the hair. Powder generously and dust off any excess. Apply a matching colour to the skin tone, powdering between layers of cream-based make-up. The final layer should cover over the face and the bald cap to ensure a perfect colour match.

6. You can now apply the fantasy design you have created. We have created a clown, laying an orange crepe hair using spirit gum. This has been shaped and styled and a red sponge nose has been added.

Blocking out eyebrows

1. Brush the eyebrows to lay them flat and apply eyebrow plastic/wax with a disposable spatula or modelling tool.

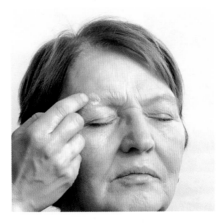

2. Use moisturiser to blend and smooth the surface of the wax.

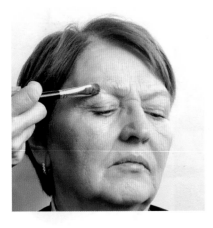

3. Apply sealer over the wax

4. Powder over the sealer, apply make-up and powder in between if adding more layers of cream base.

5. The finished look.

Other looks for media and theatrical hair and make-up

▲ Witch

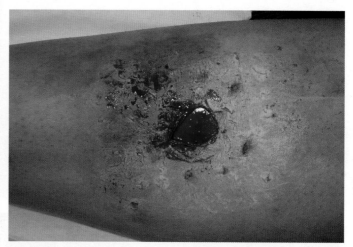

▲ Burnt arm

▲ Drug addict

▲ Theatrical look

CHAPTER 15

Provide self-tanning treatment

Units covered by this chapter:

VRQ Level 2: Apply skin tanning techniques (Note: Level 2 students can only work on the arms, lower legs, head and shoulders when providing self-tanning treatment)

VRQ Level 3: Provide self-tanning

NVQ Level 3 Unit B25: Provide self-tanning services

Chapter aims

This chapter will look at:

- Types of self-tanning treatments
- Products and their ingredients
- Benefits of self-tanning
- Tools and equipment
- Considerations when choosing a product and costing the service
- Tips for delivering safe, appealing and cost-effective tanning services
- Hygiene and avoiding contraindications and contra-actions
- Guidance in preparing for treatment and procedures for applying tanning products
- Troubleshooting tips
- Aftercare and homecare advice.

As a media make-up artist you may be required to apply self-tanning lotion or spray tan on your subject to give them a healthy glow or perhaps a tan is required for a role that they are playing. Many people are worried about the dangers associated with the damaging effects of the sun and ultraviolet (UV) tanning and are opting for sunless tanning products to give them a tanned appearance.

Recently 'self-tanning' or 'sunless tanning' treatments have become extremely popular in beauty salons. These treatments are relaxing and can be carried out without installing a shower unit and can even be completed with a 'pop up' style cubicle in which to carry out the treatment. The retail potential is massive.

▲ Tan solutions range

NVQ service times for self tanning

- Manual self-tan – 60 minutes
- Full-body spray tan – 30 minutes.

Self-tanning treatments

Manual application

This type of tanning is carried out using a hands-on method that some clients may prefer as a relaxing treatment. This method will take longer to carry out in comparison to spray tanning.

Self-tanning products these days come as a brown-coloured lotion and provide an instant tan, however the colour applied is only a guide colour and will come off the first time the wearer takes a shower. It must be explained to the client that this is not the tan coming off – only the guide colour. A few years ago self-tan came as a white lotion and it was difficult to see if the application was even and so to get an even tan. The guide colour was introduced in an attempt to remedy this problem.

The tanning process may take between 4 and 8 hours to develop before it can be washed off (refer to manufacturers' instructions).

Spray or airbrush

This method uses a compressor and a gun; the nozzle and gravity feed cup are larger for spray tanning than for some other airbrush treatments as such a large surface area needs to be covered. As technology has progressed so have the compressor units and now the spray guns tend to be larger than when airbrush tanning first became popular. The airbrush units now have a constant air flow as they are high-volume low-pressure systems (HVLPs). This has sped up the application process

▲ Types of self-tan

▲ Manual tanning products

▲ Compressor

with some brands of full-body spray-tanning treatments being completed in around 15 minutes. This means more treatments can be performed, thus maximising profit for those administering the treatment. This method of self-tanning is very quick and easy to apply, making it a very cost-effective treatment. The initial costs of setting up this treatment, however, are higher due to the use of specialised equipment such as the compressor, airbrush gun and pop-up tent.

The tan may take between 4 and 6 hours to develop before it can be washed off (refer to manufacturers' instructions).

Instant self-tanning spray

This type of tan can be administered as a homecare product or in a spray tanning booth. The homecare type usually comes in an aerosol form that is sprayed directly onto the skin however it will come off when water is applied. It may be a particularly messy treatment as overspray will touch the surfaces in the area.

Spray-tanning booths are self-contained, with jets that may be static or moving and spray tanning solution onto the client. Depending on the system this can take between 1 and 10 minutes. This system will ensure more privacy for the client but may not be suitable for a claustrophobic client. As the tanning cycle begins, the client may need to move into different positions to ensure the tanning product is applied evenly. Once full application is complete the client must be careful to leave the tanning products on the skin until dry. Excess product should then be removed from the palms of the hands and if appropriate, the soles of the feet.

▲ Self-tanning spray

Tan wipes for the face

These wipes are often a retail product sold to 'top up' the tan on the face in between professional tanning treatments. The wipes usually come in the form of a soft fabric infused with self-tanning lotion or gel and individually wrapped in a sealed sachet.

Products

- **Skin cleansing products**: These must be thoroughly removed before the tan is applied
- **Body wash**: This is a good retail product that contains no alcohol, which could decrease the life of the tan
- **Exfoliation products**: this comes in lotion or gel form and is to be used prior to manual tan application within the professional treatment. It is an excellent retail product for the client to use as a homecare treatment in between tanning treatments and prior to spray tan application. These products come either as finely ground fruit kernels or nylon spherical beads that are less damaging to the skin. Jojoba is often added to give the product 'slip' and help condition the skin

▲ Exfoliator/body polish

- **Tanning products**: these come as gel, spray, cream, foam and lotion. Gels and foams tend to come in more subtle colours
- **Moisturisers**: these often contain plant extracts such as aloe vera to help moisturise the skin and help the tan last longer. A moisturiser will also act as a barrier to give the tan a lighter appearance in areas such as the underside of the arms. Some available moisturisers give a shimmering effect to the fake tan. Moisturisers have been specially formulated for use with self-tanning products and different products within brands are often designed to be used together. Other moisturisers may react with the tan and turn it green due to the pigment contained in the tan; deodorant and perfume can have the same effect so must be removed prior to application of the tanning product.

Tanning products, body polish and moisturiser should last for around 3–4 months once opened.

▲ Tanning products

▲ Tanning gel

▲ Shimmering body moisturiser

Product ingredients

- **Dihydroxyacetone**: This is the tanning agent used in self-tanning lotions. It has no known toxicity as it is a sugar that reacts with amino acids in the skin to produce a tanned effect. It is also used as an emulsifier, humectant and fungicide. The Food and Drug Administration (FDA) in the USA declared in 1973 that this colour additive is safe and suitable for use in cosmetics or drugs that apply colour to the skin (self-tanning products). It is a white powder that becomes colourless in liquid form. It colours the skin a brown shade, giving it a sun-tanned appearance. Obtained by the action of certain bacteria on glycerol, it has a sweet taste and characteristic odour.

> **Key term**
>
> **Dihydroxyacetone** – Tanning agent used in self-tanning lotions

It is converted by alkali to the fruit sugar fructose. It has no known skin toxicity and the FDA have declared it exempt from mandatory colour additive certification.

- **L-tyrosine**: This is a tan accelerator that helps stimulate the skin's natural production of melanin.
- **Aloe vera**: This is a common fragrance used in self-tanning products.
- **Vitamin E**: This is added to some products because of its moisturising properties.
- **Erythrulose**: This ingredient helps to create a more natural looking tan, slows the rate of discoloration and is less drying to the skin.

It should be noted that some products contain alcohol as a drying agent.

Benefits of self-tan treatments

The benefits of self-tan treatments are numerous, including:

- An all-year-round tan without the ageing effects on the skin
- A single application tan lasts 5 to 7 days and just fades gradually
- Tan solutions are available in different shades to match the client's skin tone and expectations
- Those who are allergic to natural sunlight can still have a tan
- It can prolong the life of an existing tan
- Those who do not tan evenly can use it to achieve an even tan
- Self-tanning can be used as a salon or at-home treatment and can be retailed thus increasing business profits.

> **Key term**
>
> **L-tyrosine** – Tan accelerator helping to stimulate the skin's natural production of melanin
>
> **Erythrulose** – Slows the rate of discolouration and is less drying to the skin

> **Anatomy and physiology**
>
> Readers should refer to Chapter 4 Anatomy and physiology for information regarding UV radiation and its damaging effects upon the skin.

Stay Bronzed and Beautiful with Tan Solutions

▲ Self-tan benefits

Considerations when choosing a product and costing the service

There are many self-tanning products on the market, both retail and professional. When choosing a product to use professionally, there are many points to consider:

- Quality
- Reputation of product and company
- Cost
- Start-up packages (some companies have a minimum order limit)
- Application of product
- Training and backup service.

Skin colour

The skin colour dictates the degree of absorption and reflection of light from its surface. When light hits the skin, a certain amount is absorbed by the epidermis and it reflects the rest. The colour produced is a combination of three factors:

- **Melanin**: This is the natural pigment produced by cells in the epidermis and will vary in colour from client to client.
- **Fat**: Fatty matter in the skin has the fat-soluble vitamin carotene dissolved in it. Carotene is taken into the body through the diet and is contained in green vegetables and carrots. It has a yellowish colour therefore vegetarians often have a sallow skin tone because of this.
- **Blood**: The influence of blood on the skin colour depends on the thickness of the epidermis and whether the vessels are dilated or contracted. The superficial capillaries add pink to the overall skin colour.

In dark-skinned individuals, fat and blood have virtually no influence on the skin colour due to the density of melanin pigment. The paler the skin the more significant the contribution of blood and fat.

Skin colour varies greatly throughout the world, but we can categorise most skin types into three main groups:

- **African**: This can vary from light brown to darkest brown, with undertones of grey, red or yellow.
- **Asian**: Various shades of brown and Asian skin contain the yellow base of the Chinese and the cream base of the Japanese.
- **Caucasion**: This type varies from the sallow skin of those in the southern areas to the fairer skin of those in the North.

Unfortunately, sometimes the skin changes colour unevenly, which can be very distressing. See Chapter 4 Anatomy and physiology for a full description.

Hyperpigmentation

Increased melanin production causes darker patches of skin, for example with the condition chloasma.

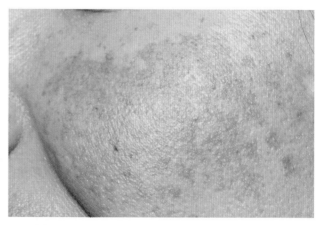

▲ Chloasma

Hypopigmentation

Reduced melanin production causes paler patches of skin, for example in vitiligo.

Hygiene

Hygiene with regard to the self-tanning treatments unit is discussed as follows.

Hygiene in general is covered in greater detail in Chapter 2 Health and safety.

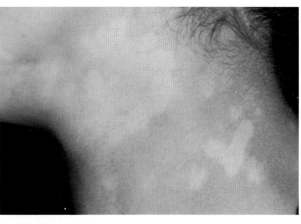

▲ Vitiligo

Cross-infection

- Avoid cross-contamination of products by using a disposable spatula to remove the products from their containers where appropriate. Many self-tanning products are dispensed from a pump-style bottle.
- Disposable consumables can be used to protect clients' modesty and privacy.
- The spray tanning cubicle or tent should be wiped down and disinfected with an appropriate solution (check manufacturers' instructions) after treating each client.

Contraindications

Prior to carrying out any self-tanning treatments the make-up artist should check the client's skin and make sure that none of the following conditions exist or have been undertaken to avoid cross-infection or client discomfort:

- **Hair removal treatments**: they should be carried out 24–48 hours prior to self-tanning product application as the hair follicles could be open and the skin could be sensitive or damaged
- **Heat treatments**: directly after heat treatments such as sauna or steam as the skin may be sensitive
- **Severe respiratory conditions**: may be aggravated by vapours or odour
- **Infestations**: contagious
- **Conjunctivitis**: bacterial infection of the membranes of the eye
- **Bacterial infections**: e.g. impetigo – a highly contagious condition that requires medical treatment
- **Fungal infections**: e.g. ringworm – a highly contagious condition that requires medical treatment
- **Viral infections**: e.g. herpes simplex or cold sores

Anatomy and physiology

These contraindications are specific to the unit. Full descriptions are discussed in Chapter 4 Anatomy and physiology.

- **Bruising**: damaged blood vessels in the treatment area; treatment may aggravate the condition, causing pain and discomfort for the client
- **Eczema or psoriasis**: may restrict treatment but if inflamed, with open sores or weeping will prevent treatment
- **Cuts and abrasions**: will restrict treatment due to risk of cross-infection
- **Rashes, redness, inflammation or hypersensitive skin**: will restrict treatment due to risk of further adverse reaction
- **Recent scar tissue**: 6 months or less – will restrict treatment due to risk of damage to tissue. Any tan may stick to the new skin, giving a difference in colour
- **Recent sunburn**: will contraindicate treatment due to risk of skin damage, sensitivity, client pain and discomfort
- **Hay fever**: sensitivity around the eye and nose area. The client may feel uncomfortable if the condition is active
- **Claustrophobia**: clients with this fear or very nervous clients may not be comfortable keeping their eyes closed for any length of time or being in the spray-tanning booth
- **During chemotherapy**: sensitivity to chemicals
- **During radiotherapy**: sensitivity to chemicals
- **Recent fractures, broken bones and sprains**: may restrict the treatment
- **Recent scar tissue**
- **Hyperkeratosis** (thickening of the skin with darker patches). The tan would exaggerate this so it is important to moisturise the skin well directly before application of tanning products.

Contra-actions

Specific contra-actions that can occur following self-tanning treatments are:

- Watery eyes
- Red eyes
- Allergic reaction
- Swelling
- Itching
- Stinging or burning sensation
- Rash
- Erythema
- Fainting and coughing – from the vapours or odour, particularly in spray-tanning techniques.

Safety

Personal protective equipment (PPE) for use during administration of tanning treatments include:

- Uniform
- Apron
- Single-use disposable gloves (powder-free nitrile or vinyl)
- Disposable underwear to protect the client
- Ventilation due to overspray mist, which can be inhaled or ingested
- Self-tanning products are suitable for pregnant women, as is the tanning treatment (check manufacturers' instructions), however body treatments shouldn't be carried out within the first 3 months of pregnancy. Some pregnant women may prefer not to have this treatment applied to their tummies. Companies administering this treatment should check their insurance cover and adjust it accordingly.
- Self-tanning will not protect against harmful UV rays from the sun
- Check the client's well being throughout the self-tanning treatment, particularly during spray tanning and use an extractor fan to improve the air quality as the spray produces a fine mist that can easily inhaled or ingested.

Anatomy and physiology

See Routes of entry in Chapter 4 Anatomy and physiology.

Skin patch test

This may be carried out 24–48 hours prior to application of tan to check for sensitivity or allergic reaction to tanning products. A small amount of product is applied behind the ear and must be left on the skin for 24 hours. This should be recorded on the client's record card along with the results.

Health and Safety

Remember to advise the client that a sun protection factor should be worn to protect against UV rays.

Matching products to service requirements

Colour

If a client has very pale skin, it should be explained that their skin will have a golden honey colour. A second application may be required to give a more tanned look. Clients often like the effect after just one application and do not wish to appear too dark. The tanning product works with your own natural melanin, and so it will look natural.

If a client is already tanned or has recently come back from holiday, the effect of the tan will be similar to that of returning from their holiday.

Modification of service

Occasionally a client may not wish to have a full-body application of a tanning product. In this case a 'half-body' application can be made, covering the face, neck, upper chest, shoulders, arms and legs.

Maintaining a client's modesty and privacy

It is very important that the treatment room is private in order that the client will feel at ease. You must remain professional at all times and thoroughly explain the treatment procedure prior to application so the client understands exactly what will happen during treatment. Many companies supply disposable underwear for use during tanning treatments.

How is a natural tan produced?

The technical term for tanning is **melanogenesis**. As the UV rays are absorbed by the skin, they stimulate into action the enzyme **tyrosinase**, which is present in **melanocytes**, the pigment-forming cells in the basal layer of the epidermis.

The tan is produced by a chemical reaction when the cream is applied to the skin, causing superficial staining of the top layer of the epidermis. If the client has sensitive skin a patch test may be applied prior to treatment to make sure they are not allergic to the product.

The chemical process causes the transformation of **tyrosin**, a colourless amino acid, into **melanin**, a colourful molecule, which migrates upwards to the surface of the skin; this is what gives skin its tan and helps to filter out harmful UV rays.

Many people will burn when exposed to UV radiation before they tan; some people burn without producing a tan. Self-tan can help with this problem. Imagine that melanin lays dormant under your skin and when the UV light activates it, it can take up to 48 hours to 'wake up' – this is when most people burn. Self-tanning creates a chemical reaction in the skin that stimulates the tyrosin, which turns into melanin and produces the self-tanning colour (in other words self-tanning works with your skin's natural melanin). It is ideal to have a self-tanning treatment before going in the sun as the melanin is already 'awake' and already producing a tan and protecting your skin naturally from burning.

Pre-treatment advice

- Clients should be given a consultation and informed as to what the treatment involves and what shade the tan will be at the end result.
- Clients should be advised to exfoliate and moisturise their skin two days before having the self-tan treatment; this will give a smoother surface for the therapist to apply the tan and therefore a much better result will be achieved.

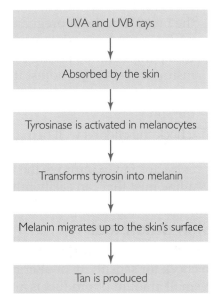

UVA and UVB rays

↓

Absorbed by the skin

↓

Tyrosinase is activated in melanocytes

↓

Transforms tyrosin into melanin

↓

Melanin migrates up to the skin's surface

↓

Tan is produced

▲ Chemical process flowchart

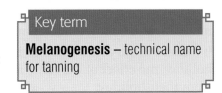

Tip Many clients have self-tanning treatments before they go on holiday so they have colour when they arrive but remember to warn them that it will not provide any sun protection factor (SPF).

Key term

Melanogenesis – technical name for tanning

- Clients **must** be advised to wear dark, loose fitting clothing when they come for this treatment (if possible, it would be better not to wear a bra).
- Clients **must** be advised to stop using any other tanning product at least four days before they have the self-tanning treatment. If this advice is ignored, the colour and quality of the resulting self-tan will not be as effective.
- Advise brides to have the treatment **two** days before their wedding, to allow them and their body to adapt to their new appearance.
- Clients should have any hair removal treatment carried out at least 24 hours before they have the tanning treatment as waxing or shaving will weaken the tan colour.
- Contact lenses should be removed prior to application of the tanning product to avoid irritation.
- A positive reaction to skin testing, if performed, should halt tanning treatment.

Preparing for manual and spray tanning treatment

A consultation must be carried out and a treatment plan agreed prior to treatment to ascertain client needs. Before you begin treatment the record card must be completed; the client's signature must be gained.

Manual tan procedure

Tools, equipment and product list

- Treatment couch
- Trolley
- Towels – dark towels may be best to avoid staining from the tanning product
- Disposable covering
- Disposable hair cap, headband, towel
- Bowl
- Spatulas
- Cleanser
- Tan
- Exfoliator
- Moisturiser
- Toweling mitt to remove exfoliator
- Bowl of warm water or sink
- Buffing mitt
- Control of Substances Hazardous to Health (COSHH) bin.

▲ Toweling mitt, buffing mitt

Set up work area

The information given on work area set up is specific to the unit. See Chapter 2 Health and safety for a more generic set up.

The set up for the purpose of this chapter is as follows:

- Large towel with disposable covering underneath: for the client to lay on
- One large and one small towel: to cover the client (only expose the areas you are working on)
- One hand towel: to be placed over the back of the bed, to wipe your hands in between product application
- Sink: it is beneficial to complete manual tanning treatment in an area that has a sink, to rinse toweling mitts when removing tan and to wash your hands etc.

 **Health and Safety**

Ensure the client thoroughly understands the treatment plan during the consultation and gain their signature before the treatment begins.

Preparing the client

The following should take place prior to commencement of treatment:

- Consultation and agreement of treatment plan: check for contraindications and carry out skin sensitivity testing, if appropriate.
- Ensure the client has followed pre-treatment advice given.
- Contact lenses should be removed.
- Ask the client to remove any accessories that may be in your working area, e.g. earrings, watch, necklace, etc. to avoid tan lines.
- Accompany the client to the treatment area and instruct them that they will need to remove their clothing and they can change into the disposable underwear if they prefer. Leave a large towel or robe for them to use as cover and explain that you will leave them to get changed and return in a few moments. Always remain within earshot for safety.
- Position the client comfortably on the treatment couch, either lying flat or slightly elevated.
- Protect the client's clothing – place a large towel over the client's body for warmth and privacy, and place a smaller towel over the client's chest.
- Gently lift and secure client's hair off their face: use a headband, turban or towel.

Manual self-tanning procedure

Exfoliation

A more even result will be achieved if the dead skin cells are removed prior to application of the tan. A mildly abrasive product should be used to exfoliate the dead skin cells. The procedure is as follows:

1. Prepare a large bowl of hand-hot water.

2. Mix self-tanning exfoliator/body polish with a little cleanser and exfoliate the face, neck and décolleté, using gentle circular movements (see Chapter 6 Skin care for cleansing routine).

3. Remove the exfoliant with dry toweling mitts followed by damp sponges.

4. Take a teaspoon of self-tanning exfoliator/body polish and mix it with the water in a cupped hand. Apply to the legs using a long sweeping movement (as in effleurage) from foot to thigh and gently back down to the starting point.

5. Use circular movements, concentrating on the areas prone to dryness, such as knees, ankles and feet.

6. Remove the product with dry toweling mitts and follow with damp sponges.

7. Ensure deodorant has been removed, then repeat the exfoliation process on the arms, beginning on the hand and working upwards towards the shoulder and gently back to the starting point using effleurage movements. Using circular movements, concentrate on the elbows, as they may be drier. Don't forget to exfoliate under the arms and axillae.

8. Continue onto the mid-section, turning the client over and repeating the process on the back of the body. Begin with the legs, then move on to the arms and then the back.

9. Return the client to their original position and remove the couch roll from under them.

 **Health and Safety**

Remember to keep the room temperature warm when performing these treatments for client comfort.

Self-tan exfoliation

All photos courtesy of Fake Bake

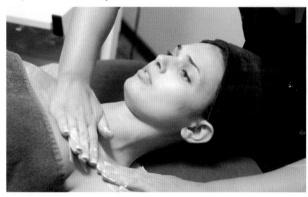

1. Mix self-tan exfoliator/body polish with a little cleanser and exfoliate the face, neck and décolleté, using gentle circular movements (as in cleansing routine in Chapter 6 – Skin care).

2. Remove the exfoliant with dry toweling mitts followed by damp sponges.

3. Take a teaspoon of self-tanning exfoliator/body polish and mix with the water in a cupped hand. Apply to the legs using a long sweeping movement (as in effleurage) from foot to thigh and gently back down to the starting point.

4. Cover all areas. Using circular movements, concentrate on the areas prone to dryness, such as the knees, ankles and feet.

5. Remove the exfoliator with dry toweling mitts and follow this with the application of damp sponges to the skin to remove any remaining product.

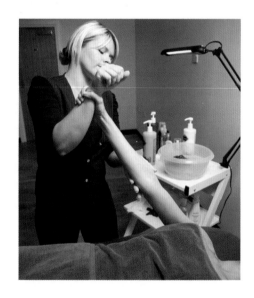

6. Repeat exfoliation. Ensure deodorant has been removed. Repeat the exfoliation process on the arms, beginning on the hand and working upwards towards the shoulder and gently back to the starting point. Use effluerage movements and concentrate on the elbows as they may be drier. Circular movements can also be used. Do not forget to exfoliate under the arms and axillae.

7. Turning the client over and repeat the process on the back of their body. Begin with the legs, and continue to the arms and then the back.

8. Return to starting position. Return the client to the original treatment position and remove the couch roll beneath them.

Manual tan application

All photos courtesy of Fake Bake

1. Wash your hands in warm water straightaway.

2. Apply moisturiser to the palms of the hands, elbows, soles of feet, ankles and knees, or any other area that may have dry skin; this will stop the tan from becoming patchy.

3. Put on gloves and make sure that they fit tightly and have no wrinkles in them as this could make give the tan a streaky appearance.

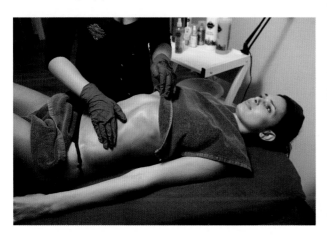

5. Apply the tanning product in line with the manufacturers' instructions. Ensure the tan is applied evenly and all areas of skin have been covered equally.

4. Remember to warm the tan slightly in your hands before applying it to the client's skin. Don't overwarm it though as this could affect the quality of the application. Warn your client that it may feel a little cold.

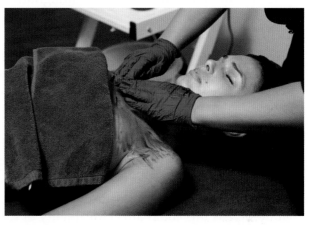

6. Most manual-tanning products are applied to the front of the body first.

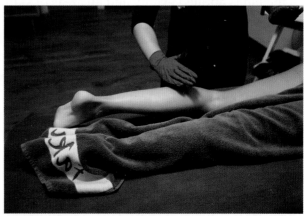

7. When applying the tan to the back of the body, complete the legs first for work up onto the back.

Face

- Use one and a half pumps of tan to one and a half pumps of moisturiser and apply all over the face, neck and décolleté. Avoid the eyes and hairline. Dispense one more pump of lotion, with the residue of tan left in your hands and mix in hands and apply to hairline, eyes and ears.
- Wash your hands in warm water straightaway.

Body

- Apply moisturiser or barrier cream according to manufacturers' instructions, to the palms of hands, in between the fingers, around the nails, cuticles, ankles and knees, or any other areas of dry skin or creases; this will stop the tan from becoming patchy.
- Now put on gloves. Make sure that they fit tightly and have no wrinkles in them as this could make the tan application streaky.
- Remember to warm the tanning product slightly in your hands before applying it to the client's skin. Don't overwarm it though as this could affect the quality of the application. Warn your client that it may feel a little cold.
- Apply the tan in line with manufacturers' instructions. Ensure the tan is applied evenly and all areas of skin have been equally covered. Ensure it is well rubbed into any creases.
- Most manual tans are applied to the front of the body first. Allow a little drying time before turning the client over.
- When applying the tan to the back of the body, complete the legs first and work upward towards the back.
- Allow the tanning product to dry for a few minutes before the client gets dressed to avoid streaky/patchy results.

Spray tan

Equipment for spray tanning

There are two types of spray-tanning equipment available:
- Compressor and gun HPLV (constant airflow)
- Airbrush-type compressor and gun (usually a storage compressor)

Recent professional spray-tanning compressors have advanced from the traditional airbrush units that are now more often than not used for nail art and airbrush make-up.

HVLP compressor

Professional compressors have an automatic air tank that produces a constant air flow, a long air hose (often around 3 m) that attaches the compressor to the gun and often two or more outlets for the gun to deliver excellent pressure for the high-volume low-pressure (HVLP) gun with a psi (pounds per square inch) set around 10.

▲ Airbrush tanning solution

⭐ *Tip* Many companies supply a starter kit that may be beneficial to begin with.

This allows a variable spray-tan pattern moving vertically or horizontally. The nozzle is usually around 0.8 mm in diameter with a larger gravity feed cup to place the tan solution in. Many have a foot pedal on/off operation as well as a finger trigger. As a general guide, 3 L of spray tan solution gives approximately 55 full-body sprays.

The benefits of using an HVLP compressor are as follows:

- It can be a little quicker than airbrushing due to around an 8 in coverage each spray in comparison to around 2 in for airbrushing
- Less overspray
- Less product may be used.

▲ Airbrush compressor

Airbrush compressor

Most tanning airbrush compressors tend to be dual action, which means they release air and tanning solution at the same time. The needle size is on average 0.5 mm. The airbrush gives preciseness when spraying and the psi used is unique to your spraying ability and experience. If your psi is high, you may find yourself having to move faster to stop the tan from beading or running.

The psi for spray tanning varies according to manufacturers' instructions but the average is around 15–25 psi. It is important that the maximum recommended psi is not exceeded as it could cause the tan to penetrate the epidermis.

The main benefit of using an airbrush compressor is its preciseness of application of the tanning product.

Tanning tent

These cubicles can be left stationary or fold away easily and quickly for mobile work. The cubicle protects clothes and surfaces from overspray of the tanning product and can be easily cleaned and disinfected as the surface is waterproof. The cubicles are usually black in colour so they do not become stained from the tanning product. Once collapsed, the cubicles can be stored in a special carry case for easy transportation.

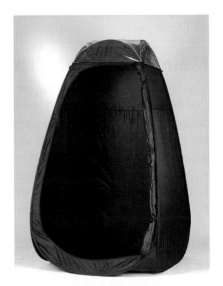

▲ Tanning tent and cubicle

Troubleshooting for spray-tanning equipment

Cleaning, maintaining and reassembly

Problems that can occur:

- Nozzle blockage
- Spitting
- Bubbles in gravity feed cup
- No air flow through gun.

Nozzle blockage

- Nozzle may not be attached correctly
- Nozzle may be cracked or damaged
- If it hasn't been cleaned properly it may have dried tanning product built up inside of it.

Spitting

- Air pressure may be too low
- Needle may be damaged.

Bubbles in gravity feed cup

- See nozzle blockage.

No air flow through gun

- Compressor may not be working
- Fuse in plug may be blown
- Air valve may be blocked
- Hose may be blocked
- Drain valve on moisture trap may be closed.

Maintenance of airbrush gun

Cleaning the airbrush is important so that it is maintained in good working order. Most manufacturers will supply a cleaning solution to be run through the gun after each use and a brush to clean the gravity feed cup and nozzle area. Many manufacturers also supply a cleaning pot in which to spray the cleaning solution; it may be useful to line this with a disposable covering to make cleaning of the pot easier. Many companies recommend running warm water through the gun before use.

The airbrush gun will need to be stripped down regularly for thorough cleaning. This will help to keep it in good working order. It is important that it is put back together correctly and always take care not to damage the needle as this will cause application problems.

Spray tan procedure
Tools, equipment and product list

- Treatment cubicle
- Trolley
- Towels: dark towels may be best to avoid staining from tanning product
- Robes (optional)
- Cleanser and body wash, if required (remember it is better for the client to be free of make-up and products such as perfume,

moisturiser, deodorant etc. prior to attending the appointment as this could add further time onto your treatment)

- COSHH bin
- Compressor and gun
- Extractor fan (optional – this can be bought for mobile use too, if required)
- Spray tan
- Disposable cap
- Disposable pedi slippers
- Disposable stickers for the feet to avoid getting tan on the soles (optional)
- Disposable thongs
- Foam cleaner
- Barrier cream.

▲ Extractor fan

Set up work area

The information given on work area set up is specific to the unit (see Chapter 2 Health and safety for a more generic set up). The set up for the purpose of this chapter is as follows:

- Tanning cubicle or tent, cleaned and disinfected
- Compressor and gun ready to use with tanning solution in large gravity feed cup
- Large towel or robe to give to the client to protect their modesty and provide privacy
- Disposable pedi slippers to hand for use after treatment.

Preparing the client

The following should take place prior to commencement of treatment:

- Consultation and agreement of treatment plan: check for contraindications and carry out skin sensitivity testing, if appropriate.
- Ensure the client has followed the pre-treatment advice given.
- Contact lenses should be removed.
- Ask the client to remove accessories that may be in your working area, e.g. earrings, watch, necklace, etc. to avoid tan lines.
- Accompany the client to the treatment area and instruct them that they will need to remove their clothing and they can change into the disposable underwear if they prefer. Leave a large towel or robe there for them to use for cover and explain that you will leave them to get changed and will return in a few moments. Always remain within earshot for safety.

▲ Spray tan in action

- Position the client in the tanning cubicle or tent.
- Gently lift and secure the client's hair off their face using a disposable cap.

Application of spray tan

Always refer to manufacturers' instructions as they may vary. A general procedure is as follows:

- Spray tan is often applied to face first, then is worked down towards the feet. This is because the spray will naturally fall to the floor and may rest on the skin as it falls.
- When spraying the client's face ensure that they close their eyes, take a deep breath and hold it until you've finished spraying their face. Try to complete this action quickly.
- Most companies recommend that spray tanning is completed by using a 'first call' or horizontal action, constantly moving and checking that are no gaps that may cause an uneven tan.
- Carefully remove the disposable cap covering the hair and check there are no white lines where it has been resting. If there are gaps, reposition the cap, ask the client to close their eyes and gently spray the area.
- Once the spraying has been completed the client should stand still for a few minutes until the tanning product is completely dry.

> ☆ *Tip* Store your airbrush gun carefully to avoid damage.

> ☆ *Tip* Ensure all areas have been fully covered including any creases!

Manual and spray tan
Aftercare and homecare advice

- If the client is very pale or requires a darker colour than was applied during the treatment, he or she can have a re-application in two days' time. The skin must be polished and moisturised before applying the tan, to ensure an even application of colour.
- Clients **must** be advised not to bathe or shower for at least four hours after the tanning treatment.
- Self-tan manufacturers recommend that clients do not swim after having had the treatment, as the chlorine in swimming pools does bleach the tan.
- Clients should be advised to purchase the body polish – it is much softer than a normal exfoliator, which could remove the tan. The body polish contains nylon spherical balls that won't scratch the skin surface. Any products that are too 'scratchy' will tear the top couple of layers of the epidermis and over a period of time would damage the skin. The skin cells should be buffed using self-tan polish every 3–4 days to keep the tan looking even and the skin soft. Self-tan moisturiser should be applied afterwards; this will help prolong the life of the tan.

Other moisturisers used should not contain perfume and should only be used after the 4-hour developing period has passed.

- The tanning lotion has a slight green pigment, which prevents it from turning orange, thus helping to achieve a more natural appearance. It is essential that the client does not use deodorant, moisturiser or liquid-type foundation after the treatment for 4 hours. It is also good to advise the client to refrain from using cream-based shower gels or soaps and not to apply moisturiser before the treatment application, as the green pigment in the tan could react with other products.

- Tans usually fade from the facial area first. This is because cleansers are more often used to remove make-up from the face than on any other part of the body.

▲ Bronzer compact

Retail products

The following are retail products associated with self-tanning:

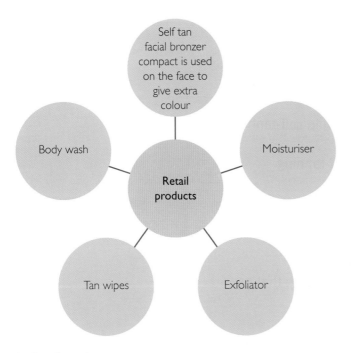

▲ Retail products

End of chapter knowledge test

1. Why would you advise your client not to use cream-based shower gels or soaps, moisturisers or deodorants before their self-tanning treatment?

2. Why do you exfoliate the client's skin before applying the tanning lotion?

3. After the treatment, how long would you ask your client to refrain from showering or bathing?

4. If a client was already using a self-tanning lotion, how long before a self-tanning treatment would you ask them to stop using it?

5. If the client has a very pale complexion or just requires a deeper tan, how long after the treatment could he or she re-apply the tanning product?

6. Why would you advise your client not to go swimming following a self-tanning treatment?

7. What is the fragrance used in self-tan?

8. Why does the tan have a green pigment in it?

9. How long does the tan last on average?

10. How long before the tanning treatment would you advise your client to have any type of hair removal treatment?

11. Why does tan fade quicker on the face?

12. Can you name the tanning agent used in self-tanning lotions?

13. Name **two** advantages of using a self-tanning treatment rather than UV radiation.

14. What is the technical term for tanning?

15. What is the name of the enzyme that is stimulated in the skin during tanning?

16. What are the pigment-forming cells called?

17. What is the name of the colourful molecule that gives skin its tan colour?

18. What does HVLP stand for?

19. Name **one** retail product for use after self-tanning treatments.

End of chapter knowledge test answers

Chapter 1

1. Salon-based make-up artist; mobile make-up artist; department store – make-up counter; make-up representative – sales; freelance media make-up artist; NHS – camouflage make-up, Ambulance service and mortuary make-up artist; Education – lecturer

2. Internet, trade magazines, newspapers, jobs fairs, in-house, word of mouth, agencies, photographers

3. To ensure targets, timings and budgets are met; to promote a professional image

4. PPE, COSHH, Health and safety, hygiene – sterilisation and disinfectant

5. Always be well organised; be punctual; be prepared for the unexpected; ensure personal hygiene is of a good standard; be well groomed; work to commercially acceptable timings; good interpretation and presentation of ideas to clients; know your job role; teamwork is vital; never gossip; treat everybody with respect – professional etiquette counts for a lot!; observe a high standard of hygiene, health and safety at all times; ensure your update on new techniques, products and training through continual professional development (CPD)

6. HABIA

7. HABIA

8. To protect themselves from litigation and to ensure permission is given to use the images

Chapter 2

1. COSHH
2. CO_2, carbon dioxide (black)
3. Label it and tell the salon manager
4. Health and Safety 1974
5. One year
6. Public liability
7. Something that can restrict or prevent a treatment
8. A reaction that occurs because of a treatment or product; this can be good or bad
9. Employers liability
10. Autoclave, glass bead, gluteraldhyride/chemical
11. UV, barbicide, disinfectants
   To find contraindications, information etc.
12. It could be voided

13. Alert people to the hazard and report to the person in charge; use a dustpan and brush (not your hands); carefully wrap in paper or cardboard and place in the COSHH bin.

14. To stop cross-infection

15. Professionalism and hygiene

16. Make sure the client record card is up to date and signed and dated by the client

   Clients can be contacted if necessary; these cards can referred back to when the client visits next; any contraindications or contra-actions should be recorded on the card

18. Total destruction of all living micro-organisms

19. Advise staff not to bring expensive items or large amounts of cash into work

Chapter 3

1. SWOT
2. Products, price, place and promotion
3. Data protection
4. Internet, website, newspaper, trade magazine, shop window, supermarkets, radio, posters, leaflets, word of mouth, other businesses
5. Cash; credit card; debit card; cheque; gift/discount voucher
6. To ensure you give accurate information to your client; to relate what you are selling to your customer's needs and wants; to work out clearly promotions and presentations

Chapter 4

1. Transportation of oxygen, nutrients, hormones, white blood cells; helps to remove waste such as carbon dioxide, lactic acid and urea; clotting
2. Sensation, heat regulation, absorption, protection, excretion, secretion
3. Transportation of white blood cells
4. Stratum corneum, stratum lucidum, stratum granulosum, stratum spinosum, stratum germinativum
5. The nucleus
6. Red patches of skin with flaky silvery scales; it may weep or bleed
7. Cuticle
8. Viral
9. Anagen, catagen and telogen
10. Terminal

Chapter 5

1. Automatic and manual
2. In line with the pupil of the eye as the client is looking straight ahead
3. 24–48 hours prior to treatment
4. 1) Petroleum jelly has touched the hairs, creating a barrier to the tint, 2) the area hasn't been thoroughly cleansed so there is a barrier to the tint or 3) the tint has been mixed too early and oxidised
5. Soothing/cooling products; eyebrow brush; eyebrow pencil; powder-based make-up (for brows)
6. Natural hair colour; client preference; skin colour; type of make-up usually worn in the area
7. Conjunctivitis; blepharitis; stye; bruising; active psoriasis or eczema; watery eyes; hay fever; any inflammation, redness, dry skin cuts or abrasions in the area; claustrophobic clients; a very nervous client (they may find it difficult to keep the eyes closed for a length of time)
8. Solvent
9. Angular; arched; rounded; straight/low arched; oblique
10. 4–6 weeks

Chapter 6

1. Effleurage, petrissage, tapotement and vibrations
2. Effleurage because: it is a way of spreading the massage medium; it is soothing and relaxing for the client; it introduces the client to the make-up artist's touch
3. Relaxation; a sense of well being; increased blood circulation that warms the skin tissues and helps ease tense muscles; blood capillaries dilate bringing blood to the skin's surface and improving its colour; increased supply oxygenated blood, improving cell renewal for the skin and muscles. The facial contours may be slightly improved as a slight toning and strengthening effect occurs; desquamation occurs as dead epidermal cells are loosened, thus improving the appearance of skin; lymphatic circulation and drainage is improved to aid the removal of waste toxins; skin temperature is raised, which helps to relax the skin's pores and follicles so that it can absorb the massage product to soften the skin; sebaceous and sudoriferous glands are stimulated, producing sebum, helping to maintain the skin's natural oil and moisture balance; sensory nerves may also be stimulated, depending which large manipulation is being performed
4. Oil, cream
5. Physical effects: those that can be seen or felt on the surface of the skin; physiological effects: those that occur in the body under the surface of the skin; psychological effects: those that the client feels
6. Dry, oily, normal and combination
7. Lacking in either moisture or sebum; pores are small and tight; skin texture is fine and thin with flaky patches; premature aging and fine lines may occur, particularly around the eyes, mouth and neck; broken capillaries may be present, often around the nose and cheek areas; skin pigmentation may be uneven; milia can be located around the eyes and cheek area as the skin is so fine here; fine capillaries can be found on the cheek area; skin may feel taut; skin is often sensitive; skin may be dull in appearance
8. To remove dead surface epidermal skin cells using a manual abrasive, peeling product or mechanical equipment
9. Opens the pores: this will aid any extraction of comedones; increases circulation of blood and lymph: improving skin colour and assisting in the elimination of waste toxins; softens the surface of the epidermis: aids desquamation; sebaceous gland activity increases: stimulating oil production to moisturise a dry, dehydrated and mature skin; relaxing: due to increased warmth and effects from essential oil if used by a qualified aromatherapist
10. Conjunctivitis; bacterial infections, e.g. impetigo; fungal infections, e.g. ringworm; viral infections, e.g. herpes simplex; bruising; eczema or psoriasis; cuts and abrasions; rashes, redness and inflammation; recent scar tissue – 6 months or less; recent sunburn; hay fever; claustrophobia
11. Creams, gels, milks, lotions, foaming cleansers and cleansing bars
12. To remove traces of cleanser; to tighten pores; to cool and refresh the skin tissues; dissolves oil and sebum; to hydrate the skin tissues; may help to restore pH of the skin
13. Distilled water: to help prevent the build up of limescale on the element of the unit
14. Setting; non-setting

Chapter 7

1. d
2. Red
3. Cream
4. For a neat application, it may last longer and for hygiene reasons
5. Dry skin type
6. Natural skin tone and try to match it
7. To avoid strain and injury; to ensure that the facial contours are in a natural position
8. Magnesium silicate
9. To even out the skin texture and provide a base for the foundation to sit on
10. Use make-up brush cleaner or appropriate gentle shampoo and lukewarm water, reshape and lie flat to dry completely

Chapter 8

1. Internet, books, photos, magazines, TV, films.
2. To help you plan the make-up and hair products needed, colours, shapes and design to be used in the final image and may also help to estimate the cost of the products used.
3. Electronic or hard copy, face charts, detailed notes, test shots, sketches, photos/pictures.
4. To improve skills and efficiency.
5. To determine if any hair pieces, extensions or wigs need to be used and to ensure that the make-up look will be effective.
6. To avoid misunderstandings and for efficiency.
7. For speed, efficiency and organisation.
8. So you have enough money to purchase the products and equipment to complete the service and professional reputation.

Chapter 9

1. Feathers, ribbons, flowers, hair gems, tiaras and chop sticks.
2. Adds shine and smoothness.
3. Cuticle.
4. Head-lice and scabies.
5. Pre-made hair pieces that can be added to the natural hair.
6. Natural human hair, fur from animals such as the goat or yak and synthetic fibre.
7. Hackle.
8. It is very delicate and may easily rip, if this happens it may be very expensive to repair.

9. Spirit gum remover or surgical spirits.
10. Spirit gum.

Chapter 10

1. Mask, apron, uniform, vinyl/nitrile gloves.
2. To meet professional standards, to achieve client satisfaction and to encourage repeat business.
3. To eliminate vapours.
4. To avoid cross infection.
5. To avoid strain and to avoid spray entering nasal passages.
6. To prevent make-up from drying out in the airbrush and clogging it.
7. Use an alcohol wipe.
8. Alcohol or oil-based cleansing creams.
9. 4–15 PSI.
10. Yearly

Chapter 11

1. To avoid misunderstandings
2. Summarise the main points and recap with the client
3. To avoid cross infection and making the condition worse
4. To avoid strain or injury
5. Complete a risk assessment prior to the event to identify the risks and how they can be managed
6. To ensure the overall total look is complimentary to the hair, costume and set
7. So the colours in the make-up look true and do not alter under different types lighting and produce different types of effects
8. To develop your own skills and be able to review, improve and adapt
9. To ensure there are no misunderstandings and to make any changes if required
10. To avoid overspending, which could result in a poor reputation

Chapter 12

1. Water-based, hypoallergenic and non-toxic
2. (REACH) – Registration, Evaluation, authorisation and restriction of chemicals.
3. Synthetic sponges, paint brush, natural sea sponge, air brush.
4. Mottling.
5. Place a dab of paint on the make-up palette and water it down to the desired consistency.

6. Use a damp cotton bud and gently roll over the mistake until in disappears. For stubborn mistakes, a clean cotton bud will need to be used every time you roll.

7. To shower using a shower gel.

8. So you can customise and mix colours accordingly.

Chapter 13

1. The client may suffer from psychological problems, causing low self-esteem and withdrawal from society and working lifestyles.

2. To help to counteract the colour pigments in the area to be covered

3. Allergic reaction; itching; swelling; erythema; sensitivity

4. Hypersensitive skin; cuts and abrasions; recent scar tissue; severe bruising; broken skin; weeping acne; eczema; psoriasis; dermatitis; eye infections (watery eyes, blepharitis, stye); skin diseases or disorders; bacterial infections; undiagnosed lumps; swelling or inflammation of the skin

5. Hypopigmentation; vitiligo; hyperpigmentation; chloasma; erythema; telangiectasia; birthmarks; atrophic scars; normal scars; hypertrophic scars; keloid scars; tattoos

6. b (Hyper pigmentation)

7. a (Avoid perspiring sports, heat and remove well)

8. b (Try a variety of shades on the area to be concealed)

9. c (After each layer of camouflage cream)

Chapter 14

1. To check for skin sensitivity or allergic reaction

2. Stop the treatment immediately, remove the product and either flush with cold water or apply a cold compress. If reaction continues advise them to seek medical advice.

3. Place a small amount of the product to be used in the make-up application either behind the ear or in the crease of the elbow and ask the client to leave it there for up to 48 hours and record it on the record card. Explain to the client what a positive and negative reaction is

4. To avoid cross infection or making the condition worse

5. Use a small brush to apply; use a tiny amount of spirit gum or prosthetics remover. Apply to edges, support the skin with one hand and gently use the brush to lift it off.

6. So that everyone on set or backstage knows their job role

7. To develop ideas and communicate them to others

8. So they know what to do in the event of a contra-action

9. Shows the order of set up for that day

10. To be develop and design make-up, the products and staff needed and where any hair and make-up changes occur within the production

11. Witch hazel, Pros-aide or acetone.

12. To plan and prepare for the products that need to be purchased, so you don't overspend and are unable to complete the job. For professional reputation.

13. To hire staff, to liaise directly with the production crew, to attend production meetings to develop ideas, to present ideas to the director and producer and manage the budget, including ordering products and equipment. Give job roles to the make-up team and keep them informed via team meetings.

Chapter 15

1. It could cause a chemical reaction and turn the tan green

2. To remove natural oils and dead skin cells from the surface of the skin, which helps achieve an even application of the tanning product

3. 4 hours

4. 4 days

5. 48 hours

6. Chlorine bleaches out the tan

7. Aloe vera

8. To stop the tan looking orange

9. Around 9 days, with care taken to maintain it

10. 48 hours before

11. It is mixed with moisturiser so it is only half-strength

12. Dihydroxyacetone

13. It won't cause premature ageing of the skin; those allergic to natural sunlight can still have a tan; those who do not tan evenly can use it to achieve an even tan; it has no implications of skin cancer

14. Melanogenesis

15. Tyrosinase

16. Melanocytes

17. Melanin

18. High volume, low pressure

19. Self-tan facial bronzer compact; moisturiser; exfoliator; tan wipes; body wash

Index